REACHING A GENERATION FOR CHRIST

GENERAL EDITORS

RICHARD R. DUNN (M.A., Ed.D., Trinity Evangelical Divinity School) is chair of the department of Christian education at Trinity Evangelical Divinity School. He is a fifteen-year veteran of church, campus, and camping youth ministries. Dr. Dunn and his wife, Teresa, have three children and live in Lake Villa, Illinois.

MARK H. SENTER III (M.A., Trinity Evangelical Divinity School; Ph.D., Loyola University Chicago) is vice president, Division of Open Studies, and associate professor of Christian education at Trinity International University. Previously, he was youth pastor for two Chicago-area churches. He and his wife, Ruth, have two adult children.

A Comprehensive Guide to Youth Ministry

REACHING A GENERATION FOR CHRIST

Richard R. Dunn
and
Mark H. Senter III

General Editors

MOODY PRESS
CHICAGO

To Teresa Dunn,
whose embodiment of 1 Corinthians 13:4–8
has brought sustenance and healing to her husband's soul

and

To Nick Senter and Jori Senter Stuart,
who were their father's primary youth group
and have become his best friends

CONTENTS

SIDEBARS

PREFACE

In Lake Wobegon, Garrison Keillor claims, all the women are strong, all the men are good-looking, and all the children are above average. Maybe that describes youth ministry at the end of the twentieth century. Strong women, good-looking men, and above average kids.

A candid look at the youth culture of this or any generation suggests that if the only young people involved with the church are above average, a whole mission field is being missed. If the staff consists only of strong women and good-looking men, then the potential pool of leaders is dismally restricted. If such restrictions exist, it is the church which is impoverished.

In some ways parents and church leaders would like for the youth group to resemble Lake Wobegon. After all, it is a fairly safe place to grow up. No stories about gang violence or substance abuse. No abortions and few out-of-wedlock pregnancies. No dysfunctional families (unless you consider the sanctified brethren as such) and few single parent homes. Yet even in Keillor's fictitious town (which time forgot), church is more of a tradition than a vital reality.

So what is youth ministry all about?

Creating safe places? In some ways, the answer is yes. But more basically, youth ministry is about hope.

Hope?

Yes, hope!

Not the whimperings of a pathetic creature out of touch with reality, clinging to a thread of religious tradition, but the confidence that God is in control of even the most bizarre circumstances in a world gone crazy. Youth ministry is driven by hope. Otherwise the culture would establish our agenda, popular culture would dictate our methodology and personal fulfillment would determine the criteria for success.

Reaching a Generation for Christ is about hope. The authors in this book are people who have done youth ministry. Along the way, most have stopped to reflect on the nature of their calling and in the process many have done doctoral research which has helped place the issues of youth ministry under the lenses of a microscope to isolate the essentials of this unique profession. Each writer shares the confidence that God is about to use a new generation of youth leaders to accomplish something new. Not necessarily different, just new.

The four lenses identified in "Part 1: A Framework for Youth Ministry" assist the youth leader in bringing youth ministry into focus. Though theology remains the queen of the sciences, the developmental, sociological, and historical lenses assist the innovative youth leader in doing theology in the environment of this generation. Even with the precise focus provided by the four lenses, youth ministry is still an art. The Spirit of God guides the insightful discipler in painting on the tapestry of growing lives.

As in *The Complete Book of Youth Ministry* (1987), this book revolves around three statements amplified in "Part 2: Structures for Youth Ministry":

1. Youth ministry begins when adults find a comfortable method of entering a student's world.
2. Youth ministry happens as long as adults are able to use their contacts with students to draw them into a maturing relationship with God through Jesus Christ.
3. Youth ministry ceases to happen when either the adult-student relationship is broken or the outcome of that relationship ceases to move the student toward spiritual maturity.

The remainder of the book attempts to answer a series of ministry-related questions. Though many enthusiastic youth workers will turn immediately to the question and answer section of the book, the editors urge that the temptation be resisted. The first two sections provide a basis for critiquing and understanding the rest of the book.

Part 2 provides two types of *structures* for youth ministry. Fifteen axioms or self-evident truths drawn from the collective wisdom of youth ministers over the years are expressed in nine *models* of youth ministry. It is the author's firm conviction that the success of any of the models is directly dependent upon the degree to which the axioms are heeded.

Part 3 focuses on the *context* for adult leaders in youth ministry. The assumption is made and developed that all youth ministry is relational. Special attention is paid to youth ministry as a profession, lay leaders as the backbone of efforts to reach a generation for Christ, and the special contributions and challenges women have in ministering to young people. Beginning with chapter 10, sidebars will provide additional information and perspectives on the topics being examined.

Skills essential for changing existing youth ministries and initiating new ministries is the focal point of part 4. Communication is at the heart of these skills. Five specific *challenges* faced by the youth minister are addressed in part 5. These include concerns related to popular culture, music, the family, students who are hurting, and ministry in small churches.

As youth ministers turn their attention to reaching this generation of young people for Christ, one profound truth has become apparent. They are not alone. *Resources* are available in organizations and people outside the local church and in methodologies and strategies within the faith community. Seven resources are explored in part 6.

To conclude the book, the editors review the state of youth ministry as the Millennial Generation comes of age. Will youth ministry in the future be a pale reflection of Lake Wobegon or will it be a compelled by new visions for ministry in the twenty-first century? The editor's reflect a firm hope in the emergence of such visions. *Reaching a Generation for Christ* is designed to be both a resource and a catalyst for those who have eyes to see and hearts to lead youth ministry, prayerfully and faithfully, into the realization of that hope.

The editors wish to express their appreciation to the authors, who squeezed their contributions into already busy schedules. In addition, appreciation must be expressed to Jennifer Isler, Linda Moffet, and Kim Pennington for the help they provided behind the scenes.

CONTRIBUTORS

Marta Elena Alvarado (B.A., Rosary College; M.A., Northern Baptist Theological Seminary; Ph.D., University of Chicago) is associate professor, department of educational ministry, Moody Bible Institute.

Gwyn Beldan Baker (B.S., University of Tennessee) is director of youth and family ministry, Lake Forest Presbyterian Church, Knoxville, Tennessee.

Scott W. Benson (B.S., Southern Methodist University; M.Div, Trinity Evangelical Divinity School) is pastor of student ministries, Winnetka Bible Church, Winnetka, Illinois.

Dewey Bertolini (M.Div., Talbot Theological Seminary) is assistant to the president, Western Baptist College, Salem, Oregon; a youth curriculum developer; and a youth speaker throughout North America.

Wesley Black (B.M., Hardin-Simmons University; M.A.R.E., Ph.D., Southwestern Baptist Theological Seminary) is associate professor of youth education, Southwestern Baptist Theological Seminary, Fort Worth, Texas.

Paul Borthwick (B.A., University of Massachusetts; M.Div., Gordon-Conwell College) is minister of missions, Grace Chapel, Lexington, Massachusetts.

Bo Boshers (B.A., Pacific University) is executive director of Student Impact, Willow Creek Community Church, South Barrington, Illinois.

Ridge Burns (B.A., Westmont College; M.R.E., D.Min., Trinity Evangelical Divinity School) is executive director, Forest Home, Forest Falls, California.

Pamela T. Campbell (B.A., Middle Tennessee State University; M.A., Wheaton College Graduate School) is director of publications, American Association of Christian Counselors, and youth director, Lisle Bible Church, Lisle, Illinois.

Mark W. Cannister (B.S., California University at Pennsylvania; M.A., West Virginia University; Ed.D., University of Pittsburgh) is chair and assistant professor of youth ministries and Christian education, Gordon College, Wenham, Massachusetts.

Christie Stonecipher Cistola (M.Div.) has been a staff member with Campus Life and ministry associate, Park Street Church, Boston, Massachusetts.

Chap R. Clark (B.A., University of California at San Diego; M.A., M.Div., Fuller Theological Seminary; Ph.D., University of Denver) is chair, youth and family ministry, and associate professor of youth and family ministry and spiritual formation, Denver Seminary.

Kevin Conklin (B.A., Taylor University) is pastor to students and families, North Suburban Evangelical Free Church, Deerfield, Illinois.

Christine Cook (B.A., Wheaton College; M.A., University of Geneva; M.A., Fuller Theological Seminary) is director of Contact-Jeunes, Switzerland.

Mark DeVries (B.A., Baylor University; M.Div., Princeton Theological Seminary) is associate pastor to youth and their families, First Presbyterian Church, Nashville, Tennessee.

Richard R. Dunn (M.A., Ed.D., Trinity Evangelical Divinity School) is chair of the department of Christian education at Trinity Evangelical Divinity School.

Teresa R. Dunn (B.A., Bryan College; M.Ed., University of Tennessee) is co-director of the Counseling Center, Trinity International University, Deerfield, Illinois.

Diane Elliot (B.A., Trinity International University) is co-founder and former director of the Association of Women in Youth Ministry, a ministry of Youth Leadership.

Donald G. Ferris is co-pastor, First Baptist Church of San Lorenzo Valley, Felton, California, and an associate staff member and trainer, Sonlife Ministries.

John Fischer (B.A., Wheaton College) is an author, speaker, songwriter, and singer.

Paul Fleischmann (B.A., Seattle Pacific College; M.Div., Western Baptist Seminary) is executive director, National Network of Youth Ministries, San Diego, California.

David J. Garda (B.A., Taylor University; M.Div., Trinity Evangelical Divinity School) is associate director, Sonlife Ministries.

Ken Garland (B.A., Biola University; M.A.C.E., Ed.D., Talbot School of Theology) is chair of the department of Christian education at Talbot School of Theology.

Stephen P. Greggo (B.A., State University of New York College at Onconta; M.A., Denver Seminary; Ph.D. and Certificate of Advanced Study, State University of New York at Albany) is a licensed psychologist and assistant professor of counseling and psychology at Trinity International University (Trinity Evangelical Divinity School).

Ronald T. Habermas (B.R.E., William Tyndale College; M.A., Wheaton College Graduate School; M.Div., North American Baptist Seminary; Ph.D., Michigan State University) is McGee Professor of Biblical Studies, John Brown University.

David S. Hart (B.A., University of Colorado; M.A., Talbot Seminary) is the editor of *Media Update,* a newsletter published by Al Menconi Ministries, and the pastor of Sanctuary, San Diego, California.

Saundra Hensel (B.A., Trinity College) is a founding board member of the Association of Women in Youth Ministry. She has served on the staff of Sonlight Express, the junior high ministry of Willow Creek Community Church, and has been student ministries director of Cedar Ridge Community Church in the Washington, D.C., area. She is a master's degree candidate in Christian education, Trinity Evangelical Divinity School.

David Hunsicker (B.S., Louisiana State University; M.A., Wheaton College Graduate School) is a doctoral candidate at Trinity Evangelical Divinity School and a free-lance author who lives in Libertyville, Illinois.

Jacob Kwon Tae Joo (B.Th., Eastern Pentecostal Bible College; B.A., University of Toronto; M.Div., Toronto School of Theology) is founder and senior pastor of the Pentecostal World Mission Church, Toronto.

Russ Knight (B.A., American University; diploma, home missions and Christian education, Moody Bible Institute) is president, Chicago Urban Reconciliation Enterprise (CURE).

Tony Ladd (B.A., Taylor University; M.A., University of Minnesota; Ph.D., Ohio State University) is professor and chair, department of physical education and athletics, Wheaton College, Wheaton, Illinois.

Greg Lafferty (B.A., Wheaton College) is pastor, junior high ministries, Amurro Mission, Viejo, California.

Mark A. Lamport (B.A., Huntington College; M.A., Wheaton College Graduate School; M.Div., Evangelical School of Theology; Th.M. Princeton Theological Seminary; Ph.D., Michigan State University) is professor of educational ministries and co-director of the Link Institute for Faithful and Effective Youth Ministry, Huntington College, Huntington, Indiana.

Kevin E. Lawson (B.S., Houghton College; M.A.C.E., Trinity Evangelical Divinity School; Ed.D., University of Maine) is associate professor of Christian education, Talbot School of Theology.

Larry Lindquist (B.A., Trinity International University; M.A., Trinity Evangelical Divinity School; Ed.D., Northern Illinois University) is pastor of Christian education, First Evangelical Free Church, Rockford, Illinois.

Sarah Katherine McDavitt (B.A., University of Mississippi) is admissions counselor, Mississippi University for Women, Columbus, Mississippi.

Wayne Mitchell (B.S., Morgan State University; M.S., Western Illinois University) is associate pastor, Oak Cliff Bible Fellowship, Dallas, Texas.

Mark Moring (B.A., University of Virginia) is senior associate editor, *Campus Life* magazine, Carol Stream, Illinois.

Helen Musick (B.A., University of Tennessee; M.A., Asbury Seminary) is instructor of youth ministry, Asbury Seminary.

Chuck Neder (B.A., University of Georgia; M.A., Columbia Theological Seminary; graduate work, McCormick Seminary) is national director of youth ministries, Presbyterians for Renewal, Chattanooga, Tennessee.

David Olshine (B.A., Ohio University; M.Div., Asbury Seminary; D.Min., Eastern Baptist Seminary) is director of youth ministries, Columbia International University, Columbia, South Carolina.

G. Keith Olson (B.A., San Diego State University; Ph.D., University of Arizona) is director and therapist, Family Consultation Service, San Diego, California.

Les Parrott III (B.A., Olivet Nazarene University; M.A., Fuller Theological Seminary; Ph.D., Graduate School of Psychology, Fuller Theological Seminary) is director of the Center for Relationship Development, Seattle Pacific University.

Steve Patty (B.S., Multnomah Bible College; M.A., Wheaton College Graduate School; Ed.D., Trinity Evangelical Divinity School) is associate professor of youth and educational ministries, Multnomah Bible College.

Ron Powell (B.Th., Eastern Pentecostal Bible College; M.T.S., Ontario Theological Seminary; D.Min., in progress, Trinity

Evangelical Divinity School) is supervisor, youth ministries program, Eastern Pentecostal Bible College; and associate pastor, Pentecostal World Mission Church, Peterborough, Ontario, Canada.

Dave Rahn (B.A., Huntington College; M.A., Wheaton College Graduate School; Ph.D., Purdue University) is professor of educational ministries and co-director of the Link Institute for Faithful and Effective Youth Ministry, Huntington College, Huntington, Indiana.

Ed Robinson (B.A., Northwest Nazarene College; M.R.E., Nazarene Theological Seminary; Ed.D., Trinity Evangelical Divinity School) is academic dean and professor of religious education, Nazarene Theological Seminary, Lenexa, Kansas.

Chuck Rosemeyer (B.S., Geneva College; M.Div., D.Min., Pittsburgh Theological Seminary) is director of the Pittsburgh Youth Network, Mission Team of the Episcopal Diocese of Pittsburgh; and parish associate of Bellefield Presbyterian Church, Pittsburgh, Pennsylvania.

David L. Roth (B.A., Fort Wayne Bible College; M.A., Ed.D., Northern Illinois University) is headmaster, Wheaton Academy, West Chicago, Illinois.

Barry St. Clair (B.A., Davidson College; M.Div., M.Min., Southern Baptist Theological Seminary) is founder and executive director of Reach Out Ministries, Atlanta, Georgia.

Quentin J. Schultze (B.S., M.S., Ph.D., University of Illinois) is professor of communications, Calvin College, Grand Rapids, Michigan.

Mark H. Senter III (M.A., Trinity Evangelical Divinity School; Ph.D., Loyola University) is vice president, Division of Open Studies, and associate professor of Christian education, Trinity International University.

William H. (Bill) Stewart (B.A., Northwestern College; M.A., Mennonite Brethren Biblical Seminary) is a writer, author, and consultant who makes his home in Kansas City, Kansas, and Indian Shores, Florida.

Jana L. Sundene (B.A., Wheaton College; M.A., Northern Illinois University) is assistant professor of youth ministry at Trinity International University.

David Veerman (B.A., Wheaton College; M.Div., Trinity Evangelical Divinity School) is partner, The Livingston Corporation, Naperville, Illinois.

Timothy Voss (B.A., Trinity College; M.S., University of Illinois) is chair, School of Human Performance and Wellness, Trinity International University.

David Warnick (B.S., B.A., University of Idaho; C.C.Ed., University of Edinburgh) is assistant to the president, National Center for Fathering, Shawnee Mission, Kansas.

Dan Webster (B.A., Biola University; graduate studies, Fuller Theological Seminary) is president, Authentic Leadership, Inc., Holland, Michigan.

Lavon J. Welty (B.A., Goshen College; M.Div., Goshen Biblical Seminary) is pastor, Lima Mennonite Church, Lima, Ohio.

Daniel J. Weyerhaeuser (B.A., Southern Methodist University; M.Div., Trinity Evangelical Divinity School) is associate pastor, Lakeland Evangelical Free Church, Gurnee, Illinois.

PART ONE

FRAMEWORK FOR YOUTH MINISTRY

1

PUTTING YOUTH MINISTRY INTO PERSPECTIVE

Richard R. Dunn

S teve surveys his new surroundings: an ancient metal desk, a recently installed phone, an older but functional computer, two worn metal folding chairs, and a file cabinet. "Pastor Steve's office," he whispers aloud, breaking into an approving smile.

Steve is the first youth pastor of Easton Community Church, a multicultural urban church plant that has grown from four families to a congregation of 225 in just five years. Steve muses that his childhood friends could never have imagined that he, the firstborn son of a dairy farming family in the Midwest, would be found living in an urban setting; Steve, in fact, is as surprised as anyone.

Recollections of his friends lead to fond memories of Brian and Joyce, the lay youth leaders in Steve's small rural church. The young married couple were used by God in significant ways to nurture his sincere though sometimes uncertain faith.

Reproducing the loving, open relational context Brian and Joyce created through their leadership is a central component of Steve's vision for Easton. Yet Steve is acutely aware that he cannot simply duplicate in a multicultural urban context the same youth ministry programs and methods he experienced in his monocultural rural youth group.

In the candidating process Steve had felt quite confident of his readiness for youth ministry. Now, on the occasion of his first day as a youth pastor, several questions are beginning to threaten that self-assurance. These questions include: How can I ever meet the needs of students from such diverse social and cultural backgrounds? How can I build maturity in the lives of the twenty junior high and fifteen high school students who attend youth Sunday school? How can I build bridges to the other five thousand students who attend schools within five miles of the church? What changes should I be making right away?

"8:47 A.M." Steve's watch informs him that he has now been a youth pastor for seventeen minutes. "This may not be as easy as I thought," he concludes.

THINKING YOUTH MINISTRY: STEVE'S CHALLENGE

Everyone in youth ministry, from college students volunteering in a campus ministry to the twenty-year veteran in a local church, has a particular youth ministry perspective. Based upon past church, ministry, educational, and personal spiritual experiences, every leader has a preconceived set of ideas about what is important in terms of values and practices in youth ministry.

Steve is realizing that he has his own youth ministry perspective. He has identified the significant influence of Brian and Joyce in shaping how he understands youth ministry. Other learning experiences that have made an impact on his ministry perspective include youth ministry training seminars and the camping ministry internship he participated in last summer.

None of Steve's past experiences, however, can act as a blueprint for the development of his new ministry at Easton. What he has previously learned cannot sufficiently provide answers for all of the new questions he is facing. Steve's challenge is both to broaden and to sharpen his current youth ministry perspective. He has been an effective "doer" of youth ministry; now he is discovering his need to become a more effective "thinker" of youth ministry.

TOWARD A MATURE MINISTRY MIND-SET: FOCUSING MINISTRY LENSES

To suggest that anyone's ministry perspective has perfect 20/20 vision would be naive. Sin, human limitations, and the diversity of human experiences guarantee that no one sees with absolute clarity. Steve, however, does not need to despair as he faces his limitations. In fact, Steve should be encouraged because there exists an ever-present potential for bringing his ministry perspective's vision into clearer focus. Robert Clinton suggests that such refocusing is an essential component for anyone called to long-term ministry:

> Effective leaders, at all levels of leadership, maintain a learning posture throughout life. . . . Leaders must develop a ministry philosophy that simultaneously honors biblical leadership values, embraces the challenges of the times in which we live, and fits their unique gifts and personal development if they expect to be productive over a lifetime. (Clinton 1988, 180)

Implicit in Clinton's statement is a challenge to Steve and all youth ministry leaders *to take responsibility for focusing the internal interpretive lenses that shape youth ministry perspectives.* Too often the urgency of an endless succession of ministry demands crowds out reflecting upon and disciplining one's ministry lenses. John Detonni observes that youth ministry leaders often become consumed by these urgent tasks:

> Most often youth workers—and especially youth pastors— are very pragmatic and oriented to the program: fun and games, Bible studies, camps, retreats, social activities, and such things. It is a little difficult to talk about philosophy and theology with such youth workers in the morning when they know they are taking care of fifteen junior highers that same evening. Further, youth workers have a reputation not of being "thinkers" but doers, being more interested in how to

do youth ministry than in the reasons and basis of it. (Deton-ni 1993, 17)

Because everyone is—consciously or unconsciously—operating out of a personal ministry perspective, it is unfortunate that so little attention is paid to such a critical component of youth ministry.

Acknowledging one's ministry perspective is one thing. Taking responsibility for evaluating and rethinking one's preconceived ideas is a separate, qualitatively different task. Clinton would suggest that this is necessary, Detonni that it is rare. What route can Steve take in his journey toward this crucial task?

A MODEL FOR FOCUSING
STEVE'S MINISTRY PERSPECTIVE

A starting place for Steve's exploration and development of his ministry perspective is presented in graphic form in Figure 1.1. The model assumes that this process is best moved along by examining three internal interpretive grids: the theological framework, the developmental framework, and the sociocultural framework. The model also demonstrates the significance of a historical framework for youth ministry. History provides insight into the dynamic nature of youth ministry perspectives. Further exploration of history's contribution is found in chapter 5, "A Historical Framework for Doing Youth Ministry," by Mark Senter.

The theological framework provides the primary base for developing one's ministry perspective. Steve's first goal is to discipline his theological thinking so that he has an increasingly accurate understanding of who God is and what it means to serve as a minister of the gospel. Human development assumptions narrow Steve's ministry vision into a more focused understanding of what it means to serve as a minister of the gospel to youth. Steve's goal here is to comprehend more of what it means to be an adolescent so that his ministry is increasingly appropriate to the developmental stages of the students. The final grid, the sociocultural framework, brings into an even more specific focus the ways in which Steve should be doing ministry in his new church. Sociocultural interpretations suggest what it means to serve as a minister of the gospel to youth in a particular context. Steve's goal is grasp the uniqueness of this particular context so that he may be increasingly adaptive to the needs and perceptions of his students.

Figure 1.1 provides a picture of how these lenses work together in a dynamic dialogue with one another. Thinking through these grids from presuppositions to practice will shape the way Steve does ministry in his new context. Thinking through these grids from practice to presuppositions will inform Steve's understanding within each grid. If Steve is to think Christianly, critically, and creatively in the unchartered, unfamiliar ministry territory he has entered he must give attention to the spiraling dialogue between each component of the model.

Theological Framework: A "God-View"

The theological framework lens could be described as Steve's understanding of "the way God sees." Based upon biblical knowledge and theological reasoning each person has a perception of who God is and how He views the created world, including people and relationships. The theological lens is the core of the leader's belief system. This lens is not limited to the leader's explicit doctrinal statements, however. Every leader, including Steve, has internalized theological beliefs that shape how he "reads and reacts" in a given context.

The significance of a fully developed, consciously reflective theological presuppositions lens can be described in these ways:

1. It provides the basic rationale for youth ministry.

Youth ministers lament the poor understanding others have of their role in the church or on the campus. Expectations to "baby-sit" or "entertain" the youth are as frustrating as the subtle messages which imply that youth ministry is not a "real job." The youth ministry leader's polemic is primarily a theological one. Youth ministry is a component of the Great Commission (Matthew 28:19–20) and the body of Christ's "ministry of reconciliation" (see 2 Corinthians 5:20–21). The vision for youth ministry should be driven by obedience to

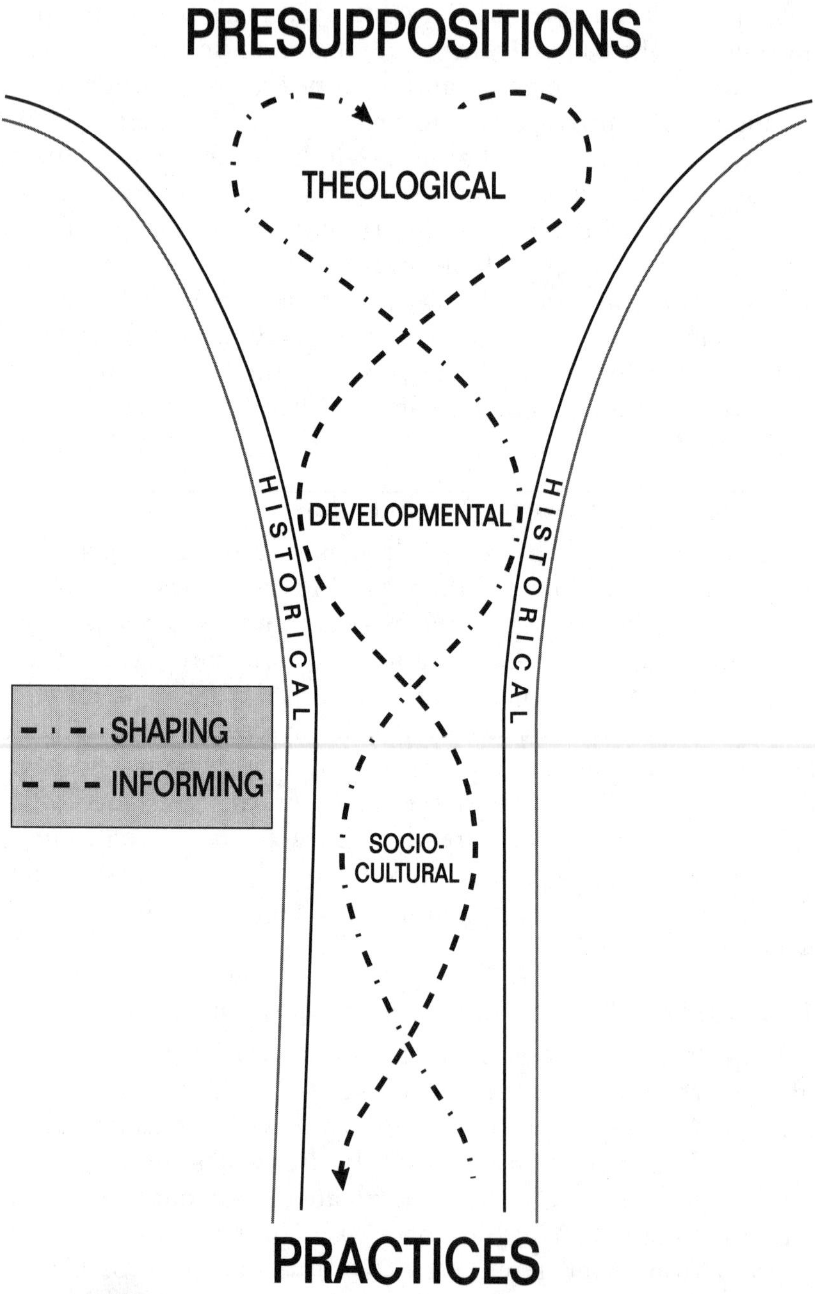

PRESUPPOSITIONS

Figure 1.1. *A Model of Youth Ministry*

God's commands to the church, not by the need to "take care of the kids."

A mature, well-articulated rationale challenges others' myopic visions of youth ministry. Rather than asking evaluative questions such as "Are the high school students active in the church?" or "Do the junior high students' parents like the youth program of the church?" the theological lens calls into question the bigger picture of what is happening in the student's spiritual lives.

2. It guides the ministry Godward.

First Peter 4:10–11 reveals the heart of the focus of ministry leadership:

> Each of you should use whatever gift he has received to serve others, faithfully administering God's grace in its various forms. If anyone speaks, he should do it as one speaking the very words of God. If anyone serves, he should do it with the strength God provides, so that in all things God may be praised through Jesus Christ. To him be the glory and the power forever and ever. Amen.

It is too easy to begin to focus ministry on one's own agenda. Increasing numbers, gaining prestige in the community or denomination, and fueling one's self-esteem can usurp the agenda of the youth ministry program. The theological lens calls leaders back to "first things."

3. It guides the ministry into the faith community.

Growth in Christian maturity is not meant to be pursued in isolation from significant relationships with other members of Christ's body (Ephesians 4:11–16). A mature theological framework considers the implications of God's design of the local church as a place where children and youth participate in an intentional, intergenerational faith community.

Guiding the ministry into the faith community is critical. Students' spiritual growth is stunted if they are lacking in spiritual relationships with peers *and* adults. Peers may have the most immediate impact on the life of an adolescent. Parents and adult mentors, however, have the most important long-term effect on students' lives. By God's design, students need to belong to and participate in the life of the local church.

4. It critiques ministry practices.

Scripture does not provide a how-to guide for youth ministers. Although some would suggest that "the biblical way" to do youth ministry exists, the reality is that there are many ways to do youth ministry that are consistent with biblical values, commands, and principles. At the same time, not all that passes for youth ministry is necessarily biblical.

A mature theological view of ministry understands that there is a difference between an idea that has biblical foundations and practicing that idea in a biblical manner. For instance, one might hold to the belief that it is a biblical practice to develop and equip student leaders for ministry. However, if in the implementation of that strategy the youth leader exhibits favoritism and partiality to these students, then the "biblical" strategy becomes an "unbiblical" practice. Being biblical, therefore, requires a continual evaluation of the *why, what,* and *how* of youth ministry.

5. It determines the content and shapes the delivery of the teaching.

Theological presuppositions will ultimately drive the teaching component of a ministry. A commitment to teach Scripture in a way that honors its unique role as specific revelation will honor God's intent that the Word is to be taught for response and life-change. Teaching for knowledge of the Bible will be foundational, but that teaching is incomplete unless one also guides the learners toward a thoughtful and loving obedience to God. Delivery, a part of the "hidden curriculum" of teaching, must also be critiqued for the implicit messages being communicated about what it means to know and love God.

6. It provides ministry motivation and challenge for service.

Nothing could read more like a youth ministry leader's heart than Paul's self-description of his ministry in 1 Thessalonians 2:8: "We loved you so much that we were delighted to share with you not only the gospel of God but our lives as well, because you had become so dear to us."

Like Paul, youth ministry leaders are aware of the substantial personal investment required for meaningful life change. In youth ministry, terms such as *relational youth ministry* and *incarnational ministry* are often used to describe that personal impartation of one's life.

Imparting one's life, however, is no easy task. After his first six months in ministry, a graduate called one day to give me a report of his experiences. His words were telling: "You told us that ministry was hard, but I never really believed you. Now I know what you meant; in fact, it is harder than you said it would be."

Ministry is more work than fun, more sacrifice than recreation. How does one stay motivated to deal with the disappointments, failures, and criticisms that are inevitably a part of the ministry experience? Paul found his motivation for enduring in the sacrificial life of Christ:

> Your attitude should be the same as that of Christ Jesus: Who, being in very nature God, did not consider equality with God something to be grasped, but made himself nothing, taking the very nature of a servant, being made in human likeness. And being found in appearance as a man, he humbled himself and became obedient to death—even death on a cross! (Philippians 2:5–8)

Leaders need a theology that has begun to develop a mature concept of the serving nature of ministry. Part of the reason youth ministry leaders have such short tenures in churches and on campuses is that they have failed to develop the theological maturity needed to weather the inevitable hurts that occur in ministry leadership.

Steve's ministry perspective can begin to be theologically focused. His first step must include identifying and evaluating his current theological presuppositions. Steve can discover the essential foundations for this step in chapter 2, "A Theological Framework for Doing Youth Ministry." Those foundations will provide the context for Steve to ask these *shaping* and *informing* questions:

- *What are my core theological beliefs?*
For example, what do I believe about God, sin, salvation, and Scripture?

- *How do my beliefs presently shape my ministry practices?*
For example, how does God's sovereignty affect the way I do ministry among the students?

- *Are there any points at which I need to make adjustments so that my practices in ministry are reshaped in a manner more consistent with what I believe to be theologically true? Do any of my practices contradict my beliefs?*
For example, am I emphasizing God's grace and holiness in my teaching, yet failing to confront students appropriately when I recognize sinful attitudes and behaviors?

- *How are my experiences in ministry informing my theological framework? What theological issues do I need to explore more thoroughly or revisit for clarification?*
For example, how do I present God as Father to a student whose father is physically and/or emotionally absent from the home? In fact, how do I understand the concept of God as Father in my own life?

Developmental Framework: A "Youth-View"

A developmental framework is Steve's understanding of the way the world is experienced in the life stage of adolescence: "the way youth see." "How do students experience and make sense of their world?" is the central question to be answered. The framework, therefore, takes seriously the role the adolescent developmental process plays in a student's personal and spiritual formation.

A developmental framework lens is an area where leaders too often develop ministry "brain cramps." Developmental mistakes are among the easiest leadership errors to make. All persons tend to see the world from their own perspective. When my daughter Jessica was only four years old I discovered that she was tall enough to ride several of the roller coasters at the Six Flags theme park near our home. My enthusiasm for roller coasters and her lack of fear of heights convinced me that she too would love them. First we tried out the Whizzer, a small but quick roller coaster. Her analysis at the end was, "I would take my children on that."

We were, in my estimation, ready for the big time. I led my daughter to the far end of the park where the great white roller coaster, the American Eagle, sat waiting to drop us down a one hundred-foot hill at fifty-five miles per hour. As we embarked, Jessica was content with looking out at the scenery. I, too, was enjoying sharing the ride with her—until we reached the top. It was at that point I realized we might have a problem. As soon as we were catapulted down the hill I knew I had experienced the equivalent of a brain cramp.

As we hurtled forward, I turned to see the look of terror on my little girl's face. As soon as we went up the next hill, she said, "Is it over?" "Well, sort of, honey. There's a little bit left," I responded, as we were launched into a next series of breathtaking, teeth-jarring hills. I felt guilty the whole agonizing three minutes (it felt like three hours) of the ride—not to mention the anxiety that overwhelmed me when I realized Jessica would definitely want to tell Mom about Dad's great idea!

Developmental mistakes in ministry can cause more damage than is caused by taking one's child on an American Eagle terror ride. I can recall a junior high retreat where I encouraged students to make a commitment to pray for thirty minutes a day when they returned home. In a desire to please God and their youth pastor, they made the commitment. I felt very satisfied about the results until about Wednesday of the week after the retreat. As I began to reflect on how much difficulty I was having in keeping that commitment, I repented for what I had done to those students in my sincere, but misguided, zeal. I had set the students up for failure in their attempts to develop a spiritual discipline. What seemed to be a good idea was actually a bad one. My ministry brain cramp led to discouragement, not discipline for my eager junior high students.

A developmental framework for youth ministry is important in several ways.

1. It overcomes inaccurate stereotypes.

Stereotypes are often made concerning adolescents as a whole, as well as in reference to individuals. Adults tend to treat adolescents as either "big kids" or "little adults." They are neither. Yet they are both. Adults must work to respect and honor the unique challenges and opportunities of this age "between the times."

Furthermore, individual students are easily misunderstood. I remember Henry, a ninth grader who bench-pressed more than most of the seniors on his high school football team. Adults who looked at Henry's six-foot-plus frame tended to project onto him a maturity beyond that of a fourteen-year-old. In fact, Henry possessed an emotional maturity that was *less* than a fourteen-year-old. Henry required patience in understanding that he was not what he appeared to be.

2. It informs theological understanding of spiritual maturity.

Adults must be careful not to mistake characteristics of adolescent development for sin. For example, selflessness is considered by Jesus as an important spiritual quality. Students in the youth group can display selflessness on missions trips or in a giving of their time which surpasses that of any adult in the church. Those same students can also make choices that reveal a decidedly egocentric orientation. Why? In some cases, these choices may truly be expressions of sinful, selfish attitudes. In other cases, they may simply reflect developmental immaturity.

Whatever the root of the behavior (maybe it is a combination of sin *and* immaturity), the attitude must be confronted appropriately, displaying sensitivity to what is taking place in the adolescents' maturation process. Too often youth are alienated from the spiritual lives of adults because of misunderstandings and, consequently, impatience on the part of adults.

3. It provides tangible "touch points" for intangible spiritual ministry.

A leader cannot physically touch the student spiritually. Yet every conversation, pat on the back, and nonverbal response makes an impact on the spiritual life of the student. How does one know how to "touch" students in spiritually meaningful ways? The answer lies in coming to a holistic understanding of how an adolescent experiences, interprets, and responds to her world. An informed developmental perspective helps to discriminate among the plethora of teaching, relationship building, and programming possibilities that exist in a given context. As a consequence, the leader is better able to prepare more purposefully for ministry students at their points of need and growth.

4. It shapes the discernment of outcomes and process of assessment.

Too often the church leadership stamps its approval on student ministries if students do not "smoke, drink, chew, or run with those who do"; if they are respectful and behave appropriately in church; and if they remain active in the youth group. However, a mature understanding of human development indicates that the goal is not to "get them through high school." Rather, the goal is to prepare them for adulthood.

Steve's ministry perspective can begin to be developmentally focused. Steve can increase the clarity of his understanding of adolescent developmental issues by reading chapter 3, "A Developmental Framework for Doing Youth Ministry." He will then be prepared to address the same pattern of critical *shaping* and *informing* questions he faced in his critique of his theological presuppositions:

- *What are the core components of my understanding of the developmental stages of the adolescents to whom I minister?*
  For example, what are they experiencing intellectually and emotionally at this stage of life?

- *How do the developmental stages of adolescence shape the way I do youth ministry?*
  For example, how has an understanding of the differences between early and late adolescents guided my strategies for using and training my adult sponsors for ministry to the students in their various stages of mental, emotional, and social maturity?

- *Are there any points at which I need to reshape my ministry practices in light of what I am coming to understand about the students' personal and spiritual development?*
  For example, does my teaching on obedience to God include ways for late adolescents to deal with the inconsistencies they discover in their own lives?

- *How are my experiences in ministry informing my developmental framework? What developmental issues do I need to explore more thoroughly or revisit for clarification?*
  For example, high school upperclassmen seem to move away from the church no matter what programs are in place. How does this reframe my questions about later adolescent developmental processes? What clues for solving this dilemma can be found in the literature on adolescent development?

- *How do the issues raised in my exploration of the developmental framework inform my theological framework? What theological issues do I need to explore more thoroughly or revisit for clarification?*
  For example, if late adolescents go through a period of struggling with "owning" their faith, how do I integrate this concept with what God reveals about spiritual growth in Scripture? What does this integration suggest I should be doing to prepare seniors for graduation and young adulthood?

Sociocultural Framework: An "Inside-View"

Whereas the developmental framework examines how the

adolescent life-stage contributes to a teenager's view of the world, the sociocultural framework addresses how their environment shapes that perspective into a worldview. The sociocultural framework is formed by the youth leader's understanding of (a) the students' views of social roles, networks, groups, and interpersonal affiliations and (b) the students' relationship to cultural symbols, myths, rituals, belief systems, and worldviews.

Social settings such as families and immediate peer groups have a profound influence upon the self-image and worldview of a student. A dysfunctional family system or a prolonged sense of rejection by friends at school can lead to patterns of self-protection and feelings of inadequacy in interpersonal relationships. Cultural values as demonstrated or communicated through the media, school system, or family lifestyle and practices likewise make a significant, though at times more subtle, impact on a student's overall orientation to life. For instance, the consumerism and materialism of the American culture can be internalized unknowingly by students. Given prolonged exposure to advertisers' seductive marketing strategies and/or parents who always feel the need to "keep up with the Joneses" (who, by the way, are trying to keep up with the Smiths), students assimilate the values that permeate their world.

In light of the power of social and cultural environments, John Detonni exhorts all youth leaders to be ethnographers. He defines ethnography as "the intentional study of a culture or subculture by someone from outside that culture or subculture" (Detonni 1993, 55). A youth worker, as a participant-observer who is among the students yet not truly one of them, performs the following tasks in response to the youth culture:

> [He] *describes* the culture/subculture, stating what it is; *analyzes* it, showing how it works; *interprets* it, stating its meaning *to* the culture's members; *predicts* it, telling what will happen, and is able to live harmoniously within that culture. (Detonni 1993, 55)

As ethnographers, youth workers must try to make sense out of youth culture. They must try to develop an insider's point of view of what it means to be saturated with this environment. The purpose of this cultural examination is twofold: to assist adults in building relational bridges to students and to assist adults in guiding students in their process of "making meaning" of their Christian faith in the midst of their world.

The sociocultural framework is significant for these reasons:

1. It bridges generational assumptions.

Baby boomers. Baby busters. Generation X. The Millennial Generation. The practice of naming generations is an attempt to identify common values, beliefs, and worldviews among a group of people born in a particular historical era. Though such identifications are broad generalizations, they speak to the differences that emerge, depending on the economic, political, religious, and moral climates within which people are nurtured. Because these differences are real, adult members of one generation must work to avoid misunderstanding the adolescent members of the next.

2. It bridges cultural assumptions.

Diversity is emerging as the rule rather than the exception in North American culture. Rural and urban, African-American and Asian-American, Hispanic and Arabic, the world in which students are growing up is full of a variety of shades of skin, first languages, and religious affiliations. The contextualization of the gospel and the development of relevant ministry strategies often require seeing the world from another cultural point of view.

3. It informs a holistic understanding of an individual's personal and spiritual development.

Although the theological framework provides the doctrines for identifying true spirituality and the developmental framework suggests how students grow spiritually as they develop personally, the sociocultural lens describes the students' relationships, which will either support or work against spiritual maturity. Every student in a youth ministry context brings with her a past of parental and peer relationships, as well as a present set of such significant relationships.

These are the "forces" that will have much to do with how she grows spiritually. Understanding these relational contexts prevents leaders from presenting one-size-fits-all approaches to spiritual growth.

4. It provides a framework for exegeting behavior.

"I just don't understand these kids." Even the most seasoned youth leader at times is at a loss to explain the "why" of students' behavior—both positive and negative. Why students like a certain musical style, dress the way they do, choose the persons they date, and spend their money the way they do can often be explained by their sociocultural contexts.

5. It critiques the relevance of practices for a moment in time.

"If it ain't broke, don't fix it" would be a poor motto for youth ministry leadership. The rapidity of social change, the diversity of contemporary culture, and the complexity of students' lives suggest that what worked before may not be the most effective approach now. City-wide rallies, process small groups, and door-to-door evangelism are among the ministry options that may be effective in one setting but not in another. The effectiveness of a strategy will largely be determined by sociocultural factors.

6. It identifies, in concert with the developmental lens, tangible "touch points" for incarnational ministry among youth.

One only has to look at Jesus' ministry with the woman at the well in John 4 and Paul's ministry in Athens in Acts 17 to discover how important understanding relational and cultural contexts can be in ministry. Knowing that Jill's parents are divorced, that Joey feels like a "loser" in his high school, that all of Mark's friends are into heavy metal music, and that Marcia's family struggles to pay their bills every month all matter when one considers how best to enable these students to understand and experience God in their daily lives.

Steve's ministry perspective can begin to be socioculturally focused. Steve will find a model for social analysis of a youth ministry context in chapter 4, "A Sociological Framework for

Doing Youth Ministry." Steve will then be prepared to address the same pattern of critical *shaping* and *informing* questions that he faced in his evaluation of his theological and developmental lenses:

- *What are the key characteristics of the students' sociocultural environments?*
  For example, what are their families like in composition and in terms of values?

- *How does the sociocultural context of my students shape the way I do youth ministry?*
  For example, how do the family backgrounds of my students inform the way I am developing this ministry?

- *Are there any points at which I need to make adjustments in my ministry practices in light of what I am coming to understand about the students' relational and cultural contexts?*
  For example, if students lack meaningful relational contact with adults, what new strategies should I be exploring?

- *How are my experiences in ministry informing my sociocultural framework? What sociocultural issues do I need to explore more thoroughly or revisit for clarification?*
  For example, if my students seem to be uninterested in corporate worship, are there sociocultural-issues clues that would guide me as I engage them and motivate them to participate in church worship?

- *How do the issues raised in my exploration of the sociocultural framework inform my theological or developmental frameworks? What theological or developmental issues do I need to explore more thoroughly or revisit for clarification?*
  For example, how do I understand true worship for these students in light of their approach to God in their music, their relational styles, and their concept of spirituality? What theological and developmental questions emerge

from their culturally relevant forms of worship? How can answers to these questions be useful in guiding their worship ever more Godward, while also enabling them to make worship their own?

TOWARD A MATURE MINISTRY PERSPECTIVE

Developing one's ministry perspective is a long-term process of focusing theological, developmental, and sociocultural lenses (see Getz 1988 for a similar development). For Steve, a new context has served as a catalyst for intentionally broadening and sharpening his particular understanding of the nature and practice of youth ministry. Ultimately, it will be his daily commitment to listen to students, to seek wisdom in God's Word, to pray with and for the students, to reflect upon successes and failures, and to submit to the guidance of the Holy Spirit that will help him form an increasingly mature ministry perspective.

Steve came to Easton to make a difference by ministering the gospel to students in the community. Little did he know that the ministry of the gospel in that community would make such a difference in him.

WORKS CITED

Clinton, Robert J. 1988. *The Making of a Leader.* Colorado Springs: NavPress.

Detonni, John M. 1993. *Introduction to Youth Ministry.* Grand Rapids: Zondervan.

Getz, Gene A. 1988. *Sharpening the Focus of the Church.* Wheaton, Ill.: Scripture Press.

Richards, Lawrence O. 1985. *Youth Ministry: Its Renewal in the Local Church.* Rev. ed. Grand Rapids: Zondervan.

Warren, Michael. 1987. *Youth, Gospel, Liberation.* San Francisco: Harper & Row.

Wyckoff, D. Campbell, and Don Richter, eds. 1982. *Religious Education with Youth.* Birmingham: Religious Education.

2

A Theological Framework for Doing Youth Ministry

Richard R. Dunn

Programs may be the flesh and bones of Elizabeth's youth ministry. They are not, however, its heart and soul. On Saturday, Elizabeth spent an entire evening with Heather, a student wrestling with spiritual doubt. Over Monday morning breakfast she searched for words of support and confidence to offer Dan, a lay volunteer experiencing a profound sense of personal inadequacy. Wednesday, in the Thompsons' living room, Elizabeth silently passed a Kleenex to Mrs. Thompson as the distressed mother related her teenage daughter's pregnancy.

Relationships, human need, and questions about how to find meaning in the midst of life's circumstances—these are the heart and soul of Elizabeth's youth ministry. Because these are sacred places, where God is met in the most intimate and personal ways, Elizabeth's relational ministry must be considered inherently theological.

Theology, however, is often perceived as a secondary rather than primary resource for the challenges Elizabeth is facing. While most youth ministry texts do provide some biblical basis for their strategies and practices, theology is arguably the least written about aspect of youth ministry.

MISCONCEPTIONS CONCERNING THEOLOGY

What prevents theology from being a more direct resource? Three misconceptions are the most immediately identifiable hindrances: theology is routinely dismissed as being *too big, too impractical,* and *too divisive.*

Too Big

My friend Dan is a youth pastor—a very tall youth pastor. Six feet, six inches to be exact. Besides being tall, he has broad shoulders and a strong, athletic frame. If it were not for his gentle spirit and warm smile, he would be intimidating. Hoping to get a closer look at this imposing figure, a toddler recently waddled over to Dan. As the little guy came close, he began to turn his gaze upward toward Dan's face. Up past the knees, above the waist and beyond, he surveyed his giant discovery. Leaning further and further back, he was soon looking at Dan's chest and . . . and . . . ummphh! The toddler fell over, flat on his back. There had simply been too much Dan for this two-year-old to absorb.

The subject of theology can feel like a "Dan" to youth ministry leaders. The idea of exploring theology can seem intimidating, overwhelming, and insurmountable.

Too Impractical

Simply mention theology and persons immediately think of terms like *amillennial* and *premillennial, dispensationalist* and *reformed, liberal* and *evangelical.* Such theological terms sound lofty, cerebral, and removed from everyday life with God. When there are students whose parents are getting divorced, whose friends are getting pregnant, and whose dreams are being dashed by economic realities, youth leaders may struggle to find value in examining the "fine print" of their faith. Leaders question how valuable theological studies could be if they do not produce any identifiable practical results.

Too Divisive

Youth ministry has traditionally been one place where denominational and ministerial distinctives among Christians have been able to be set aside for the greater good of the kingdom. Youth ministry conferences and training seminars sponsored by such organizations as Youth Specialties and Group have long been ecumenical, bringing together persons of all manner of church backgrounds. Perhaps because of the lesser attention paid to theological distinctives, the work of youth ministry has often flourished as Episcopalians ministered alongside Baptists and Assemblies of God students served on missions teams with Presbyterians. Fearing the loss of vitality that theological differences bring, many youth leaders opt for a less sophisticated approach to their particular beliefs.

A RATIONALE FOR INTENTIONAL THEOLOGICAL LEARNING

Theological issues emerge in the living of life and the doing of ministry. Discouraged by the factors just mentioned, leaders may conclude that the best approach is simply to deal with theological concerns as they surface. A preferred response, however, is to pursue theological learning before, during, and after the emergence of critical questions that explicitly demand God's wisdom. This chapter is designed to encourage youth ministry leaders toward this end by presenting the *purpose* and *impact* of intentional theological learning.

Purpose: Why Pursue Theological Learning ?

The true purpose of theological study is knowing God. Before describing what it means to have knowledge of God, James Wilhoit, in *Christian Education and the Search for Meaning,* quotes J. I. Packer in *Knowing God:*

> What were we made for? To know God. What aim should we set ourselves in life? To know God. What is the "eternal life" that Jesus gives? Knowledge of God. "This is life eternal, that they might know thee, the only true God, and Jesus Christ,

whom thou hast sent" (John 17:3). What is the best thing in life, bringing more joy, delight, and contentment, than anything else? Knowledge of God. (Wilhoit 1991, 37)

Wilhoit goes on to describe "true knowledge" of God as "facts, feelings, and proper relationship" (Wilhoit 1991, 42). Facts learned primarily in the study of God's Word, feelings experienced in response to who we have come to understand Him to be, and a personal relationship with God that has been formed from "shared experiences, commitment, and communication" comprise an authentic portrait of knowledge of God (1991, 38).

Too often Christians limit their concept of *theological learning* to the formal, systematic theological studies found in Bible colleges and seminaries. I have seen evidence of this confusion in many instances. Sometimes when I ask a youth leader or youth ministry student to describe his theological perspective on a particular topic of interest, he gives me that "deer caught in the headlights" gaze. These blank stares—and blank thoughts—are unfortunate. The whole of theology is not contained in formal statements, sophisticated systems of interpretation, and technical terms. Likewise, the ultimate purpose of theological learning is more than what can be contained in technical theological scholarship.

To balance the picture, it is crucial to recognize that disciplined systematic study of theology is an important component in theological learning. Mark Twain is credited with saying, "In the beginning, God created man in his own image, and man, being a gentleman, returned the favor." Left to a subjective, limited experiential perspective, even well-meaning Christians can easily turn their understanding of God into an image that conforms to their personal idea of what He should be, rather than the reality of who God is. The all-too-common "domestication" of God that results must be countered by the light of God's truth.

The *discipline* of theology—the formal and systematic elements of theological study—is an essential tool in the Christian's process of coming to a greater, truer personal knowledge of God. Theological studies supply the tools necessary for building a right understanding of and relationship to God. Perry Downs explains that role:

> *Theology* is systematic inquiry into Scripture. Theology is a human attempt to make sense of and draw conclusions from God's special revelation. The rules that control this inquiry are the rules of hermeneutics and logic. To do good theology one must attempt rigorous objectivity as he seeks to determine truth, but always with a degree of humility that acknowledges that only Scripture is absolute truth. Theology can be corrupted by human sinfulness and made unclear by lack of spiritual insight. (Downs 1994, 15)

Rigorous, systematic study is necessary to form and defend orthodox doctrine for the church of Jesus Christ. This disciplined theological inquiry acts as informant, corrective, and confirmer of one's personal knowledge of God. The results need not be impractical or divisive. Rather, such learning should, as Downs suggests, fuel an ongoing process of seeking, critiquing, and refining an increasingly mature knowledge of God.

God is thus seen as both source and object in theological learning. Viewed from this perspective, theology is still challenging, but far less intimidating. A child naturally wants to know his Father well.

Impact: What Difference Does Theology Make?

Impulsively one might be tempted to identify "increased accuracy in the teaching of the Scriptures" as the only substantial ministry result of disciplined theological learning. If teaching God's Truth more truthfully and faithfully is the only benefit of intentional theological learning, then the pursuit is well worth the effort. Paul instructed Timothy, "Do your best to present yourself to God as one approved, a workman who does not need to be ashamed and who correctly handles the word of truth" (2 Timothy 2:15). Although Paul's words are challenging, James's words are sobering: "Not many of you should presume to be teachers, my brothers, because you know that we who teach will be judged more strictly" (James 3:1). Because accuracy in interpreting *and* communicating

God's Word is an essential goal for all youth ministry leaders, mastering the tools of biblical hermeneutics is crucial. Even those who believe in and are fully committed to the Bible can teach in a theologically impoverished way if they have not learned how to explore its truth appropriately.

The impact of theological learning is not limited, however, to proper hermeneutics and teaching. As we have seen, the depth of one's personal relationship with God is directly affected by the authenticity of one's factual knowledge of Him. Consequently, because ministry is about relationships, the youth leader's theology has a profound effect on the depth of his youth ministry leadership. Jay Kesler says that the effect of the youth leader's theological understanding is not just profound, but pervasive.

> The theology of the youth worker is ultimately more important than his or her strategy or methodology. . . . Your personal theology will have an effect on everything you do in youth work. It will influence the type of message you bring, the response you expect, the progress of the youth among whom you minister, your method of counseling, your attitude towards others, and how you measure results. In short, all we do relates to what we actually believe. (Kesler 1983, 23)

Every believer has a theological perspective—a "life lens" based on his internalized concept of God. (In fact every person has a worldview out of which he interprets life.) Youth leaders cannot be *atheological* about life or ministry. Explicitly or implicitly, their internalized beliefs emerge. The "God questions" of ministry guarantee that the ministry leader's theology will be communicated and demonstrated. It is simply a matter of whether leaders are willing to invest the energy necessary to identify and shape that emergence.

CONSTRUCTING A THEOLOGICAL FRAMEWORK

A theological framework for doing youth ministry consists of three components: theological foundations, personal implications, and ministry applications. *Theological foundations* are the raw materials necessary for developing a life and ministry that reflect true knowledge of God. *Personal implica-*

tions address the impact basic theological foundations should have on the life of the leader. Because the leader's life is the primary teaching tool in ministry, how the leader's theology shapes her life will be what students learn most about God through her ministry. *Ministry applications* are principles and practices that directly follow from the theological foundations. The youth ministry leader should seek to make the "why" of youth ministry explicit in the "what" of youth ministry.

Six theological topics can be used as the basic building blocks of a theological foundation for youth ministry. The cornerstone, of course, would be God Himself. The other five building blocks are Scripture, humanity, sin, salvation, and the faith community of the church. The remainder of this chapter address each of these topics as a way of outlining how a youth minister could construct a theological foundation for his ministry.

Immediately following the discussion of each building block are representative *personal implications* and *ministry applications*. These brief sections provide examples of how theological foundations shape the life and ministry of a youth ministry leader. The examples by no means exhaust the implications and applications that arise from each topic. Rather, the suggested results of sound theological thinking illustrate the process and product of constructing a disciplined theological framework.

BUILDING BLOCK #1: GOD

When God speaks about Himself, He does so in personal terms. Consider, for example, His words to Solomon at the time of the dedication of the temple.

> I have heard your prayer and have chosen this place for myself as a temple for sacrifices.
> When I shut up the heavens so that there is no rain, or command locusts to devour the land or send a plague among my people, if my people, who are called by my name, will humble themselves and pray and seek my face and turn from their wicked ways, then will I hear from heaven and will forgive their sin and will heal their land. Now my eyes will be

open and my ears attentive to the prayers offered in this
place. I have chosen and consecrated this temple so that my
Name may be there forever. My eyes and my heart will
always be there. (2 Chronicles 7:12–16)

The personal pronouns, the anthropomorphisms (figures
of speech referring to God in human terms), and the call of
the Hebrews to meaningful relationship provide a clear image
of God as personal being.

God's Attributes

But how does one *describe* the "person" of God? The
uniqueness of God's self is an infinite, inexhaustible topic. An
important aspect of describing the uniqueness of that self is to
identify God's *attributes,* "those qualities of God which constitute what He is" (Erickson 1985, 265). Millard Erickson
uses the categories of greatness and goodness to describe
God's attributes. Under the heading of *greatness,* Erickson
lists "spirituality, personality, life, infinity, and constancy"
(1985, 267). In terms of *goodness,* Erickson asserts that the
attributes of goodness God possesses are moral purity (holiness, righteousness, justice), integrity (genuineness, veracity,
faithfulness), and love (benevolence, grace, mercy, persistence) (1985, 283–97). When children recite the prayer "God
is great, God is good," they are making important theological
statements about His person!

God's Trinitarian Existence

An additional aspect of God's unique being is found in His
trinitarian existence. God's three-in-one personhood is a central tenet of the Christian faith. James Buswell writes: "The
Biblical doctrine of the Trinity may well be outlined by four
propositions: (1) God is one. (2) Jesus is God. (3) The Holy
Spirit is God. (4) These three persons are in the subject-object
relationship, each to the others within the Godhead" (1962,
102).

God's existence as Trinity is indeed a profound mystery.
What emerges as a portrait of God's personhood is as wonderful as it is mysterious. As Creator/Father, God is the source of
life. In His greatness and His goodness He is sovereign over

all. As Father, He is perfectly able, perfectly loving, and perfectly holy. As Son, God has provided redemption from sin and the hope of eternal life with Him. Jesus Christ is the human incarnation of the second person of the Trinity. Fully man, fully God, Jesus is humanity's Savior, Lord, High Priest, and King. As Holy Spirit, God is "the activator and sustainer of life, the Spirit of Truth, and the transformer of persons" (Pazmino 1988, 61).

God empowers His children to know, experience, and enjoy Him in intimate relationship. This level of intimacy is a reflection of Himself. As three-in-one, God has eternally been in intimate communication and communion with Himself.

How does an accurate concept of God shape the life and ministry of the youth leader?

Personal Implications

1. My first priority is to develop my own personal relationship with God.

Gwyn Baker, a veteran youth worker, reminds young leaders that "loving kids is not your first responsibility as a youth worker. Loving God must come first." Far too many youth workers have shipwrecked their lives and ministries because they reversed this order. A proper view of God reminds us that our relationship with Him is our highest calling.

2. Because He is perfectly able, loving, and holy, I can trust Him with my daily life needs, questions, and relationships.

Youth ministry demands an enormous amount of mental, physical, emotional, and spiritual energy. When this energy is depleted, the students are not responding, and the board is questioning your approach to outreach, it is natural to begin to feel alone, unappreciated, and inadequate. Confidence in God's goodness and greatness is critical during these painful emotional seasons. Leaders who look to His faithfulness will find that they can trust God in spite of their circumstances.

Ministry Implications

1. God precedes me in my places of ministry.

When Elizabeth sits down to talk with Mrs. Thompson's daughter about her pregnancy, she does not have to wonder whether God will show up. His presence has preceded her. God has been at work to communicate Himself personally to the hurting girl in the midst of her need. Elizabeth need not look for ways to get God to act—He already has.

2. God must be presented for all of who He is, not just those attributes on which I selectively tend to focus.

To present God as holy without presenting His grace leads students to view God as a principal or policeman. To present God's grace without teaching His holiness leads students to view Him as a kind old man or Santa Claus. Neither is an accurate portrait of His character.

Mrs. Thompson's daughter needs to experience both God's holy conviction and His gracious compassion. Students need to be taught that He is a God to be feared as well as a God to be embraced. If we weight the focus one way or another we deprive students of the opportunity to encounter God's fullness.

BUILDING BLOCK #2: SCRIPTURE

The Bible is God's "propositional" and "personal" revelation. As propositional revelation, Scripture is an "uncovering" of God's attributes. Much can be learned about God by observing His creation, particularly His most precious creature, humanity. However, without His direct communication of Himself, men and women would be left with only subjective answers to the question "What is God like?"

As personal revelation, Scripture is a direct invitation to relationship. God's Word is given to provide us with an opportunity not only to know *what* He is like but to know Him *interpersonally.*

Because the inspired Scriptures are God's personal and propositional truth, the Bible is to have authority over the believer's life. Pazmino states the significance of biblical authority strongly:

The written Word of God is Scripture in its entirety and variety, and evangelicals are to teach the whole counsel of God. This stance does not imply a mindless literalism, but appropriation of the plain or commonsense meaning of Scripture as normative for thought and practice. The Scriptures are viewed as divinely inspired and believers are called to discern a biblical agenda . . . in all areas of thought and practice. The Scriptures function as the final authority and serve as the grid through which all others truths are examined for their consistency with a Christian world and life view. (1988, 50)

The Bible is explicit in its self-attestation to its authority:

All Scripture is God-breathed and is useful for teaching, rebuking, correcting and training in righteousness, so that the man of God may be thoroughly equipped for every good work. (2 Timothy 3:16–17)

Above all, you must understand that no prophecy of Scripture came about by the prophet's own interpretation. For prophecy never had its origin in the will of man, but men spoke from God as they were carried along by the Holy Spirit. (2 Peter 1:20–21)

For the word of God is living and active. Sharper than any double-edged sword, it penetrates even to dividing soul and spirit, joints and marrow; it judges the thoughts and attitudes of the heart. (Hebrews 4:12)

Far from being merely a good book or a static reference text, the Bible is God's heart *inscripturated* for personal and spiritual growth in relationship to Him.

How does an accurate view of Scripture shape the life and ministry of the youth leader?

Personal Implications

1. I must approach my reading, study, and memorization of the Word with a view towards understanding more of who God is.

Having devotions is one thing; building devotion is another. Examining a text to interpret its meaning is one task; allowing that text to examine one's heart is another. Leaders often fall victim to reading God's Word with a view toward teaching about it rather than simply being taught by it. The Bible is a personal revelation of God, and it should be read accordingly.

2. I must yield to biblical authority in my life.

James warns against those who hear but fail to do God's Word (James 1:22). God's Word is used by the Holy Spirit to convict, to comfort, and to coach. Leaders need to respond obediently to conviction, receptively to comfort, and willingly to coaching. "Religious ruts" rob leaders of the vitality of being God's child and servant. The active authority of the Word shakes leaders out of this lethargy.

Ministry Implications

1. Scripture should be taught as an alive, active, dynamic revelation of God.

The Bible should be taught so that persons see the truth in a "three-dimensional" way. The Bible should be presented in all its drama, vibrancy, and historical reality. A teenage shepherd really did kill a giant soldier, a prophet actually spent a weekend in the belly of a fish, and the twelve guys who spent the most time with Jesus were truly clueless half the time. Though the Bible is factually true, it is not written as merely a book of facts. The truth is presented as human story and should be taught likewise.

2. Scripture should be demonstrated as relevant to all of life.

The relevance of the Bible for dealing with parents, making decisions about "how far to go" in romantic physical relationships, working through painful emotions, and overcoming parental divorces should be taught. The Bible does not tell students what to do in every decision they face, but it does provide models, principles, and values that are relevant for the process of decision making.

3. Scripture should not be communicated in a way that suggests that it says something it does not.

For instance, the Bible has limited content on exactly "how far" a couple should go physically. Models, principles, and values found in Scripture can lead to the discovery of what would be consistent with God's will in this area. (See point two above.) However, to bluntly say to students, "The Bible says, 'Thou shalt not go beyond a goodnight kiss,'" is to undermine the students' overall trust of the Scriptures.

As a corollary, leaders should refrain from implying that if a person really understood the Bible all his spiritual questions would be easily answered. Student questions should be affirmed; part of this affirmation is being honest when the questions do not have simple, direct biblical responses. The Bible should be taught without apology for what it does or does not say.

BUILDING BLOCK #3: HUMANITY

The creation of man is recorded in the Bible in a simple, elegant statement: "So God created man in his own image, in the image of God he created him; male and female he created them" (Genesis 1:27). Because we are made in the image of God we are to *mirror* God and to *represent* God. Humanity was created in such a way that to see man and woman is to see "something of God" (Hoekema 1986, 67).

The "something of God" in humanity is described in a variety of ways. Being "like God" includes a self-conscious intellect, the capacity for intimate interpersonal relationships, an affective component of the self that deeply feels the full range of emotions from sorrow to joy, and the capacity to choose and thus make responsible choices in life.

Anthony Hoekema describes the mystery of the uniqueness of humanity:

> The human being is both a creature and a person; he or she is a *created person*. This, now, is the central mystery of man: how can man be both a creature and a person at the same time? To be a creature, as we have seen, means absolute dependence on God; to be a person means relative independence. To be a creature means that I cannot move a finger or

utter a word apart from God; to be a person means that when my fingers are moved, I move them, and that when words are uttered by my lips, I utter them. To be creatures means that God is the potter and we are the clay (Rom. 9:21); to be persons means that we are the ones who fashion our lives by our own decisions (Gal. 6:7–8). (1986, 6)

Dependent, yet having a form of independence, men and women are creatures of inherent dignity and worth—qualities that cannot be experienced fully apart from the One in whose image they were made.

How does an accurate understanding of humanity created in God's image shape the life and ministry of the youth leader?

Personal Implications

1. *I have personal needs that must be met. These needs include intimacy with God, intimacy with friends, loving support from a family or surrogate family, rest, recreation, and celebration.*

   Youth leaders who ignore this reality by working seventy to eighty hours a week will find that human needs have a way of surfacing at some point. Failure to care properly for oneself is the first step toward such problems as relational ineffectiveness, burnout, and moral failure (1996, 29).

2. *I have value in who I am; my self-worth is not contingent on my accomplishments.*

   Too often youth leaders feel that they are of more worth when they are seeing results in their ministries. Consequently, when these leaders struggle personally they simply work harder. Rather than working for an unattainable, externally based sense of worth, struggling leaders need to rest in God's unconditional love.

Ministry Applications

1. *Approach students' spiritual maturation as an integrated component of their total being.*

   Students are physical, emotional, rational, moral, social,

and spiritual beings. Leaders should assist students in not compartmentalizing their lives as if Sunday were more important than Monday or leading a Bible study were more important than being a friend to someone who is lonely.

2. Demonstrate and provide experiences for students' understanding of the image of God in all humanity.

The natural tendency for adolescents is to ascribe greater value to the pretty, the athletic, and the popular. Students need to be guided toward grasping their inherent worth as persons created in God's image. Leaders must be careful not to favor social "winners." Ultimately the leader's prayer is that students will see not only others but themselves from God's point of view.

Learning experiences with racial reconciliation and social justice issues can also be effective means for moving students beyond their comfortable presuppositions about human dignity and value.

3. Model the human experience of Christian spirituality.

Students seek relationships with adult Christians whom they perceive to be "real" persons. Students desire to see how leaders work out their needs, their struggles, and their dreams in relationship to God. Leaders should seek to develop personal authenticity and interpersonal availability if they are to provide this modeling.

BUILDING BLOCK #4: SIN

The human being is such a glorious creation that philosophers and educators throughout history have mistakenly come to the conclusion that humanity is inherently good. Contrary to this optimistic viewpoint, the hearts of men and women are, in fact, "deceitful above all things and beyond cure" (Jeremiah 17:9). Humanity was created "good," but as a result of the choice of sin by Adam and Eve, man has lost innocence and inherent goodness. Sin is pervasive in the human race. Downs summarizes:

Theology describes human sinfulness as *radical corruption*

or *total depravity.* The use of these terms is an attempt to capture the thrust of the Bible's teaching on sinfulness. The terms do not mean that human beings are as bad as they can possibly be. Rather, they imply that sinfulness extends to the total being. (1994, 53)

Man cannot be "good enough" to make up for what was lost. God's most precious creation has become hopelessly lost in its depravity, save God's choice to redeem humanity from its predicament.

How does an accurate concept of human sin shape the life and ministry of the youth leader?

Personal Implications

1. *I need help in becoming less self-deceptive about my personal life.*

Leaders need to be aware of their potential for self-deception. It is easy to rationalize impure motives and inappropriate attitudes. In order to have a fully reflective, "conscious" Christianity, leaders need to be receiving honest, specific, and consistent feedback from persons who know them intimately.

2. *I must actively and directly address the sinful attitudes, behaviors, and patterns I discover in my life.*

Ignoring the presence of sin in one's life will delay the process of facing one's need for growth. Acknowledging sinfulness but not dealing with it directly will also inhibit growth. Leaders must be willing to admit their specific *sins* as well as their general *sinfulness,* the former being much more difficult to accept. Confession, repentance, and intentional efforts to choose righteousness are all premised on having the integrity to address specific sins.

Ministry Applications

1. *Confront sin in the lives of students.*

Students are also candidates for self-deception. Youth ministry leaders may shy away from confronting students because of a fear of losing a relationship. However, loving confrontation that seeks to bring students into a deeper experience of God's holiness and grace is a gift. On the whole, students respond positively to an adult who cares enough to confront them appropriately and biblically.

2. Teach students how to work through failures in the Christian life.

The reality of sin will not go away on this side of eternity. Too often teaching on spiritual growth stresses "steps to success," unintentionally implying that students should be able to "get it right" if they just try hard enough.

Trying hard enough is not the issue. All students will experience personal and spiritual failures at some point. Students need a model of spirituality that enables them to know how to relate to God and how to deal with themselves in times of failure.

BUILDING BLOCK #5: SALVATION

Humanity's dilemma is clear: created as person, man was able to "deform" but not to "reform" the image of God (Augustine). Men and women lack the ability to save themselves. God, however, is not limited by humanity's inability. Paul writes:

> You see, at just the right time, when we were still powerless, Christ died for the ungodly. Very rarely will anyone die for a righteous man, though for a good man someone might possibly dare to die. But God demonstrates his own love for us in this: While we were still sinners, Christ died for us. (Romans 5:6–8)

Pazmino quotes Carl F. H. Henry's eloquent affirmation of the doctrines of Christian salvation:

> [Evangelical Christians] affirm the fundamental doctrines of the gospel, including the incarnation and virgin birth of Jesus Christ, his sinless life, substitutionary atonement, and bodily resurrection as the ground of God's forgiveness of sinners, justification by faith alone, and the spiritual regeneration of all who trust in the redemptive work of Jesus Christ. (In Pazmino 1988, 54)

God's salvation not only forgives past human sinfulness, His salvation has present and future meaning as well:

> Our salvation, as long as we are in this life, is marked by a very real tension between the "already" and the "not yet." The believer is already a participant in the new type of existence associated with the new age, but he or she is not yet in the final state. Whereas we must now continually struggle against sin, we know that someday that struggle will be over. Although we are now *genuinely* new persons in Christ, someday we shall be *totally* new. We know that God has begun a good work in us; but we are confident that one day he will bring that work to completion. (Hoekema 1989, 9–10)

How does an accurate understanding of God's work of salvation shape the life and ministry of the youth leader?

Personal Implications

1. I need to commit myself to "growth in grace."

The "not yet" of salvation indicates that there is much growth to be experienced in this life. The "already" of salvation suggests that we can experience His grace in regards to the past, present, and future. "Growth in grace" occurs as leaders stand firm in His forgiveness while pressing on toward maturity.

2. I should commit to being used by God to share His message of redemption, in all its fullness, with others.

The gospel is to be shared with those who do not know Jesus. The gospel is to be demonstrated to those who know Jesus but still struggle to accept that His love for them is unconditional. The gospel is to be so lived in my neighborhood, community, and friendships that Jesus Christ is made evident to those who observe my words and actions closely.

Ministry Applications

1. Enable students to understand the "already, but not yet" realities that face them at school, home, and in the church.

Living in God's grace, walking by His Spirit, and trusting Him with every area of one's life is a learned lifestyle. For some students, it is a particularly difficult lifestyle to practice. How can they live out Christ in a non-Christian home? What does it mean to be forgiven yet continue to struggle with a particular sin? How can they be "normal" in their schools and still stand up for Christ? Students need guidelines and guidance, challenge and support for their own growth in grace.

2. Prepare students to share their faith and provide vehicles for outreach to their friends.

Students want to share their faith, but often lack understanding, skills, and appropriate opportunities. Providing training coupled with outreach events, such as game nights, concerts, and retreats, helps students to build bridges between their faith and their friends.

BUILDING BLOCK #6:
FAITH COMMUNITY: THE LOCAL CHURCH

Pazmino describes the New Testament church as the Christian's "faith community" (1988, 27). Paul's descriptions of the people of God as the body of Christ in 1 Corinthians 12:12–31 and Ephesians 4:11–16 provide a vivid portrait of local churches as faith communities. Each member of the body is to experience a proper vertical relationship of dependence upon God and a proper horizontal relationship of interdependence with fellow believers. There is no room for individualistic independence on the part of anyone. There is a legitimate need for everyone to participate in corporate growth if Christ's purposes are to be achieved in the church.

Stanley Grenz drives home the significance of the local church:

The triune God desires that human beings be brought together into a corporate whole, a fellowship of reconciliation, which not only reflects God's own eternal reality but actually participates in that reality. Since the New Testament era the focal point of the reconciled society in history has been the church of Jesus Christ, the new covenant people. As that people, we are called to pioneer in the present the community of

love and thereby to participate in and reflect the eternal relation of the triune God, the community we will enjoy in the
great eschatological fellowship on the renewed earth.

We are the company of those who already have been
brought by the Holy Spirit to share in the love between the
Father and the Son. When we are able to lay hold of and then
articulate clearly this vision of the church, we may well gain
a renewed sense of the presence of God within the Christian
fellowship of love. And this in turn will spill over into a
renewed worship "in spirit and in truth" as we praise the triune community of love, the eternal Trinity who is our Creator and Savior. (Grenz 1993, 188)

A local church that embodies Grenz's vision of a true faith
community functions like a greenhouse to nurture the young
spiritual lives of children and youth.

How does an accurate concept of the local church as a
faith community shape the life and ministry of the youth
leader?

Personal Implications

1. I need to involve myself in the larger faith community.

Youth ministry leaders especially benefit from relationships with Christians who are not teenagers and not youth
leaders. Fellowship with peers is a real and legitimate need for
leaders. When a leader walks into the church and realizes that
all his friends are in the youth group, he should take note. By
limiting his spiritual fellowship he is missing out on an important component of his own pursuit of Christlikeness.

2. I need mentors in my life.

Every Christian grows through the spiritual nurture of an
older, wiser discipler. Mentors provide perspective on life,
feedback on personal growth, and insights into God's will.
Without mentors to shape, challenge, and guide them, leaders
are relationally poor.

Ministry Applications

1. Provide students with opportunities for meaningful fel-

lowship and relationship building with peers, with other adults, and in the broader congregation.

Students need relationships with peers—that is a given in youth ministry. Students also need relationships with adults. A teenager cannot learn to be an adult from his peers.

I have coined the term *SOAP*—Significant Other Adult Person—to refer to those important mentors who can make all the difference in the adolescent's maturation. Youth leaders in local churches must guard against developing youth ministries that are "mini-parachurches." Parachurch leaders likewise face the challenge of connecting converts to local church fellowships. Failure to address these concerns can lead to two negative results. First, in the present, students miss the rich spiritual heritage of intergenerational relationships in the body of Christ. Second, in the future, students lack meaningful connection to the broader faith community and often drop out of church following high school graduation.

2. Develop a ministry team to model the reality of Christ's body.

Students will not gain a vision for the importance of the faith community if they do not see it in the leaders. Personal implications one and two above are excellent ways to role-model the value of the faith community. Beyond this, students need to see adults in meaningful, mutually submissive, interdependent relationships. Team ministry meets the needs of the leaders, enables the leaders to be more than the sum of the parts, provides students with excellent examples of what mature adult Christian relationships should look like, and creates an environment of love and security for the students.

YOUTH LEADERS: THEOLOGICAL CONSTRUCTION WORKERS

Youth ministry becomes more experientially meaningful, spiritually vibrant, and relationally effective when leaders commit themselves to the construction of a disciplined theological framework for doing ministry. The construction process seeks to produce a consciously reflective style of leadership that regularly asks, "What is the truth?" and "How does truth shape my life and my ministry?"

Much more than what is presented in this chapter remains to be explored before a fully developed theological framework can be realized. However, the basic blueprint has been drawn. To further help the reader in this construction project, two additional building guides are provided at the end of this chapter. The "Theological Worksheet" (p. 67) outlines the process of moving from theological understanding to personal and ministry practice. At the end of the worksheet is a section for identifying questions and issues that emerge from theological reasoning or ministry practice. "Theological Topics" provides a list of the kinds of issues that were not addressed in the six foundational topics. Leaders in faith communities can use these topics to address the more specific theological nuances that belong to their particular faith communities.

My prayer is that youth ministry leaders' disciplined pursuit of the knowledge of God in their lives and ministries will produce the integrity of ministry Paul describes in 1 Corinthians 2:1–5.

> When I came to you, brothers, I did not come with eloquence or superior wisdom as I proclaimed to you the testimony about God. For I resolved to know nothing while I was with you except Jesus Christ and him crucified. I came to you in weakness and fear, and with much trembling. My message and my preaching were not with wise and persuasive words, but with a demonstration of the Spirit's power, so that your faith might not rest on men's wisdom, but on God's power.

THEOLOGICAL WORKSHEET
TOPIC:_____

Theological Foundations (Beliefs):

1. _____
2. _____
3. _____

Personal Implications: (Life Practices):

Because I believe_____, I _____
Because I believe_____, I _____

Ministry Applications (Ministry Practices):

Because I believe_____, as a youth ministry leader
I _____
Because I believe _____, as a youth ministry leader
I _____

Questions/Issues to Explore (Learning/Growth Edge):

I want to understand_____

_____

REMINDER: Completing the worksheet on one's current understanding of a topic should not be misconstrued as a closed-ended task. Quite the contrary, the worksheet or similar tool marks the beginning of the process of more intentionally disciplining what one believes, how one lives, and how one ministers. Theological learning, because of its object and source, can never be fully exhausted. The goal is increased accuracy in thinking, being, and doing according to God's truth.

THEOLOGICAL TOPICS

1. Prayer
2. Knowing God's Will
3. Evangelism and
   the Gospel Message
4. Sanctification
5. Eschatology
6. Ecclesiology
7. Forgiveness
   of Others
8. Worship

WORKS CITED

Buswell, James Oliver. 1962. *A Systematic Theology of the Christian Religion.* Grand Rapids, Zondervan.

Dausey, Gary, ed. 1983. *The Youth Leader's Sourcebook.* Grand Rapids: Zondervan.

Downs, Perry G. 1994. *Teaching for Spiritual Growth.* Grand Rapids: Zondervan.

Dunn, Richard. 1996. "What Are the Necessary Competencies to Be an Effective Youth Worker?" *Christian Education Journal* 16 (Spring): 25–38.

Erickson, Millard. 1985. *Christian Theology.* Grand Rapids: Baker.

Grenz, Stanley J. 1993. *Revisioning Evangelical Theology.* Downers Grove, Ill.: InterVarsity.

Grudem, Wayne. 1994. *Systematic Theology.* Grand Rapids: Zondervan.

Hoekema, Anthony. 1986. *Created in God's Image.* Grand Rapids: Eerdmans.

_____. 1989. *Saved by Grace.* Grand Rapids: Eerdmans.

Kesler, Jay. 1983. In *The Youth Leader's Sourcebook.* See Dausey.

Packer, J. I. 1973. *Knowing God.* Downers Grove, Ill.: InterVarsity.

Pazmino, Robert W. 1988. *Foundational Issues in Christian Education.* Grand Rapids: Baker.

Wilhoit, Jim. 1991. *Christian Education and the Search for Meaning.* 2d ed. Grand Rapids: Baker.

3

A DEVELOPMENTAL FRAMEWORK FOR DOING YOUTH MINISTRY

Steve Patty

What will it take to get through to these guys? Lauren had always found relating to junior high students to be as natural as breathing. In fact, it was the depth of her relationships with last year's eighth graders that had led her to request a place on the high school leadership team. Now Lauren is wondering what she was thinking. She simply cannot "connect" with the ideas, attitudes, and interests of the high school students. Even her beloved eighth-grade class is increasingly confounding to her.

Is it me or is it them? Have I lost my ability for youth ministry? Or are they unreachable, destined to frustrate all of their present and future leaders? she asks herself in desperation. Lauren is facing her first genuine crisis of leadership, and she has no idea where to begin to solve her dilemma.

An Unsolved Mystery

Youth ministry contains an element of mystery. Lauren is coming face to face with youth ministry's mysterious nature. Why does a message that really "hits" a junior higher fall flat with a high schooler? Is it just too simple or immature for her? Does she need something "deeper"? Why does a program so exciting to a high schooler fail to get a meaningful response out of a young college student? Does he respond better to less activity, hype, or humor? Like trying to solve a complex murder mystery, Lauren has begun to look for clues as to why her previously successful ministry approaches have suddenly, and disappointingly, lost their impact. (Unfortunately, in most cases one cannot blame this problem on the butler!) Her perplexing ministry mystery need not remain unsolved.

Unlocking the Secrets of Adolescent Development

Lauren needs to look no further than the issues of adolescent development to find help for answering her questions. The significant age differences explained by adolescent development are sometimes masked by the similarities of youth across the span of junior high through college age. In general, all ages of adolescence experience a time of discovery, identification, and consolidation of their opinions about self, others, and the world. Most teens, early and late alike, exhibit energy in thought, creativity in activity, and productivity in exploration. Similar thematic threads run all the way through the tasks of the adolescent agenda.

To the degree that there are similarities, however, so too are there distinct, meaningful differences. The process of growth is more tumultuous than placid, more developmental than static. From the time a student enters middle school until the third or fourth year of college, the pattern of growth is less like a gradual incline and more like a spiral staircase made up of a giant's steps. Whereas the agenda is not so varied between the young and older adolescent, the ways of going about the tasks of that agenda are radically different. The process is made up of distinct steps, or stages. These stages, in fact, are so distinct that from the vantage point of one stage it is difficult to empathize with the processes of the former or to anticipate the perspective of the latter. The stages of adolescence are strikingly unique in their characteristics. Consequently, effective ministry relationships and strategies for programming need to be responsive.

For years social scientists have struggled to crawl into the skin of an adolescent to describe how life unfolds. It is relatively simple to document the outward changes—to compare the means of skeletal height, describe the development of sexual organs, and note the changing patterns of perspiration that puberty incites. However, it is much more arduous to appreciate the inward changes of reasoning, feeling, and interpreting life. The observer must look at symptoms—the specific results of an adolescent's thinking, such as how he talks or what bothers him—and reason backwards, asking the question, Why does the adolescent respond like this? By examining the empirical evidence that points like mystery clues to nonempirical, intangible adolescent realities, developmental psychologists have made some critical observations for anyone working with adolescents.

ELEMENTS OF DEVELOPMENTALISM

Commitment to an accurate picture of adolescent development requires a brief examination of the broader topic of developmentalism itself. This wider framework provides a context for understanding the diverse dimensions of adolescence. One way to frame developmentalism is to see it through four essential developmental assumptions: *qualitative growth, structured wholes, hierarchical integration,* and *invariant sequence.*

Qualitative Growth

A primary axiom of developmental theory is that growth is not merely *quantitative,* but fundamentally *qualitative.* The way a younger child understands concepts is different from that of an older child. Young adolescents interpret experiences differently than adults. It is not just that older students understand more, for surely a greater exposure to facts and experiences increases the level of memorable content in the mind. More critically, older students think in a different style (structure) than younger ones. The structure of thinking changes; and with it, the structure of relating socially, reasoning morally, and perceiving emotionally.

Structured Wholes

Adolescents explore, manipulate, and seek to make sense of the world around them. Their minds are not passive receptacles. They are constantly interpreting their world and fitting the pieces of their understanding together. In the process, they develop increasingly complex and adequate structures of understanding (Kohlberg 1968). These structures are not primarily a result of the natural unfolding of genetically predetermined steps (for example, Gesell's maturationalist theory), nor are they exclusively the overlay of external social expectations (for example, Bandura and McDonald 1963). Rather, they are the predictable results of active, interpreting individuals who are growing in their means of awareness.

These structures of understanding are coherent because developmentalists assume that each individual is naturally inclined to integrate the pieces of her understanding into a whole. Like Gestalt psychologists, developmentalists see an innate drive in people to fit the various pieces of life into larger, more inclusive ways of thinking, even if doing so changes the nature of the thinker (Kitchener 1985).

Piaget suggested that this cognitive modification process can be described as "equilibration." He describes how a self-regulating pressure toward equilibration (i.e., making things fit) motivates the individual to modify his way of understanding in order to enfold areas of disequilibration (i.e., areas that do not fit). Hence, a growing child is constantly faced with the challenge not only to add more of the same kind of ideas into his knowledge bank (assimilation), but to change the structure of his understanding to embrace new ideas (accommodation). For example, the death of a pet or a loved one causes the five-year-old to reexamine issues such as death, heaven, and the love of God. The child seeks equilibration between what was previously understood about those topics and the new information he is assimilating. New ways of thinking about and relating to God emerged as a result of this accommodation of the new experiences. This growth through equilibration would not happen were it not for an innate inclination toward structured wholes.

Hierarchical Integration

Whereas each new stage is distinct and qualitatively different from the others, former stages in a person's development are not fully left behind. Old structures are reorganized, but as Werner (1948) suggests, some of their original essence is embedded in the design of the new structure. And so the old is radically redesigned, but not totally left behind.

The concept of hierarchical integration implies two important insights. First, a student will fully explore a current stage (horizontal exploration) before and in preparation for moving on to the next stage (vertical integration). Therefore, a mentor will only frustrate the rhythms of real development if she attempts to accelerate stage growth without allowing adequate time for the solidifying work of the present stage.

Second, hierarchical integration accounts for the appearance of stage regression. Though a student's abilities are forever altered by the arrival of formal operational thought, these abilities may appear at times to be more potentialities than actualities. Hence an older adolescent, fully capable of propositional thought, may in a given situation neglect to exercise anything more than concrete thinking. Understanding the process of hierarchical integration can help adults understand and be patient with an adolescent's inconsistencies. For example, hierarchical integration suggests that it is normal for adolescents to in one moment behave as a mature "little adult" and almost immediately follow with immature "big kid" behavior.

Invariant Sequence

Invariant sequence means that each stage must appear in order, and that none can be skipped (Cowan 1978). Even though the content and context of individual lives may vary radically, developmentalists affirm that the pattern of formal operational (abstract) thinking always follows concrete operations. Although the rate of progress may vary between individuals, making the age of entry into formal operations differ significantly (not all adolescents or even adults consistently achieve formal operations), propositional thinking always follows concrete thinking. The teacher may assume, then, that there is more similarity than dissimilarity in how individual students grow. No child can "skip" to adult maturity either mentally or emotionally without having taken the transformational route of adolescence.

CONTRIBUTIONS OF DEVELOPMENTALISM

Given these foundational concepts of developmentalism, the youth ministry leader can begin to assess discrete stages of adolescent development. The following discussion describes four empirical elements that are salient to adolescent stage-theory. The cognitive, social, emotional, and moral domains are accessible to observation (empirical). By examining them separately and then as a synthesized whole one can begin to explain what is happening beneath the surface of the adolescent's external characteristics. To identify these stages, a model inspired by and similar to one proposed by Fowler (1981) will be used (Patty 1992). (Stage 1 will not be considered here because of its irrelevance for the adolescent's experience.)

Stage 2: The Event Lens

Stage 2 occurs during late grade school through the first year or two of middle school. Stage 2 is event oriented. For these young people, meaning is made from the tangible, concrete elements of life. They respond to active, participatory, ordered, imaginative, practical, narrative-oriented teaching. They are capable investigators, enjoying the discovery of answers to questions of the faith in the scriptural text. Most young middle school adolescents enjoy competitive activities with clear rules but are bored by relational "non-game" activity. They have difficulty with teaching that is too hypothetical, activities that are too directionless, and ministry that has nonspecific expectations. Here is why.

Cognitive

A stage 2 student is still a concrete operational thinker. Most of those reading this chapter will be thinking in more complex ways, so it may take some imagination to climb into the mind of a young middle schooler. Concrete operational logic is tied to logically ordered rules and is highly dependent on the specific events of the student's experience. The limitation is the difficulty with hypothetical thought and inability to wrangle with combinations of observations among a full range of possibilities (Cowan 1978). Linear logic is prominent. Explicit systems of understanding are welcomed. Explained analogies are effective. Simply put, concrete operations describes a young adolescent's thinking as specific, tangible—and concrete.

Social

Selman (1976; Selman and Byrne 1974) describes how children entering early adolescence are in the process of moving from self-reflective role-taking (his stage 2) to mutual role-taking (his stage 3). In the self-reflective mode, the young person is aware of the differing perspectives of others, but he is limited to truly understanding only that which he has personally experienced. In the mutual role-taking mode, however, the young adolescent can now wrangle with a more generalized perspective. Instead of reading people primarily from what he has experienced, he can now read people from what "people like us" have experienced. Consequently, as Cowan relates, "they can be impartial spectators and maintain a point of view in which their own ideas and feelings do not intrude" (1978, 216). During the later months of stage 2, students begin to become sensitive to this generalized perspective; i.e., what is "cool" and "uncool."

Emotional

Stage 2 adolescents view themselves as active subjects and identify the discrepancy between what they do and the "correct" answer. With this budding self-awareness often comes the newly refined skill of self-judgment. As a result of this ability to evaluate the discrepancy between the actual and ideal self, it is a significant time for the development of a sense of guilt (Cowan 1978). These emotions are often so intense that young adolescents feel overwhelmed. For many, this is the time when life-long patterns for assuaging guilt, both healthy and not, are developed. How a student navigates the emotional challenges of guilt and personhood of stage 2 years is often the powerful foundation for beliefs about himself that carry on through adulthood.

Moral

Young middle schoolers see morality in terms of fair exchanges, or "deals." Kohlberg (1969) calls this *individualism and exchange*—individualism because students recognize that individuals have different perspectives on moral actions, and exchange because they believe that a fair consequence will inevitably match those actions. As a result, stage 2 students revel in investigating what they should or should not do in life situations. They are highly attuned to discovering correct answers. For a Christian, God's promises of reward for godly living are highly motivating. As could be expected, a somewhat legalistic turn of the young adolescent mind often emerges at this time as well. Still, coming to terms with a systematic understanding of faith, both in belief and behavior, can be extremely exciting for sixth graders. It provides a fulfilling way for them to wrap their minds around what God expects of them.

Summary

The stage 2 student views life through the lens of concrete, tangible events. Students at this stage see their spiritual life in "do" terms. They often interpret how they are doing by what they are doing. For instance, when asked about their walk with God, they will often say something like, "Fine, I'm helping out with junior church," or "Bad, my parents are fighting a lot right now." Teaching that exhibits immediate, clear points of application and that is mediated by concrete memory pegs will be most memorable. Bible studies that include a workbook, use a journal, or involve an activity (for example, football and a Philippians study) help frame the event of learning for the student.

This preoccupation with events is neither good nor bad; it is simply how things are for most stage 2 students. The spiritual mentor's role is not to try to push them too quickly to stage 3. Rather, the leader is to minister faithfully to the student at stage 2; the student will naturally, and in his own time, find stage 2 inadequate and reach for stage 3 development.

Stage 3: The Relational Lens

Stage 3 occurs during late middle school and in most cases extends through the better part of high school. The stage 3 view is through the lens of relationships. That which a student understands, feels, and does during this stage is interpreted through the interaction of relationships. Stage 3 students respond well to thoughtful, winsome, and provocative teaching. But they are even more profoundly affected by other elements of youth ministry. The youth group as a whole exerts tremendous implicit influence over the individual's lifestyle and beliefs. It is especially essential during this period that students are relationally close enough to see, taste, touch, and smell Christ in the life of their leaders. Here is why.

Cognitive

At least five new aspects of reasoning emerge during early formal operations (Inhelder and Piaget 1958). Cowan (1978) summarizes these by suggesting that early adolescents (1) discover the hypothetical world, (2) examine the relationship between hypotheses and data, (3) utilize sophisticated deduction, (4) form integrated wholes, and (5) are adept at wrangling with four simultaneous perspectives. Clearly a new category of critical and sophisticated thinking is now available to the adolescent. Although most late junior high and early high school students are biologically capable of demonstrating formal operational competencies, theorists admit that this level of reasoning does not come automatically in adolescent or adult years.

Social

The newfound ability to take various perspectives simultaneously opens up a variety of possibilities. Instead of focusing primarily on a stage 2 "people like us" mentality, the stage 3 adolescent can now explore and feel the perspectives of others. Because these capacities are new for the middle adolescent, and because this period of life is fraught with dramatic physiological and psychological changes, she often believes that everyone else is as obsessed with her behavior and appearance as she (Elkind 1984). Hence, the middle adolescent, precisely because of her ability to take the other's perspective, appears to be hopelessly self-centered.

Emotional

Formal operational thinking allows the adolescent to become analytically introspective and to think critically about the way he thinks and behaves. This capacity is more than merely a stage 2 acknowledgment of the discrepancy between the actual and the ideal. Rather, the individual may now think about the "why's" behind that discrepancy, explore the "what if's," and examine the "I wonder's" even about how he acts, how he examines how he acts, and even how he examines how he examines how he acts! This emerging capacity for sophisticated introspection often overwhelms a student, producing a supreme case of egocentrism while the emotions are being sorted out. Because of this self-critical capacity, the questions of "who I am" and "who I want to be" make the search for identity an increasingly critical issue (Erikson 1968).

Moral

Stage 3 students reason in a manner Kohlberg describes as *interpersonal concordance,* or "good boy–nice girl" orientation (Kohlberg 1969; Turiel 1973). A highly defined stereotype of how the ideal person behaves, or what the good Christian is supposed to do, is the guiding element in making moral decisions. They see morality as more than a stage 2 making of simple deals. They tend to focus on the expectations of family, community, church, and God. The qualities that make healthy relationships, such as character, attitude, and fidelity, are often weighted more heavily on the scale of moral importance than ethical action. Crain agrees that for this stage, "Good behavior means having good motives and interpersonal feelings such as love, empathy, trust and concern for others" (1992, 138).

Summary

Stage 3 students see life through the lens of relationships. It is not that relationships are unimportant in stages 2 and 4, but that stage 3 students are more attuned to social interactions than at any other time. They are able to look beyond concrete events, but are not quite developed enough cognitively to easily discriminate between thoughts and the people thinking those thoughts. That is why older middle school and younger high school students are more quick to ask "who is there" than "what will we be doing" about a church function. As can be expected, the youth group has a powerfully holistic influence during this time. The relational ambiance of the group effectively mediates a great deal of truth. Hence, special attention should be given to the relational health of the group so that a biblical concept of personhood is encouraged and the ties between mentors and students are strengthened.

Stage 4: The Logic Lens

Stage 4 often emerges during the late high school or early college years. It is the logical extension of stage 3: a less encumbered demonstration of the capacities of formal operations. Consequently, the lens of stage 4 is a rational one. These adolescents respond to sophisticated, ordered, and weighty teaching. They have become proficient in systematic thinking and are adept at analytic and synthetic manipulations. Here is why.

Cognitive

No new aspects of reasoning appear in stage 4. In comparison to stage 3, a stage 4 student exhibits a more functional formal operational ability in reasoning. Whereas in stage 3 the individual is consumed by the newfound reasoning ability and consequently appears ego-bound, a stage 4 individual can more adroitly and less self-consciously use higher level thinking. In fact, the ability to principalize becomes the most conspicuous cognitive attribute during these years.

Social

A stage 4 individual can distinguish between his relationships and convictions. The ideas of significant others can now be extricated from the strength of the relationship with less effort than before. As a result of an excessive confidence in the ability of the mind, stage 4 individuals interpret and judge the actions of self and others on the basis of an organized belief system.

Emotional

Stage 4 is marked by what Fowler (1981) describes as the ability to critically reflect on one's identity (self) and outlook (ideology). Springing more from inner reflection than from the assumption of values derived from the closest social subgroup (i.e., stage 3), the stage 4 student strives to find coherency between his self-identity and his worldview. This integration comes not without struggle. Fowler explains:

> Where genuine movement toward stage 4 is underway the person must face certain unavoidable tensions: individuality versus being defined by a group or group membership; subjectivity and the power of one's strongly felt but unexamined feelings versus objectivity and the requirement of critical reflection; self-fulfillment or self-actualization as the primary concern versus service to and being for others; the question of being committed to the relative versus struggle with the possibility of an absolute. (1981, 182)

Even with this struggle, there still exists a tremendous desire to arrange and explain identity and outlook in explicit systems.

Moral

A student in stage 4 uses this developed synthesis between self-identity and worldview to reason about moral issues. Kohlberg (1969) calls this stage *authority and social order maintaining orientation* because of the prominence the student's conviction plays in describing how the group, society, or church ought to act. Since the adolescent is already adept at understanding how the world could be, the student easily steps in this stage to how the world should be (Kohlberg 1971). A highly idealistic system, with a corresponding rigorous belief in the power of ideas, is often the result. This idealism can severely shake a student's beliefs of faith if she perceives inconsistency in logic or discrepancies between the real and ideal of faith practice.

Summary

Stage 4 students traffic so comfortably in the realm of concepts that they become skilled theorists about much of life. They are like novice professors, striving to fit bits of conviction into a coherent whole and then extending it to others (Patty 1992). Stage 4 students are answering questions of personal conviction, life-orientation, and purpose. They have not left events and relationships behind, but their ability to wrestle with systems of thought colors much of what they do and influences how their walk with God is experienced.

IMPLICATIONS OF DEVELOPMENTALISM

To conclude that a youth minister should take special care with events for early adolescents, relationships for middle adolescents, and theories for late adolescents is correct, but misleadingly simple. The reader experienced in youth ministry will be quick to affirm that seventh-grade boys (stage 2) desperately need relationships, and tenth-grade girls (stage 3) thrive under the stimulation of sophisticated Christian thinking. The perspective focus of each stage is not stage-exclusive in regards to content. Rather, the perspective focus describes the coordination of increasingly adequate ways of understanding and interpreting the world surrounding the adolescent. Here are simple implications in the context of a contact time, a Bible study, and a retreat:

Early Adolescents

Stage 2 is not a wrongfully immature place to be for a sixth or seventh grader. The concrete is necessary and appropriate. Relationships and logic are a crucial part of stage 2, but they are mediated through the concrete event. For example, in a one-on-one time with a stage 2 student, it is difficult to sit for an hour over a soft drink and talk meaningfully about how life is going. The contact is too intense. But to toss the football and talk, take a hike and talk, or go to the store and talk helps smooth the way for meaningful mentoring.

A Bible study about faith with a small group of stage 2 students should incorporate—even revolve around—something concrete and tangible. For instance, an inductive exploration of the adventure stories of Hebrews 11 or having the students prepare an ongoing notebook in which they describe three specific ways healthy faith will make this week different will help to move the abstract to the concrete.

A retreat designed for stage 2 students should have clear, well-planned activities. The young adolescent will be asking of the retreat, "What will we be doing?" The event is important to stage 2 ministry.

Middle Adolescents

Following the precedent of stage 2, a stage 3 student has not outgrown the impact of significant events, nor is she immune to the power of logical thought. Rather, her way of making meaning is mediated through relationships. A one-on-one contact time with a stage 3 student needs far less supporting structure than would be the case with a stage 2 student. Meaningful interaction can usually occur anytime and at any place, with only a little courageous initiative exercised by the youth minister. The student wants to know, however, "Are you talking to me because you like me and really care about me?" The social antenna is highly tuned to authenticity of motive.

A Bible study with a small group of stage 3 students would do well to encourage the exploration of the thoughts, feelings, and interrelationships of a life that is exercising faith. "How does this affect our relationships?" and "How do our friends and family affect our faith?" would be profitable tracks of reflection. At this stage the implicit messages and the silent metaphors of godly living are potent. Hence the sharing of what faith looks like, feels like, and tastes like in daily living establishes a tacit standard.

A retreat for stage 3 students should create space for

meaningful interaction. Relationships are critical for stage 3 ministry. Retreats should not be overscheduled or filled with large-group experiences only. Time should be allowed for students to hang out.

Late Adolescents

A stage 4 student loves meaningful activities and is highly motivated by relationships, but he is equally, if not more, concerned about how systems of reality fit together. This idea-centeredness does not imply an idea-fixation: Stage 4 students commonly act illogically. However, they are adept at using their formal operational reasoning abilities to define and evaluate the stuff of life. For example, a one-on-one contact time with a stage 4 adolescent is potentially stimulating even prior to establishing relational closeness. Stage 4 students seek out those they not only enjoy, but respect. Hence, a college professor with whom a student is barely acquainted can have a profound personal effect by way of the presentation of ideas.

A Bible study consisting of a small group of stage 4 students needs to regularly master information and develop explicit systems of beliefs into which both life experiences and scriptural truth can fit. Questions must go beyond surface information to explore the meaning of God's Word in the complexity of life.

For a retreat, instead of asking the stage 3 question, "Who is going to be there?" a stage 4 student will often ask, "Why are we doing this?" or "What will we accomplish this weekend?" The emphasis of leading stage 4 students should be on the development of a Christian synthesis, a putting of the parts together into a coherent whole. Meaningful thinking is essential for stage 4 ministry.

CONCLUSION

One of the most helpful insights from social science is that adolescent growth is developmental. Understanding the nature and stages of development can greatly enhance Lauren's effectiveness. She will be more sensitive to the self-consciousness her ninth- and tenth-grade students are developing in relation to the social dynamics of the Sunday school class.

She will be more aware of the students' relational antennae, which attempt to interpret how others are perceiving them. Lauren will also be more patient with the myriad questions the students ask in response to the lessons she has prepared. Instead of interpreting their "why" questions as a form of personal challenge, she will recognize the students' need to ask for deeper explanations of faith issues. In both instances Lauren will realize that the students' occasional aloofness is not a reflection of some lack of relational skills on her part but rather reflects the students' developmental processes. Over a period of time, this newly discovered awareness can lead Lauren to love the stage 3 students in a way that is distinct from and yet as meaningful as (in some cases even deeper than) the ways she loved them as stage 2 students.

In general, a disciplined developmental framework can rescue youth ministry leaders from the ineffective practice of programming the same kind of ministry across the years of adolescence, merely adding more to the program for older students. Ministry relationships and strategies should be qualitatively different in correspondence with the qualitatively different stages of adolescent development. Knowing well the general stage-characteristics of students, along with the particular needs in one's own youth group, will be a potent combination for providing strategic ministry.

WORKS CITED

Bandura, A., and F. J. McDonald. 1963. "Influence of Social Reinforcement and the Behavior of Models in Shaping Children's Moral Judgments." *Journal of Abnormal and Social Psychology* 67:274–81.

Cowan, Philip. 1978. *Piaget: With Feeling*. New York: Holt, Rinehart & Winston.

Crain, William. 1992. *Theories of Development: Concepts and Applications*. 3d ed. Englewood Cliff, N.J.: Prentice-Hall.

Elkind, David. 1984. *All Grown Up and No Place to Go*. Reading, Mass.: Addison-Wesley.

Erikson, Erik. 1968. *Identity: Youth and Crisis*. New York: Norton.

Flavell, J. 1971. "Stage-Related Properties of Cognitive Development." *Cognitive Psychology* 2:421–53.

Fowler, James W. 1981. *Stages of Faith: The Psychology of Human Development and the Quest for Meaning*. New York: Harper & Row.

Inhelder, B., and J. Piaget. 1958. *The Early Growth of Logical Thinking from Childhood to Adolescence*. New York: Basic Books.

Kitchener, Richard F. 1985. "Holistic Structuralism, Elementarism and Piaget's Theory of 'Relativism.'" *Human Development* 28 (6): 281–94.

Kohlberg, L. 1968. "Early Education: A Cognitive-Developmental Approach." *Child Development* 39:1013–62.

_____. 1969. "Stage and Sequence: The Cognitive-Developmental Approach to Socialization." In *Handbook of Socialization Theory and Research,* edited by D. A. Goslin. Chicago: Rand McNally.

_____. 1971. "From Is to Ought: How to Commit the Naturalistic Fallacy and Get Away with It in the Study of Moral Development." In *Cognitive Development and Epistemology,* edited by T. Mischel. New York: Academic.

Kohlberg, L., and R. Mayer. 1979. "Development and Its Implications for Moral Education." In *The Domain of Moral Education,* edited by D. B. Cochran, C. M. Hamm, and A. C. Kazepides. New York: Paulist.

Patty, D. 1992. "Spiritual Growth and Faith Development Structure in a sample of Adolescents from Evangelical Churches." Master's thesis, Wheaton College Graduate School.

Piaget, J. 1971. *Structuralism*. New York: Harper.

Selman, R. L. 1976. "Social-Cognitive Understanding: A Guide to Educational and Clinical Practice." In *Moral Development and Behavior: Theory, Research, and Social*

Issues, edited by T. Lickona. New York: Holt, Rinehart & Winston.

Selman, Robert. "Education for Cognitive Development. Stage Theories of Cognitive Development: Criticisms and Application." *Harvard Educational Review* 45 (1): 196–202.

Selman, R. L., and D. F. Byrne. 1974. "A Structural-Development Analysis of Levels of Role-Taking in Middle Childhood." *Child Development* 45:803–6.

Turiel, E. 1973. "Stage Transition in Moral Development." In *Second Handbook of Research on Teaching,* edited by R. M. W. Travers. Chicago: Rand McNally.

Werner, H. 1948. *Comparative Psychology of Mental Development.* New York: Follett.

4

A SOCIOLOGICAL FRAMEWORK FOR DOING YOUTH MINISTRY

Dave Rahn

Allison, are you coming to the 'New Year's Eve Bash'?"

"I don't know, Sarah. We're going to have some of my mom's family staying with us next week. Plus, I have to work the counter at the theater until nine that night. I am just not sure I will be up to it."

"Oh, Alli, come on. It won't be the same without you. Besides, Dave's got this great speaker from the university coming and he said that this year's 'mystery event' will be the most bizarre in club history."

"Yeah, well, I know I would have a good time. But, you know how it is, Sarah, there's just so much going on during the holidays."

"Sure—everybody's busy. That's why I was surprised to see how many people signed up this year. It looks like we will have almost twice as many as last year's Bash."

"Really . . . who's coming?"

"Most of the regulars, plus Ben Cameron, Justin Marks—most of the guys from our sixth period world geography class . . . let's see . . . Martha Henry is coming, too, which I am sure means Beth and Carolyn won't miss out."

"Well, maybe I should go. I think Mom would like for me to; and, after all, I would sure rather be out with you guys than at home with my relatives to bring in the new year. Besides, Justin Marks works at the mall next to the theater. Maybe he would give me a ride if I asked."

"I have seen him smile at you in class—you know he would give you a ride, Alli. The truth is, I bet he's just coming with the hope that you'll be there."

"Well, then I have to go, Sarah. It would be insensitive to disappoint him, wouldn't it?"

✝ ✝ ✝

Why do students attend youth ministry events? Is it because of the excellent program that has been planned? The truth is that youth meetings might be well paced, engaging, and meaningful—but that is not why students attend. Is it because the youth leader is cool, witty, and an excellent speaker? Fortunately—since most of us cannot live up to this stereotype on a consistent basis—the answer is no. The fact is, most students get involved in a youth ministry because it gives them a chance to connect with the people with whom they want to socialize.

Young youth ministry leaders are often blindsided by this unexpected realization. The "aha" experience can take the leader's breath away, sort of like the first jump into a swimming pool that is a little colder than anticipated. The initial awareness of this youth ministry fact of life typically produces two effects on a youth leader. The first is to thank the Lord for the unanticipated splash of humility this truth carries. After all, indulging in the temptation of self-importance can be quite a tug for any youth minister. The second is to thank the Lord for the expected benefit that this profound insight will bring to any ministry with adolescents.

Understanding the social framework for doing youth ministry is like finding the light switch in a dimly lit room. With the new and improved visibility come tremendous possibilities. For those possibilities to become realities, however, youth leaders will have to examine and evaluate what they are observing by thinking critically about the role of the social and cultural context in which they minister. Such disciplined thinking is a crucial component in the maturation process of the youth minister and the local youth ministry he has.

THE "EXEGESIS" OF SOCIAL CONTEXTS

Social contexts shape all of us. The junior high and senior high school years contributed richly to every adult's present formation. Personal socio-developmental tools—the ones that are carried into adulthood—were test-driven in adolescent years. It is not too difficult to tap into this mother lode of memories. Consider these questions adults can use as entry points to self-awareness of past socialization: Do you remember your first kiss? Or the first time your hormones seemed to be going on "red alert"? How about the first time you drove a car, or, better yet, the first time you drove solo to pick up a friend? Can you remember what it felt like in your first year of high school, and how incredibly old the seniors seemed? Did you ever experience rejection from a group of persons you wanted to belong to? Can you identify a time when you felt as if you finally belonged to a group, that they were a perfect fit for you?

Reflecting upon one's own adolescent social pilgrimage is an excellent resource for youth ministry. An important word of caution is needed, however. The human tendency to project one's experiences as normative for others may lead to unwarranted assumptions. For example, not everyone experienced a first kiss during his adolescent years, felt intimidated by older students, or struggled with fitting in. What an Anglo-American youth leader may remember about peer socialization or events in the family may be different from what the African-American or Native American students are presently experiencing in their lives. How can leaders understand what is going on in the social world of those to whom they minister without presuming that all their experiences are similar in every way?

They can do so by approaching each social context as a learner, thus going a long way toward avoiding the pitfalls that accompany errant assumptions. To assume that one's personal adolescent experience equips one as an adult to understand the social world of contemporary teenagers is like believing that because someone worked on the mission field in Tokyo he understands mission work in Haiti. The difference between Japanese and Haitian cultures is huge. It would be disastrous to conclude that "missions are missions—they're all the same." On the other hand, there is significant similarity between two missionaries who start their respective work in Tokyo and Port-au-Prince with the commitment to learn the new culture before fixing on ministry strategies. In the same way, a priority strategy for any youth minister is to get an accurate understanding of the social and cultural context where his or her youth ministry will take place.

During my Youth for Christ ministry years I led Campus Life clubs in seven different high schools. Each school had its own culture. There was a mix between urban and suburban, small town and rural. Racial attitudes were different. The sophistication of kids' experiences varied from school to school as did the level of tolerance for persons who deviated from norms. Some schools demonstrated enthusiastic unity; other schools were characterized by fractured, dissimilar interest groups. If my only motivation had been to establish a program for the teens who showed interest in spiritual things, I could have marketed Campus Life the same way in each situation and contented myself with the results. Since YFC's mission called me to think about penetrating an entire school community with the gospel of Jesus Christ, it was critical that I understood the social context of each situation and form a ministry response that was appropriately strategic.

One year it became clear that a small group of football players exercised an unusual degree of influence on what was socially acceptable at the school. For whatever reason, they had so labeled Campus Life that it was socially risky for many students to get involved. As a strategic response to this particular social context I worked hard to win the trust of this group of guys. When they subsequently began attending our meetings, Campus Life's social status changed. For a time it even became socially risky to *not* get involved!

The principle is clear. Becoming a learner of social context must precede investing oneself in ministry to that context. The pursuit of three broad questions can help "exegete" the social and cultural contexts for youth ministry in the same way that systematic inquiry disciplines biblical exegesis. Those who have led inductive Bible studies might notice a parallel to the "What does it say? What does it mean? What does it mean to me?" trilogy.

What Does It Say?

The first step is to gather snapshots of as much cold, hard data relating to teenage social life as possible. Think of this as a pictorial portfolio, with the leaders as the photographers. The question guiding inquiry is, "What are the *facts* of teenage social life in this community that can be objectively verified?" The chance of getting a handle on the big picture of adolescent social patterns increases with the number and variety of pictures collected. For instance, if the first five guys with whom the leader talked all mentioned paintball as their favorite weekend activity, the leader might make the unwarranted leap to the conclusion that paintball is all the rage among students in the area. The picture taking may have occurred among the pocket of paintball enthusiasts who hang out together. Many additional "pictures" taken from many different angles will be needed to get a truly accurate picture of social activity among the local teens.

What Does It Mean?

The second step is to uncover what the raw data means to a variety of different teens. In this step the leader is still gathering information, but the research posture is more like that of a feature reporter than a news photographer. Imagine displaying a data portfolio to a wide range of young people to seek their interpretation. The goal is to see the facts of the relevant social context through adolescent eyes. The question is,

"What does all the various social activity *mean* to the teens in the community?" The paintballers mentioned above may be the first wave of students to dive into the newest fad, but they may also be militant fringe kids at the outer reaches of the social strata. Social meaning is in the collective eyes of the beholders.

What Does It Mean to Me as a Youth Minister?

Although it is important to avoid narrowing research too soon, it is also essential to filter new insights about adolescent social life through the mission, vision, and focus of a particular youth ministry. After all, honoring the Lord Jesus as you minister to the youth He has called you to is the ultimate goal. In this final area of inquiry the strategic, reflective question is, "What does this social context—now clearly uncovered— mean for our *particular* ministry with young people?"

Now that more is known about the paintball players in our area, would it be worthwhile to invest in this activity? The conclusion may be "Yes. Paintball would be an effective means of outreach and relationship building with this group." One very effective youth ministry recently reached that very conclusion and acted on their findings by purchasing twenty paintball guns. On the other hand, the findings may lead to the thought that investing in paintball guns would yield little in terms of getting to know the five guys or in terms of interesting their friends in the youth ministry being developed.

Putting It All Together

Recall the earlier illustration about the football guys and Campus Life. In the fact-gathering phase, I was able to personally observe these guys in the cafeteria and in a few social hangout spots. As I got to know other teens, I asked about weekend activities. There were always parties, and these guys were regularly mentioned as featured attendees. I began to form a hypothesis about the role these fellows played in this school's social network and tested it by asking other students about them. The almost reverential tones used to speak of them confirmed my theory that these five football players were the gatekeepers of what was cool in the school.

My probing had also confirmed that Campus Life was not on their acceptability list. Neither was I. Notice how natural it was to move from gathering data to gathering teen interpretation of the data—phase two. Since my maximum effectiveness depended, at least in part, on Campus Life's social acceptability among those who were unchurched, I realized that my best option was to pray hard and work to build relationships with these guys. That strategic response—part of the third phase—was based on Campus Life's mission. Not every youth ministry working in this particular social context would have warranted such an effort.

SOCIAL EXEGESIS: A MODEL FOR IMPLEMENTATION

The rationale and the conceptual framework for the practice of disciplined social exegesis have been explored. What remains is to provide a practical model for implementing this practice. Remember, practice makes perfect. With experience will come new skills for gaining insight into the "who" of youth ministry so that the "what" can be done more effectively.

Just the Facts, Ma'am:
Gathering Data

One of the great shows from early TV years was "Dragnet." In this half-hour crime drama, Sergeant Joe Friday worked with his partner to solve a crime. Inevitably he came upon a witness who rambled away from the direct response he wanted to the questions he was asking. The detective's response was classic: "Just the facts, ma'am."

The first stage of exploring the social context for a particular youth ministry needs to be likewise focused. Much of the information at this stage can be quantified. After the data have been assembled they can be assembled like a large jigsaw puzzle to provide a wide-angle image of the social patterns of the young people being studied.

A particular point of emphasis is to discover *who* goes *where, when*. While any one of these W's can serve as a good starting point for investigation, the limited number of time slots makes the *when* research question useful. The question is simple. "Where are teenagers in this community at (such-

and-such time)?" Those interested in finding out about a particular hangout could begin by asking the "where" research question, "How many teenagers can be found at (such-and-such place) at any given time?" Maybe a youth leader has a burden for a particular group of teens. In that case, asking the "who" research question makes the most sense: "Where do (certain people) go at any given time?"

If the information is laid out in table form (see a limited example in fig. 4.1) it gives a quick picture of what is known and unknown about the social movements of the teens. The column dealing with percentages can help leaders to see that though they may know something about the patterns of a number of teens there are scads of others that remain a mystery. Could there be strategic ministry possibilities hidden in what is not known? For example, Figure 4.1 locates 25 percent of the student body population after school as well as 15 percent on Monday nights. What could be done to find out what the majority of kids are doing after school and on Monday evenings? Further, what sort of ministry response might convert this informative data into opportunity?

What time slots are worth checking into when trying to understand the social movements of teens? Try these for starters: before school, between class, during lunch, after school, each weeknight, each weekend night, and Saturday and Sunday. The seasons of the year lead to different nuances in the social interaction among teens. Would it be useful to know where kids spend their time in the summer? Or what they do over school holidays?

In any school community, a great number of students collect themselves into interest groups. Typical clusters include athletes, band people, drama kids, those involved in student government or student publications, socialites, and smokers. Often there are subgroups within each of these categories. For instance, football players and women's basketball players are both athletes, but it is probably not useful to lump them together in a single interest group.

There is tremendous strategic value in identifying all the different interest groups represented in a given community and then figuring out who belongs to each group. Group affil-

When?	Where?	How Many?	Percent of Whole?	Who?
After school	athletic practice	225	10%	
After school	part-time jobs	337	15%	
Friday night	cruising	450	20%	
Saturday	part-time jobs	450	20%	
Monday night	Campus Life	112	5%	
Monday night	intramural	112	5%	
Monday night	drama & music	112	5%	

Figure 4.1. *Social Movements of Teens*

iation is an important way for all of us to understand our identity. This is especially true among socially hyper-conscious teens. Many kids engage in a variety of experiences but would likely cite only one group as the one that fits them best. There are also a number of teens who, though involved in a lot of different groups, do not necessarily feel a strong allegiance to any particular group. Gathering the best data possible on these groups and their membership is a great way to approach the *who* section of the table on the previous page.

Taking a "learner first" attitude into ministry is wise in any situation, but it is perhaps nowhere so important as when working with teens from international cultures. Group membership-as-identity takes on added significance when culture and language issues become a part of the bond. Since the United States and Canada are becoming increasingly multicultural, the opportunity for engaging in cross-cultural youth ministry will likely be as close as the neighborhood high school. Cultural assumptions are among the most important shaping forces in the lives of leaders and students. The leader must apply particular discipline to acknowledging, understanding, and appropriately addressing cultural differences that may exist because of race, ethnicity, or context. Furthermore, youth leaders must be particularly sensitive to the students who straddle two cultures.

Imagine leading students in an exploration of how one's relationship with Jesus Christ ought to affect one's relationship with parents. Asian-American students in the group whose parents are first-generation immigrants will be dealing with both their parents' cultural expectations for the family and American cultural expectations. Those expectations often are in contrast to one another. Or imagine a ministry mix that includes Caribbean-American students, for whom it may not be uncommon to think of common-law marriages as part of the natural family structure. Once again cultural insensitivity —and consequent ineffectiveness—can be prevented if leaders act as learners, gathering data and evaluating assumptions.

Finally, when beginning to gather data, it is important for leaders to address any aversion anxiety over the prospect of doing "research" to collect "data." Anytime a leader enjoys a casual conversation with a student where something previously unknown is discovered that leader is engaging in a form of research. Over time, and through a number of such conversations, leaders cannot help forming some impressions about adolescent social patterns in their communities. Arming themselves with questions that will fill in knowledge gaps does not turn youth ministers into lab-coat clinicians. Neither does the process of seeking conversational opportunities with key kids. In truth, an increasingly natural curiosity to learn about the world a teen lives in is a great way to extend the unconditional love of Jesus to young people.

A View from the BK Lounge: Discerning Student Interpretations

All social context is relative. Consider the leader whose high school band involvement was one of the guarantors of his popularity among his peers. He assumed that the same sort of music affiliation would be the natural pathway to peer social status among the teens where he first ministered. Unfortunately, the school community he worked in didn't think highly of their band. He could have checked his assumptions with students in the area and saved himself a lot of head-scratching.

Do you know what the "BK Lounge" is? The term was used to describe Burger King in a locale where I formerly ministered. (In spite of my best efforts, the phrase has never caught on where I now live and work.) Just recently a friend came back from hanging around some teens where someone told him he was "in the house." He wasn't sure if that was a good or bad place to be until he checked it out with some other students (it was good!).

Other examples could be cited. Cutting-edge East Coast fashion does not fit in with many rural Midwest communities. In some social contexts wearing particular hats, bandannas, or colors may be health threatening because of their gang significance.

In each case, whether it is the use of jargon, or clothing, or specific habits, meaning is uncovered in a particular context. To be safe, leaders should work to verify their assumptions if the social context for ministry changes. This is best done by asking students to provide an interpretation of particular pieces of information. Besides being the most accurate method, this approach also communicates an appropriate respect for the students' role in their social contexts.

Asking students for interpretations can produce a variety of important insights. For example, students may agree that only a certain group of kids go to school-sponsored dances. Furthermore, they may wish aloud that they could be included in that group. Important inferences may surface regarding where social influence is taking place in the lives of key youth group students. That information may profoundly affect the next steps in the youth leader's outreach strategies.

Figure 4.2, a tool for classifying adolescents across the social spectrum, may provide a way of eliciting interpretations from teens. The chart has two intersecting axes, one labeled *visibility*, the other labeled *likability*, corresponding to the classifications of social impact and social preference used by social science researchers. Each axis has a positive and negative polarity. Teens who could be identified as "popular" are those who are both likable and highly visible. "Controversial" and "rejected" students are also highly visible, with the latter rating a negative on the likability index. "Average" students tend to get lost in the crowd to a lesser degree than those who rank a negative on the visibility index—the "neglected" student.

What labels are appropriate for persons who are likable but invisible (-,+) or barely visible (0,+) to their peers? Are there students who are unlikable and invisible (-,-) or who make minimal impact (0,-) on their peers? How could they be classified?

A number of youth ministry applications can be found for this tool. Consider explaining it to a group of teens and then asking them to put an X at the place that best describes their own likability and visibility status among their peers. They could also write down the names of peers who might best fit a particular label on the grid. Perhaps a student leader team could draw a shape that would describe the students' perception of the type of kids who comprise their youth group. It would be interesting to discuss the bulges in the polygon

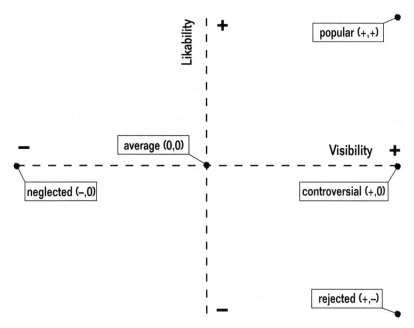

Figure 4.2. *Elements of Social Preference*

drawing. It might even be convicting to compare the social profile of the group with biblical values.

Notice that in all instances, the students are making the interpretations. What do they make of the going and coming patterns of various teens in their community? Who do they think fits a specific label? How do they feel about their analyses? What is their social status, what would they like it to be, and how could they change it? These social perceptions offer rich insights for ministry, but they represent much more than that. Teenage interpretations of the social realities in their world constitute the social context in which we must minister. Their perceptions are the only reality that counts as leaders work to understand a social framework for youth ministry.

Imagine a youth group that when asked to describe a color that most accurately represents their group collectively comes up with *gray* or *drab green*. Imagine further that the adult leadership team, separately engaged in the same exercise, uses terms like *neon green* or *hot red*. Clearly there is a disjunction—and students' perceptions are the only reality that counts in this assessment.

Having listened to and pondered student perception, it remains for youth leaders to step forward into ministry action.

The Key Filter: Ministry Mission

Jeff, Phil, Mike, and Russ are all youth pastors in the same community. It is a small city served by a single, large high school. The larger social context for their ministry to youth is identical, though each of their churches has a mediating social influence on what they do.

Jeff's church is trying to rebound from the loss of some key people over the past few years. The youth group has been impacted. Though Jeff is naturally outreach oriented, with a Pied Piper personality, he has reined himself in so that he can focus on the current roster of his youth group. They need help in forming a positive group-image before they add to their ranks.

Russ works in a church that recently merged with another. He has always seen himself as a minister to the youth of the entire community, especially those who are often disenfranchised. Russ shows up where kids are, looking for ways to serve and love them. Over the years he has actively championed teenage interests throughout the community. He looks to empower kids with the gospel, and his church's youth take much responsibility for their ministry.

Phil is the new guy in town. His ministry heart is a lot like Russ's, but he serves in a well-established church with historical expectations about the proper way of doing things. Phil has made two moves in the first few months to signal the kind of ministry he wants to create. The first is to establish a distinctive youth room with a very contemporary appeal. The second is to change the name of the youth group to "The Outsiders." Phil is working hard to let his kids know that it is no longer business as usual for the youth in his church.

Mike seems to have one of the strongest youth ministries in the community. Nested in an exciting church, it has many resources and an enthusiasm that is contagious. In fact, the church's picture of excellence in youth ministry is to offer a variety of interesting and appealing programs as an alternative to less wholesome options in the community. Mike's relational style doesn't translate very easily into being a programming whiz, but he seems to have negotiated the difficulties pretty well.

How would you expect each of these men to use Friday night's football game in their own ministry? Here is what happened.

Jeff called a few kids and went to the game with them. Fairly low-key as fans, they sat a little distance away from all the action. They ended up afterwards at Jeff's place munching on popcorn and playing some board games.

Russ showed up with his camera and planted himself by the fence. He took shots of many different kids, on and off the field. When he gets them developed he'll offer them to the kids as a way of saying that both they and their world are important to Russ.

Phil grabbed a bunch of his kids and they planted themselves in the middle of a rowdy cheer section, often leading in some of the antics. After the game, they hit each of the two fast-food places most popular on a Friday night.

Mike showed up for half of the game, and then he moved around a lot. He kept bumping into his kids, or friends of his kids, making a little small talk and reminding them about the open gym night their youth group was hosting after the game. At halftime he left with a couple of guys to set up for their program.

Ministry mission and focus will mediate the way we respond to social context. Each of the four youth ministers recognized the social significance of Friday night's football game to the teens in their community. All of them saw that the event was important to the kids with whom they wanted to minister. None of them ignored the game. Yet their ministry responses were chosen in light of their particular ministry goals. Jeff wanted the kids of his group to feel extra special, so he gave them his time and invited them to his home. Russ wanted every kid he met to feel important, so he took pictures and gave them away. Phil was working on creating a more youth-friendly image with his kids, so he left his own comfort zone to show them they could count on him to be socially aware. Mike was trying to promote a program with his kids that would enrich their overall Friday night experience.

As popular as a Friday night football game is in the social lives of many teens, there are times when our best ministry responses will take us elsewhere. Jeff could just as easily have taken his teens on a retreat for the weekend. Russ has been known to skip games so he could hang out with the anti-school crowd near the bridge. Both moves would have been consistent with their ministry foci and sensitive to the social needs of particular students. On the other hand, Mike might try to pull off an important ministry event at the same time as the big game, but he should be prepared to ask kids to make hard choices for good reasons. And there is a better chance that Mike could pull off the program than Phil. Phil's group hasn't attained the social respectability that Mike's has yet.

As important as social context is to youth ministry, the key filter in framing ministry strategies lies elsewhere. Ministry responses, though always socially sensitive, must be driven by ministry mission.

FIRST THINGS FIRST

The wise youth worker will seek to be socially savvy before designing a ministry strategy. A constant commitment to learn the social culture in any particular ministry context will serve well whether he is a guest speaker on weekend retreats or a twenty-year resident of the same community. Pursuing an exhaustive awareness of the teenage social facts of life will open the youth worker's eyes to new ministry pos-sibilities. Discovering adolescents' interpretation of their social world will inform his ministry perspectives and shape his ministry responses. Youth leaders are passionately inter-ested in seeing youth ministries experience mission effective-ness among teenagers, a population often referred to as "social animals." Success will depend, in large part, upon exploring, interpreting, and responding effectively to the social frameworks within which students live, breathe, and have their being.

FOR FURTHER READING

Bibby, Reginald W., and Donald C. Posterski. 1992. *Teen Trends*. Toronto: Stoddart.

Campolo, Anthony. 1993. *The Church and the American Teenager: What Works and Doesn't in Youth Ministry.* Grand Rapids: Zondervan.

Fields, Doug. 1991. *Too Old Too Soon.* Eugene, Oreg.: Harvest House.

Mueller, Walt. 1994. *Understanding Today's Youth Culture.* Wheaton, Ill.: Tyndale.

5

A HISTORICAL FRAMEWORK FOR DOING YOUTH MINISTRY

Mark H. Senter III

The America Online bulletin board on youth ministry innovation had been humming ever since Relater had taken on *Jesusfreek* over the question of the basis for youth ministry among Generation Xers (those born between 1965 and 1985). The two shared a frustration with the state of youth ministry, but their responses appeared to be poles apart.

Relater viewed the impersonalness of society, the insensitivity of peers and adults, and the manipulative control of students' values by the media as the hurdles to be overcome by the youth minister. His answer: hang out with kids. Be real. Let them see Jesus in your life. Live a "redemptive" life in their world and eventually you will earn the right to be heard.

Jesusfreek's reaction was strong and immediate. The local youth ministries she had been observing were merely social clubs with nothing that distinguished them as being Christian.

Since she was new in the area, she attended youth activities promoted by other churches and parachurch agencies in her town to see what was happening. To her amazement, the discussions she witnessed sounded more like either a sociology class or a twelve-step program than like a movement grounded in the Bible. What was needed was inductive study of the Scriptures.

It was not long before *ACTSman* had to add his two cents' worth to the discussion. "The key to Gen X," said *ACTSman*, "is neither relationships nor theology. It is Book of ACTS-type action. Not programs. Not boring Bible studies. Action! We need to help kids find a way to minister to people and then get all the programming junk out of the way so that they can get involved with helping people."

The problem with the on-line discussion was that everyone was right. They were like the proverbial blind men describing an elephant. One, feeling the animal's tail, described it as ropelike. A second put his hands on one of the pachyderm's massive legs and gained the impression that the creature was like a tree trunk. The final person, feeling the side of the elephant, thought the beast must be like a wall. The confusion came about because each person was focusing on only one aspect of the animal.

The history of youth ministry suggests that when ministry to students is done well, it blends three elements—warm, respectful relationships; appealing, conservative Bible teaching; and an aggressive bent for action. By contrast, when youth ministry begins to stagnate or institutionalize there comes a fragmentation of these aspects of ministry. The on-line discussion suggests that youth ministry may be in just such a situation—at least in the communities where *Relater,* *Jesusfreek,* and *ACTSman* live.

Classic Example

Dwight L. Moody began his ministry as a youth worker. A Sunday school teacher, to be exact.

Later world renowned as an evangelist, Moody volunteered to teach God's Word to boys on the north side of Chicago while working as a shoe salesman. Unlike much of youth ministry today, Mr. Moody was not given his own class of young men from Christian homes. Instead his Sunday school superintendent brusquely told the young entrepreneur to go out onto the streets of Chicago and recruit his own class and then he would be given a place to teach the boys.

Into the streets he went, first gaining the friendship and then the loyalty of young boys who had not known him a few days before. Moody played with the boys, gave them prizes for bringing friends, and eventually became dynamic in the way he taught the lesson. More came. Some left, but most returned week after week. The Sunday school grew to more than six hundred children, which is an impressive number by any youth worker's standard. The year was 1859.

When asked why he attended Mr. Moody's Sunday school when he could be doing so many other things in the streets of Chicago, one boy replied, "They love a boy down there."

Youth ministry in its purest forms has always been relational, theological, and action oriented.

ROOTS

Cycles of youth ministry have usually been initiated by an event outside youth ministry that is pivotal in shaping the world of the adolescent. In fact, youth ministry as such did not come into being until late in the eighteenth century. The Enlightenment in the seventeenth and eighteenth centuries created an intellectual climate in which theology was no longer considered the queen of the sciences. Biblical Truth was reduced to truth. No longer did theology define the sciences. It gradually became just another discipline of study. Religious convictions and values were rejected by many and were hotly debated by the intellectuals of the day.

The changes initiated by the Enlightenment reached the level of the common person and became a concern for Christian parents with the birth of the Industrial Revolution in the eighteenth and nineteenth centuries. With the rise of technology, the sheltered world of the village, extended family, and church was shattered. Industrialization caused jobs to be concentrated in urban centers. Families needing income left the nurturing environment of the small village and followed the promise of a better life to the city. Lost in the transition was the spiritual and moral accountability, for good or bad, which was present in extended family and parish life. Youth fell prey to the temptations that abounded in the city.

Families and congregations felt helpless to stem the tide of worldly influences around their young people or rescue the impoverished children of the street. It was into this spiritual vacuum that there arose a series of ministries that appealed to youth and allowed adults to pass Christian values from one generation to the next. The Sunday school, Young Men's Christian Association (YMCA), and Young Women's Christian Association (YWCA) provided the first wave of youth ministries. Though these movements began in England, their greatest impact was actually felt in America between 1824 and 1875.

A second wave or cycle of youth ministry emerged between 1881 and 1925, taking its impetus from the Society for Christian Endeavor founded in 1881 by Francis E. Clark. Encouraged and threatened by the success of Christian Endeavor, denominational leagues and societies were formed in order to provide nurturing activities to youth while maintaining denominational loyalties. The focal point for these societies was the local church. Soon other club activities followed. Groups such as Boys' Club of America (1906), 4-H Clubs (1907), Camp Fire Girls (1910), Boy Scouts of America (1910), and Girl Scouts of America (1912) shared a Judeo-Christian value system but were not necessarily religious in nature. Similar groups were appearing across the British Empire during this same period.

The third cycle of youth ministry took its cue from the public high school. Between 1935 and 1987 agencies such as Young Life (1941), Youth for Christ/Campus Life (1945), and Fellowship of Christian Athletes (1954) established strategies which were soon copied by local churches in a fashion similar to the manner in which denominations cloned Christian Endeavor activities during the previous wave of youth ministry. Club programs for the evangelical church, modeled after scouting and similar programs, were established by Christian Service Brigade (1937), Pioneer Girls (1939), and AWANA (1950).

Parachurch agencies even shaped the training of youth workers for the church. Youth Specialties (1968), *Group Magazine* (1974), and Sonlife Ministries (1979) led the way, while Christian colleges scrambled to include youth ministry majors in their curricula.

DISCIPLESHIP BALANCE

Youth ministry, when it has been most effective, has blended three emphases into a balanced approach to discipleship. Productive youth ministries have come upon the scene because insightful leaders, responding to the needs of their day and the guidance of the Holy Spirit, have blended relationships, theology, and purposeful activity to appeal to the youth with whom they had contact. These three components have formed a creative triad that remains effective in discipling young people (fig. 5.1). (Parallels can be drawn with the cognitive, affective, and motor skill domains of learning.)

In youth ministry, as everywhere in the work of the church, God has worked through people. People, in turn, have created systems that reflect their giftedness, the needs of

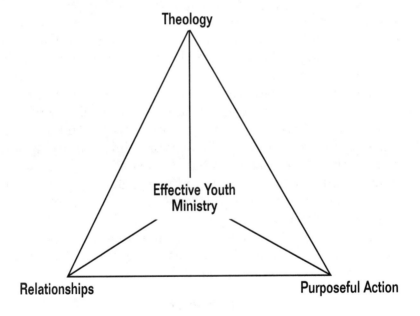

Figure 5.1. *Discipleship Triad*

their generation, and the resources available at the time. In time, those systems have been appropriated by other people who have held the founder's passion but who brought a different set of gifts and abilities to the ministry. Inevitably the discipleship triad has changed.

At times the changes made the ministry more effective because of important refinements. The Miracle Book Club was founded by Evelyn M. McClusky in 1933. On the strength of articles published in the *Sunday School Times* the club program spread rapidly across the United States and to other countries. Although Mrs. McClusky was a talented writer, communicator, and innovator, her organizational abilities and effectiveness with high school boys were limited. Jim Rayburn became the Texas state director of the Miracle Book Club but his abilities and vision far exceeded those of Mrs. McClusky. Within a matter of months Rayburn had broken with the founder to establish the Young Life Campaign in 1941. The split, while contributing to the demise of the Miracle Book Club, made possible some of the most significant innovations in youth ministry in more than fifty years.

More frequently, however, changes tended to bring imbalance in the creative triad of youth ministry and begin a gradual slide toward ineffectiveness. The Society for Christian Endeavor from its beginning balanced a formal pledge by young people to report on their "endeavor" to know God, with a program system that used officers and a structured program to keep youth involved in order to fulfill the pledge. Denominational groups quickly began appropriating the program structure of Christian Endeavor while modifying and softening the pledge that stood at the heart of Francis Clark's theology and system of youth ministry. Between 1889 and 1895, six major denominations established leagues or unions that paralleled the national program of the Christian Endeavor system and adapted it for denominational purposes. Purposeful action became defined as *program*. As a result, relationship and theology suffered.

DISCIPLESHIP SYSTEM

An important question to consider when looking for his-

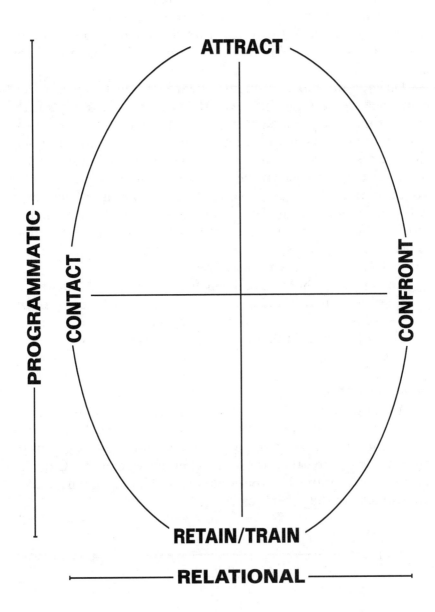

Figure 5.2. *Discipleship System in Youth Ministry*

torical patterns in youth ministry is, *What constitutes a youth ministry discipleship system?* As patterns have appeared, there has been a tendency for innovators to lock onto one component of the system and boldly proclaim that it is the hoped-for change.

Perhaps the most frequently heard cry over the past two centuries of youth ministry was the concern of Moody's little friend that youth ministry be a place where a guy is loved. Concerned Christian adults have consistently found that good theology is best lived out through loving relationships. Incarnational theology has served as the foundation of effective youth ministry for nearly two centuries, although the concept was only identified by Young Life leaders in the 1940s. But strong adult-adolescent relationships without a more comprehensive discipleship system will merely exhaust even the most spiritually motivated youth worker.

Consistently there have been four components to such a discipleship system: *contact, attract, confront,* and *retain/train.* These are placed along two axes: *programmatic* and *relational.* The roles within this discipleship system are given in Figure 5.2.

Relational Axis

Along the relational axis have been two functions: contact and confront (present with the gospel) (fig. 5.3). Youth ministry generally began when a Christian adult found a way to enter the world of an adolescent. Contact was made. Conversations were enjoyed. Experiences were shared. Each discovered a niche in the other's world.

Contact ◄─────────────────────────────────► Confront

Figure 5.3. *Relational Axis*

Contact has been established in many ways. The YMCA provided living quarters, gymnasiums, and reading rooms for urban youth in an attempt to provide contact between Christian men and boys as well as among Christian peers. The original Sunday schools were situated in neighborhoods and communities where youth needed positive adult role models and many times teachers became mentors and friends to the ruffians from the street. Christian Endeavor built a society where mature young adults in their late twenties led younger people in their endeavor to know God. Similarly, Young Life and Campus Life staff members have built ministries by hanging around practice fields and drama practice rooms in order to get acquainted with students and eventually invite them to club activities.

Natural contact occurred when a Christian adult built a friendship with a student while at work, in the neighborhood, or through mutual interests. *Adult-initiated* contact took place when a youth worker found a way to participate in activities the student enjoyed. *Program-initiated* contact took place when a church or parachurch agency sponsored an activity attractive to students and understood to require an adult presence. *Parental* contact took place when the relationship between parent and young person was based on trust and respect. This latter contact many times extended to a circle of the adolescent's friends. *Issue/need driven* contact resulted from mutual concern over something that threatened the security of the young person's world (drugs, alcohol, violence). All of these set the stage for incarnational ministry.

Confrontation with the Christian gospel was the other end of the axis. God's truth related to God's holiness, human sinfulness, and Christ's provision for salvation has been viewed as vital for students so that the message is understood and acted upon. Union meetings, youth rallies, camp experiences, and, in some cases, special club meetings provided opportunities for the good news of the gospel to be presented and a response to be invited. In most gospel presentations there was drama. Although the logic of the gospel was there, music, testimonies, storytelling, even humor and other appeals to the emotions were important parts of the gospel presentation.

Although effective witness is essentially an individual matter, three strategies of confrontation have dominated the history of youth ministry. Youth rallies (though not called that until just prior to World War II) were meetings to which young people could be brought to hear the gospel. The pattern most frequently recorded suggests that effective rallies were attended by large groups of youth and adults. Speakers were gifted in evangelism though many were not ordained ministers. More recently, seeker strategies in churches have proved effective when the program can attract a critical mass of young people to hear and experience the gospel.

Camps and conferences provided a second venue for confrontation with the Christian message. Young Life camps were a classic illustration of the strategy. Contact had culminated in confrontation with Jesus Christ.

Jack Wyrtzen connected his Word of Life camps with rallies, a national radio broadcast, and a church-based club program to gain a hearing for the gospel. Fellowship of Christian Athletes used a similar strategy using regional and national training camps. Youth for Christ promoted regional and national conferences to accomplish similar ends, as did denominational and independent camping programs.

The third approach to witness focused on individual activity. One of D. L. Moody's Sunday school teachers hired a carriage in order to visit all the children in his class and explain the way of salvation before he returned to his home in New York. Evelyn M. McClusky recorded story after story in her articles and books about young people who came to faith in Christ through personal witness. Student Venture, originally (and under a different name) the high school ministry Campus Crusade for Christ established in 1966, built its entire strategy around personal witness by high schoolers to peers.

The more intimate was the relationship between adult and youth, the narrower the gap between contact and confrontation (fig. 5.4). But the more people who were involved in the discipleship system, the more structure was required. Spontaneity had to be carefully planned.

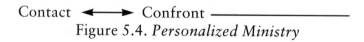

Contact ◀──▶ Confront ────────────────

Figure 5.4. *Personalized Ministry*

Programmatic Axis

Along the programmatic axis were two functions: *attracting* and *retaining/training* (fig. 5.5). Programs were the vehicles whereby groups of people could be brought with comfort and integrity to experience the Christian gospel. There they could continue to grow in their relationship with the eternal God to the point where they become part of the process of bringing others into contact with Jesus Christ.

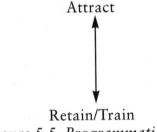

Attract

Retain/Train

Figure 5.5. *Programmatic Axis*

Attracting young people to attend an event where the Christian gospel would be presented was the main feature of the discipleship system. Over the past fifty years the primary models have included using clubs as a means of teaching and as a way of attracting fellow club attenders to Youth for Christ rallies. Willow Creek's youth ministry built teams to compete in wacky competition events in order to attract teenagers to the seeker events sponsored by the Student Impact program. In Young Life, students who had attended clubs that might not have been heavy in biblical content were invited to conclude their school year by going to one of the resort camps owned by Young Life. There they found that for the first time the gospel made sense. For still others, locally sponsored coffee houses or gymnasium ministries provided the basis for getting young people to consider the claims of Christ. In each of these approaches, discipleship systems were dependent upon adults to create and young people to invite their spiritually seeking friends.

Earlier systems that bridged the span between contact and

confrontation included the Sunday school activities. Some of these were contests and incentives, a variety of YMCA/YWCA athletic and social activities, as well as the church-based youth societies that allowed young people to have a safe and socially acceptable place to gather in a day when few other options were offered.

Retaining and training was the logical outcome of the programming axis. Rather than an event or a series of events this was a long-term process whereby spiritual commitments were strengthened and leadership qualities were developed. From formal classes in which the Bible and spiritual disciplines were taught to small accountability groups, and from Christian service opportunities to leadership development occasioned by being an officer of the group, the retain/train process provides structure designed to nourish the adolescent in spiritual growth.

Publishers of Sunday school and youth group materials assisted even the smallest of churches to train their youth. Christian youth magazines and—beginning in the 1960s—recordings of gospel artists for young people helped reinforce the learning and training process. Bible quizzing, traditional camp programs, and mission trips were other means of helping adolescent believers to grow to maturity in Christ.

The more the student was involved in direct evangelism, however, the less formal structure was necessary for the retain/train process. Discipleship became a by-product of evangelistic encounters. Students had to grow spiritually in order to survive (fig. 5.6).

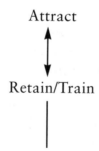

Attract

Retain/Train

Figure 5.6. *Evangelism-Based Ministry*

The cycle of youth ministry was complete when an unbelieving teenager had been contacted by a peer or adult, was attracted to attend events where the Christian truth confronted him, and was assimilated into a formal nurturing process. The end of the process saw young people actively involved in contacting spiritually sensitive peers in hopes of bringing them to Christ.

CONCLUSION

The problem *Relater, Jesusfreek,* and *ACTSman* faced in their E-mail discussion was a lack of perspective. Although each had a valid point to make and all could support their perspectives from Scripture, they had missed the big picture. A historical perspective may have helped them to find a strategic balance that would lead to enduring ministry.

When youth ministries are healthy, they have retained a balance among relational dynamics, theological thinking, and a bent for action—which in turn shapes a system of discipleship. A balanced system will include contacting unbelieving youth, attracting them to activities that result in a confrontation with the Christian gospel, and a training process by which the new believer is discipled.

WORKS CITED

Chaplin, William Knight. Ca. 1931. *Fifty Years of Christian Endeavor: A Jubilee Record and Forecast, 1881–1931.*

Erb, Frank Otis. 1917. *The Development of the Young People's Movement.* Chicago: Univ. of Chicago Press.

Hopkins, C. Howard. 1951. *History of the Y.M.C.A. in North America.* New York: Association.

Loftis, Michael G. 1988. "A Historical Survey of Evangelical Youth Ministries in the United States, 1935–1985." Chattanooga: Temple Baptist Theological Seminary.

Lynn, Robert W., and Elliott Wright. 1980. *The Big Little School: 200 Years of the Sunday School.* Nashville: Abingdon.

Rice, Edwin Wilbur Ca. 1917. *The Sunday School Movement, 1780–1917.* 2d ed. Philadelphia: Union.

Senter, Mark H. III. 1989. "The Youth for Christ Movement as an Educational Agency and Its Impact upon Protestant Churches, 1931–1979." Ann Arbor: University Microfilms International.

_____. 1992. *The Coming Revolution in Youth Ministry.* Wheaton, Ill.: Victor.

PART TWO

STRUCTURES FOR YOUTH MINISTRY

6

Axioms of Youth Ministry: The Context

Mark H. Senter III

As excellent as last year's youth ministry was at Bloomingdale Evangelical Church, this year has been bad. Really bad," confessed Ned to the youth workers in his workshop session. "If I had done this session last year, I might have titled it 'All You Ever Wanted to Know About Youth Work but Were Afraid to Ask.' This year I am tempted to call it 'The Youth Ministry Blues, Brothers.'"

The development of the church's youth ministry had been like a fairy tale during Ned Burgess's first three years in Bloomingdale. Village, church, school district, and youth group all seemed to mushroom in tandem. Although a significant proportion of the new students and leaders had moved to the community from the racially changing urban area twenty miles away, Ned's greatest joy had come from the non-Christians who had been reached and were now being discipled into the church.

But that was last year.

June had seen the graduation of the key student leaders Ned and his youth sponsors had been discipling over the past three years. Now the greater spiritual maturity and leadership potential appeared to be in the freshman class. Numbers had dropped off. Non-Christians were not being reached in any significant manner. Momentum seemed to have been lost.

Yet there was Ned, standing in front of forty-five youth workers, explaining how the ministry should be done. He had two options. Either tell the expectant audience the glory stories from the last three years or honestly confess that hard times had come to Bloomingdale's youth ministry and attempt to discern what had been beginner's luck and what had been biblically sound ministry principles.

The next two chapters are an effort to isolate ministry principles that apply in all of the models of youth ministry. The ideas are referred to as *axioms,* or propositions regarded as self-evident truths. Although some supporting evidence will be provided for certain axioms, the various propositions are offered as insights based on the successes and failures of a generation of youth ministry practitioners.

The idea of axioms for youth ministry was introduced in 1987 in *The Complete Book of Youth Ministry.* As I concluded the doctoral research which laid the foundation for *The Coming Revolution in Youth Ministry,* I found three other axioms that need to be considered if this chapter is to be considered complete. In the days since, I have challenged others to propose and defend other axioms, so in the days ahead more axioms may be identified.

This book will divide the fifteen axioms into two groupings: *context* and *dynamics.* The context axioms give perspective on the environment in which youth ministry can best take place. For the most part they deal with the role of adults and what they do to make youth ministry happen. The dynamics axioms focus on the ingredients within the youth ministry itself. The focus here is the chemistry among the young people. Admittedly, the axioms are not as distinct as the division may suggest, but I hope the division will be helpful in understanding youth ministry.

An important distinction must be made at the outset. *Youth ministry* has to do with adults whose primary desire is to disciple students in their Christian faith; *youth work* is a broader term that does not necessitate Christian discipleship; *youth movement* in a Christian context describes young people discipling other young people, a process in which adults play a decidedly secondary leadership role.

Thus the Student Volunteer Movement and Student Foreign Missions Fellowship, as well as many aspects of the Jesus People movement, are not considered youth ministry because they were student led. Similarly, the activities of the YMCA, Boys Club of America, most aspects of Scouts, and youth athletic leagues are not youth ministry because Christian discipleship is peripheral to their primary purpose.

AXIOM 1

Youth ministry begins when a Christian adult finds a comfortable method of entering a student's world (Green 1981, 61–66).

Though some adults feel comfortable spending time with adolescents, a large proportion of Christian adults would feel rather awkward attempting to build a relationship with a high school student without some kind of excuse to do so. Parents of students similarly might look with skepticism on adults who appear to be spending time with their children without apparent rationale. Consequently, the comfort zone must to some degree include student, parent, and Christian youth worker.

Entering a student's world can be described as contact work. The idea was capsulized by Young Life staff member John Mackay when he spoke of "earning the right to be heard" (Cailliet 1963, 62). The idea was not new, for adults had been earning a right to be heard by youth through organizational systems for years. Young Lifers merely applied it to a new area, that of relationships. Their contention was that the basis of evangelism and discipleship is a relationship, not a system.

Today at least five kinds of contact work can be identified. *Natural contacts* are made by people who, by virtue of personality and position, attract young people to themselves. Certain schoolteachers, employers, athletes, and media people would fall into this category. Students, for one reason or another, find them fun to be around, and so the contact that can lead to discipleship has been made.

A second kind of contact is *adult-initiated contact.* This contact is by people who may not be with students on a normal basis but who use a skill or interest to meet a need in the life of a student. Tutors, nonprofessional coaches, mechanics, computer specialists, musicians, and youth ministers could all use their abilities in fields of interest to young people to gain a hearing for the gospel.

Program-initiated contact is a third way for adults to gain a hearing with youth. Sunday school, youth group activities, youth choirs, camps, retreats, and clubs are activities in which adults make contact with students . The young people come to be involved with a formal organization geared to their interests or needs. Thus the program provides the comfort zone for adults, students, and parents.

A fourth kind of contact work is that of *parental contact.* When youth ministers were asked who had been instrumental in shaping their spiritual development, one answer was heard frequently: their own parents or the parent of a close friend to whom they went in time of need. Though this could be an extension of *natural contact,* it deserves special attention because so frequently parents forget that they, too, are youth ministers (Senter 1986, 40–44).

A final kind of contact is *need-driven contact.* With so much of an adolescent's life at risk, specific movements have emerged to help young people discover a safe place in society. Alcohol and drug abuse, pressures to engage in premarital sex (and the consequences of teen pregnancies), dysfunctional families, and communities endangered by gangs are but a few of the dangers adolescents face. These all have given rise to contact between adults and young people. Students Against Driving Drunk (SADD), Teen Moms, True Love Waits, foster parenting, runaway shelters, and urban youth centers can provide a framework for contact between students and Christian adults.

Implications

1. The most comfortable method for an adult to earn the right to be heard by students will differ from person to person as well as from situation to situation in any *one* person's life. There simply is no one right way to enter a student's world.

2. At the same time, youth ministry will not happen unless someone has earned the right to enter the student's world. Just as redemption would not have happened if the God-man had not entered time and space to live, die, and live again, so the Christian discipleship of students will not take place without flesh and blood relationships (John 1:14).

AXIOM 2

Youth ministry happens as long as a Christian adult is able to use his or her contact with a student to draw that student into a maturing relationship with God through Jesus Christ (see Goetz 1978, 164).

Maturity, like excellence, is much easier to recognize than to describe. When one focuses on an aspect of maturity that is as elusive to describe as spirituality, the idea of defining spiritual maturity becomes exceedingly difficult (see Towns 1973, 155–67, for a useful discussion of the subject). Yet, for the purpose of discussion, a definition is in order.

> Spiritual maturity for a high school student is that stage in his or her relationship to God when he or she is capable and willing to allow biblical truth to shape his or her values, decisions, and actions.

Youth ministry happens only as long as the youth minister's efforts are moving students in this direction. The progress will not be smooth, for adolescence is a period of idealism and doubt, of success and failure, of growth and relapse. There may be periods when nothing appears to be happening. Then evidences of spiritual maturity will appear. Yet all of the youth minister's activity has one objective in mind: spiritually mature students. Everything else is merely "youth work."

An important gauge of youth ministry is the question, How often and to what extent do the students tell me their fears and doubts, triumphs and joys, hopes and dreams, mistakes and sins, moods and feelings? These are the teachable times. These are the maturing times (for further treatment of facilitating relationships, see Richards 1985, 119–39).

At least three evidences of spiritual maturity can be found in Luke's description of the church following the Day of Pentecost (Acts 2:41–47). First, people were being converted, signified by their baptism (v. 41). Second, they were learning biblical truth as explained by the apostles. They evidenced its impact by participating in the church's love feast, including Communion and prayer (v. 42). Third, they were learning to love each other, accepting the implications of that love by making material sacrifices for each other (v. 44).

The various models of youth ministry provide a context in which adults can assist young people in their spiritual pilgrimages. Team competition provides an opportunity for captains to confront team members with the claims of Christ. Drama, under the wise direction of a qualified adult, becomes a vehicle for ministry. Core groups, when guided by a caring leader, exemplify a redemptive community. Planning teams, when coached by nurturing adults, bring about leadership skills in the next generation of church leaders.

There is a link between time spent with youth and the success of the program. Towns, citing a study by E. Michael Rustin, points out that the "average time spent by each youth sponsor per week was highest in the most successful churches: most successful youth groups spent 11.4 [hours per week with youth sponsors]; other sponsors . . . spent 3.9 hours. Most successful churches devoted an average of .7 hours per week per youth, while the average for the others was .1" (Towns 1973, 197).

Implications

1. Models of youth ministry are *vehicles* for assisting the spiritual maturation process in young people, nothing more. They are neither biblical nor unbiblical, right nor wrong, appropriate nor inappropriate in and of themselves.

2. Spiritual maturation appropriate to the youth group and the individuals within the group is the ultimate standard of success for the ministry. It is also the means by which adults working with youth should measure their effectiveness.

AXIOM 3

Youth ministry ceases to take place when the adult-student relationship is broken or no longer moves the student toward spiritual maturity.

It is quite possible for a strong youth ministry, or even part of a youth ministry, to slip unwittingly from youth ministry to youth work, from assisting young people in their spiritual maturation process to providing mere activities for the same students. In fact, if youth workers are not aware of this downside of youth ministry, their efforts may become frustratingly ineffective.

The two major aspects of axiom 3 may be linked in an apparent cause-and-effect connection, but for purposes of this discussion they will be examined separately. The first is broken relationships. Relationships can be severed in youth ministries in three primary ways. Adults and students can physically move away from each other, and though a discipling relationship can continue, more often than not new loyalties are established.

A second and more subtle manner in which ministry relationships can be broken is through adult and student drifting apart. As a student begins to take greater responsibility for his or her own spiritual growth, he or she may find that the need the adult had previously met is no longer an issue. Or the mutual interest that initially drew adult and student together, such as sports, drama, music, or camping, is no longer a significant part of the student's life. New interests supersede older commitments. Relationships fade.

The least obvious and most detrimental way in which ministry relationships can be broken is through a loss of respect by one or both of the adult-student tandem. For example, unfulfilled expectations, perceived inconsistencies, unconfessed sin, unresolved interpersonal conflict, and unkept promises on the leader's part will undermine his authority and bring about a loss of respect, especially if the young person he is working with has not developed skills in conflict resolution. Whereas the "drift factor" may merely be developmental, the "respect factor" has its roots in spiritual matters and thus needs to be identified and resolved lest long-term damage results (Elkind 1984, 109–13).

Adult-student relationships, though not broken, may become unproductive from a spiritual standpoint and thus bring youth ministry, at least for those people, to an end. A friendship can degenerate to a "buddy-buddy" arrangement wherein the adult is more like one of the students than the loving adult role model the young person needs. That is most common when an adult youth worker has an identity problem and is gaining his or her sense of worth from the students to whom he or she is ministering (Goetz 1978, 170).

Nonproductivity can result when the student outgrows the spiritual leadership that an adult has to offer, especially in later adolescence when young people are the most capable of coming to grips with the social, economic, political, and moral implications of the gospel. The adult's need at this point may be to refocus his activity toward the young people who do need what he has to offer.

Romantic relationship between adult and student usually brings about unproductive youth ministry. Although stories have been told of the youth minister who marries a girl who had recently been a member of his group, actual examples are rare. More often ministry becomes unproductive on three fronts. First, the student becomes so emotionally involved with the adult that he or she loses perspective on spiritual values. Second, other members of the youth group feel ill at ease about the relationship and may withdraw trust from the two involved. Finally, parents of other students may become resistant to the youth sponsors for fear that this will happen again. And this is not to speak of the temptations to sexual sin, "breaking up" woes, and abuse of power issues.

Nonproductivity can also result from the adult sponsor who focuses so exclusively on the specific skills around which the ministry model is built that the goal of spiritual maturity is obscured. Athletic activities, music, drama, and Bible quizzing can all fall into this trap. It is a matter of the good becoming the enemy of the best.

Implications

1. Adults must accept their adultness in order to maximize their ministry potential. Youth ministry is no place to resolve a postponed identity crisis.
2. Adults must maintain their focus on bringing students to spiritual maturity through the ministry model employed. If the model becomes an end in itself, the ministry will tend to be lost by default.
3. By contrast, adults must be willing to release students when spiritual independence is necessary. The youth worker's "empty nest syndrome" may be as difficult for the loving youth worker as it is for the nurturing parents. Endless accountability, however, will become counterproductive.

AXIOM 4

The influence of the student's family on his or her value system will exceed the influence of the youth worker on most occasions.

There is a tendency among youth ministers to see themselves in isolation from any other sources of influence on the young person's spiritual development. Fortunately and unfortunately that is not true. It is fortunate because a majority of youth ministers have not gained the wisdom necessary to be solely responsible for a young person's spiritual development. It is unfortunate because the spiritual convictions of many parents are discouragingly vague.

Yet research points out that for the most part the church, and more specifically the youth minister, is only a temporary, though sometimes pivotal blip on the radar screen of a young person's life. Reginald Bibby and Donald Posterski, in their 1984 survey of Canadian youth fifteen to nineteen years of age, concluded: "Teenagers readily adopt their parents' affiliation and religious self-image, along with some basic Judaic-Christian beliefs and selected practices. However, the majority

neither profess religious commitment nor want extensive involvement with 'their' religious groups" (Bibby and Posterski
1985, 128). Commenting on that group's view of organized
religion, the same researchers observed that Canadian teenagers "exhibit 'a polite posture' towards formal religions. A
two-thirds majority indicate that they have a fairly high level
of confidence in church leaders, similar to the confidence they
accord educational, scientific and judicial leaders" (119–29).

Similarly, in their study of 8,156 young adolescents and
10,467 parents, American researchers Merton and Irene
Strommen suggest that adolescents

> share the personal conviction of their parents about the
> importance of religion. A majority of the young adolescents
> say it is the most important or one of the most important
> influences in their lives. . . . The enigma, however, is this:
> though religion is identified as important by both parents
> and adolescents, it is almost a taboo subject at home. (Stom-
> men and Stommen 1985, 133)

Despite this resounding silence in their homes, the Strom-
mens conclude that "young adolescents in this study tend to
experience religion as more liberating than restricting. In part
this means that young adolescents focus more on God's love
than on God as judge or rule-giver" (137). It would appear
that the absence of religious instruction in the home has allowed each young person to construct a concept of God that
closely resembles parental attitudes gained informally in the
home.

Admittedly, neither study was looking specifically at
churches that employ youth ministers, but the findings did
not indicate that a difference might be found in such populations. Young people, comments Michael Rutter, "tend both to
share their parents' values on the major issues of life and also
to turn to them for guidance in most major concerns" (in
Richards 1985, 27).

George Barna, basing his conclusions on a 1995 nationwide (USA) telephone survey of 723 randomly selected kids
whose ages were thirteen to eighteen, found

What is most interesting, though, is whom the teens of our day turn to for reliable and useful guidance. Tops on the list, by a wide margin, is Mom. Three quarters of all teens said if they had an important question about life, Mom would be among the handful of "must see" advisors. About half of the teen population would also consult their best friends, and half said they would probably consult their fathers. (Barna 1995, 64)

Perhaps that is why Jehovah was so explicit in explaining to the Jewish parents in Deuteronomy 6 exactly how they were to go about passing the law from generation to generation. It was not through the priests or through the synagogue (which emerged later) or even through the prophet Moses that spiritual values were to be shaped. It was the family's responsibility.

What, then, is the function of the church and, more specifically, the youth group in discipling young people today? Perhaps the best way to describe the youth group's function is as a laboratory in which to test the appropriateness of parental spiritual values in the students' lives. Of course that is not the only laboratory in which young people are experimenting, but it is a very important one.

Implications

1. A youth worker is only fooling himself if he thinks that the few hours he spends with a young person each week can offset the many years of informal education amassed by that young person as he observes his mother and father. That is not to say the Holy Spirit is bound by a family conditioning process; it is merely to suggest that the Holy Spirit does not limit the young person to the exclusive stewardship of the youth worker.

2. At the same time, the youth worker is not a baby-sitter for someone whose spiritual life has already been determined and over which he has no influence. He is called of God to assist the young person in examining biblical values and making them his own.

AXIOM 5

When everything else is said and done, the role of the Christian youth group is to pass biblical values from one generation to the next.

The primary reason youth ministries were created in the nineteenth century was that families needed help raising their children as Christians. Previously, the public school had been the Christian parent's ally. But secularization, affluence, and social mobility had broadened the sphere of influence that shaped the values of young people. Christian convictions were being lost. Youth were not growing up with a Christian worldview. Although some churches created parochial schools to combat the negative influences of society, by the turn of the century virtually all Protestant churches had some type of youth society to assist young people to live Christianly.

The values churches desire to be passed from generation to generation vary from church to church. To ethnic churches of European background, the cultural heritage and Christian traditions of the land of their origin are part of the package. In highly confessional churches, a knowledge of doctrine is an important component. In non-confessional churches, values such as justice, reconciliation, and simplicity are prominent themes. To seeker-oriented churches, evangelism and follow-up discipleship set the agenda for youth ministry. In holiness traditions, brokenness and sanctification are vital ingredients. In conservative churches, issues related to lifestyles distinct from the dominant culture are core focuses.

Unfortunately, negative values that exist in the larger church will similarly show up in the youth group. Racial bias, apathy toward social issues or evangelism, cliquishness or tolerance of sexual infidelity, abuse of drugs or alcohol, and ethical compromise in a youth group will usually reflect the values of the adults who lead the church.

Youth ministry will reflect not only the values of its church or denomination, but it will also exhibit convictions prominent in the broader culture in which it is housed. Reading-based discipleship systems may not be highly effective in the speaking oriented African-American church culture. Individualized responsibility for spiritual development may not prove useful in authoritarian cultures. Democratic principles of leadership may not work in youth groups in the two-thirds world.

The role of the youth ministry is prophetic in nature. While affirming everything that is of value in biblical perspective, questions need to be raised about the values that find their source in the sinful nature of the human species. These two must be kept in balance or else the youth ministry will alienate the very people it seeks to serve, and soon the ministry may deteriorate to mere youth work.

The idea that any one youth ministry system will fit all church or parachurch cultures is a bit idealistic. Although core values may be shared by many and even most youth ministries, the more profound difference lie in the values shared by the dominant adults in a given church. Youth ministry people will succeed to the extent that they can incorporate the positive values and challenge the sub-biblical biases of the parents of the church.

Implications

1. There will always be tension between the prophetic vision of a youth ministry's visionary leadership and the need for pastoral care felt by parents on behalf of their children.
2. In periods of relative calm within the culture, youth groups will not have the same intensity and momentum that naturally exist during periods of unrest.
3. Youth group strategies used in the Western world may be totally ineffective in authoritarian cultures (such as the former Soviet bloc countries) or in traditional societies (such as are found in the two/thirds world).

AXIOM 6

Youth ministry prospers where the Bible is taken seriously and is used as the basis for faith and life.

"The vast majority of teenagers in America own Bibles," reports George Barna, and "an amazingly large proportion of teenagers argue that the Bible contains useful and valid information." Among the 86 percent of the adolescent population who call themselves "Christian," "6 out of 10 maintain that the Bible is 'totally accurate in all of its teachings.'" Although only 42 percent of students surveyed claimed that the Christian faith is important in their lives, this level of interest still provides a solid basis for doing youth ministry at the end of the twentieth century (Barna 1995, 75, 80).

It is no wonder that many churches are retaining their young people and experiencing significant numerical growth. In these churches the Bible is taken seriously, presented in a relevant manner, and the students are living as loving Christian brothers and sisters. The postmodern student who is looking for a source of truth that is verified by a corresponding reality in life responds well to this compelling witness.

Although orthodox Christians throughout the history of youth ministry have viewed the Bible as revealed truth, the greatest impact on young people has been made where the authority believed has become the authority lived. Unfortunately, today youth ministry is vulnerable to an emphasis on living the truth without a corresponding emphasis on knowing and understanding revealed truth. Such an imbalance is sustainable for only a short time. When the authority of God's Word is lost, effective youth ministry is not far behind as witnessed by the change in the YMCA and some mainline denominational youth ministries.

Evidences of taking the Bible seriously are seen in the lives of students both in the cognitive and affective domains. Students will acquire a knowledge of Bible content, understand principles that flow from the content, apply the principles and direct commands in daily life, analyze the component parts of the biblical text, put the truths discovered back together using relevant means of communication, and gain the ability to evaluate new ideas based on a Christian worldview.

Students who value the Bible will show a willingness to receive biblical truth, respond by being obedient to Scripture, value opportunities to discover more about God's Word, organize their activities so that contact with the Bible is frequent, and ultimately are characterized as being people who have been transformed into fully devoted followers of Jesus Christ. Although the youth ministry alone cannot bring about these responses to the authority of Scripture, the Word of God will need to be handled in the youth group activities in such a manner that these values are fostered.

Implications

1. Students need to be equipped with Bible study skills as much as with Bible knowledge.
2. The more the youth group is dependent upon large group meetings and activities to maintain momentum, the less likely is the development of Bible study skills by students; the more the youth group is dependent on small group activity to maintain fellowship, the less likely is the small group to focus on the development of Bible study skills. Balance is essential.
3. In most cases expositional teaching tends not to be effective with high school students; therefore youth workers should attempt to employ teaching methods that drive students back into the Bible for themselves.

AXIOM 7

A youth ministry will reflect the vision of its adult leaders.

Remember, we are not talking about *youth movements.* Those reflect the vision of young people. When God sees fit to bring about a youth movement, adult leaders would be well advised to set aside their visions and assist the rising generation to do God's work in a manner that is new and at times uncomfortable to the people who have seen God work in previous years (for an excellent summary of youth movements, see Howard 1970).

Greg Gregoire defines *vision* as "perceiving God's desires based upon the absolutes of His Word and your circumstances." In comparison, *objectives* state those desires in measurable terms, and *programs* help you to organize activities that will fulfill those objectives (Gregoire 1981, 2). Thus *vision* can be thought of as the broad strokes of the paint brush, the big picture, the dreams that others can perceive and follow.

"It is easier to serve God without a vision," suggested Oswald Chambers, "easier to work for God without a call, because then you are not bothered by what God requires;

common sense is your guide, veneered over with Christian sentiment" (46, for March 4th). Chambers used *vision* in a very narrow sense, which stressed receiving a clear understanding of what God wants a person to do. It is possible that this observation was taken from a talk given while he was doing youth ministry with the YMCA in Egypt.

There are two kinds of visions current in youth ministry. One is *process vision,* which is most concerned with what will happen to the young people involved in the ministry while they are en route to a specific objective. Success or failure of an activity is measured in terms of the extent to which the events assisted students in their spiritual maturation process.

The other is *product vision,* which is more focused on the expected outcomes of youth group activities. The reason for this greater goal orientation is that spiritual maturity is difficult to measure so it may seem better to focus on visible results.

Most visions include both process and product. That is a healthy blend. The key question, however, is not, Which vision is best? Instead, it should be, Can the other adults and students catch the vision and build the ministry around it?

In order for a vision to be transferable it must be significant, attractive, and attainable. Significance has two primary foci. The first is biblical. Does the vision further the kingdom of God as revealed in Scripture? The second is cultural. Do the students of this generation view the activities implied by the vision as important? Without the former, youth ministry has degenerated to mere youth activity, and without the latter, students will tend to view the activities as petty, Sunday school busywork.

Attractiveness has to do with the appeal that the vision has. Is the vision capable of capturing the imagination of students and adult leaders? Many activities that are theologically significant and culturally acclaimed are simply boring to youth group members.

For example, a suggestion that the youth group spend two weeks ministering in an impoverished section of an urban center would be highly significant but might not be at all attractive to suburban high school students. Does that mean this kind of vision should not be selected? Not at all. It merely suggests the vision may not be transferred into reality without a great deal of effort to make the idea attractive.

A transferable vision must be perceived by students and adult leaders as attainable. No matter how significant and attractive a dream may be, unless the young people and their sponsors can see themselves as a part of the big picture, the leader's vision will remain just that—the *leader's* vision.

Mediocrity and past failures are the primary enemies of a vision appearing to be attainable to students. If the philosophy that "it is good enough for church work" has dominated the church's approach to youth ministry, it may take a while to raise the group's sights to expect excellence. By contrast, if someone has previously raised the group's expectations and then for some reason or other failed to deliver, the resistance to trying again may be greater than if the group had not tried to live out the vision.

Implications

1. A youth group that is without a vision is a youth group that is doomed to perpetuate the past. It is in a rut. It tends to be governed more by sociology than by theology. The student and adult leadership tends to have a high turnover rate. Creativity is limited. The spiritual impact is minimal.

2. A leader's vision, when shared by students, is the starting point for planning. Each leadership meeting will be structured in reference to the vision. Each decision will be made with the youth group's vision in mind. Each evaluation will measure the contribution that an activity has made toward achieving the vision.

CONCLUSION

A youth ministry is like a pond situated on a gently flowing stream. If the ecosystem of the stream and pond are healthy, the pond will support a wide variety of life, from simple algae to larger fish and even animals from the surrounding countryside that rely upon the pond for food and water. These seven *context axioms* help define the environment in which the pond of youth ministry can flourish.

If there is pollution within this youth ministry ecosystem, the pond and the life it supports will begin to die. Pollution results when any of axioms one through seven are absent or are ignored. For example, some youth workers might want to turn the pond into a lake but in so doing forget about the healthy influence families or relational adults play in the lives of adolescents. Unless appropriate care is given, the nutrients that had been provided by the family structure and other Christian adults may be undermined and even lost in the larger body of water.

Other creative youth leaders may see youth ministry in performance terms. If the program is exciting and well organized, and the publicity dynamic, ministry will flow. What results, however, is pollution. The pond or lake may look healthy when in reality the fish are no longer able to feed themselves or reproduce. It may only be a matter of time before even swimming is impossible because of pollutants.

Healthy youth ministry, however, is more than a type of spiritual ecology. It requires purposeful action directed at channeling the energies of young people into decision making that balances the truth of Scripture with the realities of their life situations. The next step will be to incorporate the *dynamic axioms* into the maintenance of the youth ministry pond.

WORKS CITED

Barna, George. 1995. *Generation Next.* Ventura, Calif.: Regal.

Bibby, Reginald W., and Donald C. Posterski. 1985. *The Emerging Generation: An Inside Look at Canada's Teenagers.* Toronto: Irvin.

Cailliet, Emile. 1963. *Youth Life.* New York: Harper & Row.

Chambers, Oswald. 1987. *My Utmost for His Highest.* Westwood, N. J.: Barbour.

Elkind, David. 1984. *All Grown Up and No Place to Go.* Reading, Mass.: Addison-Wesley.

Goetz, William R. 1978. "Adult Leaders of Youth." In *Youth Education in the Church,* edited by Roy B. Zuck and Warren S. Benson. Chicago: Moody.

Green, Ken. 1981. *Insights: Building a Successful Youth Ministry*. San Bernardino, Calif.: Here's Life.

Gregoire, Greg. 1981. "Developing a Vision for Ministry." In *Insights: Building a Successful Youth Ministry*. See Green, Ken.

Howard, David M. 1970. *Student Power in World Evangelism*. Downers Grove, Ill.: InterVarsity.

Richards, Lawrence O. 1985. *Youth Ministry: Its Renewal in the Local Church*. Rev. ed. Grand Rapids: Zondervan.

Senter, Mark H. III. 1986. "What Contributes to Spiritual Maturity?" *Youthworker* 3, no. 1 (spring): 40–44.

Stommen, Merton P., and A. Irene Stommen. 1985. *Five Cries of Parents*. San Francisco: Harper & Row.

Towns, Elmer L. 1973. "Maturity: The Goal for Church Youth." In *Successful Biblical Youth Work*. Nashville: John T. Benson, Impact.

FOR FURTHER READING

Benson, Warren S., and Mark H. Senter III, eds. 1987. *The Complete Book of Youth Ministry*. Chicago: Moody.

Black, Wesley. 1991. *An Introduction to Youth Ministry*. Nashville: Broadman.

Boyer, Ernest L. 1983. *High School*. New York: Harper & Row.

Dausey, Gary, ed. 1983. *The Youth Leader's Source Book*. Grand Rapids: Zondervan.

Dettoni, John M. 1993. *Introduction to Youth Ministry*. Grand Rapids: Zondervan.

Dudley, Roger L. 1992. *Valuegenesis: Faith in the Balance*. Riverside: La Sierra University.

Ratcliff, Donald, and James A. Davies, eds. 1991. *Handbook of Youth Ministry*. Birmingham: R.E.P.

7

AXIOMS OF
YOUTH MINISTRY:
THE DYNAMICS

Mark H. Senter III

Becky's youth ministry library was the best in a three-county area. She had books on small groups, teaching strategies, youth culture, program helps, and just about every other category that would help a youth leader put together a program that would attract and hold the attention and loyalty of young people.

Training seminars were another part of her youth ministry pedigree. At times she kidded that she had heard Tony Campolo speak in more contexts than Tony had actually spoken. Regional, national, denominational, or local church sponsored, she was there. Workshops at Sunday school conventions, seminary in-service opportunities, even on-line chat rooms and bulletin boards had been a part of the maturing youth worker's educational process.

Yet something seemed to be missing. Her ministry appeared to be a rough mosaic of seminar ideas and textbook strategies. What Becky needed were spools of thread with which to weave the patches of youth ministry into a ministry quilt. The *dynamic axioms* identified in this chapter may serve as those spools of thread. Various models or strategies might be employed by the youth worker, but these axioms provide a structure for making the program effective.

AXIOM 8

Most youth groups reach peak effectiveness when attendance reaches twenty to thirty high school students.

One of the great frustrations to a new youth minister is the manner in which youth group growth stalls once the average attendance reaches about thirty students. The reasoning goes something like this. Because group attendance was averaging close to twenty people each week before a youth minister was employed, the average should double or triple as a result of the extra amount of time a full-time youth pastor can invest in the ministry.

But that kind of reasoning is focused on the wrong factor. Unless the youth minister is an especially charismatic person with excellent communication skills, the mere injection of additional ministry time into the youth group is not enough to overcome the social dynamics of the group.

C. Peter Wagner points out that the average person feels known and accepted by no more than thirty people. There is a natural cohesion in such groups. People know each other's names, interests, frustrations, skills, and attitudes. People sense that other people care for them, and as a result they develop a high degree of commitment to that group (1976, 97–109).

Donald C. Posterski, in his book *Friendship: A Window on Ministry to Youth,* supports Wagner's idea. "Healthy young people," comments Posterski, "want to influence their environment. They are attracted to circles of relationships in which their presence matters." Based on his research among 3,600 Canadian youth, he further observes that "bigness is not necessarily better when trying to touch people who have tasted intimacy and have experienced what it is to belong. Large size alone is threatening; it can alienate the very people the organization intends to help" (1985, 14).

Adults working with such groups need to have a clear perspective on what they can and should be doing for their students. Two primary functions stand out. Adults assist the group in finding a sense of direction that reflects biblical priorities and ensure that each student retains a feeling of belonging within a loving, caring fellowship. These can be thought of as teaching and shepherding functions.

If a youth group is to grow beyond the twenty to thirty attendance range (and in many cases that is both desirable and necessary in order to do God's work in a community), youth workers will need to ensure that the students do not view one or two adults as essential to the unity chemistry of the group. Friendship clusters, as Posterski calls them, with other adults involved, will need to be established within the large group in order to provide the social security necessary to reach out to more people.

Implications

1. Working harder may not increase the size of a youth group beyond a certain point. The youth minister could put in eighty-hour work weeks and not be able to break through the average attendance barrier that has developed. Better talks, more effectively organized committee meetings, stronger links with the students' parents, and more creative activities only assist growth to a certain point. Then, in most cases, growth stops.

2. Working smarter is the key that allows growth and continuity to happen beyond that given point. Working smarter invariably focuses on multiple leadership. As Gary Downing warns, "Don't do it alone! Some things are dangerous when done alone" (1982, 35). Volunteer youth workers with significant roles in the youth ministry are essential to working smarter and thus more productively.

AXIOM 9

A high school student will not be theologically mature until he or she is sociologically comfortable.

Perhaps the most frequent critique of a high school youth

group that has ceased to be a ministry to students is that many of the members are cliquish. Students from "the other high school" feel excluded by students from the school where the majority attend. Those who buy their clothes at J. C. Penney feel rejected by the more well-to-do shoppers. National Honor Society members feel scorned by the athletes, and everyone looks down on the "nerds."

Although it is important to point out that small groups in which one feels loved and accepted are the building blocks of social relationships, exclusive groups (or cliques) have a highly detrimental effect on the spiritual development of youth ministry. Psalm 23 beautifully illustrates the comfort level that is important for a normal growth process. The lamb is part of a flock and finds comfort in the shepherd, the environment, and even the support system available when danger occurs.

Dennis Benson and Bill Wolfe suggest that the primary reason for the emergence of cliques in a youth group is the need for protection and security among the members, "a homemade social insurance policy" (*Basic Encyclopedia* 1981, 70). In many ways this problem sounds like the infighting described by Paul in 1 Corinthians 3. Such strife resulted in the Corinthians believers remaining "mere infants" (v. 1).

The proponents of "mastery learning" are helpful in assisting the youth worker in understanding why theology and sociology are linked in youth ministry. Three domains of learning have been identified, two of which have special relevance to this discussion. The *cognitive domain* deals with knowing. The *affective domain* focuses on valuing. The two are distinct from each other (Bloom 1956; and Krathwohl, Bloom, and Masia 1964). Thus it is possible for a student to know a biblical principle but not to value it; or worse yet, to value abusing what is known. At best that would have to be considered theological immaturity.

A warning is in order at this point. Just because a student will not be theologically mature until he is sociologically comfortable does not mean that when he is sociologically comfortable he will become theologically mature. Unfortunately many youth programs settle for creating social comfort zones that never lead to theological maturity. That, as distinguished in the previous chapter, would merely be youth activity, not youth ministry.

There are several ingredients that will contribute to developing theologically mature students. The first is models of openness on the part of student and adult leaders. It is a rare freshman who will feel at ease with upperclassmen unless the older students take deliberate steps to make the newcomer feel at home. Many times it is the adult youth worker who is the key in opening the doors of friendship in the youth group by demonstrating love and concern for each one who attends, while urging student leaders to do the same.

The second ingredient in the sociological/theological maturation process is creating structures that break across the offending social network. Sunday school classes may have to be restructured. Ministry projects may be planned and staffed with people who are not well acquainted with each other. Core groups may be created with a mix of upper- and underclassmen. Teams may be organized at camp or on a retreat that include no more than two people from the same high school or other natural grouping.

The final ingredient is that of vital spiritual life within the students and leaders. One could hardly expect students who are spiritually dead to demonstrate the evidences of love described in 1 Corinthians 13. Similarly, one could not expect great theological insight from students or adults who lack theological conviction. Spiritual life breeds both loving actions and theological sophistication.

Implications

1. Sunday school may unteach more theology than it teaches. Students who do not feel a part of the social structure of the youth group may throw out the theological baby with the sociological bathwater. They may learn the doctrinal information and reject spiritual commitment.

2. A more subtle response that leads to the unteaching of theology is apathy. Students may learn but not value the biblical information to which they are exposed. The

result is environmental Christians who have been condi-
tioned to respond in culturally appropriate ways without allowing the Holy Spirit to grip their lives.

3. Well-developed shepherding skills, both in student and
   adult leaders, are as important as accurate theological
   convictions. The sovereign Lord, speaking through the
   pen of Ezekiel, gave a beautiful picture of how He
   would care for the flock of Israel (Ezekiel 34:11–16).
   The product of that careful shepherding was a theological awareness as the people of Israel realize that Jehovah is their God (34:31). The skills of a shepherd
   produced the insights of a theologian.

4. A possibly more intriguing implication is that contemporary Christian music may become the primary source
   of theological perspectives for the current generation of
   young Christians. Unless the church provides a sociologically comfortable context in which to learn theology, young people are likely to find that context through
   the community atmosphere created by Christians in the
   performing arts. The unfortunate aspect of that is the
   theological inadequacy of the words sung. They may
   come nowhere close to the doctrinal maturity of the
   Sunday school materials published by the leading evangelical publishers.

AXIOM 10

*In youth ministry the group performs three functions:
identification, contribution, and consolation.*

Scattered around my desk as I write this chapter are nearly
twenty of the best-known books on youth ministry. Yet I have
sought in vain to find an author who has dealt with the question, What contributions does a youth *group* make to the
development of a mature Christian young person? Not the
leaders of a group, not the other people in the group, but the
specific dynamic that comes from the young person having
associated himself or herself with a group.

Church growth literature, on the other hand, has been
much more conscious of the *group factor* (see Gibbs 1981,
275–312; Wagner 1976, 97–109). As adapted from the writ-

ings of Peter Wagner and Eddie Gibbs, three functions of groups might be identified. The first is that of *identification.* The youth group provides the young person with a place to belong, not in the "joining" sense but in the "place to be" sense. There is a feeling of dignity in being associated with the people who make up the group and in participating in their activities.

The second function is that of *contribution,* for it is within the youth group that a young person can first begin to discover his or her niche within the church. "Where do I fit in?" "What do I possibly have to offer?" Those are questions felt by teenagers as they attempt to discover their personal identities by testing out different roles apart from school and home. For most, the youth group is a new beginning both socially and spiritually.

For some the niche would appear to be negative to the adult observer—clown, rebel, loudmouth, flirt, skeptic, "airhead," even "nerd." Yet the important thing is not the role but that the young person has a distinct place within the group.

For others the positive leadership roles are readily available. Team captain, organizer, care giver, consistent witness, up-front communicator, spiritually sensitive person, and even loyal follower are usually respected niches in the youth group. Thus the student finds a distinct place to make a contribution, hopefully of spiritual value, within a safe environment outside his or her home.

A third function of the youth group is that of *consolation.* When a student is feeling insecure, has had an argument with parents, or has broken up with the person he or she has been dating, a support system is in place. When a young person has doubts about God, moral standards, or issues of life and death, there are specific people from the group to whom that person can go. When someone misses a youth group activity or two, he or she is missed. Each of these is evidence of consolation.

In small groups these functions happen rather naturally. As a group grows, special care must be given to ensure each function, or else the group will revert to a size small enough for identification, contribution, and consolation to happen spontaneously.

Large group or small, a sense of identity generally comes from the group as a whole. Contributions, by contrast, decrease as the youth group grows in size. Once the size exceeds thirty to forty students some people are going to begin feeling as though their contribution does not count anymore. From that time onward the group will need to be subdivided in order to allow every person to have a context in which to make his or her contribution. Such groups will need to be large enough for new niches to develop. Frequently that means a dozen or more members in each new subsystem.

Consolation is best provided by two to five people who genuinely care for a hurting person. In larger groups it becomes essential that a structure be established so that hurting people who do not have a high profile in the group are immediately missed or responded to as needs dictate.

Implications

1. The larger the group becomes the more spontaneity must be carefully planned. It is a continuing concern for adult and student leaders. A plan to provide all of these functions tends to break down the day after tomorrow. Therefore, they must be stressed repeatedly, monitored continually, and repaired constantly. The purpose for all of this calculated spontaneity is the continual enfolding of all students for whom the group has a stewardship.

2. The tendency in a larger group is not to realize a person has been missing from the group activities until he or she returns. If he or she does not return for a prolonged period of time, a disengagement process begins as the absentee emotionally withdraws from the group. Should that process extend over three or more weeks without a response from a caring friend, the student may be lost to the group and possibly to the Lord.

AXIOM 11

Student ownership of youth ministry guided by respected Christian adults is essential for the ministry to remain healthy.

Youth ministry begins when an adult earns the right to be heard by students, but it reaches its peak of effectiveness when the adult has earned the right to be silent. Students, willing and capable of providing spiritually sensitive leadership for the youth group, assume ownership. Seldom will a youth ministry reach the point where the students will have so much ownership and maturity that their adult leader will be able to remain entirely silent, but that should be the goal for at least some aspect of the ministry.

Negative ownership by students is a distinct possibility as well. The ingredient that turns student ownership sour is an absence of respect for the adult leader. The adult has attempted to impose his ideas on the students without earning the right to be heard. The result is that the adult leader cannot be heard even when he needs to be. Students are controlling the direction of the youth group, even if it means going around in ever smaller circles.

Worse than negative ownership is an absence of ownership. Some call it apathy, others refer to it as a lack of commitment, but it amounts to the same problem. The adults are the performers, whereas the students are mere spectators (Green 1985, 67–71). The weight of responsibility is placed on the adult leaders to provide constantly improving entertainment or students do not attend youth group functions.

The best illustration of student ownership is a high school state championship team. The coach has done most of his work behind the scenes, working long hours to refine athletic skills and team coordination so that when the final buzzer sounds, all of the players, even those sitting on the bench, have a sense of being champions. The students have done the work. The coach has merely found a way to bring out the best from each player.

Ownership is a tricky factor, and adult leaders handle it in different ways. Some will concede ownership to the students ("It is their youth group, let them do with it what they want"). Others will respond favorably to student ownership

("If that is what you really want to do, let me help you do it the best we possibly can"). A few will sell ownership to the students ("I've shared this idea with the student leaders, and they are pretty excited about it, so they've asked me to explain it to you. What if we . . ."").

Certain adults will discover mutual ownership with the students ("What do you think we could do for God's glory if we had no fear of failure?"). A relatively few have the personal charisma to succeed in demanding ownership by the students ("If you don't take the challenge of this ministry, then God will raise up students who are willing to do His work"). Still others have the joy of seeing students adopt the ownership of an obviously successful ministry ("Welcome, freshmen, to one of the most exciting youth groups in the Midwest. Many of you have begged me to allow you to join earlier, but now is the time").

Styles of adult leadership will differ. Student motivation for ownership may not be the purest. But without student ownership the youth ministry of the local church will produce neither numerical nor quality results.

Implications

1. When students sense ownership in a youth ministry, their capacity for leadership is amazing. Their spiritual insights, creative expression, capacity for work, and willingness to persevere under adverse conditions will encourage even the most optimistic adult leaders.

2. Traditions and symbols are closely associated with student ownership. Group names, a logo, and annual activities known for reasons that the group values all contribute to the building of a greater sense of group identity. To ignore or violate such symbols or traditions without group permission will invariably bring about problems.

AXIOM 12

Long-term growth of a youth ministry is directly dependent on the ability of the youth worker to release ministry responsibilities to mature and qualified lay volunteers.

Delegation has a ring of General Motors, impersonal bureaucracies, and the worst aspects of big business. The stereotype is that of dumping unwanted jobs on unwilling workers. But the image of such coercive leaders as the corporate ideal, criticized by some youth ministry writers (Richards 1985, 109), has been replaced more recently in management literature by the concept of networking. John Naisbitt states in *Megatrends:*

> The vertical to horizontal power shift that networks bring about will be enormously liberating for individuals. Hierarchies promote moving up and getting ahead, producing stress, tension and anxiety. Networking empowers the individual, and people in networks tend to nurture one another. (1982, 204)

Robert C. Coleman, in his classic book *The Master Plan of Evangelism,* suggests that one of the essential elements of the Lord's ministry was delegation (1963, 82–93). The idea was not at all of purging undesirable tasks from a busy leader but of sharing crucial responsibilities with carefully selected co-workers who could work together to accomplish the goal.

Early in my ministry, Kenneth Wessner, former chairman of the board of Servicemaster Industries, shared this idea with me: "Delegate the things you do best." When I reacted with surprise, he went on to explain that the things one does best are the easiest for him to adequately supervise because he will be able to tell at a glance if they are being done well. By contrast, tasks that a person does not do well take more time to adequately supervise because he has to figure out what should be done and evaluate how well the person is doing it.

So what does releasing ministry responsibilities mean in youth ministry? It means shifting to other people the authority to minister to young people while sharing the responsibility for the quality of that ministry with them. That definition suggests that real authority is given to volunteer workers so that they do not have to fear being second-guessed by the professional youth worker. At the same time, responsibility is shared so that both professional and volunteer youth workers have a vital interest in effective ministry to youth.

Simple enough, right? So then why is releasing ministry responsibilities so difficult? Several reasons come to mind.

"I want to do it" is the implied comment from some big-hearted youth workers. It is not that they distrust other youth workers or fear incompetence on their co-workers' parts. They simply enjoy the ministry so much that they never want to lose the opportunity to spend a majority of their time in face-to-face communication with students. Consequently, effective long-term growth is stymied.

"What will I do if I release my responsibilities?" questions another delegation resister. There may be a fear that the church people will mistake delegation for laziness or that volunteer workers will resent the "glory" the professional is receiving while they are doing all the work. It might simply mean that the professional youth minister does not know how to supervise once he has delegated specific aspects of the ministry to people who lack natural talents in youth ministry.

"Students will come to me anyway" is another smoke screen placed in the path of delegation. That feeling is frequently found in churches where the youth pastor is a very charismatic figure who lacks an adequate understanding of the dignity of the people of God (see the discussion of the "people of God" in Richards and Martin 1981).

"I can't get qualified staff" is a fourth reason given for failing to release ministry responsibilities. Although this is a real problem in many churches, and may be the very reason a youth minister was employed in the first place, the situation must not be permitted to persist. Even if he must grow his own staff from within the youth group, qualified staff must be developed.

As a youth minister learns to delegate ministry responsibilities, he will pass through three stages. In the first stage nothing is delegated, for the youth worker is learning how the ministry should be done. Stage two is the experimentation stage in which some tasks are delegated and initial skills in supervision are learned. The final stage is the growth period when most of the primary ministry responsibilities are accomplished through nonprofessional youth workers.

Implications

1. As a youth worker grows, the focus of his or her ministry must change from primary ministry to secondary ministry or else the effectiveness of his or her efforts will be severely limited. A resistance to change in ministry style is a vote to kill a ministry.

2. Shared leadership responsibilities coordinated by a resourceful leader is more likely to generate numerical and qualitative growth than non-shared leadership. Though one plus one may not always equal two in ministry terms, one alone will never equal two.

3. Released authority and shared responsibility in ministry is one method of inhibiting burnout. All the weight of the youth group does not rest squarely on the shoulders of only one person. This allows the youth worker to retreat from time to time in order to rebuild his ministry resources.

AXIOM 13

The development of a youth ministry will not exceed the public communication skills of the primary adult leader.

Jesus Christ is a prime example of marvelous public communication skills. After all, five thousand people do not come to listen to a person who is dull or boring. He did not do extensive expositions of Old Testament passages and show their relevance to the modern Jewish culture. He told stories (parables), used catchy phrases that were easily remembered (Beatitudes), and chose examples to which the hearer could relate (children, the weather, trees).

Let there be no mistake, our Lord's primary task, as A. B. Bruce has pointed out, was the training of the Twelve (1898), but His personal communication skills provided the context in which that training would take place. The attracting of crowds in Christ's earlier ministry and the rejection by crowds because of hard sayings later in His ministry provided examples that Peter and the other apostles would follow after the Lord returned to heaven.

As a person looks at the public communication skills of the leading youth ministers of this century, four common de-

nominators emerge. They are *story oriented*. Most are craftsmen in the art of bringing narratives to life. Many, if they
wanted to go commercial, could give Garrison Keillor and Bill
Cosby a run for their money. They are able to capture the
seemingly insignificant details of life and weave them into a
verbal picture in which each listener can place himself. Jim
Rayburn, the founder of Young Life, was a master of the art.
Using a conversational tone, he could spin a tale which captured the attention of the most unsuspecting young person.

The story is not an end in itself, and yet it is. Many times
the listeners will walk away without a Bible verse in mind and
yet have a marvelous grasp of a theological concept due to the
masterful way in which the speaker has wedded the story to
the concept it illustrates.

Effective communicators to young people are *need oriented* in their presentations. They know their audience, their joys
and pains, pressures and fantasies, struggles and achievements, loves and rejections. They raise questions that students
are asking ("If God is love, why can't I get my locker open?")
and then take them to principles of Scripture that assist them
in dealing with these tensions.

For the novice communicator the tendency is to speak in
abstract philosophical terms, in words borrowed from
respected communicators, or in response to his own needs
that are fancied to be of concern to the listener. Each
approach reflects the background of the speaker rather than
the struggles of the hearer. To be effective, the rookie youth
speaker must move from a "Here is what I have to say" posture to a "Can I help you solve that problem?" stance.

Biblically based is a third common denominator of effective youth speakers. There is an authority to what they have
to say. Though they draw from the social sciences and current
events, from the arts and media, from literature and sports,
from history and politics, the ultimate interpreter of human
experience is the Word of God. Without that source of authority the speaker is little more than another source of entertainment, and youth ministry degenerates to youth activity.

Youth ministry communicators are *results focused*. They
know which results to expect each time they speak, and they

are surprised if God does not intervene in the lives of the young people being addressed. Not all appeals for response are focused on salvation, although that is appropriate some of the time. Many touch on changes in daily living that would honor the Lord of Scripture. Dedications and rededications to Christ are neither overworked nor ignored. God the Holy Spirit is assumed to be working and willing to give visible results.

Implications

1. Much of the identity (see axiom 8) that a youth group has will be associated with the public presentation of the primary spokesman for the group, usually a professional youth minister. Thus the youth worker would be wise to work continually on improving his or her public communication skills for the sake of the ministry.

2. Motivation on the part of the speaker is very important. If speaking is nothing more than an effective method for gaining the status or attention that was not afforded an individual earlier in life, the speaker has become merely a "resounding gong or a clanging cymbal." Speakers get caught in all kinds of questionable practices if their motives are not pure before God. Stories can be enhanced for dramatic effect. Emotions of immature adolescents can be manipulated in a quest for greater responses. Personal biases can be pawned off as the will of God.

3. Public speaking in behalf of God is an awesome responsibility. It must be handled wisely.

AXIOM 14

The most effective youth ministries are those that rapidly move students into ministry postures.

In his book *Dedication and Leadership,* Douglas Hyde contrasts the manner in which Communists and Christians disciple new converts. The Communists, says Hyde, immediately send newly enlisted followers out to sell copies of the party's newspaper or some similar activity. The enthusiasm of the fresh party loyalty sells papers. At the same time the experience teaches the novice what he does not know about his newly embraced cause. When he returns from his assignment, he is the most willing learner in the party. He demands answers. He tests his spontaneous responses to the official party line and makes appropriate modifications in his thinking. No one has to urge him to study Communism. It rapidly becomes an obsession with him (1966, 21–26).

By contrast, Hyde points out that Christians take new converts and assign them to a classroom for the first three years after their conversion under the pretense that they do not want to shove immature believers out of the nest before they are ready to provide answers to non-Christians. By that time their newly found enthusiasm has worn off, and the witnessing for which they have been so carefully prepared never takes place.

Glenn Heck, former vice president of National-Louis University, applies this same principle in the realm of youth ministry. Heck suggests that at the very time when early adolescents begin feeling adult instincts to nurture (baby-sit, work in the church nursery, help with the little kids in vacation Bible school), traditional Christian education wisdom has insisted that those students be the receivers rather than the conveyers of nurture. So by the time they are deemed ready to serve, the lessons of non-service have already been learned.

There are four kinds of ministry postures that are common in youth ministry today. The first is ministry within the youth group. Though most models of youth ministry make a sincere effort to reach beyond the limits of their youth groups, a majority of the youth ministry models sees ministry within the group as their primary ministry focus. That is especially true of the youth fellowship model (Benson 1987, 264–67), in which a majority of the activity is focused on serving the group through the presentation of Sunday evening programs by the students themselves.

The second approach involves ministry within the church but beyond the scope of the youth group. The community model (Benson 1987, 240–43), which tends to treat students as full participants in the life of the congregation, urges early and full involvement in the serving of non-peers within the church. Teaching of Sunday school, even as early as the junior high years, service on church committees, visitation of the elderly, and participation in the worship services are advocated.

Service outside the church is a third ministry posture. The phrase most frequently heard in that regard is "reaching your campus for Jesus Christ." The competition model is as conscious of that kind of ministry as any of the models. Student leaders are constantly reminded that the only people who have free access to students on campus are those who attend, not youth pastors or Christian rock groups. No parachurch leaders or even schoolteachers and administrators have the freedom that students have to be salt and light on their campuses.

Other services outside the church could include certain kinds of musical ministries, tutoring of special-need student groups, ministries to latchkey children, and community service. Clown and puppet ministries, backyard Bible clubs for children, and other outreach activities can also fit into this category.

Ministries outside the culture would be a final kind of ministry posture. The ministry model is a primary example as it attempts to focus the entire youth ministry on "Samaria, and to the ends of the earth" (Acts 1:8). Ministries to minority groups within the country as well as specific ministry activities in other countries would be the primary concern of this ministry posture.

Dann Spader, founder of Sonlife Ministries, suggests that different types of ministry require seven distinct levels of spiritual maturity. Though some people would suggest that cross-cultural ministry by high school students is the zenith of their involvement in ministry, Spader contends the opposite. Although ministry in another country or in another culture may be exciting and appealing to high schoolers, ministry to nonbelieving peers in the local community requires far more spiritual maturity. Spader's distinctions are offered, not as a means to pigeon-hole students in their spiritual development, but to encourage a progression from adventure-filled ministry in cross-cultural settings to the personal vulnerability required for ministry to peers, especially those who profess no spiritual commitments.

Implications

1. Perhaps the greatest hindrance to rapidly moving the young people into ministry postures is the myth of "know before do." Most of life is just the opposite: people do in order to know. Children learn to walk by walking, they learn to talk by talking, and they learn to keep their rooms neat by keeping their rooms neat (usually with strong encouragement from Mom). Patterns are formed early in life. The sooner service activities are provided, the sooner a theology of service will be integrated into a student's worldview.

2. The priority of service in youth ministry may determine the curriculum or at least the curricular materials for youth ministry. Depending on the intensity and complexity of the service experience (witnessing on the street is much more intense and complex than ministry in a nursing home, although both are valid ministries), the formal educational time (Sunday school or group Bible studies) may have to be dedicated to responding to immediate student needs for answers and skills.

Axiom 15

When evangelism of high school students is left to high school students, it will not get done.

Most youth workers can think of at least one exception to this axiom. In some cases a high school student acting completely on his or her own initiative has won scores of peers to faith in Christ. Unfortunately, the youth evangelizer is no more the rule in high school society than lay adult evangelists are in the broader church setting.

To complicate the matter, when high school students are involved in peer evangelism, they find their greatest success among people from the same social grouping within the high school. If they hang around with athletes, it is athletes who are touched with the gospel. If they are in the band, it is band members who are reached. The reality of the situation is that a majority of the youth ministry that takes place in local churches is targeted at students who are planning to attend college. So when these students attempt to reach their peers, their primary target group is the 62 percent of the high school population who plan to attend college (Department of Commerce 1995, 178). This leaves 38 percent of the average high school out of meaningful contact with Christian students.

In a series of informal surveys conducted among youth ministers in the United States and Canada over the past several years, the consensus appears to be that the target audience for church and parachurch youth ministry consists of about 25 percent of the high school population. Though signs of change are appearing in local settings, most of the efforts appear to be competing for the same 25 percent of the high school population.

There are encouraging signs of ministry activity on the high school campuses. The National Network of Youth Ministries reported that an estimated 2 million students participated in See You at the Pole in 1994 (*Network News* 1994, 3). Although is amazing, the total number of high school students in the United States that same year was 13,649,000 (Department of Commerce 1995, 151). The turnout was 15 percent of the high school population.

In a statistical report of secondary school campus clubs in the state of Arkansas, Randy Brantley of the Christian Club Campaign reported that 34 percent of the 450 campuses in the state had some type of Christian club. National club programs accounted for only 28 percent of these; the rest appear to have been grass roots initiatives. The average club had 55 members with 6,650 total members. That same year 5,900 students graduated from Arkansas high schools. If the statistics are an accurate picture of the campus witness in the state, fewer than 25 percent of the students in the state were involved with local Christian campus clubs (Brantley).

Nor does this appear to be unique in America. At the Conference on Youth Ministry, convened in Oxford, Fuzz Kitto, a youth ministry consultant in Australia, reported that 75 percent of the efforts that go into Australian youth ministry focus on 15 percent of the population. It appeared that the consensus of the conference was that this was true in Great Britain as well. John Allan, writing in England's *Covenanters Leader,* observed, "Someone has said that 95% of youth work in

Britain is aimed at 5% of the youth population; I don't think he was exaggerating" (1994, 4).

The key to the evangelization of high school students appears to be strategic use of adults who are willing to make contact with youth in the other 75 percent of the high school population and begin ministries which are autonomous from existing ministries.

Implications

1. The role of the youth minister should focus on what is known as *Youth Group Plus One*. The Plus One factor should be a subpopulation of the local high school that does not have a natural contact with Christian students. Although the youth minister may not be able to establish contact with that subpopulation, others within the church's ministry may be capable and should be empowered to do so.
2. Students, while capable of ministering outside of their normal sphere of friends, should be encouraged to concentrate on evangelizing their peers, for very few of the 30 percent with whom they have normal contact have a vital relationship with Jesus Christ.

CONCLUSION

Webster defines *axiom* as "a maxim widely accepted on its intrinsic merit." The fifteen maxims presented here have been widely accepted on their own merit. They are an indication of the manner in which youth ministry in the local church has matured in recent years.

There may be youth ministers who take issue with these axioms or who would like to offer additional axioms to further refine the ministry skills of a rising generation of youth ministers. The editors of this book welcome continuing dialogue on the subject.

WORKS CITED

Allan, John. 1994. "Christian Youth Work: The Challenge to the Church." *Covenanters Leader* (Winter): 4.

The Basic Encyclopedia for Youth Ministry. 1981. Loveland, Colo.: Group.

Benson, Warren S., and Mark H. Senta III, eds. 1987. *The Complete Book of Youth Ministry.* Chicago: Moody.

Bloom, Benjamin S., ed. 1956. *Taxonomy of Educational Objectives: The Classification of Educational Goals.* Handbook 2, *Cognitive Domain.* New York: Longmans, Green.

Brantley, Randy. "Christian Clubs: Arkansas Secondary School." The Christian Club Campaign, 525 W. Capitol, Little Rock, AR 72203.

Bruce, Alexander Balmain. 1898. *The Training of the Twelve.* Edinburgh: T. & T. Clark.

Coleman, Robert C. 1963. *The Master Plan of Evangelism.* Old Tappan, N.J.: Revell.

Downing, Gary. 1982. "The Care and Feeding of the Volunteer Youth Worker." In *Working with Youth: A Handbook for the '80s,* compiled by Ray Wiley. Wheaton, Ill.: Victor.

Gibbs, Eddie. 1981. *I Believe in Church Growth.* Grand Rapids: Eerdmans.

Green, Jim. 1985. "Helping Youth to Take Charge." In *The Youth Worker's Personal Management Book,* edited by Lee Sparks. Loveland, Colo.: Group.

Hyde, Douglas. 1966. *Dedication and Leadership.* Notre Dame, Ind.: Univ. of Notre Dame.

Krathwohl, David R., Benjamin S. Bloom, and Bertran S. Masia. 1964. *Taxonomy of Educational Objectives: The Classification of Educational Goals.* Handbook 2, *Affective Domain.* New York: David McKay.

Naisbitt, John. 1982. *Megatrends.* New York: Warner.

The Network News. 1994. Vol. 12, no. 3:3.

Posterski, Donald C. 1985. *Friendship: A Window on Ministry to Youth.* Scarborough, Ontario: Project Teen Canada.

Richards, Lawrence O. 1985. *Youth Ministry: Its Renewal in the Local Church*. Rev. ed. Grand Rapids: Zondervan.

Richards, Lawrence O., and Gib Martin. 1981. *A Theology of Personal Ministry*. Grand Rapids: Zondervan.

U.S. Department of Commerce. 1995. *Statistical Abstract of the United States*. Washington, D.C.

Wagner, C. Peter. 1976. *Your Church Can Grow*. Glendale, Calif.: Regal.

FOR FURTHER READING

Christie, Les. 1987. *How to Recruit and Train Volunteers*. Grand Rapids: Zondervan.

Coleman, Lyman. 1984. *Youth Ministry Encyclopedia*. Littleton, Colo.: Serendipity.

Green, Ken. 1981. *Insights: Building a Successful Youth Ministry*. San Bernardino, Calif.: Here's Life.

Griffin, Em. 1982. *Getting Together*. Downers Grove, Ill.: InterVarsity.

Hargrove, Barbara, and Stephen D. Jones. 1983. *Reaching Youth Today: Heirs to the Whirlwind*. Valley Forge, Pa.: Judson.

Search Institute. 1984. *Young Adolescents and Their Parents*. Minneapolis: Search Institute.

Senter, Mark H. III. 1990. *Recruiting Volunteers in the Church*. Wheaton, Ill.: Victor.

Spader, Dann. 1981. *Sonlife Strategy of Youth Discipleship and Evangelism*. Chicago: Moody Bible Institute, 1981.

Ward, Pete, ed. 1995. *Relational Youthwork*. Oxford: Lynx Communications.

8

BASIC MODELS OF YOUTH MINISTRY

Mark H. Senter III

The story is told of three former youth group members who met in heaven and began discussing their experiences in the different churches they had attended in life.

"Our group was so exciting," reflected one, with a trace of cheerleader-like nostalgia. "We were constantly on the go with our teams, and the team captains were the greatest. In fact, it was John, our team captain, who led me to Christ. I can remember it as clearly as yesterday. It was at the end of a Christian rock concert."

"Rock concert?" interrupted an athletic-looking companion. "Your group attended rock concerts?"

"Christian rock concerts," replied the first person, a bit unsure of the point of the question.

"Our group always stayed clear of those kinds of activities," responded the athlete. "We felt there were much better ways in which to bring people to Christ than allowing our-

selves to imitate people who were living lives nearly indistinguishable from the values of the secular culture. Witnessing,
for instance. Every Saturday morning our group went out witnessing. That's how I came to know the Lord."

"But what about justice?" inquired the third member of
the heavenly trio. "We all know how important it is to make a
personal commitment to Christ, but what about the role of
being salt and light in the world? That's what our group did.
It was never easy, but we learned to share in the sufferings of
Christ before a watching world."

The conversation continued, perhaps for millennia, each
person periodically expressing surprise, disbelief, and admira-
tion as the activities of the other youth groups were described.
The three youth group members seemed so dissimilar, yet
there they were, all in heaven, discussing their differences.

Though the preceding story is apocryphal, it points out the
diversity of youth ministry at the end of the twentieth century.
In the two decades since the models were first identified in
Youth Education in the Church (See Senter 1978, 267–83)
and then in *The Complete Book of Youth Ministry* (see Senter
1987, 239–69), a number of changes have been made within
the models as they were presented. The *community, gift development,* and *youth society* models, while still in existence, are
not a significant part of the youth ministry scene in the United
States and Canada. Therefore, they have not been included in
this chapter. The names of two models (*fundamentalist* and
urban models) have been changed to reflect a broader usage.
They are now called the *Christian school* and *safe place* models respectively. This chapter will discuss the Christian school
model, the competition model, the discipleship model, and the
safe place model.

Four new models have gained prominence, and although
they may not have as clear a definition as the others, they
appear to be viable options for youth ministry. These include
family based, high school subpopulation, meta, and *youth
church* models. These will be described in the next chapter.

CHRISTIAN SCHOOL MODEL

Scenario

Mary Robbin's oral report on a Christian view of Creation was due the day before spring break. It was the busiest time of the school year. Girls' basketball season (she was sixth person), *The Music Man* (she was Zaneeta), and spring choir tour (it began the afternoon she gave her report) were all competing for her attention.

Mary Robbin loved it. She was involved in everything. Not all the kids at Christian High were as multitalented as Mary Robbin, and some resented her presence in so many activities, but the junior honor student was quick to listen to their frustrations when expressed. Her prayer partners had been a major help to Mary Robbin. Several days each week they met before school to hold each other accountable in their Christian walks and to discuss the problems they were facing.

The pressure was the worst part of Christian High. Ninety-two percent of last year's graduating class had gone to college, and the competition for grades was fierce. Student leaders felt tension to lead exemplary Christian lives. After all, parents had sacrificed to provide an education where Christian values would be reinforced. Chapel services, while often dull, frequently had outstanding speakers and musicians who seemed to keep raising the bar for the Christian high jumpers. But the real pressure came from Mary's peers. Especially hard to take were biting comments from some students who really did not want to be at Christian High. They seemed critical of everyone and everything.

While Mary Robbin attended church and was somewhat involved in the youth group, the focus of her activity and source of most of her spiritual growth was Christian High. After all, she was involved in activities associated with the school six days a week (sometimes seven). Mary's parents were satisfied with this arrangement since they saw very little that a youth group could add to her life.

It was 11:00 P.M. and the creation report was almost done. She had done her research. She was good on her feet, and besides, she had her prayer group standing with her in this time of need.

Philosophy

The Christian school model builds young people into well-rounded Christian adults using the Christian high school as a social, academic, and spiritual laboratory, shaped by Christian teachers and administrators who share and foster a Christian worldview, so that as adults the graduates will live as Christians in a non-Christian world (fig. 8.1).

Background

The foundations for the Christian school movement were laid in Massachusetts when in 1647 the legislature enacted a law, sometimes called the Olde Deluder Satan Act, which required towns to provide educational opportunities for their youth. The purpose of this public education, similar to the Christian schools of today, was to ensure that children would be raised as proper Christians.

Not everyone was comfortable with the Calvinist worldview advocated in New England schools. In the Middle Atlantic states the Catholic, Dutch Reformed, Quaker, and Lutheran churches established parochial schools as an alternative to the type of Protestant teachings found in many public schools. As Lutherans and Reformed Church people migrated from northern Europe and Catholic people came from southern Europe, parochial schools spread west, for they felt the best way to maintain their religious convictions was to establish schools associated with local churches. Later, this seemed even more necessary because of the secularization of public school systems (Gangel and Benson 1983, 241–56).

In the mid-nineteenth century, before public high schools were available, private academies, such as Wheaton Academy, were established to provide educational opportunities for Christian youth. After the turn of the century, a variety of Christian high schools came into being for various reasons. In Chattanooga, Tennessee, McCallie Schools (military) and Girls Preparatory High School served the children of affluent southern Christians. Ben Lippen Schools (Asheville, North Carolina) and Hampden DuBose Academy (near Orlando, Florida) provided schooling for children of missionaries and Christian workers as well as a cross section of evan-

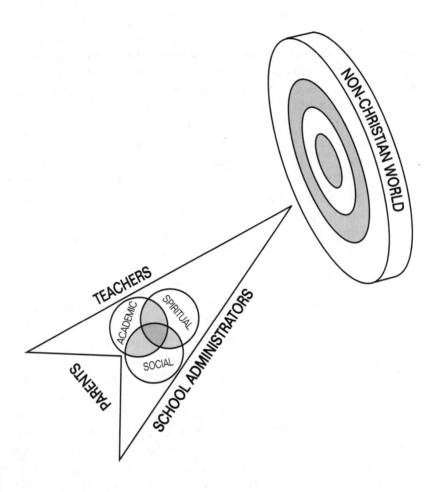

Figure 8.1. *Christian School Model*

gelicals. Stoneybrook School on Long Island, New York, provided a Christian alternative to the eastern prep schools.

But it was the 1970s and 1980s that gave rise to a new generation of Christian high schools. With the spread of such schools has come a decreased need for traditional youth groups in the churches associated with them. The relational aspects of the churches' ministry to students have shifted to the Christian high school. The loser is the teenager who attends a public high school but attends a church that supports the Christian school.

Some youth ministers unfamiliar with the Christian school model might question whether this is a valid model since it limits the effectiveness of the church youth group. Yet that is the precise point. Everything that a church youth ministry seeks to accomplish can be accomplished in the Christian school. When done well in an appropriate context, that may be even more effective than the local church youth group.

Major Activities

The *Christian high school* provides a Christian worldview as well as social activities for the majority of students from Christian homes, thus decreasing the need for traditional youth group functions.

Service opportunities such as choir tours and mission trips during vacation periods provide chances for students to touch the lives of people outside the world in which they live most of their high school lives. Discipleship groups and other service options, similarly, are part of the co-curricular offerings of the school.

Camps, retreats, and *special meetings* or concerts are normal parts of the Christian school's youth ministry.

Church youth groups provide a support role to the ministry of the Christian school where a few students may build relationships with students from public high schools.

Leadership Roles

The *headmaster and faculty of the Christian high school* play the primary role in the discipleship of students who attend. Social activities of the school (formal and informal) as well as biblical teaching take place primarily through the school.

Parents provide vital support for the Christian school approach to youth ministry; they pay the not insignificant tuition and they volunteer time to sponsor activities in which their children are involved.

The *youth pastor* may be a participant either by helping bridge the gap between public and private school students or by becoming an unpaid spiritual adviser to students attending the Christian high school.

Preferred Context

The Christian school model tends to work best in situations where the congregation has a predominance of what S. I. Hayakawa has called bimodal thinkers. Bimodal thinkers tend to see life in mutually exclusive categories. Things are seen as black and white, good or bad, right or wrong. In this context, authoritarian leaders who are willing and able to lead people in the "right" way are highly respected.

Another location in which the model may flourish is in places where the public school system is dysfunctional. The violence of urban areas, combined with dwindling economic resources available to school systems, may make this model a dynamic alternative both as a means to build Christian character and to evangelize young people seeking an adequate education.

Since the up-front expense of the model is enormous, a critical mass of highly motivated parents with the financial wherewithal to sustain the school must be present and willing to work for the good of the school. In urban settings these ingredients may not be available, so alliances may have to be built with faith communities where the resources are available.

COMPETITION MODEL

Scenario

The narthex of the church is a sea of teenage faces. Dress ranges from prep to freak. Most are still hyper from the game time just completed. All are waiting for the same thing.

In a few moments the doors of the sanctuary will open and the Student Impact band will greet the human wave of high school students with a modified rendition of the Beach Boys' song "Be True to Your School." Only the vocalist will sing, "Be true to your *team*," as hundreds of students pour into the sanctuary carrying banners declaring themselves to be on one of eight teams named after colors. Video footage of the competition earlier in the evening flashes on a screen behind the band while the students stand and clap and whistle, awaiting the announcement of the scores for the night and month.

But competition is not the main point of the competition model; discipleship is. Competition is merely a way to gain a hearing from secular students for the life-changing truths of the Bible. Within a half hour this same sea of vibrating teenage bodies will be prepared by music, media, and drama to listen with rapt attention as the youth minister focuses biblical truth on an area of need common to the listeners in the room.

Many will respond. Some will never return. Others will be left to reflect on the events of the evening until next week. A few will seek out team captains or the youth minister in order to commit themselves to an ongoing life of Christian discipleship.

Philosophy

The competition model uses natural leaders from the high school society, trained to serve as servants and motivators to their teams in the context of team competition, to attract and hold high school students for an articulate confrontation with biblical truth, both in a large group setting and in smaller discipleship groups (fig. 8.2).

Background

In 1972 Dave Holmbo, youth music director at South Park Church in Park Ridge, Illinois, formed a musical group called the Son Company in order to reach high school students with their own kind of music. By the fall, Bill Hybels had been enlisted to develop a ministry that would use Holmbo's music and other ministry vehicles to evangelize high school students. Using a group of thirty high school students who were willing to

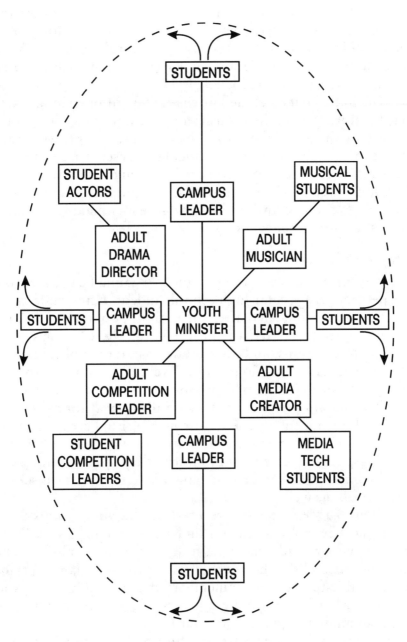

Figure 8.2. *Competition Model*

discipline themselves in Bible study, prayer, and presenting the gospel, Hybels created a new mix of youth ministry ingredients that within a short time was drawing more than a thousand students each week to the Son City program of the four-hundred member church (Cousins 1985, 191).

The ingredients included intense competition among teams led by student captains; music, drama, and media presentations that were on a par with the best theatrical presentations of the local high schools; and articulate presentations of biblical truth as it related to specific needs of high school students. Its rapid success soon led to similar programs springing up all over the nation, with hundreds of students making commitments to Christ each week.

Major Activities

Weeknight meetings are designed to gain a hearing for the gospel from the secular high school student. Using team competition, music modeled after the current popular music, dramatic vignettes related to the theme of the evening's talk, media presentations, and topical talks based on biblical truths, the student is swept along in an exciting experience that is both enjoyable and thought-provoking.

Discipleship meetings provide biblical meat for those students who want to experience further spiritual growth. These may be part of the Sunday school structure or meet on Sunday evenings, but the discipleship meetings are usually led by the youth minister. Many groups have another layer of discipleship groups as well.

Team leader meetings are used by the youth minister to train the key student leaders and develop ministry skills in people who already have natural leadership abilities. The meetings also allow the youth minister to hold team captains accountable for their team members and their spiritual development. Many times young adults serve as team captains in order to maintain quality and continuity.

Camps and retreats are relation-building times for the youth minister and his staff while the students are being guided into new levels of spiritual character development. Larger programs may run as many as eight to ten weeks of camp during the summer months.

Leadership Roles

The *youth pastor* is a skilled communicator who has a vision for reaching the local high school population with the gospel of Jesus Christ. Most often he has organizational skills that allow him to administer a complex combination of moving parts.

Youth staff members provide technical and administrative assistance to the youth minister. They will work with talented students to provide the music, drama, media, and staging aspects of the evening's program.

Team leaders are, for the most part, high school students who organize team activities and shepherd their members. Leaders will include a captain, co-captain, and others, if needed by the team.

Parents have little contact with the youth ministry.

Preferred Context

The church in which the competition model is located must have a vision for reaching the current high school generation in its city or town. The pastor, as well, must provide unqualified support for the program, or else the resistance from people with special concerns will inevitably bring the ministry to an unceremonial end.

The program requires a significant financial investment. Sound systems, media equipment, athletic paraphernalia, and staff salaries are just a few of the costs the competition model will incur. It is best that these costs be paid by the church, although in some cases the youth program has been able to pay for itself through fund-raising activities.

Creative people who are committed to Jesus Christ are another aspect of the context. In most cases the competition model needs to be located near a college community in order to draw on the talent of Christian students as youth sponsors.

The competition model can be adapted to junior high students by de-emphasizing the competition aspect of the game time. Noncompetitive games that create excitement and yet do not focus on finely developed skills to the embarrassment of rapidly growing early adolescents are strongly preferred. Team captains should be taken from older age groups in order to perform the functions essential to the model.

DISCIPLESHIP MODEL

Scenario

"What's been happenin' this week?" asked Juan as the six sophomore guys settled into comfortable positions on the floor of his apartment. The weekly core group meeting was under way.

Juan Martinez had been involved with the church's youth ministry since he had come to know the Lord as a sophomore at Forest View High School eight years ago. For the past two years he had been responsible for building relationships with seven high school students with the purpose of helping them grow in their spiritual lives. Six of the seven were present. Tony had called earlier to let Juan know that he had been grounded by his parents and therefore would not be at the core group meeting tonight.

Juan usually began their Wednesday evening get-together with an open-ended question in order to allow his guys to tell him what had been happening in their lives. Most of the time the responses were anticipated by the young leader because he had been in contact with his charges by phone or in person earlier in the week. Yet it was important for the boys to learn to express their feelings, joys, and concerns before their peers as well.

The sharing time varied in length. Sometimes it was five minutes. Other times it dominated the hour and a half they spent together.

Tonight it lasted about fifteen minutes before Juan focused the attention of the group on the Bible passage assigned for the evening's discussion. Part of the commitment to the group was to come prepared to share insights gained from studying the passage during the week. Though it was not always easy to guide the discussion, this evening the conversation flowed smoothly. The group members had obviously done their homework by studying the passage on their own.

The core group meeting was concluded in a prayer time. One of the key prayer requests had been mentioned by the youth pastor in Sunday school the preceding week. It involved a girl in another core group who was having tests at Mercy Hospital the following day for a suspected tumor. Other prayer requests focused on the non-Christian friends at school, problems with parents, and the upcoming high school retreat.

The clock struck 10:30 P.M. as Juan opened the refrigerator to get a cool glass of orange juice. Most of the group had left by nine o'clock, and then, as usual, Juan had driven Scott and Rob home. It had been a productive evening. The fellows appeared to be taking their faith much more seriously this year. Juan just hoped that the other core groups were enjoying a similar response.

Philosophy

The discipleship model trains students to be God's people in an ungodly world, equipped with Bible study and prayer skills developed in a caring atmosphere with a view to reproducing their Christian lives in others (fig. 8.3).

Background

The idea of discipleship groups is nothing new. James A. Davies has pointed out that "students of church antiquity know that Baptist, Moravian Brethren, Methodists, Quakers, as well as Lutherans used petite cells for religious nurturing" (Davies 1984, 43).

The Wesleyan revivals were a prime example of small groups in action. Converts were placed into tightly disciplined groups, or class meetings, with ten to twelve members from the same neighborhood. The purpose of the weekly gathering was to examine the needs and spiritual progress of each member of the group, thus keeping the Wesleyan movement pure. John Wesley later commented that he had found that one of these group members had "learned more from one hour's discourse [in a class meeting] than from ten years' public preaching" (Davies, 44).

The Navigators, founded by Dawson Trotman, employed similar strategies during World War II in order to evangelize

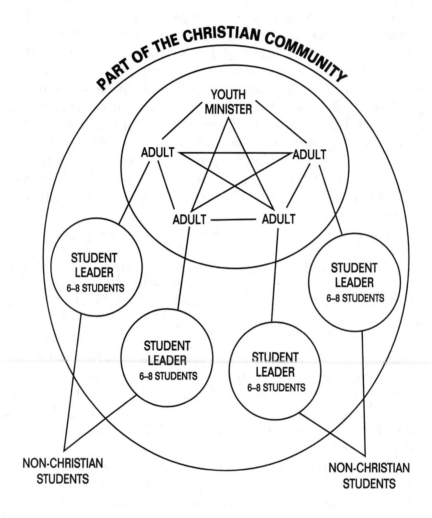

Figure 8.3. *Discipleship Model*

and disciple military personnel all over the world. With the end of the war, many of these men and women enrolled in colleges and universities where they employed the strategy to reach their campuses for Jesus Christ (Glovach and Sholund 1978, 379).

It was not until the late fifties that people working with high school students began to take the strategy seriously. Perhaps the most influential location in this shift was the Wheaton (Illinois) Graduate School under the leadership of Lois and Mary LeBar. It was from this context that people like Chuck Miller and Bill Gothard emerged with a discipleship strategy for doing high school youth ministry (see LeBar 1958, 161–62; Gothard 1961; and Miller 1982, 57–59).

In 1966 Carl Wilson started the high school ministry of Campus Crusade for Christ, now known as Student Venture, using discipleship principles he identified through his study of Scripture and adapted from the organization's college ministry (Wilson 1976). In 1979 Dann Spader began what came to be known as Sonlife Strategy Seminars for creating a Great Commission mind-set in church youth ministry. The strategy, which has been embraced by a number of denominations in North America, is built upon discipleship principles and placed a strong emphasis on developing student leaders to evangelize their peers (Spader and Mayes 1991).

Major Activities

Core group meetings are the heart of the discipleship model. Usually consisting of six to eight students and an adult leader, core groups meet weekly to hold members accountable for Bible study, prayer, and (in some cases) evangelistic efforts. Core groups sometimes have social activities and may take on short-term ministry efforts (Musselman 1983, 141–51).

Large group meetings provide both a sociological and theological function. Because students are divided into core groups for a midweek meeting time, it is essential that the youth group meet as a body at another time during the week for the students to feel part of the larger whole (sociological function). Usually this is during the Sunday school hour, although it may be on Sunday evening or at other times throughout the week.

During the large group meeting the youth pastor usually teaches from the Bible and relates the Scripture to the problems encountered by students in daily life. Frequently the large group meeting includes group singing, skits, media presentation, and announcements that affect the entire group.

Core group leaders' meetings are essential to keep the ministry to high school students moving in a unified direction. Held at least every other week, the meeting allows the youth pastor to provide in-service training for core group leaders, assist in dealing with problems that have arisen in individual core groups, and maintain a level of support and accountability to and from the volunteer workers in the high school ministry.

Camps, retreats, and *big events* are a regular part of the ministry to high school students. The function of these activities is to reach non-believing peers and edify the students while allowing them to have common experiences that are wholesome and entertaining. Camps, retreats, and big events play a major role in maintaining the unity of the youth group.

Leadership Roles

The *youth pastor* has two major functions: communicator and administrator. As a communicator, he rallies the group to enjoy and respect the biblical truths that are presented in large meetings. As administrator, the youth pastor works through other people who care for students and hold them accountable for their own spiritual development.

Core group leaders are the undershepherds of the youth group. They are the flesh and blood of the whole youth ministry, for they are the people with whom students share their experiences en route to maturity. The core group leader is not primarily a communicator. His or her responsibility is to win the right to listen and then provide the structures in which students will talk about their spiritual development.

Student leaders either take on short-term tasks, such as working with the youth pastor to plan and promote a retreat, or they emerge as core group leaders for younger students. Student leaders are expected to be involved in peer evangelism and encourage others to do so as well.

Parents tend to provide a supportive environment for the discipleship model. Christian parents view the model as an extension of their parental function, whereas non-Christian parents tend to appreciate the care being provided for their adolescent.

Preferred Context

The church in which the discipleship model functions best tends to be a church where the teaching of biblical truth is highly revered. Church leaders realize that the way to produce a spiritually mature youth group is not through a constant diet of entertaining activities but through developing biblically literate volunteer leaders who are adept in passing their skills along to a generation of high school students.

The organizational arrangement of the church must permit the youth pastor to take control and, if necessary, significantly change the high school Sunday school hour rather than allow it to function in the traditional manner.

A community where college students and young working adults want to live is important (though not essential) for the discipleship model to function well. They tend to be the people with the amount of discretionary time necessary to perform the functions of an effective core group leader.

The model can be used with junior high students, though the intensity of accountability of students should be decreased.

MINISTRY MODEL

Scenario

The airport terminal was jammed with little brothers, banners, cameras, and parents of all shapes and descriptions. The students who would enter the terminal through gate H5 were returning from three weeks of ministry among orphan children in Mexico. And three life-shaping weeks they had been, for many of these normal American high school students had never before ventured out of their cultural cocoon. Parents, families, and church awaited the impact of the trip.

The expectations were not the result of wishful thinking. This was the seventh summer missionary trip sponsored by the church, and each year the impact among the students seemed to be more tangible.

Last year's post-trip response was perhaps the most significant. Within days of her return from three weeks of ministry in one of the major urban centers of the nation, Dawn, a high school senior, began to ask, "What can we do here at home during the rest of the year?"

A survey of the community by Dawn, her youth pastor, and several other students revealed the presence of hundreds of "latchkey" children, preschoolers and grade schoolers who come home to empty apartments because their parents are not yet home from work, jobs that often pay no more than a subsistence wage. From that survey emerged a five-afternoon-a-week ministry sponsored and led by high school students from two churches.

Demands for high school social activities decreased as the students began sponsoring parties for their latchkey children. Tithing became as natural as breathing when the students determined to raise the six hundred dollars a month required to support the latchkey ministry. Ministry had become a way of life for these high school students.

Philosophy

The ministry model develops student ministry skills and a context in which to use those skills through carefully planned exposure to human and spiritual needs outside the cultural context of the church, enhanced through meeting similar needs in the community surrounding the church and supported by accountability groups within the youth group (fig. 8.4).

Background

The vision of students making valid though short-term contributions to the worldwide mission of the church was not new when George Verwer and students at Moody Bible Institute founded Send the Light (later called Operation Mobilization) in the late 1950s. However, the idea was never the same after Verwer began taking college students during vacation periods to distribute literature in cross-cultural situations.

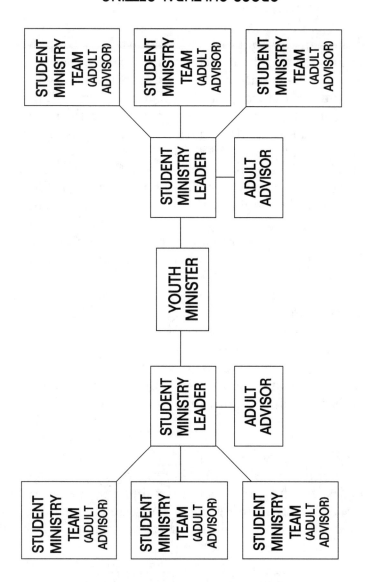

Figure 8.4. *Ministry Model*

Within a few years the idea of including high school students in similar efforts began to emerge in missionary-minded local churches. Initially most of those missionary trips were focused on Native Americans, but quickly more ambitious trips were undertaken as high school students were sent around the world. Names like Missionary Internship, M.O.P. (Missionary Outreach Project), and Project Serve began showing up in magazine articles about the missionary involvement of students in local churches. The problem with the concept, however, was that once the trip was over, the experience of service tended to stop until the next missionary trip (Bynum 1978, 330; Sloat 1969, 23–28).

Soon *Teen Mission,* with the slogan "Get Dirty for God," began sponsoring missionary trips all over the world for high school students. Although their "boot camp" experience better prepared the students to serve, and though the missionary trips were more task oriented, the follow-through in the local churches during the rest of the year was still lacking (Bland 1985, 269–75).

Ridge Burns and the students of the Wheaton Bible Church in suburban Chicago were among the first to turn summer missionary trips into the essential core of a church's youth ministry throughout the year. Though others had enjoyed limited success with similar ideas, Burns was able to incorporate elements of other models into the ministry model and in the mid-1980s sustain a youth ministry around the idea (Burns 1984, 64–68).

Major Activities

Student missionary trips, providing cross-cultural ministry experiences, are the activities that tend to engage the students in the model. Taken during vacation periods (usually spring or summer), the trips are designed to mix manual labor with the meeting of human and spiritual needs.

Weekly community ministry is an outgrowth of the missionary trips. When functioning best, these are student led, staffed, and supported. These ministries are not an extension of the existing church program but are expressions of student visionaries.

Sunday school or a weekly large group meeting gives the youth group a sense of being part of a larger body of committed high school students. Bible teaching and discipleship training along with skit announcements are major features of this whole group function.

Core groups of six to eight students meet during the week to hold each other accountable for spiritual development. These are usually led by adult sponsors.

Retreats and *camp* experiences are used to build group unity, interpersonal relationships, and Christian character.

Leadership Roles

The *youth pastor* is a skilled communicator of biblical truth, a shepherd of adult sponsors and student leaders, and a stimulator of student ministry visions.

Student leaders dream of, organize, and lead their fellow students in actual ministry efforts, including major cross-cultural trips. Though working closely with the youth pastor, the students actually are the missionary leaders.

Youth sponsors serve as coaches on cross-cultural trips and shepherds of core groups at home.

Parents are strong supporters of the concept and practice of allowing the Christian mission to be the focal point of the youth ministry. Usually this means a significant financial commitment to underwrite the expenses of the missionary efforts, and it may even mean being patient until their student is willing to make a commitment to the ministry concept.

Preferred Context

The ministry model tends to work best where the adults of the church have a strong commitment to the world mission of the church. This most frequently can be seen in a significant missionary budget in conjunction with active programs of outreach in the local community.

The model is not built overnight. In most cases the process of adapting the ministry model has taken place over a period of three or more years. Therefore, it is essential that the youth pastor have a long-term commitment to the church.

Because the model is a break from the average expectations of a youth group, it is necessary that the concept have the unqualified backing of the senior pastor and the church board.

SAFE PLACE MODEL

Scenario

When Tom first walked into the locker room at Roosevelt High School, the situation seemed hopeless. Equipment was old and inadequate. Facilities were worn. There was not even a full-time football coach. "Bud" Johnson, the head coach, was really a math teacher who was paid a small stipend to head up the football program, but what could he do with so few resources? There was not even a weight room for developing the strength of the players.

During his first year as an unpaid assistant coach at the four-thousand-student urban high school, Tom earned the right to be heard by the students both on and off the playing field. Relationships were built, even though he was candid about being the youth minister at the Jefferson Memorial Presbyterian Church. Yet few of his athlete friends ever showed up at church.

Then an idea occurred to the urban youth worker. The school had no weight room. Besides, even if it did, the school would be locked up as tight as a steel drum over the summer months, and that was the most important time for the football players to build up their strength. Why not buy a Nautilus™ machine, set it up at church, and sponsor a weight-training program for the athletes and their friends all summer long?

It took some convincing to get the church session to go along with the idea and a lot of hard work to raise the money for the weight machine outside the church budget, but by July 1 the machine was in place and the athletes were streaming to the church.

Stipulations were made for people enlisting in the program, and soon Bible studies and discussion groups were filling the youth pastor's hours when the weight room was not open. Local Christian athletes were brought in at the end of the summer to address the program participants, and a number of students made personal commitments to Jesus Christ and began regular attendance at Jefferson Memorial Presbyterian Church.

That was four years ago. In the meantime, the weight machine concept has expanded to a year-round program that puts volunteer Christian youth workers in contact with urban teenagers and allows them to gain a hearing for the liberating news of the gospel.

Philosophy

The safe place model uses the equipment and facilities of the church or youth center in conjunction with the presence of loving Christian adults who have earned the right to be heard in the world of the students who are at risk. Those adults then have the opportunity to reach the kids and build spiritually accountable relationships with them. The context is a sustained contact with mature Christians at a local church or youth center (fig. 8.5).

Background

In the mid-nineteenth century the YMCA and YWCA were among the first to provide safe places for young people. As young people, many of them very naive, left their rural communities to seek jobs in urban areas, many fell prey to the deceptive pleasures of big city bars and dance halls. The early "Ys" were primarily places for Christian youth to hang out. Soon living quarters were added. Bible study and prayer groups led to training sessions for Christian service. Gymnasiums were available for physical exercise and helped to create a safe environment that was congenial to Christian young people and their friends (Hopkins 1951).

In the mid-1930s, Lloyd T. Bryant, the first full-time youth minister of Manhattan's Calvary Baptist Church, was instrumental in starting forty or so youth centers along the east coast of the United States. During a period when the nation was economically depressed, youth needed places that were safe for Christians and their friends (Senter 1992, 111).

Bill Millikan, working with Young Life in Harlem, found that the strategy still worked in the sixties (Millikan 1968). Teen Challenge under the leadership of Dave Wilkerson built

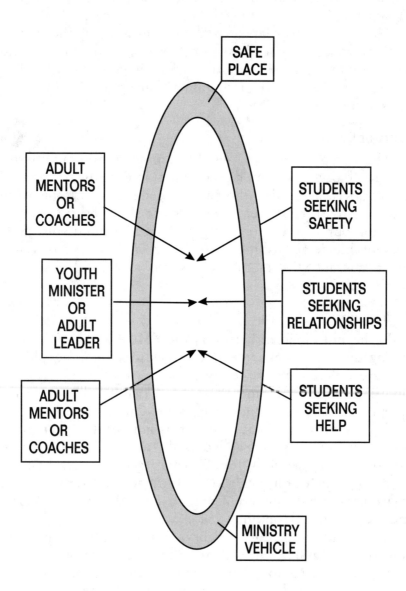

Figure 8.5. *Safe Place Model*

an entire ministry to troubled teens, especially those involved with drugs, by providing a safe place where the Holy Spirit could transform their lives (Wilkerson 1963).

Ray Bakke attempted some of the same strategies when he formed the Innercity Athletic Mission to reach beyond the walls of a church on the north side of Chicago in the late 1960s. More recently, Wayne Gordon at the Lawndale Community Church, on Chicago's southwest side, has blended the strategies of the parachurch agencies with the continuing presence of a local church and in the process has typified the safe place model of youth ministry (Young 1983, 1–2).

In rural settings, a youth center that is open on weekends and guided by Christian adults provides opportunities for the adults to build relationships and attract youth into a vital relationship with Jesus Christ. Unlike urban settings where the danger may be physical, the rural context, with its absence of alternative activities, may find more subtle dangers to conform to pressures that compromise Christian values on a variety of levels.

Safe places take the forms of group homes for young people, tutoring labs, and Christian coffee houses. The effectiveness of these ministries is built upon the ability of the leadership to remain focused on the power of the gospel to transform lives.

Major Activities

Contact work on campus and on the streets by an adult youth worker builds a relationship between adult and student while earning the right to be heard.

Activities using a ministry vehicle, such as a recreation room, gymnasium, weight machine, coffee houses, or a group home, provide an opening to build relationships with students who may otherwise remain untouched by the church. The activities are not an end in themselves but are an opportunity to gain a hearing for the liberating power of the gospel.

Bible studies, which tend to be more like challenges from the Scripture by the adult leader, are tied closely to the activities using the ministry vehicle. Generally these must begin at a very basic level because of the absence of background in biblical teaching.

Camp, when possible, tends to be a vital catalyst in a young person's breaking detrimental habits he has acquired. The camp setting is conducive for experimenting with Christian principles for living.

Leadership Roles

The *pastor* or *youth pastor* must be a person who gets out of the church building and meets students on their own turf. He must be a risk taker, a visionary, and a person who is willing to do whatever is necessary to bring his dream to fulfillment.

Youth workers, frequently brought in from local colleges or from among young professional people, are an extension of the pastor's "presence" to more students. The activities are relational and discipleship oriented.

Student leaders perform a role within their peer groups as they influence student opinions, bring their friends to meetings, and play an important part in maintaining discipline.

Parents usually have little active part in the active role in the safe place model.

Preferred Context

Perhaps the best place for the safe place model to function is in a new urban church or in a setting where the youth ministry to church families is nonexistent or at least limited to the Sunday school hour. Otherwise there may be significant tension felt by church members over the people with whom the pastor or youth pastor should be working (Carney 1984).

In the safe place model, the Sunday school must not be a sacred cow or it may keep the program from achieving significant growth. The Sunday school is generally not compatible with the lifestyle of many of the at-risk youth reached through this model.

A supportive church board is essential in this model because the students brought into the church building through this kind of ministry usually do not have the same value system and respect for property that more established members of the church have. Board members who see a hole in the wall of the gymnasium as a desecration of the church rather than an evidence of ministry may make the model difficult to employ.

CONCLUSION

Models of youth ministry seldom appear in a pure form such as is described in this chapter. Youth ministers most frequently take program elements from a variety of possibilities and form them into a ministry package that conforms to their giftedness and the abilities of the staff they have recruited.

Yet even with this customization process, the youth leaders still tend to cluster their ministry philosophy around one primary model or another. Smaller youth groups, especially those that do not have paid youth workers, may revert to the community model or youth fellowship model described in *The Complete Book of Youth Ministry* (Benson and Senter 1987, 239–69) and still find these systems effective for their local ministries.

WORKS CITED

Benson, Warren S., and Mark H. Senter III, eds. 1987. *The Complete Book of Youth Ministry.* Chicago: Moody.

Bland, Robert M. 1985. "Involving Youth in Missions." In *Evangelizing Youth.* See Smith.

Burns, Ridge. 1984. "Report from the Front Lines: New Hope for Latch-Key Kids." *Youthworker* 1, no. 2 (Summer): 64–68.

Bynum, Bill. 1978. "Missionary Education of Youth." In *Youth Education in the Church.* See Zuck and Benson.

Carney, Glandion. 1984. *Creative Urban Youth Ministry.* Elgin, Ill.: David C. Cook.

Cousins, Don. 1985. "Son City: A Youth Program That Works." In *Evangelizing Youth.* See Smith.

Davies, James A. 1984. "Small Groups: Are They Really So New?" *Christian Education Journal* 5, no. 2 (Glen Ellyn, Ill.: Scripture Press Ministries).

Gangel, Kenneth O., and Warren S. Benson. 1983. *Christian Education: Its History and Philosophy.* Chicago: Moody.

Glovach, Vic, and Milford S. Sholund. 1978. "Parachurch Youth Movements and Organizations." In *Youth Education in the Church*. See Zuck and Benson.

Gothard, William. 1961. "A Proposed Youth Program for Hi-Crusader Clubs." M.A. thesis, Wheaton College, Wheaton, Ill.

Hopkins, C. Howard. 1951. *History of the Y.M.C.A. in North America*. New York: Association.

LeBar, Lois E. 1958. *Education That Is Christian*. Old Tappan, N.J.: Revell.

Miller, Chuck. 1982. "Discipling: A Holistic Ministry." In *Working with Youth: A Handbook for the '80s*, compiled by Ray Wiley. Wheaton, Ill.: Victor.

Millikan, Bill. 1968. *Tough Love*. Old Tappan, N.J.: Revell.

Musselman, John. 1983. "Ministering Through Core Groups." In *The Youth Leader's Source Book*, edited by Gary Dausey. Grand Rapids: Zondervan.

Senter, Mark H. III. 1978. "Youth Programs." In *Youth Education in the Church*. See Zuck and Benson.

_____. 1987. "Models of Youth Ministry." In *The Complete Book of Youth Ministry*. See Benson and Senter.

_____. 1992. *The Coming Revolution in Youth Ministry*. Wheaton: Victor.

Sloat, Bette. 1969. "Operation 'MOP.'" In *High School Leaders' Resource Book*. Vol. 1. Wheaton, Ill.: Scripture Press.

Smith, Glen C., ed. 1985. *Evangelizing Youth*. Washington D.C.: Paulist National Catholic Evangelistic Association; Wheaton, Ill.: Tyndale.

Spader, Dann, and Gary Mayes. 1991. *Growing a Healthy Church*. Chicago: Moody.

Wilkerson, David. 1963. *The Cross and the Switchblade*. New York: Pyramid.

Wilson, Carl. 1976. *With Christ in the School of Disciple Building*. Grand Rapids: Zondervan.

Young, Cathleen. 1983. "Pastor, People Send Their Hopes Aloft." *Chicago Tribune*, 24 November, Tempo section, 1–2.

Zuck, Roy B., and Warren S. Benson, eds. 1978. *Youth Education in the Church*. Chicago: Moody.

FOR FURTHER READING

Foster, Charles R., and Grant S. Shockley, eds. 1989. *Working with Black Youth*. Nashville: Abingdon.

Myers, William. 1991. *Black and White Styles of Youth Ministry*. New York: Pilgrim.

Robertson, Fern. 1968. "Sunday Evening Youth Programs." In *Youth and the Church*, edited by R. G. Irving and R. B. Zuck. Chicago: Moody.

Stewart, Ed, and Neal McBride. 1978. *Bible Learning Activities: Youth*. Ventura, Calif.: Regal.

Yaconelli, Mike, and Jim Burns. 1986. *High School Ministry*. Grand Rapids: Zondervan.

9

EMERGING MODELS OF YOUTH MINISTRY

Mark H. Senter III

I t is not always clear what will emerge as a model of youth ministry and what will merely be a springboard for other new ideas for youth ministry. Usually the change is gradual, so innovations can be observed as they develop. The last decade of the twentieth century appears to be different. Four rather distinct models have appeared quite abruptly. All four have roots in youth ministry and yet have taken on innovative forms. The *family-based* model, although refreshingly new, may reach the farthest into history in its attempt to restore the family and faith community to a central place in the nurture of young people. The *youth church* model draws upon the church experience of ethnic minorities to shape a strategy for ministry to youth.

The *meta* model, while new as a complete system, is heavily influenced by the small group movements of the past. The *high school subpopulation* strategy comes as a recognition that the fabric of the public high school has come unraveled, leaving groups of students isolated from each other. These four models may not sustain themselves through the coming decade, but if they do not, it is most likely that related models will emerge to take their places.

FAMILY-BASED MODEL

Scenario

Saturday morning was sacred for the eight fathers who met at Harry's house to pray for their children. All had high school students, but that is where the similarities ended.

Harry's large house was known in the country by police and social workers as the place where homeless kids could find a meal and a place to sleep. Whoever was there at 6:00 P.M. ate; whoever was there at 11:00 P.M. slept. One closet in the family room was reserved for sleeping bags, which were aired out each morning. The family had grown up participating in the ministry. It was a source of pride to the children as well as a source of satisfaction to Harry and his wife, Julie.

Stan's wife Sylvia was still home-schooling their two high school boys and junior high daughter. Stan and Sylvia were part of a network of parents from several churches who pooled their talents when appropriate, banded together to pressure the local school board for specific services, and provided volunteer services in the park district where their children gained social contact with peers through athletic competition. Stan helped with the swim team on which his two boys competed.

Joe and Dale had been to Promise Keepers for two years before they realized the potential of including their sons in the experience. Despite the fathers' fears that their boys would be bored by the long meetings, the younger set got caught up in the drama of the event and began insisting that they be included in the "Next Step" small group that followed the weekend. Although the groups were not as exciting as the youth group, boys and dads were bonding with Christ and each other.

All eight of the men were involved with the church's student mentoring program. When a student reached his or her thirteenth birthday, the youth pastor took the student and his or her parents out to dinner (at the church's expense) and explained the mentoring concept. The student would select an adult of his or her sex from the church to be his or her mentor. If the person agreed, and most of them did if asked, the adult would meet with the student as a friend at least once a month until graduation. Structure was provided by the youth pastor, and if things were not going well he would intervene and sometimes even provide another mentor.

The prayer time, however, seemed to be the power that drove the wheels of the youth ministry at their church. Several prayer groups, including one just for working mothers, were taking place weekly. The result was that the church functioned more like a large family than like a string of programs.

Philosophy

In the family-based model, parents, aided by their faith communities, guide their children to intellectual, emotional, social, moral, and spiritual maturity while using their distinctive giftedness to witness to the broader community of adolescents and their families (fig. 9.1).

Background

Before the Industrial Revolution in the nineteenth century the family was the center of Christian nurture. Church buildings were used primarily for worship services and, in some circles, revival meetings. No Sunday school classes, youth groups, or even choirs existed. Education was assumed to be the responsibility of the school and the home. Communities shared Christian values, so it was entirely possible for a child, as Horace Bushnell advocated, "to grow up a Christian and never know himself as being otherwise" (Bushnell 1861; reprint 1979, 10).

With the coming of the Industrial Revolution and the technological changes that followed, families and communities were no longer insulated from non-Christian values. Perhaps they really never had been, but rapid change forced a realization of the need for help in discipling youth. While the family quietly remained at the heart of Christian nurture, agencies such as the Sunday school, YMCA, church youth groups, para-

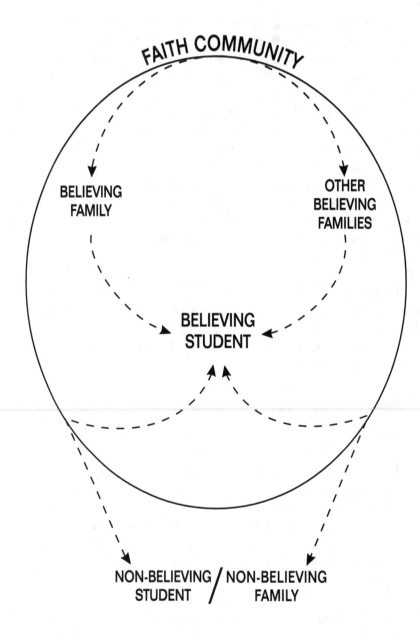

Figure 9.1. *Family-Based Model*

church ministries, and camps came into being to support the family's efforts.

It did not take long until publishers and church leaders, while giving lip service to the role of the family, appeared to place all of their emphasis on educational experiences that excluded parents. With the emergence of the youth pastor in the sixties and seventies, this trend spiraled, and soon well-meaning youth pastors even viewed parents as obstacles to the spiritual development of their teenagers.

Bill Gothard, with his Institute for Basic Youth Conflicts, was among the first evangelicals to shift the responsibility for the training and nurture of young people back to the home. In the three decades after the founding of the Institute in 1961, more than 2.5 million people were reported to have attended his seminars, now called the Institute in Basic Life Principles. To supplement the seminars, Gothard became a major publisher of home schooling materials that further empower parents in their educational responsibilities toward their children.

Perhaps a turning point in the church's view of the family's role in youth ministry came as the result of James Dobson's radio broadcast, "Focus on the Family." From his background in psychology, Dobson recognized that the problems young people faced could not be seen in isolation from their families. The entire family system was at risk. Dobson's program laid the groundwork for parents to begin assuming greater roles in the spiritual training of their young people.

Although few church groups have attempted to keep a family emphasis in their youth ministries, several books have emerged in the nineties that have brought family-based youth ministry back into the mainstream of youth ministry. Mark DeVries's book *Family-Based Youth Ministry* provided an excellent framework for rethinking the role of youth pastor and parents in youth discipleship (DeVries 1994). Lavon J. Welty provided a mentoring guide for congregational youth ministry in his book *Side by Side* (Welty 1989). The mentoring concept is but one of many ideas that have been in use for some time but which are now finding a broader hearing.

Outreach-oriented family-based youth ministries include foster parenting for teens, shelters for runaway or throw-away youth, as well as programs for families with codependency problems.

Major Activities

Adult prayer and support groups bring together the people who are involved in family-based youth ministries so that they can support each other before God and through sharing experiences and resources. This could include twelve-step programs.

Structured parent-student activities provide opportunities for the large majority of parents who need coaching and a pattern for building the kind of relationship with their children that they could only dream about otherwise.

Support from the church leadership both in spirit and in action is essential if family-based models are to be proved effective over time. Pastors and youth pastors must be cheerleaders, bringing the encouragement and resources of the faith community into networks of parents.

Leadership Roles

Parents must be active participants with an intense desire to disciple their own children. This is not the type of program that can be imposed on unsuspecting parents and run by surrogate parents in the form of youth sponsors.

Conveners of prayer and support groups encourage fellow parents to maintain the course when difficult times occur.

Students must be active participants. Student leaders must value their involvement with their parents and establish a climate in which other students will want to participate.

The *youth pastor and/or church leaders* will need to view the model as a vital part of what the church should be doing with young people. Although the youth pastor may have other ministries in which young people participate, the family-based model is at the heart of his/her youth ministry.

Preferred Context

Although components of the model could work just about anywhere, to have a family-based youth ministry it is essential that the parents of the church have a sense of community within the church. Trust and mutual concern are key factors, for without them parents will not take the risk of making themselves vulnerable in the prayer and support group.

Small youth groups lend themselves to a family-based youth ministry. As the number of youth in the church approaches thirty, the complications related to maintaining viable relationships between students and adults for intentional conversations become time-consuming. A creative youth pastor may need to become the continuity agent.

HIGH SCHOOL SUBPOPULATION MODEL

Scenario

The divinity school's modular master's program attracted an interesting cross section of youth ministers for the week-long seminar on strategies of youth ministry. Lunch on Tuesday found six people representing both church and parachurch agencies, discussing their ministries.

Kim worked with high school girls who are mothers in a program called Teen Moms. It had been a difficult year, then suddenly four of the girls made professions of faith within two weeks. It had taken a long time to earn their confidence, but after they tested her for nearly six months, two results surfaced—not only did they trust Kim's Lord but they brought other girls, some of whom were still pregnant, to the weekly gathering.

Lloyd struck the rest of the class as a nerd. That was only because he, in fact, was a nerd. Not just any kind of nerd, Lloyd was a computer nerd. Yet it was his love for young people that had gotten him to hang out in a computer store in the mall and begin meeting high schoolers who shared his passion. Soon they were talking that kind of talk that only computer geeks can understand. Some of them were into some heavy computer gaming and were beginning to find their minds getting messed up before Lloyd became their friend.

Brian's idea of ministry was an enormous garage with a half-pipe where freestyle skateboarders could "catch air" all winter long. They were willing to pay the fee and abide by the safety rules because Brian was willing to hang out with them after school and on weekends. Every freestyler in town knew

Brian since the time during the summer when he talked the president of Midtown Bank into letting his friends use the parking garage after the bank closed to do their skateboard tricks. But Brian was the most excited about the openness to Christ's love he had found after he spent the night in the emergency room with Tony after he had lost control in the middle of a simple wheelie and broken his arm.

The others had similar stories. Pamela worked in a drop-in center where she talked with kids who were referred to the center by the courts. Oliver, as a volunteer, coached a chess team that had won the regional championship and placed second in the state. The school paid his way to the state tournament and the kids loved it. Roy managed a fast-food restaurant where he only hired minorities who wanted to learn how to succeed in business. In the process of teaching them entrepreneurial skills, he taught his business philosophy, which included his faith in Jesus Christ.

Their common conviction, as it turned out, was that they had all given up the hope of reaching their entire high school for Christ and had decided to focus on one subgroup within the high school population. As a result of this paradigm shift, each youth worker had found a whole new world of ministry.

Philosophy

In the high school subpopulation model, Christian adults with similar interests or backgrounds to youth within specific subpopulations of adolescent society discover a means by which to build relationships with that group of people and share both a love for the common interest and a love for Jesus Christ. The desire is to elicit an interest in spiritual matters that might lead the young person to faith in Jesus Christ and participation in the believing community (fig. 9.2).

Background

Prior to 1973, high school society consisted of two groups, the "innies," consisting primarily of athletes, cheerleaders, and student body officers, and "outies," which included everybody else. The assumption was that, despite their protestations, in their heart of hearts the "outies" really wanted to

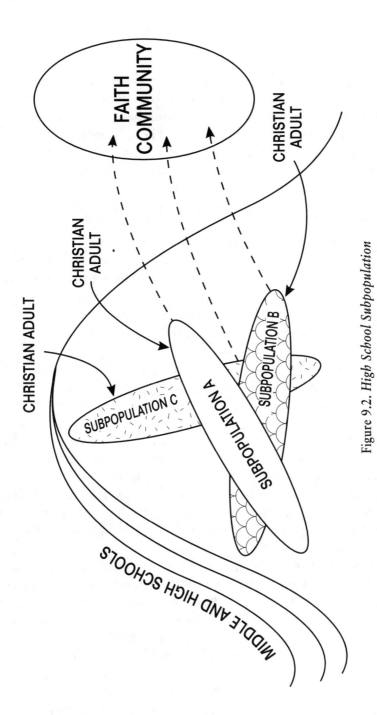

Figure 9.2. *High School Subpopulation*

be "innies" (Keyes 1979). Some insisted that there was a third group, the "greasers," who despised the "innies" and all who wished to be like them.

As simplistic as this analysis of the high school social structure is, most of the models for parachurch ministry even well into the eighties were based on these assumptions. The strategy was to reach the student leaders. If they would attend club meetings, activities, or camps, other students would follow just to be associated with the student leaders. Of course there were still the "greasers." Most ministries ignored them or set up completely different programs for them, with names like "Lifeline," which implied a rescue operation.

Whether the social analysis was accurate or not, the strategy appeared to work. Young Life, Campus Life, Fellowship of Christian Athletes, and many other club programs did it much the same way. Since it was the only strategy in town, no one got a fair look at any alternatives to it.

Then came the entitlement legislation for high school students beginning in 1973. No longer could high schools put all of their resources into programs dominated by student leaders. Programs for handicapped students, female athletic teams, music groups, math teams, and a host of other activities had to be funded by the local high school. The freshman soccer team soon had its own set of cheerleaders, the chess team was traveling to tournaments, and swing choir was attracting players away from the football team. The net effect was that there was no longer a small set of student body leaders everyone wanted to know. The school had fragmented into a multitude of social circles, many of which had little or no contact with the others.

Youth workers at the grass roots recognized the change well before national parachurch programs and local church ministries became aware of it. By the mid-nineties, experiments with a wide variety of youth ministry strategies were underway. E-mail allowed youth workers all over the world to communicate directly with each other about ministering to sub-populations of high school students without having to go through journal editors or institutional bureaucracies to access that information. With those "filters" no longer in place, youth workers have had to do their own work of sifting the useless advice from the truly worthwhile, but on balance this access to information has been helpful for youth workers. In time local youth workers will have distinguished one from the other and applied the best ideas to their work.

Major Activities

Identify high school subpopulations that need to be touched by the gospel. This may be done by professional youth workers, volunteer leaders, or other interested adults in the church.

Discover people who can establish contact with the "unreached people" in a high school subpopulation. For the most part these will be adults who have a heart for ministry.

Empower leaders to experiment with ways of building relationships with the target group. The professional youth worker may become more of a cheerleader than a coach for the empowered leader because, in all likelihood, the professional has never attempted to minister to that group of students.

Hold leaders accountable for evangelization and discipleship of new believers. It is very easy to build a relationship with a young person but never bring the gospel into the friendship.

Build appropriate strategies to expand the ministry to other young people in the same subpopulation.

Leadership Roles

The *visionary* is the person who can identify the high school subpopulations that can be reached in a community. This person may be a professional or volunteer youth leader.

The *authorizer* is the person who grants permission for the resources of the church or parachurch agency to be channeled toward the subpopulation that has been identified. This person will hold the person doing the ministry accountable for completing the ministry cycle (i.e., evangelism and discipleship).

The *point person* leads the way in building bridges of friendship with the group identified.

Preferred Context

The subpopulation model is heavily dependent upon volunteer leaders to establish and maintain the ministry. Thus the model can only work where there is a ready supply of volunteer leaders or where volunteer leaders can be attracted to serve.

META MODEL

Scenario

"What do you mean, this church has no youth group?" asked the startled newcomer. "All churches of this size have youth groups of some kind or other."

"Well, when you put it that way," replied Dennis, the youth pastor, "we do have youth *groups,* but I thought you meant the traditional kind that has thirty or forty kids who meet so that the youth pastor can teach them."

"Actually that *was* what I had in mind," replied Mrs. Swanson, a thoroughly confused parent.

"Then the answer is no!" smiled Dennis. "We do not have a youth group (singular); we have youth groups (plural)."

For the next fifteen minutes, the youth pastor explained how the high school ministry was spread all over the city, meeting in what he called meta groups, which operated like (and only a youth worker could describe it this way) cancer cells. By that he meant that they were growing at an abnormally rapid rate. The reason for this growth, Dennis went on to explain, was that each small group was designed for evangelistic growth. Each group was required to have an open chair each time they met for the explicit purpose of reminding the members that the non-Christians for whom they had been praying were the ones who should be occupying that seat next week.

If the group exceeded fifteen, it was divided into two groups so that the growth process could continue. If it failed to grow at all, it was disbanded so that a "healthy" cell could be formed. (Since when is a cancer cell healthy? Only in youth worker analogies.)

The whole idea seemed like quite a change from what Mrs. Swanson had associated with youth ministry. Soon enough she would realize that the "meta" was based on a Greek word meaning change. The very purpose of the model was to respond to the changing needs of postmodern young people, sometimes called Generation X.

Philosophy

In the meta model, adult and student leaders equip and empower caring Christian cell groups to multiply in amoeba-like fashion in order to create an expanding network of friendship clusters in which students share their lives with each other and discuss the life of Christ with spiritually open peers (fig. 9.3).

Background

The growth of the Central Church in Seoul, South Korea, to more than 200,000 members captured the imagination of church growth specialists in the West during the 1980s. At the heart of the dynamic growth was a highly effective use of cell groups to evangelize and disciple.

Two books published at the beginning of the last decade of the twentieth century captured the imagination of youth workers who were dissatisfied with the existing models of youth ministry. Ralph Neighbor's *Where Do We Go from Here?* (1990) and Carl George's *Prepare Your Church for the Future* (1991) focused attention on cell groups as the basis for church growth and stimulated wide discussion in youth ministry circles.

Perhaps the greatest boost to the meta model came when Willow Creek Community Church's Student Impact program began to experiment with the new approach to their youth ministry. In their Student Impact Leadership Conferences, Bo Boshers and Troy Murphy began stressing the building of balanced small groups as the key to reaching high school youth and de-emphasizing the large group activities. The transition to a meta-based program is far from complete, but the effort at Willow Creek demonstrates that at least one of the premier youth ministries in the United States is attempting to either incorporate the meta model into its existing structures or move completely to the change-based model.

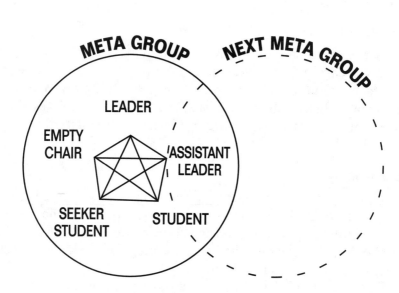

NEXT GROUP FORMED WITHIN
SIX MONTHS

Figure 9.3. *Meta Model*

Major Activities

Leadership development of small group leaders and apprentice leaders sets the stage for the creation of groups that are capable of reaching out to new people and including them in a caring Christian cell of students.

Open groups, while allowing for continuity of relationships among high school students, constantly include new friends who have been drawn to the group through the integrity of a friendship with a loving Christian peer. It is here that the gospel is both lived and presented.

Cell growth happens when groups reach about fifteen in number and the apprentice leader and some of the group form a new cell group that looks to build genuine friendships with new people and draw them into a place where they are cared for and introduced to Jesus Christ, the master care-giver.

Celebrations take place periodically, where the various cell groups come together to worship and receive instruction.

Leadership Roles

The *youth pastor* serves as the visionary, leadership trainer, and celebration leader, but he does them in that order. His primary responsibility is the development, support, and encouragement of small group leaders.

Small group leaders and apprentice leaders have as their responsibility the creation of groups of students that have an "empty chair" in the midst as a symbol of their desire to include spiritual seekers in their groups. Apprentice leaders are people in training to assume leadership when a new cell group is ready to be formed.

The *celebration team* creates worship experiences that engage both the minds and emotions of students and provide opportunities to be part of the larger gathering of Christian young people in the faith community.

Preferred Context

It would appear that the meta model works best in situations where the authority of the leadership is highly respected or where authoritarian leadership is a recent memory. The best contexts for the meta model are probably youth groups

composed of oriental students, churches where the leadership
resides primarily in the hands of a trusted pastor or youth
pastor, and possibly countries where authoritarian govern-
ments have existed or still do.

A context where change is a normal expectation will provide fertile soil for the model to develop. The strategy is so
entrepreneurial that innovation is a necessary part of the
dynamics. Yet there needs to be a solid leadership structure
that can provide a theological framework for the emerging
leadership, or else the culture beyond the church will shape
the teaching within the youth ministry.

YOUTH CHURCH MODEL

Scenario

When Tommy Kim came to the United States from Korea
he was eighteen months old. While his mother and father
worked at and eventually bought a dry cleaning business in
suburban Toronto, Tommy was being educated in the public
schools. He spoke English like any other Canadian and,
although his parents were concerned that he did not respect
his Korean heritage, Tommy was more concerned with fitting
in with the society in which he and his family lived.

It was only in their home and at church that the Korean
language still predominated. As Tommy and his Korean
friends reached their teenage years they continued to gather
from all over the Toronto area at their church on Friday nights
and on a majority of the Sundays. At first it was the Friday
night activities that changed as the program was allowed to
take place in English. Then, in a rather dramatic concession
from the pastor, the young people were allowed to hold their
own service, in English, on Sunday morning. He called it the
Youth Church.

As the church grew, so did the English service. The worship
leaders were all adolescents or young adults. Preaching was
done by a seminary student from a nearby school. In time, the
English service become the dominant worship service, and the
people who attended the Youth Church—now a bit older and
more sophisticated—became elders in the church and continued to lead the church service. By leading their peers in wor-

ship, the Korean youth of the church became the Christian leaders their parents had hoped they would be.

Philosophy

In the youth church model, the youth minister and spiritually gifted and qualified adults prepare young people to be spiritual leaders by taking responsibility to establish a new church either within an existing church, as a spin-off of a church that seeks to plant a new church. It could also be the logical outcome of the ministry of a parachurch organization (fig. 9.4).

Background

The "Holy Club" at Oxford University led by John and Charles Wesley had no fantasy of becoming a church, but a few decades later the Methodist Church was the product of their activities. In the 1730s, the members of the "Holy Club" might not have called it a youth church, but, in retrospect, that probably would not have been a bad description.

The Sunday school movement, unlike what is known as Sunday school today, was primarily a means of ministering to young people who were outside the reach of established churches. During one short period, known as the Great Valley Campaign, several thousand churches were established by Sunday school missionaries in the Mississippi Valley. These were hardly youth churches in the sense experienced by Tommy Kim, yet churches were built as extensions of youth ministries.

Hal Merwold, former director of Young Life in Brazil, reports that a decision was made in the mid-seventies to create communities of adults who had been reached by the ministry of Young Life but who had been unable to find churches that manifested the incarnational qualities that had been so much a part of their secondary school experience with Young Life. In effect these were youth churches. They were led by people who had no formal theological training but who had been developed as Christians and as leaders by the informal training process of Young Life. These communities are thriving today.

The initial motivation was as much economic as anything.

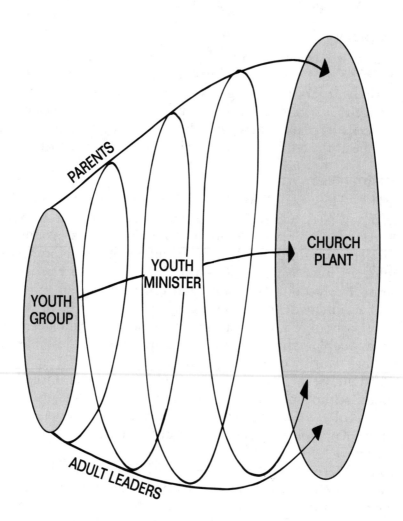

Figure 9.4. *Youth Church Model*

Young Life workers knew that if they did not create an economic base in Brazil the ministry would continue to be dependent upon American dollars. The effort has worked. Brazilian Young Life is autonomous and until recently functioned under the same leader Merwold appointed when he left in 1976. At that time the young man was twenty-six years old.

A number of nonethnic churches are experimenting with youth churches as well. Their desire, sometimes driven by some poor motivations (such as avoiding the question of musical styles in worship), has given birth to church services primarily for young people that encourage youth to participate and lead.

Major Activities

Worship services planned for and led by young people are at the heart of the model. Most meet on Sunday morning and are usually an alternative to the church's normal worship service. The youth pastor usually does the preaching.

Worship teams composed of young people prepare the component parts of the worship service. This could include music, drama, dance, media, Scripture reading, and sometimes other forms of visual art.

Shepherding groups provide a way for all who attend the youth church to be present or accounted for. Spectator Christianity becomes a possibility when attendance at the service exceeds thirty of forty young people.

Leadership Roles

The *youth pastor* is usually the driving force behind the formation of a youth church. The collective impact of the service is usually based on his creativity and communication skills.

Worship team members take the framework created by the youth pastor and create worship experiences that are appropriate to the audience.

Shepherds assume responsibility for six to twelve young people and make sure each person is enfolded into the faith community.

A *supportive senior pastor* is necessary, or else the idea will never get off the drawing board. He will be the person who will take the greatest amount of criticism because of the youth church.

Preferred Context

Youth churches work best where there is a great amount of contrast between the worship styles the adults and young people embrace. When the adults are willing to adapt to the preferences of church young people, the model becomes less attractive to all involved.

The youth church model may also be used as a strategic design for church planting. The leadership of a mother church may ask the youth pastor to adopt a philosophy of youth ministry that would train young people and volunteer staff for the task of establishing a daughter church in a nearby community several years down the road. This strategy could be adapted by parachurch agencies, especially those operating at major universities.

Choosing a Model

The models presented in chapters 8 and 9 are not all appropriate for every situation. Some very sincere and enthusiastic youth workers could still fall flat on their faces in attempting to implement the model of their choice for one of three reasons:

1. The situation might not be appropriate.
2. The youth worker's abilities and gifts might not be suitable.
3. The Holy Spirit might be working to bring about something unforeseen by either the youth worker or the people in the church.

The first two reasons can be analyzed ahead of time. The final "obstacle" is the "checkmating" of the Holy Spirit. That should be viewed as the starting point for a whole new set of lessons for both the youth worker and the church.

The following series of questions, when compared to the description of models presented in these chapters, should provide an adequate basis for selecting a model.

1. Does the church have a distinctive philosophy of ministry that must be reflected in the youth ministry?
2. Is the church willing to hire and capable of employing a youth pastor, and will it provide a budget sufficient to support the model?
3. How well developed are the communication skills of the youth worker, especially in front of large groups?
4. How competent are the organizational skills of the youth worker?
5. How adept is the youth worker at meeting and gaining a hearing from non-Christian students?
6. What kind of vision does the church have for ministering to the community immediately surrounding the church building?
7. How strong are the family ties within the church, especially as they relate to spiritual nurture?
8. To what extent are mature and talented adults available to implement the model selected?
9. Are the students presently in the youth group sufficiently eager to make the changes necessary to implement a model that would have a significant spiritual impact on their lives?
10. What kind of facilities does the church have that would enhance or weaken the model chosen?

WORKS CITED

Bushnell, Horace. 1861; reprint 1979. *Christian Nurture.* Grand Rapids: Baker.

DeVries, Mark. 1994. *Family Based Youth Ministry.* Downers Grove, Ill.: InterVarsity.

George, Carl F. 1991. *Prepare Your Church for the Future.* Tarrytown, N.Y.: Revell.

Keyes, Ralph. 1979. *Is There Life After High School?* New York: Warner.

Neighbor, Ralph W., Jr. 1990. *Where Do We Go from Here?* Houston: Touch.

Welty, Lavon J. 1989. *Side by Side: Mentoring Guide for Congregational Youth Ministry.* Newton, Kans.: Faith & Life; Scottdale, Pa.: Mennonite.

FOR FURTHER READING

Barker, Steve, et al. 1985. *Good Things Come in Small Groups.* Downers Grove, Ill.: InterVarsity.

Black, Wesley. 1991. *An Introduction to Youth Ministry.* Nashville: Broadman.

Dettoni, John M. 1993. *Introduction to Youth Ministry.* Grand Rapids: Zondervan.

Hestenes, Roberta. 1983. *Using the Bible in Groups.* Philadelphia: Westminster.

Peace, Richard. 1985. *Small Group Evangelism.* Downers Grove, Ill.: InterVarsity.

Ward, Pete. 1993. *Worship and Youth Culture.* London: Marshall Pickering.

PART THREE

CONTEXTS FOR YOUTH MINISTRY

10

HOW CAN LEADERS
BUILD A RELATIONAL
YOUTH MINISTRY?

David Veerman

A day (and night) in the life of Youth Pastor Todd:

8:00 A.M.	Check "to do" list for today
8:15 A.M.	Prepare talk for Friday's outreach event
9:30 A.M.	Write quarterly report for Elder Board
10:00 A.M.	Pastoral staff meeting
11:00 A.M.	Initial planning for Winter Retreat (check on hotels, bus rental, potential speakers, etc.)
12:00 noon	Racquetball with Kevin, area Young Life director
1:00 P.M.	Fast-food lunch in the car
1:15 P.M.	Errands (refreshments and supplies for tonight and Friday)
2:30 P.M.	Personal prayer/devotional time

3:00 P.M.   Attend to office details: phone, mail, paper-
             work
3:30 P.M.   Prepare for tonight's youth ministry volun-
             teer staff meeting
5:00 P.M.   Home with the family for dinner
6:45 P.M.   Set up for staff meeting in youth room
7:30 P.M.   Lead staff meeting. Tonight's topic: "The
             Importance of Relational Youth Ministry"

The term echoes from settings as diverse as the classrooms of colleges offering youth ministry courses to the lobbies of hotels hosting Youth Specialties conventions to the basements of churches where adults meet for youth ministry training. Sometimes casually, at other times with a great conviction the words *relational youth ministry* are spoken. *Relational* has become the defining adjective for many leaders attempting to define to others the distinctives of their approach to youth ministry.

But why is it so important to have a relational youth ministry? What characterizes a truly relational youth ministry? Furthermore, how does one actually go about the process of initiating and sustaining such a ministry?

WHY RELATIONAL MINISTRY?

Life-change occurs in the context of close relationships. Television and radio programs, videos, curricula, books, tapes, CDs, on-line services, and other media play an important role when used effectively as communication tools. Creative programs, including church services and classes, youth meetings, camps, conferences, retreats, conventions, and special trips, can provide tremendous help in the communication process. But usually it takes a *person* to get through. Programs initiate and provide opportunities for relational interaction, but it is the relationships themselves that change lives.

Reflect upon what you consider to be the significant, life-changing moments in your spiritual walk. Certainly your "scrapbook" includes the time you professed faith in Christ. Other events may have occurred at youth camps or retreats, in a youth group setting, or a small group Bible study during your college days. In each case, however, regardless of the venue, context, and program, the turning point in your life probably was tied to a person—a relationship. In my case, my *mother* led me to Christ; a Sunday school *teacher* played an important role in my life as a young Christian; my *family* provided a context for growth; my *pastor* encouraged me to develop my ministry gifts; a close *friend* helped me dig deeper; my *wife* challenged me to be a man of God.

Beyond being personally meaningful for each of us, relational ministry is also *biblical, responsible,* and *effective.*

Relational Ministry Is Biblical

God's entire plan for humankind unfolds through relationships. At creation, "The Lord God said, 'It is not good for the man to be alone. I will make a helper suitable for him'" (Genesis 2:18). People were created for relationships. All of biblical history records God's relationship with His chosen people, the Jews, and then the church. Then God became a person, a human man, through the Incarnation, to identify with us, communicate on our level, and suffer and die for our sins. Now, through faith in Christ, we can enjoy the closest of relationships with God, as His dearly loved children (see, for example, Luke 20:36; John 1:12–13; Romans 8:16–17; 1 John 3:1–2), born (John 3:3 and 1 Peter 1:23) and adopted (Ephesians 1:5) into His family, and as His bride (see, for example, Revelation 21:2).

Biblical ministry models are characterized by close relationships, one-on-one and in small groups. Look at Jesus. He called His disciples individually, spent time in their homes, and built into their lives. Within those relationships He demonstrated great compassion as He touched and healed the leprous, the blind, and the physically and emotionally disabled. God expects His people, as disciples of Jesus, to minister through relationships as well. In fact, Jesus commanded His disciples to go into the world (Matthew 28:19), loving as they went (John 13:34).

Relational Ministry Is Responsible

In this age of information and impersonal technology, peo-

ple often feel like faceless numbers defined primarily by
demographic statistics. Impersonal "personalized" junk mail
and telemarketers assault households daily, trying to sell some
product or service. Voice mail removes people yet another
step from interpersonal contact. No one likes the feeling of
being perceived as a number, a statistic, or a "sale."

A number of years ago a Jewish high school student told
me that some Christian friends had been trying to get her to
attend their church youth group. During her conversation
with them, it came out that these students were to receive
points for every visitor they brought. After explaining the situation, the girl said to me, "How'd you like to be a 'point'?"
This student felt as though her "friends" didn't really care
about her as a person, only as a target—an object—a way to
earn points for their team. That is the very definition of *irresponsible* ministry.

Youth ministers are also being irresponsible when, consciously or not, they *use* kids to meet their needs. Wanting to
have a large ministry in order to feel good about themselves,
such leaders insist that students come to meetings. Hoping to
impress their peers with the breadth of their ministry, irresponsible leaders keep students busy and insist that student
leaders sacrifice everything else for the youth group. Desiring
to have a good report to the board about the number of conversions to Christ, they pressure students to make "decisions."

In fact, all evangelistic efforts that treat people like products on an assembly line ("go through these motions"; "pray
this prayer"; "use these words") smack of irresponsibility. So,
too, do mass-production evangelism efforts ("Now, all of
you, together, pray this prayer after me"). Perhaps the most
irresponsible ministry activity is leaving recent converts to
fend for themselves alone. That is like leaving a newborn baby
in the delivery room, expecting him to grow, develop, and
mature on his own. Yet that often happens in youth ministry.

In contrast, responsible youth ministry, including youth
evangelism, treats each person as a valuable creation of God
and handles them with care, not using young people but loving them and meeting *their* needs. Responsible youth ministry

is characterized by building strong, close relationships that move toward the goal of changed lives.

Relational Ministry Is Effective

Imagine that you have just sat down to dinner and are about to dish up a hot casserole. Brrrring! Pushing away from the table, you hurry to the phone, pick it up, and say "Hello." Instead of a friend, relative, neighbor, or business associate, the voice on the line belongs to a stranger trying to sell you something. (Why do they always call at dinner time?) As the persistent telemarketer gives his canned presentation, you barely listen while you worry about your food getting cold and think of ways to cut the conversation short.

The caller may have had a terrific offer, an opportunity of a lifetime, or a fulfillment of your wildest dreams, but you will never know because you did not care and were not listening. And you did not listen because the caller's voice joined the chorus of so many other pitches, proposals, and promises that you had heard before. There is simply too much clutter in the marketplace.

Relational ministry is effective because it breaks through the confusing marketplace clutter.

When adults build relationships with students, they break through the noise and distortion. Instead of dismissing adults *and* their message by lumping them together with all the other ideas vying for their attention, students listen carefully because their friends are speaking. Take the telephone call that interrupted your dinner. Suppose that this time, instead of a sales-stranger, the caller was a close friend who wanted to tell you about an important piece of news or a personal breakthrough. Even if you could not talk right then, you would have listened closely, spoken carefully and warmly, and arranged another time when the two of you could meet. Friendship would make all the difference.

Relational ministry is effective because it builds communication bridges.

In Youth for Christ, this is often termed "winning the right

CLUTTER
DAVE VEERMAN

Bible and Christian book sales are booming. The sales of records and CDs by Christian contemporary artists have skyrocketed. Religious radio and television ministries have multiplied. And the Christian Coalition has burst onto the political scene. With all of this activity, sound, and press, one might conclude that the nation, if not the whole world, must be nearly evangelized. Considering all the Christian voices, how could anyone not know about Christ?

In reality, Americans, especially young Americans, are more lost than ever. Just consider the growth of drugs, gangs, violence, sexual activity, gambling addiction, and other problems among young people these days. Unfortunately, the books, records, and broadcasts by all the preachers, teachers, and performers seem merely to have added to the din, the noise, and the clutter. All of it is easily dismissed or ignored by kids today. We do not need to make the message louder or flashier or prettier or even give it more often. But we *do* need to be more effective—to break through the clutter so that we can present the life-changing message of Jesus Christ to needy young people.

to be heard." Imagine that you are shopping in the mall, casually looking in the store windows. A complete stranger approaches and begins to speak enthusiastically about a vitamin she has been taking that has cleared up her skin and given her incredible energy. Undoubtedly your first thought might be that the woman is mentally unbalanced, an aggressive salesperson, or perhaps even an extreme extrovert. Your natural response would be to escape the conversation as quickly as possible. Suppose, however, that instead of a stranger, the woman is a friend, someone you know and trust. Once again, relationship makes all the difference. You would be genuinely interested in the vitamin because of the credibility of the person as an authentic, concerned friend.

Relational ministry is effective because it gives kids the chance to see the Christian life in action, in our lives.

This process is often called "modeling," providing positive role models for young people to follow. Jesus said that people would know His disciples by watching them (John 13:34–35), and Paul told young Timothy to "set an example for the believers in speech, in life, in love, in faith and in purity" (1 Timothy 4:12). As adults get close to students, they will be observed for how they live out their mature faith. Students will notice the difference that Christ makes in the adults' lives —they will see what it looks like for a person to put God first in relationships, recreation, job, and finances.

Whether they want it or not, entertainment, sports, political, and even religious celebrities are set up as examples to be emulated. Often, however, when the private lives of those stars are exposed, hypocrisy, immorality, and illegality are revealed. Talk is cheap—anyone can make bold, grand pronouncements and promises. Living them out is another story.

Living out the commitments adults have made as leaders, and living them out close enough for students to see and "touch" that reality, is just what today's youth need. They are hungry to see God's truth in action as mature adults apply Scripture to their lives. Young people will see that when they see believing adults "up close and personal"—as *friends*. Relational ministry is incarnational ministry, an authentic model of the Christian life. As it was with Jesus' ministry, so will it be with youth ministry—relationships will make all the difference.

WHAT IS RELATIONAL MINISTRY?

Before going any further, a misconception should be put to rest—*building relationships is not merely a means to an end.* In other words, a leader should not get to know students and become friends with them *simply* to build a communication bridge that can be used to initiate evangelism. Yes, communicating the life-changing message of Christ and helping students mature in the faith are our goals, but leaders must not play with relationships, using them as only a means to an end.

Students need to know that if they never accept Christ as Savior or become leaders in the youth group, they can still be our friends. Building an authentic relational ministry requires being genuine and honest, accepting and loving students for who they are and not for what they do or how they respond.

Leaders should not expect to have a deep friendship with every young person with whom they come in contact. Some students will remain at the *acquaintance* level; some will be *casual* friends with whom we can carry on a conversation about school, activities, family, and peers; others will move *deeper and closer,* getting to know us quite well; a few will become *very close.*

The long-term impact of relationships at these various levels may surprise you. Recently a young adult wrote:

> You probably don't remember me because I didn't come to Campus Life when I was in high school. But I used to see you at my school all the time and knew what you stood for, and that made an impression on me. I was impressed that you cared enough about us kids to keep coming to the school. In college I became a Christian, and one of the reasons was your example. Thanks.

That young man and I had the *lightest* of relationships— we weren't even at the "acquaintance" level—yet my relationship-building efforts had made an impact on his life. Of course we want to move deeper with kids, but God can use us at every relationship level—all are valuable.

HOW DOES ONE BECOME A RELATIONAL MINISTER?

The answer to this question is simple: just be a friend to kids. What does it take to be a friend? Think of a best friend —what did it take to begin and develop that relationship? That same process and those same qualities apply to relationships with students in the youth ministry context.

Friendships begin when people spend time with each other. Often a common interest or activity brings them together.

Crises or special events will also bond two individuals together. Many years ago, my wife, Gail, drove four hours through a snowstorm to be at the side of a friend who was suffering a miscarriage. From that moment on, they have been extremely close (I have the phone bills to prove it!). Friendships grow and deepen through shared experiences and mutual respect. Friends find themselves enjoying simply being with each other. They have fun together, often laughing, singing, celebrating, and feasting together. A person will drop everything and rush to a friend in need. And good friends are loyal—they are our cheerleaders.

Come to think of it, this description of friendship sounds a lot like Paul's description of love in God's Word:

> Love is patient. Love is kind. Love isn't jealous. It doesn't sing its own praises. It isn't arrogant. It isn't rude. It doesn't think about itself. It isn't irritable. It doesn't keep track of wrongs. It isn't happy when injustice is done, but it is happy with the truth. Love never stops being patient, never stops believing, never stops hoping, never gives up. (1 Corinthians 13:4–7, PARAPHRASE)

Relationships Take Time

There are no shortcuts to building close friendships. In this day of E-mail, drive-through fast-food restaurants, and media sound-bites, it is tempting to think that there is a fast way to do everything. That simply is not true with relationships. They take time—both to establish and to build.

The need for time is especially true when two people have very little in common, such as an adult and a teenager. A normal, relatively mature adult will have as his closest friends men and women of his same age group—co-workers, people at church, college buddies, neighbors, and so forth. Most adults do not have teenage friends with whom they hang out. And most adolescents find their friendships among their peers at school, in the neighborhood, or on the team. So adults will have to commit to spending time with kids—it will not "just happen."

Relationships require time spent in their world.

When someone asked a famous thief why he robbed banks, he answered, "Because that's where the money is!" In the same way, to build relationships with kids, adults have to go where they are: on campus during and after school, at school events, at teenage hangouts, where they work.

The most obvious of these locations is the local high school. Some campuses are open. You will have freedom to contact kids during lunch, between classes, and after school. Some campuses are closed. Except for official business or a school event, you will not be allowed on campus. Whatever the case, creative leaders can always find ways to get to know kids and to spend time with them.

In the Campus Life ministry, we were required to spend at least ten hours a week per school, on campus. Yet early in my ministry I found it easy to make excuses for not going there (I had office work to do, the campus was closed, I was too tired). In all my years as a youth worker and for the last seven as the parent of teenagers, I have seen *very few* church youth ministers on campus, even for school events. Leaders of the high school ministry team at my church spoke often about relational ministry, yet over the four years, not one person on that team came to a single volleyball game to watch my daughter play.

Talk is cheap; excuses come easy. You will have to make time in your busy schedule to be with kids. Remember, Jesus didn't tell His disciples to wait, put up posters, or hold meetings and then hope people would come. He told them to *go!* So be prepared to go—that's what relational ministry is all about.

Relationships require time spent on their schedule.

Meeting and building must occur when the students are available, not just when the leader has time. If school gets out at three o'clock, leaders should attempt to schedule being available at that time. If the soccer games are played during the time the youth minister usually prepares for Sunday youth meetings, preparation times should be changed. If a student

STUDENT BILL OF RIGHTS
—Current Law Regarding Religion in the Public Schools—

STUDENT PRAYERS

Students have a right to pray or to discuss their religious views with their peers, as long as they are not disruptive.

TEACHING RELIGION

It's fine to teach the history of religion, comparative religion, the Bible as literature, or religion in history. Any genuine scientific evidence for any explanation of life may be taught in a science class. Religious critiques or beliefs unverifiable by scientific methodology may be taught in social studies class.

RELIGIOUS ACTIVITY

Teachers may not engage in religious activities in their official capacities. But they can engage in private religious activity in faculty lounges.

STUDENT ASSIGNMENTS

Students may express their religious beliefs in reports, homework, and artwork. Teachers may not reject such submissions just because of a religious theme or symbol.

PERSUASION VS. HARASSMENT

Students have the right to speak to, and try to persuade, their peers about religious topics. They have the right to invite their peers to church. But harassment is something like a repeated invitation in the face of a request to stop—and that's not permitted.

CLASS DISCUSSION

Religious or antireligious remarks made in the course of classroom discussion are permissible and constitutionally protected. But teachers may disallow religious remarks that are irrelevant to the subject at hand.

RELIGIOUS LITERATURE

Students have the right to distribute religious literature, subject to the same restrictions placed on the distribution of any other non-school literature. Outsiders may not distribute religious or antireligious literature in school.

SEE YOU AT THE POLE

Students may participate in before and after school events such as "See you at the pole" prayer times.

EQUAL ACCESS ACT

Student religious clubs in secondary schools must be permitted to meet and to have equal access to campus media to announce their meetings if a school permits any student non-curricular club to meet during nonclass time.

RELIGIOUS HOLIDAYS

Public schools may teach about (but not observe) religious holidays and may celebrate secular aspects of that holiday.

EXCUSAL FROM LESSONS

Schools generally must excuse individual students from lessons that are objectionable to that student or their parents on the basis of their religion.

GRADUATION PRAYER

School officials cannot mandate or organize prayer at graduation. They can't organize a religious baccalaureate ceremony. But if the school rents its facilities to others, it must rent them to private sponsors of a religious baccalaureate. The issue of student-led graduation prayers is still unresolved.

TEACHING VALUES

Schools may teach civic virtues like honesty, citizenship, sportsmanship, courage, respect, etc. Just because most religions also hold these values doesn't make it unlawful to teach them in school.

STUDENT DRESS

Religious messages on T-shirts cannot be singled out for suppression. Students may wear religious attire such as yarmulkes and head scarves.

RELEASED TIME

Schools can dismiss students for off-premises religious instruction. But outsiders cannot teach religion on campus during the school day.

Used by permission of the Christian Legal Society. This is a summary of "Religion in the Public Schools: A Joint Statement of Current Law." The complete text of this document may be purchased for $3.00 from Christian Legal Society, 4208 Evergreen Lane, Suite 222, Annandale, VA 22003–3264.

goes to the hospital, drop the "important" committee meeting and go directly to be there for her and her parents.

Unfortunately, some youth ministers think they can plan the times and places for relating to young people (on Sundays during Sunday school and youth group, at special events, on trips). However, one cannot schedule quality time with teenagers the same way one schedules staff meetings or planning committee meetings. Relational ministry requires going to kids where they are, being there when it is convenient for *them.*

Relationships Take Effort

Relational ministry is not easy; in fact, meeting with kids on their turf can be threatening. (Walking into a crowded high school cafeteria can feel like walking into a party you haven't been invited to—you think everyone's looking at you and wondering who you are and why you are there.) The truth is, it may require hard work. Leaders must be persistent in their attempts to get to know certain kids, to gain their trust, and to build friendships with them.

In addition to persistence, leaders will need creativity, especially when dealing with busy kids, closed campuses, and suspicious parents. On one high school campus that was closed to outsiders, a youth minister scheduled a series of appointments with the school newspaper editor, the yearbook editor, the athletic director, the choir director, a counselor or two, the student council sponsor, the student council president—at least one appointment a week for the whole year. Each time, he showed up early so he could be in the halls with all the kids during the passing period. During the appointment, he introduced himself and his ministry and then spent time finding out all he could about the person he was meeting with and his or her organization. He also asked how he could help the person and his or her work in the school. Afterward, he took the long, slow way out of the school in order to be on campus as long as possible.

Teachers, counselors, coaches, and club sponsors always need willing helpers, and most youth workers have areas of expertise they can share (experience with and knowledge of music, art, drama, athletics, sports medicine, journalism, dance, debate, computer science, and on and on). One youth worker picked up towels after basketball practice and another held the down markers at football games. One of my staff members became the official photographer for the football team; another one chaperoned trips with the ski club; one energetic youth leader became a cheerleader sponsor; I know several youth ministers who served as assistant coaches.

The point is this: Regardless of the situation at the high schools, *leaders can get on campus*. It will require creativity and effort, but it can be done. Furthermore, it *must* be done.

STEPS TO FOLLOW IN BUILDING A RELATIONAL MINISTRY

Broken down into the simplest terms, there are three steps in building relationships with kids. These steps apply to contacting and getting to know kids for the first time as well as for building relationships with the students you already know.

1. Be Seen

The first step is simple but imperative. Any relationship begins with being seen, and, as has already been mentioned, with young people this means being seen *in their world*. Regardless of what happens beyond this first step, the leader's presence in the halls, at the games, backstage after the performances, at the bus stop, and in the hangouts will speak volumes. There are a number of critical components in the process of establishing a presence in the midst of an adolescent world.

Pray. Every time a leader goes to be with students, she should pray. Leaders need to be asking God to help them keep their focus on Him and on their mission. This will stand in contrast to the leader who is continually keeping a focus on herself. Leaders also should be in dialogue with the Holy Spirit, asking Him to direct them to the students who should be contacted today.

Be strategic. Think about the most strategic settings for being seen. Look for opportunities to be where most of the kids will be gathering (in the halls between classes, at an all-school assembly or pep rally, at the big game). Then, do not hide—make a point of being seen, walking in front of the stands during halftime, mingling with the crowd during the intermission, standing in line at the refreshment stand.

Other strategic places for being seen include athletic, drama, and music practices and at events where parents are usually the only spectators. Leaders are rarely seen by the masses, but those who do see them are impressed and thankful that they took the time to come. Such strategic visitations provide an opportunity after the cross-country meet to congratulate John on a great race and maybe even meet his mom or dad. After the play practice, a conversation can be initiated as to why a particular student chose to be in this play and why she enjoys acting.

Be friendly. Greet people with a warm—not superficial or forced—"Hello." When the opportunity arises, strike up a casual conversation with an individual or a small group. While you watch a basketball practice, start a conversation with a couple of students who have also stopped by to watch. Ask about this year's team—the best players, the outlook for the season, who is the team's strongest opponent.

Look for clues for what to talk about. A girl carrying a chemistry book would be a good candidate for a discussion about chemistry (How does she like it? Why is she taking it? What is the teacher like?). A boy carrying an instrument case probably would talk about the band or orchestra, the school's music program, and what he wants to do with his music. Other clues include letter jackets, magazines, and the logos of popular music groups. Students are often eager to offer an opinion on the school, restaurant, auditorium, store, or location where you have encountered them.

Be yourself. Be casual and relaxed. Do not yield to the temptation to try to be someone or something you are not. Talk briefly, introduce yourself, and be sure to get the student's name. *Adults should never go into detail about themselves or their ministry program.* This first step—*be seen*—is light, so do not expect to have deep conversations. Also, remember that the goal is to form a friendship, not to recruit someone to a meeting.

Be disciplined. Work at remembering names. Intentional

efforts to remember a name and something distinctive about a person will be appreciated and will make a lasting impression that may lead to the reward of a new friendship.

2. Be Known

This next step goes beyond being seen. The focus now turns to leaders getting to know students and helping students get to know them. Learning about individual students, especially those from the youth group and those who seem most interested in building a friendship, can lead to meaningful conversations. Some leaders find it advantageous to keep a file, with an index card for each young person. On the card leaders note the person's interests, background, talents, and other relevant information.

Going to the games and performances of students is important for building relationships at this level. Next to calling a young person by name, this is the most effective way for an adult to demonstrate his or her interest in being a friend. This is especially true when adults attend events that usually have very few spectators: underclassmen athletic events, mu-

FRIENDSHIP AS COMMUNICATION
CHRISTINE COOK

One of the greatest challenges facing youth work in Switzerland today (as well as in the rest of Europe) is the need to develop a relational style of ministry. Traditionally, in the area of education as well as in the church, Europeans have not communicated relationally. In order to successfully complete their high school degree or to finish catechism and be confirmed in the church, young people had to learn a set curriculum and pass a certain number of required tests. There was very little contact outside the classroom or the church hall with teachers or pastors. The style of learning was very formal, with little or no dialogue between teacher and students.

In the last ten years or so, this style of communication has been proved to be much less effective than more personal ones. Young people are dropping out of school and church at an alarming rate. I mention education to show that the phenomenon of teenagers deserting the church is not only related to matters of faith, but is a general trend with young people today. The programs offered, either in school or in church, are no longer sufficient to maintain a young person's interest or participation.

Contact-Jeunes (contact to youth) is a relational outreach ministry to teenagers. We base almost everything we do on a friendship style of evangelism. By this we mean that young adults invest a fair amount of time getting involved in a teenager's life, not only to share the love of Christ with that young person, but to take an interest in everything that affects him or her, much as a friend would.

A high majority of the young people we in *Contact-Jeunes* are working with have had little or no contact with the church. What we are discovering is that we are able to communicate much more about God's love for these young people through the friendships we are establishing with them than through a formal teaching/learning situation.

Young people today need to experience friendship, care, interest, and love before they can relate to the fact that God cares for them, loves them, and is interested in them. The divorce rate in Geneva is one out of two; drugs, black magic, Satan worship, and pornography are a "normal" part of life in Geneva. The AIDS rate is higher in Switzerland than in any other country in Western Europe. It is no wonder that young people are having trouble believing in a God who cares for them and is interested in them.

The young people who come to a weekend or a camp we organize (usually invited by a friend we already know) are first of all taken aback by the friendship they are shown. We usually remember their first names. We are not put off by their aggressive behavior, bad language, or insecurity.

Recently a fourteen-year-old girl came to our summer day camp invited by a friend. Her Egyptian mother has not been able to take care of her since her father's death when the girl was eighteen months old. The girl is under the responsibility of the State of Geneva and lives in a home for girls. At our camp, she found an acceptance that she does not usually find. The men leaders appreciated her for who she was and not just for her cute body. At the end of the week when we talked about how Jesus treated women in his day (I used the story of the woman caught in adultery), she was really touched. She now wants to come to our meetings every week. If she had not first of all felt accepted by us, had several days of fun activity with us, and been able to start a relationship with us as her friends, I seriously do not think that the gospel story would have had the same impact on her life.

We communicated as much about Jesus' love by the way we treated her as by the telling of a gospel story. She could then relate the story of Jesus to her own experience. In that way, it took on a different and more real meaning for her.

sic recitals, honor society inductions, and so forth. After a concert, play, recital, or musical, leaders can go backstage and seek out the performers they know. Congratulating the participants and thanking them for the invitation are other ways to communicate individual interest. Likewise, a leader can clip out a newspaper article about a student's accomplishments and send the clipping with a note congratulating the student and offering the clipping to the family as a record of the event.

The most effective way to get closer and *be known* by students is through shared experiences. Leaders must look for ways to do things together, one-on-one or in small groups. Warning: adults must be sure to do this with members of the same sex or with a mixed group—leaders should not go one-on-one with a member of the opposite sex. Ideas for these activities include shooting baskets, going shopping, driving to an away game, taking in a movie, going out for pizza after a game, going to a concert, taking a study break, watching videos at someone's house, going to the beach, working on a project, planning a party for a friend, and much more.

The more time spent with a student, the more the friendship will grow and deepen. In the process, the student will get to know the adult better. The friends will learn to share likes and dislikes, goals and dreams, strengths and weaknesses, gifts and idiosyncrasies. They will, in the midst of this process, have a natural and personal means for discussing matters of the heart and the spirit, particularly in relationship to the gospel of Jesus Christ.

During these times and in such conversations, adults must respect students' individuality as well as their maturity. They should not stereotype them, condescend to them, or belittle them. Rather, adults should look students in the eye when they talk together, listen carefully to what they say, and let them know that, as a friend, there is an expectation of honesty. When the opportunity arises, adults can also communicate respect by asking the student for insight or assistance. Students typically respond enthusiastically when an adult values their input and help.

At this stage of relationship building it is appropriate to invite students to ministry events. In fact, leaders may even want to design an event with a particular group of new student friends in mind: a ski outing, a trip to a big mall in another city, a basketball marathon, a small group discussion. Again, as students become friends with adults, they will begin to learn about Christian values, priorities, and faith.

3. Be Understood

The last major step in relational ministry is the point where students understand who Jesus is and His claim on their lives. As adults spend the time it takes to get to know individual young people, the opportunity will arise to meet them at their point of personal need. The adult will become a source of encouragement, counsel, and support.

At this stage, however, just as with the other two, leaders should be prepared to take the initiative. If the right to be heard has truly been won, then the adult should look for opportunities to share Christ with the student. Ask for a time to get together—set up an appointment and take time to eat a meal together with the intention of discussing the student's life and his relationship with God.

Relational ministry at this level is not without difficult issues to be addressed. There may be times when an adult has to confront a student about his or her lifestyle. This will not be easy, but "speaking the truth in love" in the context of a meaningful relationship is a powerful gift to the student. Some youth workers who believe strongly in relational ministry are afraid to confront kids with the claims of Christ—or about anything else for that matter. They fear that they will jeopardize the relationship or will alienate the student and scare him away. Usually those fears are unfounded. If a true friendship exists, important, life-related matters are appropriate topics for discussion.

Another difficulty is that some young people are so needy that they will cling to and dominate a youth worker's life, if they possibly can. Such students need to understand where the line has been drawn: they are accepted, appreciated, and enjoyed, but the adult must honor personal and family commitments as well. Without attention to these commitments, the leader's life will begin to tumble like a row of dominoes.

RELATIONAL MINISTRY: GOD'S TOOL

The goal in youth ministry should be changed lives—watching God work to conform young people into the image of His Son through the Holy Spirit (Romans 8:29). Deep, life-changing ministry occurs in the context of loving relationships. No other method, technique, material, or program can take the place of relational ministry. It is biblical; it is responsible; it is effective. Relational ministry takes time and effort, but the rewards are eternal.

FOR FURTHER READING

Christie, Les. 1994. *How to Work with Rude, Obnoxious, and Apathetic Kids*. Wheaton, Ill.: Victor.

Robbins, Duffy. 1990. *The Ministry of Nurture*. Grand Rapids: Zondervan.

Simone, Mark A. 1993. *Ministering to Kids Who Don't Fit*. Denver: Accent.

St. Clair, Barry, and Keith Naylor. 1993. *Penetrating the Campus*. Wheaton, Ill.: Scripture Press.

Veerman, David. 1988. *Youth Evangelism*. Wheaton, Ill.: Scripture Press.

_____. 1995. *Reaching Kids Before High School*. Wheaton, Ill.: Scripture Press.

Ward, Pete. 1995. *Relational Youthwork*. Oxford: Lynx.

11

WHAT IS THE STATUS OF PROFESSIONAL YOUTH MINISTRY?

Mark A. Lamport

Kevin is entering his third decade as a youth pastor. He describes his current youth ministry as the most challenging and most rewarding thus far. Kevin has found "life after lock-ins" to include meaningful peer relationships with parents and significant mentoring relationships with lay staff members.

✝ ✝ ✝

After five years of effective youth ministry in a local church setting, Aaron begins his seminary education. He chooses a Master of Arts in Youth Ministry because he has committed his life to youth ministry. His denomination has encouraged him to pursue this degree with the hope that he will reinvest his education in the lives of succeeding generations of youth ministers.

✝ ✝ ✝

Mark serves his parachurch missions agency as a youth ministry leader in Europe. Having completed his doctorate, he also serves as a teacher in the local seminary. His seasoned longevity in this place has led to opportunities he could never have even imagined in his earlier years of youth ministry. Far from being an "outsider" who "comes over" to do missions, Mark and his family know they can only be home when they are with these people.

✝ ✝ ✝

Youth ministry has come of age. The long-term call to youth ministry is being taken seriously by churches, seminaries, and mission agencies.

Unfortunately, this has not always been so. In previous decades, those who worked with adolescents in the church were often viewed with lower regard than those who served in "real" (pastoral) ministry. A career in youth ministry was seen as a pre-professional position rather than a legitimate occupation—hence the term *stepping-stone ministry*. The job was thought of as including little more than organizing fun and games and sprinkling in a little Christian moralizing. Some thought youth ministry could be administered with only a modicum of common sense and an animated disposition. It was thought of as not worthy of serious study or long-lasting commitment.

Today the image of youth ministry and youth ministers has moved far beyond the limited perception of past generations. One of the long-time advocates of the profession of youth ministries, Tony Campolo (1988, 21), has summarized this dramatic change:

> When I entered youth work some 30 years ago, it was assumed that working with young people was for seminary students until they were graduated and got churches of their own. . . . Now, however, youth ministry is perceived as a lifetime vocation rather than an early stage in budding clergymen and women.

SIGNS OF READINESS
FOR YOUTH MINISTRY
MARK A. LAMPORT

Rate yourself on the following signs of readiness for youth ministry. Assess which areas you need work on for increased proficiency. I believe these are basic requirements to enter the profession.

1 = low to 10 = high

_____ 1. Senses a personal calling.

_____ 2. Is able to articulate a biblical philosophy of youth ministry.

_____ 3. Demonstrates an ongoing relationship with God.

_____ 4. Shows competence in handling Scripture.

_____ 5. Knows basic counseling and referral skills.

_____ 6. Effectively communicates the faith to teenagers.

_____ 7. Can administer people and program resources.

_____ 8. Understands adolescence and youth culture.

_____ 9. Deals capably with adult leaders and parents of youth.

_____ 10. Exhibits both creativity and critical thinking skills.

_____ 11. Understands the history and mission of the church.

_____ 12. Can evaluate curriculum.

_____ 13. Is able to work within (and around) organizational structures.

_____ 14. Has and instills vision.

_____ 15. Is a person of integrity.

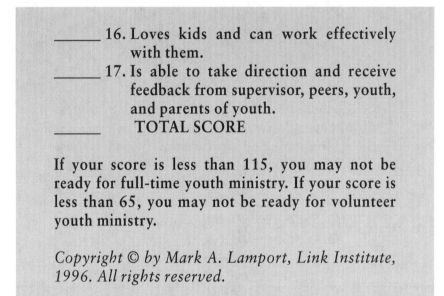

_____ 16. Loves kids and can work effectively with them.

_____ 17. Is able to take direction and receive feedback from supervisor, peers, youth, and parents of youth.

_____   TOTAL SCORE

If your score is less than 115, you may not be ready for full-time youth ministry. If your score is less than 65, you may not be ready for volunteer youth ministry.

Copyright © by Mark A. Lamport, Link Institute, 1996. All rights reserved.

The profession of youth ministry has indeed emerged as a long-term, viable vocational option for service in the kingdom of Jesus Christ. Literally thousands of full-time opportunities in local churches and parachurch organizations exist. Over three dozen colleges in the United States currently offer a formal degree in youth ministries. Most of these programs have emerged in the last decade. A myriad regional and national training conferences and organizations give vision to the youth ministry enterprise.

THE CALL TO YOUTH MINISTRY

Insiders in the field of youth ministry have always taken their calling seriously. Dedicated youth ministry leaders have long felt that being in ministry with youth was the most significant responsibility and most wonderful privilege a Christian leader could possess. These men and women recognize that whether they are volunteers or full-time ministers, the sheer potential inherent in the task they face is monumental. Ecclesiastes 12:1 exhorts all to "remember your Creator in the days of your youth, before the days of trouble come." Two of three people who become Christian do so *before the age of eighteen.* The investment made in reaching and nurturing children and youth in the Christian faith will pay significant dividends for the future of the church.

A Definition of Youth Minister

What does it mean to be called to be a youth minister? A youth minister is one who is committed to

> the purposive, determined and persistent quest by both natural and supernatural means to expose, transmit or otherwise share with adolescents God's message of good news which is central to the Christian faith. Its ultimate end is to cultivate a life transformation of youth by the power of the Holy Spirit that they might be conformed to the revealed will of God as expressed in scripture, and chiefly in the person of our Lord and Savior, Jesus Christ. (Lamport 1996, 62).

The Significance of Calling

Research seems to indicate that a clear and certain call is the preeminent reason people give for remaining in their youth ministry jobs (Roehlkepartain 1988). In response to the question "Why do you continue in your ministry?" youth ministers cited God's call (76 percent), the ability to reach youth (66 percent), good relationships with youth (56 percent), feeling needed (37 percent), and self-fulfillment (32 percent).

Without the confidence of this all-important "call by God," youth ministers are more likely to change professions within ministry or even leave the ministerial profession. One of the most discouraging realities of the profession is the startling dropout rate for this career. Some estimates indicate an average ministry of less than five years and the swift change from one youth ministry position to another, some youth ministers staying as short as two years in a given location.

Anyone who wants to be a professional youth minister must evaluate his or her motivations for pursuing that career. If the person is thinking of going into youth ministry simply to prolong adolescence, or to "finally be popular," or to meet parents' expectations, or to gain experience until becoming a "real" minister, frustration and failure is bound to come, and the youth worker may even put youth at risk.

People who plan on being professionals in youth ministry need to ask themselves the following questions:

1. Why am I doing this? What motives do I have for becoming a youth minister? How do I know God has in some way called me?
2. What do my parents and other family members say? What are my spiritual gifts and natural abilities? Can my family see a fit between me and this profession?
3. How do mature Christian friends respond? Do they advise me to pursue this calling?
4. What do my previous ministry experiences suggest concerning my call to ministry? In what ways do these experiences affirm or call into question the appropriateness of my giftedness for youth ministry?
5. What do the leaders in my church say? Will they recognize my ministry calling and formally support this move?

THE COMMITMENT TO YOUTH MINISTRY

Smith (1995, 21) says: "Youth work is more passion than profession." Anyone who will be effective in youth ministry must be relentlessly and passionately committed to two things: youth and youth ministry.

Commitment to Youth

Picture a home engulfed in flames. A crowd stands by helplessly, in awe of the tenacity of the heat and its swift destruction. Some are constrained to observe from afar. They may be sympathetic toward those trapped inside, but they cannot bring themselves to help. Others are more daring. Their boldness, compassion, and willingness motivates them to rescue those inside. Youth ministers are in business with God as "life-rescuers." They must have this kind of commitment to be effective ministers with youth.

John 10:10 teaches: "The thief comes only to steal and kill and destroy; I came that [you] might have life, and have it abundantly" (NASB). The seductive (but patently false) propositions offered to our youth by the world compel us to vigorously labor in telling the truth. Youth ministers are called to

UNDERSTANDING
YOUR SENIOR PASTOR
WILLIAM H. (BILL) STEWART

Youth ministry workers look for an encouraging, warm, stable place in which to do their work. With this expectation, the youth pastor may see the senior pastor as a father or grandfather figure who provides the church and its staff with the hoped-for or anticipated security. The pastor, in the meantime, is normally looking for help. Each has his own agenda. They are both looking for someone to minister to or for them.

Some pastors reject the image of a "father figure." Paul did not (see 1 Corinthians 4:14–17). Why would a pastor reject his father role? He may be tired. He may not want another kid. He may be pressed or pressured by his own driven nature. He may be more interested in what the youth worker will do to enhance the church's ministry and thereby his own image. He might not consider ministry as beginning with his own staff before ministry to the church. He might assume that a person in a staff position is an adult and relatively self-sufficient.

Jesus said, "Whoever wants to become great among you must be your servant . . . just as the Son of Man did not come to be served, but to serve, and to give his life as a ransom for many" (Matthew 20:26, 28).

The senior pastor's age and stage development factor will help shape ministry expectations. We understand from Daniel Levinson's work that men in our culture can be expected to face predictable issues at various stages of their lives. The thirties are the time to climb the ladder in establishing family, professional life, education, and the church.

Where does church staff fit in? Said one pastor, "Staff? I pay them to be successful."

When the forties come on, a pastor is trying to decide if he likes the ministry, this church, or even himself. With sermon preparation, books to write or at least read, and more professional recognition, a busy life is the rule of the day. Youth ministry may be less central in mind and ministry as his own progeny are out of high school and soon out of the home.

Now the big five-O knocks on the door. The fifties are showdown or slowdown for some. If you work with a pastor who does not pace himself well, look carefully to yourself. If, in the mid- or late fifties, retirement becomes your pastor's focus, there will be a different feel to the picture and ministry. I had the good fortune to work with two different men of this age who did not even consider retirement.

The sixties may mellow a staff pastor or cause one to become a grouch of the first degree. The public patriarch, loving bear of a man, may be more godly with age or he may be more political, sneaky, and difficult. Survival skills may develop an ungodly side of the man. "Not many great men of God finish well," said one observer.

The bottom line is, besides looking for how he can be your mentor or father figure, you will need to minister to your pastor. Look for how you will help him develop his godliness and keep his perspective. If you fear him, then fear will destroy your relationship.

combat this "thief" and propagate Jesus' message of authentic, rich, and extravagant life.

The shortest and perhaps one of the most profound verses in the Bible is John 11:35: "Jesus wept." He expressed this tender emotion not simply because of the loss of His friend Lazarus. (Jesus had already said He would raise him from the dead.) His emotional expression came from His sharing the pain of those surrounding Him—persons grieving over a death and in need of life themselves. Jesus yearned for them to know the Father's love and the life He was making available to them in the Son. Jesus said earlier in this chapter, "I am the resurrection and the life. He who believes in me will live, even though he dies; and whoever lives and believes in me will never die. Do you believe this?" (vv. 25–26).

Youth ministers must be certain of their call, deeply committed to serving youth, and firmly committed to the profession of youth ministry.

Commitment to Youth Ministry

In the foreword to *The Youth Leader's Sourcebook* (Dausey 1983, 9), Jay Kesler contends:

> Most people don't take church youth work seriously. When they would ask me what I did and I would tell them I was a youth worker, they would often say, "What do you plan to do when you grow older?" or "Have you ever thought of going into the ministry?" Over the years I began to counter with, "I am in youth work just like the president of the state university is in youth work, or the principal of the high school, or the superintendent of schools, or the math teacher." The reason these people are respected is because they take their work seriously.

One should not enter this profession unadvisedly, but once called and determined, one should not turn back too hastily. Perhaps if candidates knew more about themselves and occupational realities, the high turnover rate would be diminished. Literature on career selection can be summarized as an ongoing process involving five variables or influences (Lawson 1994, 3).

KEYS TO LONG-TERM MINISTRY
LARRY LINDQUIST

From my days in public education, I recall the value of gaining *tenure*. The credibility and security it brought made the effort worthwhile. Although there may not officially be a process of tenure offered in ministry, credibility, security, and effectiveness come conceptually with long-term ministry. Listed below are six practical tools in establishing tenure in your ministry.

T *Training.* Although many ministers do a fine job without going to college or seminary, those training environments provide a purging process. Not only will you receive valuable preparation for ministry through the years you invest in a degree, but it is also true that only those with a firm conviction of their call to ministry will persevere through the training process.

E *Establish a clean reputation.* I have observed some in ministry who seemed fully equipped for long-term ministry fall morally. Beyond just maintaining a pure lifestyle, those who wish to continue in long-term ministry must not let "even a hint of sexual immorality" be spoken of them (Ephesians 5:3). Don't be alone in counseling the opposite sex. Have windows on your office door. Make it laughable when others would accuse you of immorality.

N *Nurture relationships with others.* Remember that ministry is people, not program. Discipline and programming will be more effective when you have nurtured relationships with those you lead. Beyond that, you need good friendships. Even the Lone Ranger needed a Tonto.

U *Untangle your life.* Don't try to be your predecessor or meet all the expectations of everyone. You will fail at both. God has given you abilities to minister to those in your care. Discover those gifts and center on them. Surround yourself with individuals who are gifted in areas you are not.

R *Reserve time for yourself and your family.* Make it clear that you need time away from ministry. Long-term ministry, as with long-distance runners, is a matter of pace. Take a day off regularly. You need to respire! Burnout is a rookie mistake.

E *Evaluate yourself and your ministry regularly.* Journal your ministry experience. Set personal goals and ministry goals, and take time each year to review them.

- "Personality characteristics and ego development of the individual" (for example, abilities, strengths, weaknesses, personality style). Candidates for youth ministry should not be lulled into thinking that there is one stereotypical personality model most suitable for the job. Various kinds of youth need various kinds of adults.
- "Societal norms concerning life transitions" (for example, beginning a job, moving to management, retirement). Some might get the idea that people beyond thirty years of age should not continue in youth ministry. This view is changing. A growing number of role models are forty, fifty, even sixty years old—persons committed to youth for the long haul.
- "Job context and content factors that result in job satisfaction or dis-satisfaction" (for example, work conditions, salary, level of autonomy, organizational culture). Because of the emerging nature of full-time youth ministry positions, too little regarding job description and compensation issues is standard. Be aware of the tenuous climate in the marketplace.

- "Broader societal influences affecting job availability and status" (for example, national economy, desirable vocations). Pressure may be exerted your way at various points in your career path to consider more prestigious or lucrative occupational choices. Remember your calling.
- "Unique influences of sustained relationships with others" (for example, mentors, work relationships, personal contacts, family support). Relationships in youth ministry are a double-edged sword: They bring great joy but their intensity can drain the youth minister to the point of exhaustion.

A commitment to the profession of youth ministry is critical. Ministry is not like other professions; it is a holy calling based on spiritual giftedness. The most frequently used Greek and Latin words for ministry (*diakonia* and *ministerium*) are rooted in the notion of service. To minister is to serve. Yet the ministerial office carries with it the temptation to power. "The idea that ministry is set apart does not imply that it is

A CAREER, NOT A STEPPING-STONE
KEN GARLAND

Not too many years ago, students graduating from Christian colleges and seminaries viewed a local church youth ministry as an interim position, a ministry to be endured while preparing oneself for a "higher calling" to Christian education pastor, associate pastor, or even senior pastor of a church. Today the scene has changed considerably. More and more students graduating from Christian colleges and seminaries are viewing youth ministry as a career choice. These students seek to prepare themselves to serve the church in a professional way as a youth minister, committing themselves to a career of ten years or longer.

In light of that, more and more Christian colleges and seminaries are developing curricula to give professional training to the student who desires such a career. In the fall of 1994, a group of twenty-six professors of youth ministry met for two days in La Mirada, California, to identify competencies and qualifications that should be present in a man or woman who desires to be a professional youth minister. The group met for the second year in Chicago in October 1995, and more than forty professors participated in the two-day discussions.

Looking at another aspect of increased length of service, churches seeking youth ministers are increasingly asking for people who will make a commitment of more than just a year or two. Churches are realizing that even a highly qualified youth minister may be well into his or her third year at a church before starting to have a significant ministry to a youth group. One characteristic of effective, stable youth ministry programs nationally is that in almost all cases they are led by youth ministers who have been at their churches for longer than five years.

An indication of the increased longevity of individuals currently involved in the profession of youth ministry could be found at the 1995 Christian Ministries Training Association Convention in Pasadena, California. Twenty-five youth ministry professionals taught more than forty workshops. The average tenure in youth ministry of those twenty-five youth ministers was more than eleven years. Two of the workshop leaders had been involved in professional youth ministry for more than twenty years! More and more, people involved professionally in youth ministry are in it for the long haul.

designated for honor, but rather for service, for representative caring, for authentically proclaiming the good news" (Oden 1987, 87).

Above all, you are a person of God. Unlike being a lawyer or a physician, being a youth minister is primarily a calling rather than a position aspired to and gained simply through learned skills. Youth ministers above all need to know Jesus. What other competencies are nonnegotiable?

THE COMPETENCIES OF THE YOUTH MINISTER

In *The Rainmaker* (1995, 20), best-selling legal novelist John Grisham describes neophyte lawyer Rudy Baylor's thoughts on his training in the law:

> Law school is nothing but three years of wasted stress. We spend countless hours digging for information we'll never need. We are bombarded with lectures that are instantly forgotten. We memorize cases and statutes which will be reversed and amended tomorrow. If I'd spend fifty hours a week for the past three years training under a good lawyer, then I would be a good lawyer. Instead I'm a nervous third-year student afraid of the simplest of legal problems and terrified of my impending bar exam.

Have you wondered if receiving formal education course work in youth ministry and related areas is necessary for a career? Rudy Baylor seems to have resented the impracticality of being trained in a classroom apart from hands-on experience in actually practicing the law. I know a number of very effective youth ministers who do not have a degree in youth ministry. However, my recommendation is to spend a significant time in a Christian college or seminary preparing for the profession of youth minister and also to volunteer to help at a local church or in a parachurch setting. The insights of your professors and fellow students, coupled with the classroom reading assignments and extensive practical experience, will make for a solid foundation that will increase your chances of success in the profession.

Recently one of my former youth ministry students wrote to me wondering aloud if his role as full-time youth minister

FOOTBALL PLAYERS AND BRICK MASONS
MARK H. SENTER III

Can the youth ministry profession validly be compared to that of medicine or the law? Or can it be compared to education, a profession that has struggled for identity over the years? My contention is that it can be compared to neither. Although youth ministry looks like an "in the office" profession, the specific training it requires looks more like that for two other callings we do not associate with offices—football and brick masonry.

Jay Kesler, the former president of Youth for Christ USA, was the first person I heard draw the parallel between youth ministers and football players. Some football players last only a few years on the professional level and do not even qualify for an NFL pension after they retire. These players then go on with their lives using their college major, life skills, and personal contacts to develop a second career, which may or may not be related to football. A majority of youth ministry professionals follows this pattern. They minister to young people during college and/or seminary, continue for a few years after graduation, and then go into other professions—the pastorate, Christian education, real estate, teaching public school.

A second group of football players are more successful (like the Chicago Bears offensive linemen) and continue their careers for eight to ten years before hanging up the pads. A few superstars and specialists (field goal kickers) may continue for as many as fifteen years or more before retiring from their playing careers. Most of these then leave football behind and start a second career, but for some this second career is closely related to the sport—coaching, broadcasting, selling athletic equipment, or even marketing or managing NFL products. Parallels in youth ministry might be working for a teen-oriented publishing house, directing a camp, or teaching youth ministry on the college or seminary level.

A third set of football players continues to play for extended periods of time. These are the George Blandas of the world, who continue their active playing careers over four decades. They are a rare breed but survive as a result of their ability to adapt and provide services necessary to the team. Yet these too eventually retire and find life after their playing days are over. Bill Stewart, Bill Eakin, Sonny Salsbury, and a handful of others fit into this category.

The educational parallels between football and youth ministry are interesting. Both find their initial instruction in the informal sector. Football is learned on playgrounds, in neighborhood activities, in clubs, and eventually in leagues coached by volunteers from the community. Only when one gets into high school is football formalized by training camps (double sessions) and "classes" (chalkboard sessions). Finally, the college football player may begin taking classes for academic credit. Formal training is slow in coming and is only supplementary to what happens on the practice field and on game day. I would contend that the profession of youth ministry is learned through a similar process.

In the second profession I would use as an analogy, brick masonry, in order to become a card-carrying brick mason, the young laborer must go through an educational process, but not in the traditional educational institutions. Actually, the process is much older than seminaries and Bible colleges, for it finds its roots in the medieval guild system. In that system, young tradesmen progressed through a sequence of educational experiences, beginning as apprentices, then becoming journeymen, and finally emerging as master craftsmen.

Today, effective youth ministers are more likely to have come up through an apprentice-type system (similar to masons) than through an internship system after formal education (similar to doctors). The reality of the current youth ministry profession is that formal education, whether at the college or seminary level, is supplementary to the hands-on (apprentice-like) experience youth ministry professionals gain in the churches and parachurch agencies of the land. Formal education is not the primary basis of preparation.

was really necessary considering the very competent volunteers in his church. I wrote back to him:

Great to hear things are going well at the church. You may remember me saying in class that "the wise youth minister will try to work himself or herself out of a job" by effectively training others to take more and more ministry responsibilities (Ephesians 4:11–17). It sounds like you have set up tremendous programs based on a strong theoretical understanding of ministry principles. You say, "I sometimes wonder if the church pouring time and money into a youth ministry is really worth it." I say, "It is," because they cannot do the things you have done. Yes, they can do great ministry, but they do not have the background that normally comes from a formal study of youth ministry principles that informs one how to develop the programs and philosophy you have set up.

In *Eight Habits of an Effective Youth Worker* Tim Smith says:

There are principles for effective youth ministry. These are to be contrasted with practices which are culturally, demographically or situationally specific. . . . Principles differ from practices because they are proven, fundamental truths that have universal application. . . . Our goal is to study the habits of effective youth workers and personally integrate timeless truths into our thinking. (Smith 1995, 15)

Smith's eight habits (or competencies) of effective youth workers are these: They should be lifelong learners, be service-oriented, radiate the positive power of the Holy Spirit, believe in others and their growth, lead balanced lives, see life as an adventure, be team players and synergistic, and be committed to personal renewal.

THE CHALLENGES OF YOUTH MINISTRY

The best days of youth ministry lie ahead. Yet even as much may change about what is considered effective youth ministry, we must constantly return to study the pattern of Jesus' ministry and extrapolate principles that govern our practices. Several important issues need to be faced in the profession at large and by youth ministers individually.

Contentment

The myth that greener grass exists elsewhere smacks too often of escapism. The semi-nomadic careers of some in youth ministry positions are not comforting. Discontentment in this profession may arise for a variety of reasons: apparent lack of tangible results, conditional support from constituents or supervising agents, unfulfilled expectations. One of the major reasons for job turmoil in youth ministry is conflict a youth minister has with his or her immediate supervisor. Yet conflict and difficulty do not automatically signal that the youth minister should move to another job. There will always be another supervisor, another irascible personality.

Continuity

Often the consequence of discontentment is an abbreviated stint in ministry. A steadfastness to remain, except in unusual circumstances, is a more desirous virtue. High turnover in youth ministers sometimes leads to confusion among and even hostility by the youth. They may infer that they are unworthy of the youth worker's time and blame themselves for his or her departure. By leaving early the youth worker will also not realize the fruits of longevity.

Listen to these words that should be heeded by youth ministers: "I have learned to be content whatever the circumstances. I know what it is to be in need, and I know what it is to have plenty. I have learned the secret of being content in any and every situation, whether well fed or hungry, whether living in plenty or in want" (Philippians 4:11–12). Paul speaks elsewhere and essentially says, "Stay put and bloom where you are planted" (1 Corinthians 7:17, PARAPHRASE).

Compensation

Some gifted, called, and committed youth ministers are forced out because of lack of financial support. These men and women must take other jobs to support their families because of inadequate compensation. I commiserate. One of the leading deterrents people have to beginning a career in youth ministry is the fear of not making enough money to care for the essential needs of their families.

Yes, I am aware that some youth ministers are provided for fairly and generously. I have friends in youth ministry who drive late-model cars, wear fashionable clothing, go on summer vacations, and send their children to college. I am also aware of the other side. Leaders of churches and parachurch organizations need to evaluate the pay they give youth ministers in light of the apostle Paul's admonition: "The elders who direct the affairs of the church well are worthy of double honor, especially those whose work is preaching and teaching. For the Scripture says, 'Do not muzzle the ox while it is treading out the grain,' and 'The worker deserves his wages'" (1 Timothy 5:17–18).

Continuing Education

Many professions have discovered the value of an ongoing personal and professional development plan. The investment in time and money is well worth the effort in the long run.

TOO BUSY:
REFLECTIONS OF A PERSON GOING MAD
WITH THE BUSY ADDICTION
CHUCK NEDER

Too busy. Schedules to meet, planes to catch, bills to pay, people to be with, ball games to watch, phone calls to make. Life takes and takes, and the more it wants the more it takes—until I find myself functioning as a machine. Nike says it best: I "Just Do It!"

Too busy to stop. To smell the roses. To enjoy a sky full of stars. To notice little eyes that look to me longing for time with Daddy. To notice hands across the bed that reach out to be held.

Too busy to spend time with my Lord. To pray with my wife. To tuck in my children. To call my friend. To thank the many who help me. I am a busy person with so many important things to do. Do I know or do I care that my busy life destroys relationships, kills the dreams of my spouse, discourages and alienates my children?

I protest to anyone who says, "Slow down, you are sucking the life out of all who love you." *They* are to blame. Don't my kids know my busy schedule doesn't have time for them? Doesn't my wife understand that my wedding vows are less important than my busy schedule? Haven't they got it? I never see them because I'm working for Him and for them. Don't my friends know I can't just hang out? I am too busy. The answers to these questions would be nice, but I am too busy to take the time to find them.

Unexpectedly my busy life is *attacked*. My sister dies. My friend finds out she has cancer. My child needs me and I don't know how to be with him. I wake up wondering if I have any friends, realizing my best friend long ago gave up on me. I'm lonely and alienated, yes, but still busy. Busy covering the pain a life-out-of-control brings. But I will tell you a secret: The healings I need will never be found by a busy schedule that cushions my denial and need for control. On the contrary, it is in stillness and quiet, not busyness, that God makes Himself known.

My choices are to run from the pain or embrace the pain, owning the destruction my life has caused, allowing my denial to be cracked and exchange my busy life for a life at peace. To learn to walk in the woods, enjoy a sunset, embrace silence and not run from the thoughts and fears that attack when the pace slows and the Lord begins to do His surgery. To allow silence and solitude to be my companions and the Word to be my guide is my quest.

I will go to my Father's home and say, "I have sinned against . . ." and hear Him and those who love me say, "Welcome back into our lives; we have missed you."

By God's grace I will never fall into the busy trap *again*.

What good will it be for a man if he gains the whole world, yet forfeits his soul?

Even after a solid undergraduate education in youth ministry, many want to become more informed and pursue some form of continuing education. This may be a formal graduate degree program (for example, in youth ministries or educational ministries or biblical studies or counseling) or an informal individualized program of reading and study. One study reports that youth ministry graduates would advise their college and seminary departments to offer "more supervised field work and direct experience in ministry; teach how to work with volunteers; courses in leadership; how to deal with local church and denominational conflict and politics; multiple-staff ministry" (Lawson 1994, 37–38).

Summary

Youth ministry has matured into a well-respected profession with solid scholarship behind it. Youth ministry has come of age, yet it remains to be seen what it can become as this generation of professional leadership emerges. For the full potential of the field of youth ministry to be realized, leaders must continue to be men and women who are sure of their calling, faithful in their commitments, and increasing in their competencies.

WORKS CITED

Campolo, T. 1988. "How Youth Ministry Is Maturing." *Youthworker* (spring).

Grisham, J. 1995. *The Rainmaker.* New York: Doubleday.

Kesler, Jay. 1983. Foreword to *The Youth Leader's Source Book,* edited by G. Dausey. Grand Rapids: Zondervan.

Lamport, M. 1996. "What Is Youth Ministry?" *Christian Education Journal* 16, no. 3 (spring): 61–70.

Lawson, K. 1994. *Educational Ministry Staff: Perspectives on Vocational Ministry.* An occasional paper funded by the North American Professors of Christian Education and Cook Communication Ministries (June).

Oden, T. 1987. *Becoming a Minister.* Vol. 1. Classical Pastoral Care Series. Grand Rapids: Baker.

Roehlkepartain, E., ed. 1988. *Youth Ministry Resource Book.* Loveland, Colo.: Group.

Smith, T. 1995. *Eight Habits of an Effective Youth Worker.* Wheaton, Ill.: Victor.

12

HOW CAN WE FIND
AND SUPPORT
VOLUNTEERS?

Barry St. Clair

A revolving door. That was the best way Clyde could describe the volunteers who ducked in and out of his youth ministry.

The pattern seemed the same with each new worker. The recruit would begin with enthusiasm and optimism but within six months would be lucky to show up even for major activities. Next it was "out the door," and the leader would be gone.

"Why did you quit?" Clyde asked Polly after she had been AWOL for several weeks. "I have to do the ministry whether you show up or not. I really need you."

"That's the problem," responded Polly in measured tones. "*You* do the ministry whether I show up or not. It is *your* ministry. Somehow I don't seem to fit in."

✝ ✝ ✝

I admit it. I still get the rush of success when young people pack out my meetings. But in defining success I keep coming back to a man who often avoided the crowds in preference to a small group of potential leaders He called His disciples. Jesus loved the multitudes, but He knew His long-term ministry would be accomplished through training key leaders. We would do well to follow Christ's example.

THE VALUE OF VOLUNTEERS

They round out an otherwise lopsided ministry. Perhaps youth ministry is more a field of service—a calling—rather than a gift. Some youth pastors have, for example, the gift of teaching. They employ this gift in their God-given ministry field—youth ministry. But many other gifts, such as mercy, administration, helps, and exhortation are needed to lead a successful youth ministry. No youth minister has all the gifts. In order to take the theology of the body of Christ seriously (Romans 12; 1 Corinthians 12; Ephesians 4; 1 Peter 4), we must staff volunteers to complement our weaknesses.

Someone has said that a church can be compared to a football game—twenty-two athletes on the field desperately in need of rest being cheered on (or booed) by ten thousand people in the stands desperately in need of exercise. The model for biblical ministry should be like the credits run at the end of a movie that cite scores of workers of various kinds: scriptwriters, director, actors, grips, caterers, all doing their part to produce an excellent product. A good question to ask ourselves regularly: "If I ran the credits after this week of ministry, how full would the screen be?"

Youth ministry flows through relationships. Jim Burns states, "today we realize that long-term influence with lasting results comes from significant relationships and role models" (Burns 1988, 15). Although our love for youth and ability to relate to them probably influenced our decision to go into youth ministry, we can significantly relate to only a small group of young people. We may never relate well to certain youth, or even an entire subculture of youth. If indeed youth are primarily changed through relationships, we must multiply our ministry through godly volunteers who also love youth. Then we will find our greatest joy in seeing our volunteers successfully ministering to youth.

A broad ministry can only stand on a broad foundation of volunteers. The minister who shoulders the entire responsibility for teaching, evangelism, administration, and counseling will end up either burned out or severely limited, or perhaps both. We need help. But we also need camaraderie, accountability, and vision.

One youth pastor led an unusually successful ministry. According to one volunteer, search committees called almost daily, urging him to join their teams. "What's his secret?" someone asked the volunteer. "Love your volunteers," she said. "Sometimes we have almost as many adults as youth on trips."

First Things First: The Life of the Leader

"Love your volunteers." We might have expected her to answer, "He loves youth." I'm sure he did, or he would have never gone into youth ministry. But at some point his heart went out to those volunteers who shared his heart for young people.

This youth minister didn't *use* volunteers to accomplish his goals and expand his ego. He sincerely *loved* them, wanting to see his volunteers blossom in their ministries.

To exhibit the kind of life that a volunteer would want to follow, the leader must walk with Jesus and draw security from Him. Then the leader can take delight in young people bypassing him or her to lift up a volunteer as their most significant spiritual influence.

One volunteer is pursuing early retirement to spend more time doing volunteer work for his church's youth ministry. "What makes your youth minister so successful?" someone asked the volunteer. "Is he a powerful teacher?" Answer: "Boring." "Then he must be a great administrator?" Answer: "Others administrate for him." How did he lead the largest youth group in his area so ably? The committed volunteer proceeded to describe an incident where the youth pastor spontaneously prayed with a group of distressed youth and adults. The youth leader loved God and loved people. His character evoked the best from his volunteers, bestowing upon him that elusive quality of leadership that made others want to follow.

TYPES OF VOLUNTEERS

Different types of volunteers require different qualifications and training.

Those who will provide spiritual leadership correspond most closely to the twelve disciples during the life of Christ or to the elders in the New Testament church (Mark 3:13–15; 1 Timothy 3; Titus 1). The qualifications include having a good reputation and self-control, being above reproach and gentle, and having the ability to communicate with and relate to youth. Speaking skills alone are not enough. In order to fill the roles of teacher or discipleship leader, volunteers must exhibit strong character and be adequately trained. It is better to shut down a certain ministry than to shove an unqualified warm body into such slots. "Not many of you should presume to be teachers," James warns us, "because you know that we who teach will be judged more strictly" (James 3:1).

Those who will provide services correspond most closely to others besides the disciples who accompanied Jesus and to the deacons in the New Testament church (Acts 6; 1 Timothy 3:8–13). These invaluable volunteers keep records, organize retreats, set up rooming charts, and lead the decorations committee. Although their qualifications are nearly as stringent, their training is less extensive and more specialized.

Don't forget that youth can be volunteers! Tony Campolo well said that if we lose this generation of youth, it will not be because we have challenged them too much, but because we have challenged them too little. One youth minister recruited some intellectually inclined middle school students as research assistants for a book he wrote for a major publisher. He never told the publisher that several of his research assistants were ninth graders!

An active student council or student leadership team can provide a structure through which youth serve. Their leadership is invaluable in evaluating events and planning. Some churches elect youth council members by presenting the qualifications of deacons to the entire youth group and adult leaders and then having them vote by secret ballot to elect peers who qualify.

Outside the leadership team, students can assist in leading worship, planning events, assisting in research for messages, decorating classes, planning parties, doing outreach. If youth simply attend meetings planned for them by the youth minister, they may never discern their own gifts and provide church leadership for the next generation. When youth are involved in leadership, they sense ownership of a ministry and push hard to make it succeed.

FINDING VOLUNTEERS

Pray. Jesus set the example by spending a whole night in prayer before choosing His disciples (Luke 6:12). On another occasion, He challenged His disciples to pray for laborers (Matthew 9:38).

Keep a list of potential volunteers. Ask youth for their ideas. Then, when approaching adults about a position, you can let them know, much to their delight, that some youth recommended them. Also, ask other adult leaders, including church staff and parents, for recommendations.

Keep the congregation abreast of youth activities. The congregation needs to know that God is alive among the youth! This makes more people eager to be a part of what God is doing.

Invite new volunteers to fill short-term, helping roles. Check them out before placing them in long-term, teaching roles. An attentive observer can learn a lot from watching new staff chaperon a retreat. Do they love youth? Are they comfortable with who they are, or are they trying to perform for the young people's acceptance? Are they here to serve, or to be served? Do they draw students closer to Christ?

If they are faithful in a little, they can be trusted with more (Luke 16:10). Give a potential teacher an assistant's role. As the volunteer meets weekly with a small group of youth, occasionally substituting and assisting with the teaching, and shepherding under a teacher's supervision, both you and the volunteer will discover whether or not teaching youth is his forte. Much better for you to discover this when the volunteer is still an assistant than when he or she is four months into a teaching position!

Get to know them and observe their character. Ask around about their reputation (1 Timothy 3:10), particularly leaning on the input of other church staff. We should ask ourselves, "Is this the kind of person I want my students to become?" (Luke 6:40).

If all signs are go, provide them with short-term and ongoing training.

PREVENTING ABUSE

Unfortunately, people who have a tendency to abuse young people entrusted to their care will be attracted to active youth ministries. They would be easy to detect if they conformed to the stereotype of a shifty-eyed pervert in an oversized trench coat. Instead, like Satan himself, they appear as angels of light.

Even if a volunteer is asked a direct question about abusive activities in the past, if he wishes to hide those sins he will simply lie about them. Some abusers are merely sick people who are actively looking for venues in which to exploit vulnerable young people. Others think they have overcome the sins of their past and are desperately looking for a new beginning. In rare cases, a volunteer may have completely blocked out the memory of abusive activity.

BALANCING BEING A MOM, WIFE, AND YOUTH LEADER
HELEN MUSICK

It is a great struggle being a mom, wife, and youth ministry leader. Juggling time, energy, and devotion can be a struggle. It can be difficult because teens want all of your devotion, but your own kids also need you. I feel torn between leaving my family and working with teens. I have learned to move from entering the teens' world to incorporating them into mine. I allow the teens to come into my family and spend time with me. The girls, especially, see how I relate to my family and see how a Christian family can operate. This is my first suggestion for balancing all three.

Second, my husband is not in the ministry. This allows me to express my own self as an individual and develop my own gifts. The time I spend in ministry allows my husband time alone with the kids, which is also very valuable. My husband completely supports me in ministry and sends me with his blessing.

The transition from your being single to being married can be hard for the kids. You now have someone else to spend time with. Whether or not he is also in the same ministry will also affect this transition. In this scenario you are seen as the big sister. With each transition comes age and experience.

The transition from being married to being married with a child was difficult for my ministry. The kids were excited about my being a mom, but they were also jealous. My baby took the attention off them. Teens need to understand the transition. Let them experience the joy of the baby also. Be sensitive to this transition. Talk about it. In this scenario, you are looked at as the mother figure.

Remember with each transition what is important overall. God needs to be first, husband second, children third, and ministry fourth. Make sure that the church leadership also understands your many roles. Being the best wife and mother you can will also help your ministry.

Adapted from interviews with Helen Musick and from *Breaking the Gender Barrier,* edited by Diane Elliot and Ginny Olson, Chariot Victor Publishing, copyright 1995. Used by permission of Chariot Victor Publishing.

Steps must be taken to protect both the young person and the at-risk volunteer. The following steps would be a start.

Require written applications. Every volunteer should be asked to fill out an application form that includes a question about abusive activity. The question should focus on previous actions, not on accusations or actual convictions. The application may serve as a filter that allows vulnerable volunteers to avoid detection by withdrawing quietly and not following through with the process necessary to become involved as a youth leader.

Interview every volunteer. Whether the person wants to teach or merely to organize social events, the interview is essential. The volunteer should be pointedly asked: "Have you ever abused or molested a child or young person?" Though it may be uncomfortable at first for the interviewer to ask this question, it will become natural with use. Look the interviewee in the eye as the question is asked, and watch for any hints of deception.

Avoid using people new to the church. Certain abusers move from place to place, hoping their reputation will not catch up with them. After a year of involvement with the broader church fellowship, a person's reputation should be established. If the person has been a loner, be careful. Be sure to ask people whose judgment you trust for their impressions of the volunteer.

Network with other youth ministers. Make sure you have a forum with other youth ministry professionals for discussing the problems related to abuse. Social workers and educators are helpful in understanding local laws and resources. Their insights and perceptions may be invaluable.

Avoid letting volunteers be alone with young people. The current climate may have precluded one of the most important youth ministry tools, the warmth and confidence that come from private personal conversation. The youth worker must now work to create the same dynamics in more public locations. Remember, even Christ seldom placed Himself in one-on-one situations. When such situations are appropriate, the youth worker must be sure to notify someone else ahead of time.

QUALIFICATIONS OF VOLUNTEERS

We have mentioned the different types of qualifications needed for different types of responsibilities. In addition to these, look for the following for all positions.

Faithfulness

Do they carry out responsibilities as needed, or do they need constant prodding?

Availability

Some volunteers are eminently qualified but too busy to commit to training or ministry.

Teachability

Jesus' entourage was not eminently qualified when He called them. Not an M.Div. with vocational Christian service experience among them. But they were eminently teachable. Successful youth volunteers must constantly learn. This year's small group of athlete-dominated youth may respond very differently from last year's social-fringe youth.

Love of Young People

Walt wanted to teach Sunday school, but he had only a sixth-grade education. The superintendent said there was no place for him. Undaunted, he rounded up thirteen kids in the community and started his own class. He was not dynamic, but he was real. He loved the youth. He took them hiking and on other outings. Nine of the young people came from broken homes. But eleven went into vocational Christian service. One of them was Howard Hendricks, today one of the foremost Christian educators (Hendricks 1987, 21–22).

A Servant's Heart

A teacher should not be above cleaning tables, setting up chairs, or throwing away trash. Our master set the example by washing feet. He "did not come to be served, but to serve" (Matthew 20:28).

Notice what is distinctly lacking in these qualifications. First, outward appearance. Our culture idolizes the outward appearance. When a tall, handsome, athletic young man volunteered to teach a class of middle schoolers, one man said, "Students will have to respect him, for his very size if nothing else." But his class ran over him. He couldn't control the class.

In fact, in all my years of youth work I have found little correlation between outward appearance or athletic prowess and impact upon youth in a local setting. "Man looks at the outward appearance, but the Lord looks at the heart" (1 Samuel 16:7). The only exception to this may be in target-oriented ministries where, for example, a spiritual college athlete can reach a high school football team more effectively than the computer whiz. In this case, he can more easily "become all things to all men" (1 Corinthians 9:22), following the example of the apostle Paul.

Similarly, age neither qualifies nor disqualifies a person from youth work. Once youth get to know a good-natured, fun-loving senior adult, they may pick him or her for a chaperon over an emotionally distant college student.

THE TRAINING

Content

The type of training depends on the type of position we are filling. A Sunday school record keeper would not need the training of a discipleship leader. The list below includes some elements the youth minister can cover in a general volunteer training program.

Personal spiritual life

This has to do with the lordship of Christ, prayer, Bible study, church involvement, Christian character, and discovering one's spiritual gift. We are not simply grooming people to fill slots in our youth program. Rather, we are developing men and women of God, helping them find and develop their gifts, and finally helping them find their niche and succeed in ministry. If no pre-existing niche exists, these people may start new ministries that fit their gifts and visions (for example, ministry to unwed mothers, to delinquents, to intellectuals, to athletes). Volunteers don't exist to help fulfill our dreams. We equip them to fulfill their God-given dreams.

"BEEN THERE, SEEN IT, DONE IT, LIVED THROUGH IT" PEOPLE
DONALD G. FERRIS

Which of these looks like your youth ministry? Select one.

_____ You can't tell the difference between the staff and the kids.

_____ The staff's collection of sixties music isn't on CDs.

_____ You have more dating problems with your staff than your kids.

_____ The entire net worth of your youth staff is under $100.

Every youth ministry needs "been there, seen it, done it, lived through it" people on the staff. Older volunteers can bring rich and much needed spiritual depth, valuable life experience, and well-worn wisdom.

Mentoring younger staff,
providing mother/father figures for
    some students,
calming fearful parents, and
championing the ministry before the leader-
    ship of the church and the church at large
    are just a few of the things they bring.

*If you don't have volunteers
over thirty-five years of age in your ministry,
your ministry is shallower than you think.*

Most youth leaders would love to see the "older and wiser" generation involved on their team. The issue isn't one of desire. The challenge is one of recruitment. *How do I get someone so far removed from his or her own high school years involved with my kids?* you think.

Luckily, it's easy. You just have to change the way you think. Your kids and your programs need to become their opportunity rather than their mission field.

> *Key:*
> *At thirty-five years of age*
> *the question changes from*
> *"Where do I serve?"*
> *to*
> *"How do I fit?"*

If you keep in mind the following equation and how it works, you will never lack volunteers in the boomer generation.

> *Fit Equation:*
> *What the ministry can use*
> *+ What the volunteers want to do*
> *= God-breathed enthusiasm for*
> *your youth work.*

Give me a person who wants to do what I can use and I can develop a formula for success every time.

Phil wanted to get involved. He was a traveling trainer for an engineering firm. His passion was affecting people. He loved training. He loved outdoor adventure. He especially loved small groups. We designed a spot for him in our ministry—discipling a small group of boys and developing adventure experiences for our group.

MAKING IT HAPPEN

1. Have a plan. It is important that the youth leader knows enough about youth ministry and ministry direction to know what is needed. Be clear and specific. Don't be afraid to color outside the lines.

2. Interview properly. Have two interviews at least. Make sure that the first interview revolves around the question, "What do you enjoy doing?" References will give you valuable insights. The second interview should center on the person's fit.

3. Love and encourage them. Everyone needs to know he or she is doing well, even "been there, seen it, done it, lived through it" people. Let them know what you think. Tell them what the students are saying about them. Let them know where they can improve.

4. Contribute to their spiritual development. We have been told consistently by our staffers over the years that this is the single most important thing we have done for them. Many ministries fail to contribute to the lives of their workers. If you feel too young or over your head doing this with people older than you are, find someone who can make a contribution in this area of the ministry.

General ministry skills

This has to do with witnessing, teaching, leadership, follow-up, time management, and counseling. A survey asked people to list their greatest fears. The number one choice came as a surprise to many: Speaking in public. The most confident, energetic worker may wilt before an audience. Training can give such volunteers the confidence they need to prepare talks and group discussions.

The possession of the gift of teaching or the gift of evangelism does not preclude the need to develop that gift. Dan DeHaan led a Bible study group from a small home study to over one thousand people attending weekly. His powerful teaching was one of the main draws. But an early speech teacher once told DeHaan, "Whatever you do, don't go into public speaking!" Gifts must be developed.

Student skills

Skills in this area have to do with developing relationships, understanding youth, penetrating the student culture, and presenting Christ to students. We may be comfortable relating to youth, but we dare not forget that for many, the thought of picking up a phone and calling a youth is intimidating. The prospect of chaperoning a retreat can beget sheer terror! Volunteers must see youth as people who, like themselves, long for acceptance, love, and understanding. They also need to know certain dos and don'ts as they go cross-cultural with their faith. "Don't quote rock lyrics to those guys in the pick-up trucks. They can't relate."

Task-oriented skills

These are specialized skills for different ministries: leading the drama team, teaching a discipleship group, planning a retreat, leading small groups. For certain ministries, such as puppet or drama ministries, we can rent videos or use seminars to provide instruction and inspiration far beyond what we have to offer.

Methods

A "leadership family" composed of the leader and adult volunteers provides an ideal setting for training leadership. Volunteers commit themselves to attend meetings. Beyond covering training material, the spiritual accountability and relationships that develop will provide fertile soil for followers to grow into leaders. Although some leadership groups meet monthly or bimonthly, the ideal is usually weekly.

Meetings can include training, sharing, prayer, and evaluation of youth programs or recent events. And don't forget to plan for some fun! A game of softball, volleyball, or a potluck supper can go a long way toward building relationships. The informal atmosphere of a home is conducive to fostering friendships.

Try to spend personal time with volunteers. Let them know you care. Talk to them about their interests. Do something with each of them that they like to do. If you become interested in their world, they may become interested in yours. This caring not only develops a cohesive team but models what we want them to do with students.

Developing ministry skills requires the additional input of on-the-job training. This well-used process has yet to be improved upon:

1. I do it.
2. I do it; they watch.
3. I do it; they do it with me.
4. They do it; I watch.
5. They do it.

Materials

Without good materials, the leadership family meeting may become a lecture time. With something in their hands to prepare, the meeting can become a time of mutual sharing. Some leaders assign a book to be read. Others use training materials. Sometimes an expert on crisis counseling or teen suicide can lead the group. (For a detailed, step-by-step guide to training volunteer leaders in youth ministry, see St. Clair 1991.)

Continuing Education and Motivation

The leadership family group should continue to meet after the leaders are in positions. Volunteers will need this support group to share their victories and discouragements. Skills need fine-tuning. Volunteers also need our individual praise for jobs well done (Hebrews 10:24–25). They need us to give them the perspective of their part in the overall youth ministry and the kingdom of God. Sherri isn't just shepherding a group of giggly seventh graders; she is performing a vital role in impacting the world for Jesus Christ!

Take volunteers with you to youth worker training conferences. They can pick up the fire along with you and help you dream about the future.

Consider planning a volunteer staff retreat at least once a year. Use the time to plan, pray, reflect, recreate, and build relationships.

WARNINGS

1. Beware of training only one or two people. If one or two are all you have, train them. But remember that the group dynamic can make training more meaningful and effective. Also, expect attrition. People move, spiritually fail (think Judas), or get recruited for other ministries.

2. Don't wait until positions are needed before seeking and training volunteers. It's easy to come to the end of the ministry year and desperately need three small group or Sunday school leaders and then frantically look for people to fill slots, rather than placing trained people in ministries suited to their gifts.

3. Be careful about recruiting teachers through mass appeals. Some may respond out of the wrong motives, such as the desire for acceptance, the desire to impress, or a sense of pity for the poor youth class with no teacher. Our local high schools would never resort to such begging ("Willing Teachers Needed. No Qualifications Necessary!") to fill an open slot for a biology teacher. Is a study of God's Word less important?

4. Make job descriptions clear. Some volunteers fear being put in a perpetual teacher's position. A job description calling for a one-year commitment can alleviate those fears. Time limits can also make terminating a teacher less traumatic. It's easier to allow someone "to complete a term of service" than to "fire a teacher."

Put the descriptions in writing. Without a job description, volunteers may never know if they are failing or succeeding. When you recruit, let volunteers know exactly what is expected of the position. If you want Sunday school teachers who can minister as well as teach, include such requirements as these:

1. Contacts students during the week by phone.
2. Plans at least four class activities during the year.
3. Knows and prays for specific student needs.
4. Writes regular notes of encouragement to students.

5. *Don't always expect visible success.* One executive in a major corporation made a decision that cost his company thousands, perhaps millions of dollars. He faced his superiors expecting to be fired. "Are you kidding?" they exclaimed. "We just spent a million dollars training you!" In order to insulate ourselves against failure, we sometimes stifle creativity and risk taking, two essential ingredients in the growth of a ministry. Look at the success/failure rate of Jesus' disciples, and don't be so harsh with your volunteers.

6. *Prepare for rejection.* Some people are too busy to work with youth. Be glad that they know their commitments well enough to avoid overcommitment. Others will drift away spiritually, even after you have invested years of love and training in them. Don't be discouraged!

7. *Don't overprogram, especially in your first year.* By starting more programs than you can staff with qualified leaders, you set yourself up for failure. Better to start with a few programs and give yourself time to invest in your leaders.

ISSUES IN VOLUNTEER WORK

The Best Place for Parents to Serve

Where can parents best volunteer? Some would argue against extensive parental involvement on the following grounds:

1. Their presence can inhibit the independent spiritual growth of their children.
2. Sometimes a conflict of authority develops when parents allow their children to do things on retreats (skip a session to go out to eat, for example) that have been forbidden by the youth worker.
3. College students are closer to the age of teens and can thus relate to them better.

EMPOWERING YOUR VOLUNTEERS
JANA L. SUNDENE

I'll never forget the first volunteer I supervised. Her name was Lisa and she only stayed around for a few months—largely because of my inability to empower her. She had been running the ministry for several months in the absence of an "official" staff person, but when I came in I decided that I (the expert) should take over. After all, she was just a "volunteer"! So, I proceeded to gently push her toward the background while I stepped in. In the process I learned everything you ever wanted to know about how to *de*power a volunteer.

My mistakes with Lisa remind me of an unfortunate experience I had recently. As I was driving to work, the left front wheel of my car shot dramatically across the road in front of me, causing the car to skid perilously on its axle toward the grassy shoulder. The problem? I had had some work done on the brakes, and the lug nuts for one of the wheels were not properly tightened, so off went my wheel! As a result, my car was rendered undrivable. I think our volunteers are like those lug nuts. Sure, we may be the "big wheel" of the ministry, but if our volunteers are not properly attended to, we may end up with a ministry that is in many ways skidding to an unhealthy halt.

Our volunteers are one of the moving forces behind what enables a ministry to meet the students at their points of need. If we truly understand that our volunteer staff is one of the most important keys to ministry effectiveness, then we will be motivated to empower them. Too often, through neglect or ignorance we depower the people who have the potential to bring the most energy and care to our ministry. Carefully consider the following ways to empower your most important helpers—volunteers. How are you doing?

1. *Respect and value their unique contribution.* What does this volunteer bring to the ministry? How can I provide opportunities for him to share that gift or skill with the students? We must put to death our tendency to want to shine brighter than those around us, find ways to express appreciation for others' strengths, and give them a chance to shine too.

2. *Entrust them with roles of importance and meaning.* Don't limit your volunteers to being your gofor or tell them that just hanging around the students is all they need to do. Help them to find a meaningful place in the vision and purpose of the ministry. Assist them in understanding the importance of their role to the students and to the vision of the ministry.

3. *Be concerned about their spiritual health.* Spiritual ministry will only occur as spiritually growing people interact with students. This means that knowing about and encouraging the spiritual lives of your volunteers needs to be a priority. Do your staff meetings only cover information? Do your conversations only focus on finding out what is happening in the lives of the students they are working with? Make sure that you are personally interested in the spiritual lives of your staff as well.

4. *Facilitate their connection to one another* (thus helping them to establish a support network). Try as we might, we cannot fully understand the frustrations, challenges, and joys of being a volunteer. Even if we have "been there," they may still perceive us on a different level just because we do this for our "job." I've found it is essential to help provide opportunities for volun-

teers to connect with each other to commiserate, problem-solve, and encourage each other in the trenches of ministry.

5. *Equip them with the skills they need to effectively minister to youth.* This is an obvious but important area. We must never expect more of our volunteers than we are willing to train them in. Invest some time here, and you will be amazed at how much more confident and effective your volunteers become.

Fans of parental involvement try to offset the problems just described by emphasizing the following benefits:

1. They often understand youth culture well, having viewed it through their children's friendship clusters.
2. They often have many contacts with unchurched youth through school and other venues.
3. They often want to chaperon and are willing to put in some effort for all you do for their children.
4. They are often great friends to other youth and can pick up valuable insights on emerging problems or opportunities in the group that the youth minister would be the last to discern.
5. Their presence on trips assures other parents that their children will be well-chaperoned.

Terminating Ineffective Leaders

How can we terminate (ask for the resignation of) ineffective leaders? First, try to help the leader succeed. He or she may simply need clarification of the job description or may need additional training.

Moral failure requires a one-on-one confrontation, in a spirit of love (Galatians 6:1). Certain sins, such as sexual immorality, may disqualify the person from a teaching position (1 Timothy 3:2–7). Such terminations must be done respectfully, with love, and in consultation with the leadership of the church or organization. But don't lose contact with the person or give up on him. The purpose of all our dealings with such volunteers is to see their complete restoration.

If it becomes apparent that a faithful volunteer is working outside his or her area of giftedness, help the volunteer to find another niche in the ministry. Faithful workers will be relieved to be free from a frustrating ministry, and eager to find a more effective way to serve.

CONCLUSION

If Clyde, our friendly do-it-all youth pastor, is to survive and have an effective ministry, he will have to learn the words *we* and *our*. Just as mom needs the help and support of dad (and vice versa), if she is to be an effective parent, so youth pastors need to be complemented by volunteer workers. Although some single parents do an outstanding job of being both mom and dad, the norm God designed is for cooperation in the parenting task. Clyde may be a "single parent," but the chances are he would be far more effective "married" to some volunteers.

WORKS CITED

Burns, Jim. 1988. *The Youth Builder.* Eugene, Oreg.: Harvest House.

Hendricks, Howard. 1987. *Teaching to Change Lives.* Portland, Oreg.: Multnomah.

St. Clair, Barry. 1991. *Building Leaders for Strategic Youth Ministry.* Wheaton, Ill.: Victor.

FOR FURTHER READING

Christie, Les. 1987. *Unsung Heroes: How to Recruit and Train Volunteer Youth Workers.* Grand Rapids: Zondervan.

Coleman, Robert. 1964. *The Master Plan of Evangelism.* Old Tappan, N. J.: Revell.

Ilsley, Paul J. 1990. *Enhancing the Volunteer Experience.* San Francisco: Jossey-Bass.

Johnson, Douglas W. 1978. *The Care and Feeding of Volunteers*. Nashville: Abingdon.

McGinnis, A. 1985. *Bringing Out the Best in People*. Minneapolis: Augsburg.

Senter, Mark. 1990. *Recruiting Volunteers in the Church*. Wheaton, Ill.: Victor.

Stone, J. David, and Rose Mary Miller. 1985. *Volunteer Youth Workers*. Loveland, Colo.: Group.

Wilson, Marlene. 1983. *How to Mobilize Church Volunteers*. Minneapolis: Augsburg.

13

WHAT ARE THE ISSUES WOMEN FACE IN YOUTH MINISTRY?

Diane Elliot

In the field of youth ministry all men—and women—are not created equal. You can blame it on theology or on an ancient patriarchal system. Blame it on opposing biblical interpretations of women in Christian leadership or on traditionalism and stereotypes. Or better yet, maybe it's time we stop blaming and take a hard look at the issue and become part of a healing solution that can break down gender barriers so that all of us can get on with the business of influencing students for Christ.

Instead of adding theological fuel to either side of the burning debate, in this chapter we are going to start by making the assumption that women *are* in youth ministry and that women are *needed* in youth ministry. The current trend in youth ministry is diversity of leadership, and women are emerging as a key component. With this in mind, it is the purpose of the chapter to give a glimpse of the realities women face as they investigate youth ministry as a career option; to assist veteran women in identifying and overcoming the obstacles they now face, or might; to encourage all women to be as active as they can within their own theological persuasions; and last, to challenge men to understand and encourage the women with whom they serve.

My journey in youth ministry started over ten years ago; during the last seven I served as a full-time volunteer in both parachurch and church settings. I fell into youth ministry at first. Someone asked if I would teach a Sunday school class, and without too much thought I said, "Sure!"

I don't actually know when the "call" came. I just knew it felt right for me to be working with kids. After a few years I started getting more serious about my ministry and being a student of my students. Somewhere, with the joy of serving mixed in with the challenges, I realized that this was where God wanted me all along. However, especially in recent years, I have questioned God's call on my life. Although many of the challenges I have encountered are common to most youth workers, one of the most constant and debilitating struggles I have come up against is the one thing I have no power to change, my gender.

CURRENT CONDITION OF
WOMEN IN YOUTH MINISTRY

1. Women are in the minority. If you have been in ministry any length of time you know that women are in the minority. You only have to look as far as the next youth ministry conference brochure that passes over your desk to see that the majority of speakers are men. *Group* magazine states that 33 percent of youth workers are women (Schutz 1991, 6). *Youthworker* journal estimates that 10 percent of their readers are women (Rice 1990, 3). However, a survey by *Journey Publications,* a membership organization for the leadership development of women in youth ministry, found that in the Chicago metropolitan area there are more women in youth ministry (professional and volunteer roles) than men. If this is reflective of a nationwide norm, it is ironic that most training events, conferences, and publications are produced by men, for a target audience of men.

In fact, in the mid-eighties, 14 percent of *Youthworker* journal contributors were women. In the last two years, almost ten years later, only 18 percent of its contributors were women. At that rate we should reach some semblance of gender equity around 2035. Unfortunately, if that is the case I won't be around to celebrate.

2. Few resources are available that specifically target women in youth ministry. Over the last fifteen years *Youthworker* journal has published one article about women in youth ministry approximately every five years, with the winter 1990 journal being dedicated to the entire issue. *Group* magazine, on the other hand, has had even fewer articles about women, but more female contributors on a regular basis.

It is understandable, then, that a 1992 survey found that 93 percent of the women in youth ministry surveyed felt that current youth ministry literature did not adequately address the issues that women struggle with.

3. Youth ministry is slow to change—but it is changing. Over the last ten years there has been little change regarding the issues that women face. The only minor change is that there has been a little less anger or frustration in the more recent articles. The majority of the articles, however, still center around finding a woman's "place" in youth ministry and developing ways to gracefully overcome the obstacles. Even the assumption that there needs to be a "place" or a specific "role" for women rather than accepting women wherever they are needed or called to is a concept that needs to be eliminated.

Although there is little likelihood of the pendulum swinging to the extreme of complete acceptance, there does seem to be greater openness to women's involvement in ministry in the last decade of the century. In 1992 "eighty-four Christian denominations ordain[ed] women, leaving approximately eighty-two that still do not. . . . Over 21,000 ordained women now serve in these churches. Analysis of Christian seminaries show that between 1977 and 1987, the number of women graduating with Master of Divinity degrees increased 224 percent, while the number of male recipients rose only 4.6 percent. Presently, over 30 percent of all seminary students are women: a dramatic increase from 1972 when women accounted for only 10.2 percent" (Burrei 1992).

4. *Women are still walking a fine line.* While the feminist movement has had controversial effects on our culture, the debate itself has created a simultaneous awareness and fear of women's ministry involvements in the evangelical community.

> Some conservative Christians have reacted so strongly against the movement that they have created a backlash. Possibilities once open to women (assisting in worship leadership or directing educational programs involving men) have now closed. This in unfortunate. Feminism is a diverse and multi-faceted movement that includes many Christians in it and that should not be totally rejected by Christians. (Hestenes 1990, 26)

In spite of the calmer seas we are now experiencing, many of us are still feeling the adverse reaction to the tidal wave of militant feminism that slammed our culture in the 1970s. Unfortunately, recent memory influences the way women are often perceived. A woman in leadership who openly verbalizes her passionate and strong convictions may still be misinterpreted as overbearing and ungodly. So what does a woman need to do to communicate her convictions and yet be clear in her honorable intentions?

> As women, we are to be aware of times when we are being treated differently because we are women, but we are still to remain gentle and Christ-like (Note I said Christ-like, not passive.) If we are constantly demanding our rights, we will be greeted with closed doors and cold shoulders. If we are always ready to fight with our fist up, others will follow suit and we will accomplish little for the kingdom of God. (Eckman, 2)

5. *Tearing down the walls.* Maybe it is naive to imagine, but my hope is that someday gender will not be an issue in youth ministry. As opposed to a "woman in youth work," it is

my dream to be just a "youth worker," judged solely on my spiritual commitment to Christ, my giftedness, education, and skills. The challenge for the future of youth ministry is to continue tearing down the walls of gender separation. We can best work toward that end by understanding the challenges that women face in youth ministry, exploring the opportunities, and preparing ourselves to go the distance.

CHALLENGES OF WOMEN
IN YOUTH LEADERSHIP

Theology

One of the first challenges women face in youth ministry is their understanding of Scripture regarding female leadership. I struggled with this issue for several years before I finally found a comfortable place of understanding. In fact, in addition to personal study, it took an in-depth seminary course dealing with the issue that finally challenged me and eventually led me to the place where I currently reside. For both men and women it is important to wrestle with this issue until each person comes to a comfortable place, confident in the resulting interpretation of Scripture.

One thing to be aware of, however, is that many of us do not grapple with the issue enough. Many people neglect the hard work of personal study and blindly adopt the views of others. I heard one woman say, "I don't care what the elders decide the role of women should be in the church, I just want them to decide, then I'll just do whatever they say is acceptable." This laissez-faire attitude is unfortunate and yet all too common. What we must not forget is that each *individual* is personally held responsible before God for her theological beliefs. There is no substitute for personally doing the work of theological investigation.

What happens if you do the work of studying the Scripture and find that you are not in a place where you can minister to the fullest extent that you feel called and theologically empowered? That's a tough question, but one I have heard often. Depending on the situation, it might be best for you—and all concerned—to submit to the leadership's interpretation of Scripture and remain in your current position. However, sometimes individuals feel that by doing so they will be going against their specific call to ministry, or they feel frustrated in not being able to use all their gifts. In those cases, perhaps it would be better for the women to move to another position where they can feel more comfortable and more fulfilled in ministry.

Although I was raised in a conservative evangelical background, at one point I felt that I was being stifled in the church where my husband, David, and I attended. After working through the issue with David and talking with the elders, we decided that it would be best for us to move to a church where I was freer to use my gifts and abilities.

The reality is that I have struggled with the gender issue all of my life. I didn't realize how ingrained the challenge was for me until recently. While on a job interview with a denominational organization, I was surprised by the question, "Now, you should know that we fully accept women as active leaders in this denomination. Is that a problem for you?" At first I though he was joking! A problem? For half of my life I have been waiting to hear those words, but they still shocked me. Although I was thinking, *Of course it's not a problem. A gift, absolutely! A problem, never.* But the words that came out of my mouth were something profound like, "I . . . I . . . don't think so."

Stereotypes and Tradition

Youth ministry has traditionally been considered a male-dominated field. Ironically, according to Mark Senter, the parachurch club concept of youth ministry was originated in 1933 by a woman, Mrs. Evelyn McClusky, with the Miracle Book Club (Senter 1992, 74). During the decades following, however, it was primarily adventurous young men who responded to the call, creating the stereotype that the typical youth worker is a suburban, white, twenty-seven-ish married male. With the stereotype came the hangin'-with-the-guys informal networking and male pronoun vocabulary that is still dominant in youth ministry arenas.

Recently, I attended a youth leadership breakfast. I was one of about eight women in a group of about fifty people. I had no problem with that. That ratio is about the norm. However, when a seminary youth ministry professor got up and gave a motivational pep talk to the "guys" about being *men* of God, and encouraged them to not neglect their wives at the expense of ministry, I must admit, I was a little put out. As a grown woman and a longtime follower of Jesus Christ, I understand that he meant me, too. But as a *daughter* of Christ, I have become tired of being called a *son*. I am frustrated when in a mixed audience I am referred to as a "man," or when all the illustrations are examples of men. When I am in a forgiving mood I can write it off as verbal laziness. Other times, each *he* pounds in my ears, taking a whack at my self-esteem. I am not a *he*. And I do not want to be forced to translate the *he* word every time I hear it.

Realizing that the topic of gender-appropriate language is dangerously close to that fine line of feminism discussed earlier, I believe the topic is important enough to the future of youth ministry that it needs to be addressed, if not for the women currently in youth ministry, for the girls with whom we minister. As one author states, "Inclusive language seeks to enhance communication by removing the roadblocks of sexism, racism, 'age-ism,' and 'handicap-ism' from our speech. Far from being mere linguistic gymnastics, our use of language fundamentally impacts the way we view and deal with our world" (Nielsen 1990, 48).

Admittedly, I have often thought that perhaps God did make a mistake when He created me, a woman, with the giftedness of a pastor. I have conservative roots, and had been raised to accept that pastors—youth or otherwise—were supposed to be men; that the *sons* of God had unlimited potential for Christian service, whereas the *daughters* had limited opportunities. No, of course that's not what the leaders said, but nonetheless that was the impression subtly communicated to me. So, as a woman, the questions then became, Where does that put me? Is there any place for me in ministry other than in the kitchen, with young children, or serving other women? Where do I fit in? My hunch is that multitudes of women have asked the same question.

What do we do to dispel the stereotype? I believe that current leaders in youth ministry today need to be proactive in their acceptance of all diversity, including gender diversity. Regardless of gender, age, or ethnicity, a variety of individuals are needed to reach the diverse student populations we encounter. Practically speaking, this means we need to be deliberate in our efforts to help women develop their leadership gifts and the more visible gifts of speaking and teaching. (The good news is that there are women with these gifts out there.) Another positive step Christian leaders can take is to affirm their female staff by using gender-inclusive language. Some may not think this issue warrants deliberate efforts, but women will notice and appreciate the effort.

Discouragement

Battle fatigue is one of the most difficult obstacles to overcome. Youth ministry by nature is a high-energy, low-refueling field. However, with the added gender obstacles women face, the burdens can often seem overwhelming. In *Breaking the Gender Barrier in Youth Ministry* one author eloquently sums up the issue of discouragement.

> One of the most puzzling barriers we face is the reaction to our ministry of those closest to us. It's puzzling because we hope and even expect that those who surround us will be supportive of our choice to be in youth ministry. It's discouraging to have well-meaning friends, family members, church members, and even senior pastors question the validity of our being in ministry. These people can be subtle—not asking any questions about our ministry, hoping if they ignore it long enough, it will go away. They can also be blatant, sometimes to the point of being cruel—cutting off communication with us because they disagree with ministry as a career choice. These people can question our being in ministry because of a theological disagreement ("women shouldn't be in leadership in ministry") or because they don't think youth ministry is a valid career. (Olson 1995, 105–6)

I have found that it is especially important for women to carefully guard their hearts. No amount of anger or bitterness will speed the progress of women in youth ministry. In fact,

YOUTH MINISTRY:
COMING IN OR GOING OUT
CHRISTIE STONECIPHER CISTOLA

There are many reasons that a woman may choose to enter youth ministry. Regardless of how a woman describes her calling, biblically and/or personally she should be able to answer these questions:

1. How has God led you in the past?
2. How do you understand the Scriptures to be speaking to you in your choices and directions now? Are the biblical norms and principles clear or at least focused enough for you to begin?
3. What counsel have you received from your parents, elders, and peers? Are you affirmed, or do you find resistance? How would the youth you have ministered to respond to your desire?
4. Are you realistic about what lies ahead? Can you anticipate, in part, where you will be strong and where you will fail? How will you face those situations?

Do women leave youth ministry? Yes, and you too might leave. Therefore, as you contemplate entering youth ministry, be aware of what might lead you out of the field. Here are some of the factors that might provoke you to such a decision:

1. A heart for primary or secondary youth work changes: you do not want to focus your ministry on youth any longer.
2. Economics, low salary, or lack of job possibilities: you cannot save money or stay abreast of your financial obligations.

3. Balance of life decisions: you might desire to marry and/or start a family, and you do not want to balance the relationships of a family with those of the youth in your church.
4. Lack of support or supervision from staff, parents, or youth: regardless of how motivated and effective one is, burnout creeps in when affirmation and support are missing.
5. Your skill level has peaked: you are not sharp anymore, and you are facing situations beyond your ability.
6. A change in your personal belief system: your philosophy of ministry or goals may be different from when you began.
7. You have reached a plateau personally, professionally, and spiritually. You need to move in a new direction to accommodate a new interest and growth.
8. You possess unrealistic expectations of yourself: a negative attitude or continual sense of failure and inadequacy surrounds you.
9. You cannot balance your personal life and your ministry: you have not had a date in two years, and you want one.

Contemplating the reasons women (and men) leave youth ministry enables you to think through how these could possibly affect you and your career choices. But just as there are reasons women leave youth ministry, there are signals that will serve to confirm and validate an ongoing ministry. The signals are:

1. *Listening ears:* someone or some others listen and support you.
2. *Financial support:* though money may be strained at times, it is there when the needs exist.

3. *Helping hands:* people are available to serve physically and spiritually.
4. *Individuals* appropriately confront you in love and compassion.
5. You know the *freedom to fail.*

Not every ministry situation will be perfect and encompass all five of these signs. But if all or most of these elements are missing, there needs to be a reevaluation, a touching base, and a going back to identify where the breakdown is and why.

anger will only drive women further away from Jesus Christ and diminish the effectiveness of their ministries.

Fear

A few years ago I was asked to speak at a high school Bible camp. Nervous but adventurous, I said, "Yes!" From that moment to the day of the camp I regretted my decision and tried to finagle a way out of the commitment.

The day finally came. As I sat in a room full of excited youth workers, I kept being introduced as "the speaker." As awkward as it felt, I really *was* the speaker, although I didn't feel like one. In the moments that followed, camp counselors relayed the best and the worst of the previous eight years of speakers. The one that kept coming up as the most notable was Duffy Robbins, the first and seemingly the greatest. They kept saying that he was so funny and that the kids loved it when he played sports with them. I knew then that I was in trouble. I had been scared before, but by now I was petrified.

The problem is that, unlike Duffy, I am not "funny"! Thought provoking—perhaps, sensitive and engaging—definitely; but never *intentionally* funny. That's just not who I am.

But in spite of my fears I took the risk. I was no Duffy Robbins, or even a Becky Tirabassi, for that matter. I was, however, the best "me" that I could be. And the good news is that through God's strength I was able to connect with the students and effectively communicate the words God wanted *me* to say. But it took a risk. Long-time youth worker and author Ginny Olson encourages us to be risk takers, not only for ourselves, but for our students and for those leaders who will follow in our footsteps.

> Sometimes we have to realize that in order to do what God calls us to do, we must be uncomfortable and take some risks. Is it less risky to pass up a speaking opportunity? Absolutely. You don't fail if you don't try. But you don't succeed either. And the loss is that students don't get to experience a woman being in a visible leadership position. In schools, both boys and girls are being taught that women can do anything they put their minds to. Yet, when it comes to the church, many women feel they need to check their God-given gifts (and personalities) at the door. If God opens up an opportunity to stretch, take it. Put yourself into a risky situation. Grow. Do it for the students in the audience who need to see what a godly woman looks like in leadership. They see plenty of ungodly ones throughout the week. Offer a strong alternative. Follow Esther's example. She sure wasn't comfortable in what she was called to do. But she did it anyway, putting personal fear aside. Maybe God has called you to this situation for such a time as this. (Olson 1995, 109)

OPPORTUNITIES

Remember the debate, about what came first—the chicken or the egg? Women in youth ministry today find themselves in a similar debate. Should women be trained for youth ministry when there are still relatively few jobs, or should women wait to be trained until there are jobs available? I believe that if God has touched your heart and you feel that you are called to youth ministry, follow your dream and get ready for an adventure.

Because of the diversity of ministry opportunities there is no one list of qualifications a woman should possess, nor is there just one way to prepare for ministry. There are some commonalities, however.

Suggested Qualifications

Youth workers should have a growing commitment to Christ, be sensitive to the Holy Spirit, and be teachable. Past that, women need to have some of the following gifts: pastoral, administration, leadership, teaching, and encouragement. Because ministries in general are diversified and have relatively few people doing much of the work, it would also be helpful to be entrepreneurial, creative, self-motivated, assertive, flexible, thick-skinned—and possessed of a good sense of humor.

Education

The good news is that there are dozens of seminaries and Christian colleges specializing in youth ministry and Christian education. While "surfing" the Internet I found more than sixty-eight colleges and seminaries that currently have youth ministry majors—and that is a survey of only the institutions listed on the net.

Education is a great way to improve and prepare yourself at the same time. For me, education opened many doors that would have otherwise remained closed. However, it is important to note that although education does increase employment potential, it doesn't guarantee a position. Also, it seems that, all things being equal, unfortunately all things are *not* equal. Women still need to have more education in their field than their male counterparts to acquire the same position. Perhaps this will be an area that will change in the near future.

Vocational Ministry or Volunteer?

Another issue to consider is the capacity in which you feel called to serve: full-time, part-time, or volunteer. Whether you have three or ten hours a week to give to student ministry, your involvement is significant. Many times full-time professional youth workers get so bogged down with the administrative aspect of ministry they do not have enough time to enjoy the reason that they got into ministry in the first place—students. I actually prefer being a volunteer because I am able to keep my emphasis on ministering to the needs of students rather than on administrative tasks.

Availability often is dictated by the season of life a woman finds herself in. For some reason, we have the idea that there are acceptable capacities in which we can minister to youth. I disagree. I have seen a retired man invite a few guys over to work on an old car, or a mother of preschoolers invite teenage moms to bring their children over and bake cookies. Although these are not the traditional ways of ministering to youth, they are creative and viable means through which we can touch students' lives.

Being a professional youth worker has its own challenges and concerns for women, not the least of which is that there are fewer opportunities to serve and thus greater difficulties in finding paid positions. A 1992 survey of Southern Baptist women in ministry found that 77 percent of ordained women found placement to be average to very difficult, and 70 percent of unordained women found placement to be average or very difficult (Felice 1992). Although this is only one denomination, in my experience women find that placement is difficult, yet not impossible. Generally it is easier for women to find positions in parachurch organizations. One of the issues that then presents itself is whether an individual is willing to personally raise funds, which is often required by parachurch organizations.

Salary is another challenge to consider when evaluating youth ministry in general and specific positions in particular. A survey published in a 1992 issue of *Youthworker* found that the average male youth worker earned $30,866 and the average female earned $25,887 ("*Youthworker* Salary Survey" 1993, 85). In other words, in comparison to men, women earn $.84 on the dollar. Although the inequity is unfortunate, it is not as extreme as in the secular world, where women generally earn $.72 on the dollar (Lewis 1991, 1).

Finding a Ministry Position

Although a challenge, finding a ministry position is possible. One author says, "When looking for a position in youth ministry, women need to be open to alternatives beyond the church. Parachurch organizations have historically been more open to women in leadership" (Olson 1995, 109).

In addition to canvasing ministry listings at your local Christian college or seminary, there are several other resources you can check. Probably the most complete ministry listing at this time is *Intercristo* (there is a small fee for the service). If you have access to the Internet, Christianity Online, a service of America Online, has a ministry/job classifieds section. *Youth Specialties* generates a free listing published every Friday. Just send a self-addressed, stamped envelope and they will send you a free copy. For specifically women in youth ministry, *Journey Publications* has a free posting in its bimonthly newsletter for individuals looking for ministry opportunities, or ministries looking specifically for women youth workers. Although probably the most difficult and time-consuming process, networking with others in the field of youth ministry has been the most effective way women have found placement in youth ministry positions.

Going the Distance

When I started working with students, I never thought that I would be in ministry past my mid-thirties. I always thought that I would "settle down" and start focusing on my family. However, that wasn't the plan that God had for me. His plan, although drastically different than mine, has been the adventure of a lifetime.

Although I realize that not all individuals will be lifetime youth ministers, I believe that if we have a ministry mind-set God will allow us to minister throughout our lives. To do that, we need to prepare ourselves spiritually, mentally, and physically to go the distance.

How do we prepare to go the distance? It means taking care of yourself so that you can remain true to God's calling in your life. It means taking the time you need to nurture your relationship with God, knowing that your ministry flows out of your relationship with Him. And last, it means recognizing the freeing truth that God doesn't need you to accomplish His plan.

Too many youth workers feel they are the only individuals God can use to carry out His plan, thus setting themselves up to experience a destructive, out-of-control lifestyle. Rather, God allows us the awesome privilege of *participating* in His plan to carry the Word of God to students. Living under a false obligation and pressure is destructive and dangerous. Even God, in human form, took time to rest, retreat, and reflect.

We, too, need to protect ourselves so that our spiritual, mental, and physical weaknesses do not leave us vulnerable and open to attack. At our best, ministry is difficult. In a weakened state, ministry can be deadly. In recent years we have all heard of ministers who have let down their guard and fallen into sin. Or we have heard stories of skilled, gifted youth workers who have left the ministry after only a short time, feeling burned out and disillusioned. There is no need to walk into the same trap.

Pacing ourselves means not trying to live up to others' expectations. It also means making careful lifestyle choices with regard to life and ministry. What good is it for a youth worker to spend years in preparation only to burn out in a few years?

You are the only person who can take care of yourself. You are the only person who can make healthy choices for yourself. And you are the only person who can pace yourself to go the distance.

THE JOY OF MINISTRY

There are few things in life as rewarding as shaping the spiritual future of students. Although students will seldom verbalize their feelings of gratitude, your contribution will be apparent in this life and the next.

Yes, there are significant obstacles for women to overcome, but the future of women in youth ministry looks promising. Pioneers have blazed a bumpy but useable trail. All we need now is brave women and men willing to continue smoothing the path for the next generation to follow. It's all part of the journey.

WORKS CITED

Burrei, Deeni. 1992. "The Role of Women in Youth Ministry." Unpublished paper, Trinity Evangelical Divinity School.

Eckmann, Kara. "Gentle Strength." *Journey Publications,* 12:2.

Felice, Toni. 1992. "Southern Baptist Women in Ministry: Summary of 1992 Survey Results." Univ. of Louisville.

Hestenes, Roberta. 1990. "Redefining Roles in Youth Ministry." *Youthworker* (winter), 26.

Lewis, Robert. 1991. *AARP Bulletin* 32, no. 10:1.

Nielsen, Annette. 1990. "The Case for Inclusivity." *Youthworker* (winter), 48.

Olson, Ginny. 1995. "Barriers Along the Way." In *Breaking the Gender Barrier in Youth Ministry*, edited by Diane Elliot and Ginny Olson. Wheaton, Ill.: Victor; Colorado Springs: Chariot Victor.

Rice, Wagne. Editorial. 1990. *Youthworker* (winter), 3.

Senter, Mark H. III. 1992. *The Coming Revolution in Youth Ministry*. Wheaton, Ill.: Victor.

Schutz, Tom. Editorial. 1991. *Group* (June-Aug.), 6.

"Survey of Volunteer and Professional Women in Youth Ministry." 1994. Unpublished survey compiled by *Journey Publications* staff.

Unpublished survey compiled by Diane Elliot and Ginny Olsen of *Journey Publications*. 1992.

"*Youthworker* salary survey." 1993. *Youthworker* (spring), 85.

FOR FURTHER READING

Bilezikian, Gilbert. 1985. *Beyond Sex Roles*. Grand Rapids: Baker.

Cistola, Christie Stonecipher. 1987. "Women in Youth Ministry." In *The Complete Book of Youth Ministry*, edited by Warren S. Benson and Mark H. Senter III. Chicago: Moody.

Elliot, Diane, and Ginny Olson, eds. 1995. *Breaking the Gender Barrier in Youth Ministry*. Wheaton, Ill.: Victor; Colorado Springs: Chariot Victor.

Schaller, Lyle E., ed. 1982. *Women as Pastors*. Nashville: Abingdon.

Tucker, Ruth A. 1992. *Women in the Maze*. Downers Grove, Ill.: InterVarsity.

PART FOUR

SKILLS FOR YOUTH MINISTRY

14

HOW CAN WE BE CHANGE AGENTS IN YOUTH MINISTRY?

Mark W. Cannister

Emerson Park Church had always maintained a youth ministry through volunteers and seminary interns, but I was the first full-fledged youth minister they had ever hired. The first month I began building relationships with the youth leaders, most of whom had grown up in the church. I visited the students, got to know the church staff, and observed the youth meetings. I concluded very quickly that some things had to change, and so I decided to bring in a big gun to help with the innovations.

Ellie had been the regional director of Christian education for our denomination for some twenty years. I called the Youth Committee and the youth leaders together and begged Ellie to bring these people up-to-date on recent trends in youth ministry. The first thing she did was break out four old flip charts and ask the group to create four lists. The first list contained everything they could remember about growing up as teenagers in the fifties and sixties. The second contained everything they knew about the growing pains of contemporary teenagers. The third contained everything they could remember about the youth ministry in which they grew up. And the fourth contained everything they knew about the current youth ministry program.

Ellie then stepped up to the four flip charts and in her gentle wisdom noted that the first and second lists were very different. Growing up as an American teenager had changed dramatically over the years, and these adults recognized that fact. Then the moment I had been waiting for—Ellie pointed out that the third and fourth lists were nearly identical. The youth ministry had not changed in decades. Why was it that these bright church leaders recognized changes in the youth culture but continued to minister through a program that was geared to meet the needs of a previous generation? Primarily because they were afraid of change.

One of the greatest fears of our congregations is the fear of change. Talk about innovation makes people nervous. It is usually more comfortable to maintain the status quo than to take the risk of change. Yet to be effective in youth ministry we must be innovative. We must be driven by a vision and provide transformational leadership for our constituency. This chapter explores the difficulties of being an innovator and provides a road map for strategically bringing about changes necessary for effective youth ministry.

COPING WITH THE FEARS OF INNOVATION

The great common denominator in our fears is the fear of the unknown, and innovation usually brings a degree of the unknown. If we are unable to overcome the fears felt by parents, organizational leaders, and even teenagers themselves, then we will never move our ministry beyond the status quo.

Organizational Fears

Whether a ministry grows out of a church or a parachurch setting, there are pastors, associate pastors, regional directors, secretaries, custodians, elders, officers, committees, financial supporters, volunteer leaders, etc. who will fear our innovations and resist any type of change we may propose. The primary reason for such resistance within organizations is the fear that, in one way or another, one person's bright idea will affect others in a negative way.

When Gary proposed to the church staff that the youth ministry sponsor a coffee house once a month in the church gym to reach unchurched kids, the normally dull staff meeting exploded with questions:

CUSTODIAN: Who will clean the building late on Saturday night so that the church will be ready for Sunday morning?

SECRETARY: Does this mean I'll be sending *another* monthly mailing?

PASTOR: Will the noise be disruptive to the neighbors? I don't want the neighbors complaining to me on Sunday morning about these coffee houses.

BUSINESS MANAGER: What liability risks are we taking if the coffee house gets out of hand? I'd better check with our insurance company first.

CHOIR DIRECTOR: How will this impact the Sunday morning youth choir rehearsal?

Each person had a legitimate concern. Other concerns about innovations may be raised regarding expenses, theology, staffing, community image, or even the value of the new proposal. Many times, however, this resistance can be alleviated if we have a detailed plan of implementation that shows that the new idea will not negatively impact the responsibilities or ministries of our colleagues.

In Gary's situation, he was given permission to hold the coffee house because he had done his homework *before* he presented his idea to the church staff. He talked with the three neighbors the noise might affect, and they all approved as long as the coffee house was over by 11:00 P.M. He arranged to pay the assistant custodian for working late Saturday night out of the proceeds from the coffee house. He spoke with the local police, who agreed to drive by the church a few extra times that night and be prepared for any trouble. He recruited a few parents to help with the extra mailing, and he made a deal with the choir and Sunday school kids that if they didn't show up on Sunday morning they couldn't attend the next coffee house.

Over the years the church coffee house ministry attracted hundreds of unchurched teenagers who came to know Christ and become active in the discipleship groups of the ministry. This innovation was possible because Gary was able to allay the fears of the organization during one very intense staff meeting.

Parental Fears

When parents hear of a radical new idea from our ministry they naturally raise one question: How will this affect my child? Mike faced this question when he proposed that his Campus Life group take a mission trip to Haiti. Parents who had nurtured, cared for, protected, and loved their children

WHEN CHURCHES FEAR CHANGE
GREG LAFFERTY

Churches are collections of people—and since people fear change, churches do too.

In Acts 11, Peter is called on the carpet for dining with the uncircumcised. Such a breach of etiquette struck a sour chord on the old social conventions. Only with the strongest of arguments could Peter persuade Jewish believers to acknowledge that "God has granted *even the Gentiles* repentance unto life."

Was the change embraced?

Hardly. The passage that follows describes mass Gentile conversions in Antioch. When the news hit Jerusalem, believers there immediately dispatched Barnabas to investigate. (Committees embrace change at the speed of molasses; they resist it at the speed of light.) Fortunately, Barnabas was a man of substantial spiritual stature. He actually was glad when he saw the evidence of God's grace. But I'll bet they could have sent others who would have been much less enthusiastic.

So the precedent was set right on the pages of Scripture, and churches have followed suit ever since. That leads me to the following principles.

1. *Face the fact that all churches fear change.* I've ministered at two very different churches. The first was a traditional, conservative church in the Midwest; the second, a contemporary, seeker-targeted megachurch in southern California. Interestingly, both feared change. Human nature dictates that stress and anxiety levels rise when we leave the familiar. However, beyond this common ground of fear, the two churches differed tremendously. The first entered the icy waters of change slowly, one toe at a time. The second did fully clothed "cannonballs." The difference is not in the fear; it's in the response.

2. *Know what can't change.* Generally speaking, the longer a church exists the more nonnegotiables it has. The church I currently serve is a fifteen-year-old adolescent, young and pliable. The only nonnegotiables we have are our core values. We fear change—everyone worried about what would happen when we moved into our new worship center—but we also embrace it. We're one of those "people matter to God" churches that will do almost anything to reach the lost, including scrapping Sunday school, burning the hymnals, redesigning the bulletin, and changing the order of worship.

My former church, on the other hand, is a sixty-five-year-old senior citizen. It's not so sprightly anymore. Over time, many nonessentials have crystallized into rigid standards. You can see it in their two sacred texts, the Bible and the Policy Manual. (Fortunately only one is in the pew racks.) In that church, I fought for my inalienable right to use the photocopier and carry office keys. Touching the Sunday school or the pipe organ would have been out of the question.

It's not that change can't occur in an older or more resistant church—it just takes greater energy to make fewer gains.

3. *Assess the cost of change and make sure you can pay it.* Every church has a CPI, a Change-Price Index. It's the cost of support, trust, and credibility to make the changes you propose. The problem here is twofold. First, the older the church, the higher the price of change. Second, the younger the minister, the less he or she has to spend. In other words, many times we just don't have the clout. We make changes without the support, trust, and credibility to see them through. Shrewd ministers will prove themselves faithful and trustworthy within the system before they try to change it. Sadly, though, many youth workers put themselves in a deficit position just by *proposing* changes before their time. Even proposals cost. John Maxwell warns, "Before you change, check the change in your pockets."

4. *Enlist the support of key influencers.* In church leadership, the Lord rarely works through lone individuals. Teamwork is the rule. If key leaders, advisers, parents, and volunteers get on board, there's a strong possibility the Lord is in the change. If they don't, reassess your vision. By testing the waters with your teammates and enlisting their support, you amass more "change" in your pockets. If they don't back you and you're

still convinced the change is necessary, there's a good chance your supporters are at another church. Go find them. There's nothing like ministering in a church that embraces necessary change and innovation.

5. *Expect problems; expect pain.* Assuming you've chosen to tackle an area that can and should change—and that you have the "change" to pay—get ready for war. It may be relational mortal combat, or it may be subtle spiritual warfare. Either way, even the most innocent of changes tends to spark a counterattack.

When I arrived at Saddleback, the first change I made was to bring order to a chaotic, uncontrolled group. Call me crazy, but I actually decided to expect a baseline of good behavior from kids. If someone repeatedly disrupted a meeting, after two or three clear warnings I kindly asked him to leave. Initial results: kids called me too strict, a quarter of the volunteers quit, and one family made a point of letting me know it was leaving the church. It hurt. I wanted to be loved and followed by everyone. My changes were simple, fairly risk-free, and necessary, but people still drew a target on my back.

Thankfully, in a very short span of time, those who left were replaced by multiples more. And through the transition phase, the key influencers—those who hired me and some key volunteers and parents—backed me solidly. But best of all, successfully negotiating the problems and pains built a stronger, higher platform from which to dive into deeper change. And ministry revolutions are made by the platform divers, not the poolside dippers.

were now being asked to send their precious kids to a Third-World country that was in political turmoil, spoke an unknown language, and had little sanitary drinking water. Mike was ready for some tough questions about his risky idea because, just like Gary, he had done his homework.

Parents may cringe at programming surprises, so, rather than letting them find out about the Haiti trip from their kids or a postcard in the mail, Mike held a parents advisory meeting.

At that meeting he laid out his idea and explained how the kids would benefit from such a trip. He involved the parents by asking them to team up and do some research on the trip. Some parents called travel agents and the State Department to assess the safety of traveling to Haiti. Other parents focused on finding leadership for the trip by contacting a variety of missions organizations that took groups to Haiti on a regular basis. The parents who were most opposed to the trip were asked to research alternative mission experiences that would accomplish the same goals proposed for the Haiti trip.

After a month of meetings the parents had taken ownership of the trip. To relieve their fears, one change was made. The group went to *Mexico,* where many kids had life-changing experiences. Yes, Mike had to make a compromise on the country, but the resulting experiences could not have been any better in Haiti.

Students' Fears

Students resist change whenever they feel comfortable in a situation. It has been said that many people are as excited to reach heaven because of the people who won't be there as they are because of the people who will be there. Teenagers often think the same way about their youth group.

When Beth gave a talk titled "Ten Ways to Make Our Group Grow," the kids responded coldly. They didn't want to invite others; they didn't want to go on retreats with other groups. They just wanted to keep their little Sunday night club to themselves.

In order for people to grow spiritually or socially they must move out of their comfort zone. Moving kids out of their comfort zone is most difficult if kids are unable to see any benefit to making a change. Most student resistance to innovation can be overcome through developing a vision with them that provides a clear picture of the possible end results. If the results have meaning to the students, they will often make major sacrifices to accomplish them. If the results are seen as superficial, then the students will resist changes at every turn.

Beth found she needed to throw away her "top ten" list. Instead she worked through the book of Ephesians with her students, teaching them the importance of sharing their faith with their friends. Eventually, the youth group doubled and then tripled in size.

Even if we deal with the fears associated with innovation, change may not happen because youth leaders try to force inappropriate changes or are not aware of the conditions that give birth to innovation. Such inventiveness, however, is not a magical process, limited only to highly creative people. In fact, it is little more than shifting low productive energy into highly productive ministries.

SOURCES OF INNOVATION

Peter Drucker suggests there are seven sources of innovation—four internal and three outside the organization. When applied to youth ministry, the dynamics to which the youth minister will respond include four sources within the youth group (Drucker, 1985).

The Unexpected

Whether success or failure, the unexpected may be an opportunity for change. The unexpected may be the sudden invasion of young people who use drugs at the coffee house, or it may be that no one comes to the well-planned coffee house. Either result should be the occasion for taking the ministry in new directions.

An Incongruity

An incongruity between what is and what ought to be provides another occasion for innovation. When a group of

WHEN YOUNG PEOPLE RESIST
DAVID HUNSICKER

Have you ever heard a pencil snap?" asked Brian as I was taking him home.

"Yes," I replied.

"Ever noticed that right before it snaps, you can hear the paint cracking?" he continued.

"Never really noticed," I responded.

He lowered his head and stared at the floor for a few moments. There was complete silence. Then he looked at me and said, "I can hear the paint cracking in my life. I feel like it's about to snap. I don't know what to do."

I felt the pain in his words; I knew he was struggling. He was reared in an affluent neighborhood, but his parents had struggled financially. Added to this, being a freshman in an affluent high school had only magnified the difficulty of entering high school. He was also still hurting deeply over the senseless death of a close friend. Confused and lost, he had turned to alcohol for help.

Things came to a head one day during the holiday season. He had gotten wasted so many times that he had begun to scare himself. He called AA. Two men came and spent the morning with him, then he called me asking for help. We met together for months and talked about God's love. I knew in my heart that if there was ever a kid who needed a relationship with Christ, it was this kid. Unfortunately, he eventually decided that Christianity was a "crutch," and he could change without any help. It was my turn to feel helpless. What do you do when a young person resists?

Thankfully, Jesus did not leave us without a clue; He suffered the same rejection during His life that we see after His death. Scripture provides examples. When a person resists Christ's message of forgiveness and acceptance, we need to remember some very basic principles and examples from Scripture. First, God's generous expression of love was rejected. When His arms were outstretched on a cross for the world, only a criminal accepted His message of love. When the rich young ruler rejected His offer to be a disciple, Jesus may have felt the kind of hurt I felt when the young man rejected Christ.

Scripture lays out many promises for us, but none quite as poignant as this: Anyone who dares to share the gospel will face rejection. This is as true a promise as our promise of hope and redemption.

Second, impatience and busyness cripple us to the point that we look past the person in front of us, but Christ never did. Imagine the feelings of Jairus (Luke 8:40–56), whose daughter lay dying, when Jesus stopped to deal with the bleeding woman who touched His robe. The father's anxiety must have swelled to the point of near anger. Jesus could have told the woman that He did not have time for her because Jairus's daughter was more important, but He did not. In this small narrative within the larger story of a dying child we see an enduring lesson for all disciples: Though we do need to see the big picture, we must also look at what God has placed directly in front of us.

A final thought that has always comforted me in the face of rejection is the reminder of *who* is at work. Early in my youth ministry experience I was constantly reminded that God does not need my *ability;* He has all the ability imaginable. Yet, He does need my *availability* because that is how He has chosen to function in our world; that is,

He has chosen to work through believers. God commands our obedience, faithfulness, and willingness to be witnesses to the truth of the gospel.

It was, and still is, difficult for me to place young people like Brian on the altar of prayer and trust in God's providential hand to bring others to them at His chosen time. But as a laborer of the harvest, I am comforted in realizing that the wheat can only be harvested when it is ripe; only God determines that time. Our task is to be ready and available when He ripens the hearts of people.

Christians becomes an exclusive clique instead of hosts to a place where the shy person and beauty queen are treated with equal honor and acceptance, it may be time to reexamine the structure of the youth program.

Process Need

This refers to a situation where something that may have worked well in the past is no longer working and as a result new systems are needed. This is especially true when groups grow past forty or fifty attenders. Ways of knowing when a person is absent that work spontaneously in a group of twenty kids may need to be creatively modified in a group that has doubled in size.

Changes in the Structure

A change in the structure of the church may cause innovation that catches the youth ministry unaware. The addition of a contemporary worship service that suddenly attracts and uses young musicians, actors, and media people may leave the youth ministry hurting for student leadership.

In addition to internal sources of innovation, three sources of innovation come from outside the youth ministry and even outside the church. These become opportunities for creativity.

Demographic Shifts

When there is a shift in the demographics of the neighborhood around the church, that may call for new approaches to youth ministry. An ethnic neighborhood may change rather suddenly as a younger generation grows up and moves to more affluent communities, leaving the youth group to those who commute back to the old neighborhood and a new mix of youth from other ethnic backgrounds.

Changes in Perception, Mood, and Meaning

Other changes in the larger culture may render old forms of youth programming obsolete. In a culture where hanging out with a few friends is the dominant social value, youth rallies and concerts may find little appeal even to loyal youth from church families.

New Knowledge

New knowledge may cause a redirection of ministry energies. When youth ministers realized that they tended to compete with other church groups and parachurch agencies for the same 25 percent of the high school population who were achievement oriented, some churches decided to refocus their attention and attempt to reach students in the other 75 percent of the high school world.

With eyes open to the sources of innovation in youth ministry, the youth worker should build a system to bring about change. The following steps will facilitate action when the conditions are appropriate.

BRINGING ABOUT CHANGE IN YOUTH MINISTRY

Identifying Needs

Assessment is the foundation upon which any significant innovation will rest. The assessment should investigate three areas: the schools, the community, and the ministry.

The School Assessment

The school assessment is a natural place to begin and should include all the private and public middle schools and high schools in the community. Once the schools have been identified, talking with the principals or assistant principals, students, parents, teachers, coaches, and reading the school newspaper and yearbook will paint a picture of these institutions that will help you assess the needs of teenagers in your local area. (See "Key Questions for a School Assessment" elsewhere in this chapter.)

The Community Assessment

Assessment of the community should include any aspect of community life (besides the schools) that may impact the lives of teenagers. Interviews with community leaders such as police officers, clergy, YMCA and YWCA directors, other youth ministers, store owners, etc. will help to describe the community in which you have been called to minister. (See "Key Questions for a Community Assessment" elsewhere in this chapter.)

The Ministry Assessment

Assessment of the ministry should include the specific aspect of the current and past ministry along with an assessment of how the youth ministry fits into the overall ministry of the church or parachurch organization. If you are assessing a church ministry, then an interview with the pastor, elders, and/or parents will be helpful in answering questions concerning the place of the youth ministry within the church. If you are assessing a parachurch ministry, then interviews with a number of pastors, parents, community leaders, and the regional director or area staff of the organization will help put the ministry in its proper community context. (See "Key Questions for a Ministry Assessment" elsewhere in this chapter.)

Once an assessment of the schools, community, and ministry has been completed you are ready to assess the actual needs of students and plan for any changes or innovations that may be necessary for the ministry.

STRATEGIC POINTS
OF MINISTRY

Entry Points

My experience in strategic planning with numerous ministries has led me to conclude that we need four strategic points of ministry. Every ministry needs *Entry Points,* where new students can feel comfortable joining the group. Entry Point programs are usually very social with little or even no proclamation of the gospel. These programs revolve around activities such as ski trips, coffee houses, wilderness outings, fellowship or club meetings, and outreach contact work.

Growth Points

Our ministries also need *Growth Points,* where students who have shown an interest in the faith have the opportunity to learn about Christ and respond to the message of the gospel. These programs still maintain a strong social element (and a lot of pizza), but there is also a clear and significant amount of teaching that enables students to make faith decisions.

Discipling Points

Once students have accepted Christ as their Lord and Savior they need to link up with the *Discipling Points* of our ministry as they learn to be followers of Christ. This element of ministry may involve small group Bible study, one-on-one discipleship, quiet time challenges, prayer groups, and so on. The key of a discipling point is that students are willing to take responsibility for their spiritual growth.

Leadership Points

Having taken responsibility for their own spiritual growth, students can be challenged to take on the responsibility of ministering to others through *Leadership Points.* Leadership Points could be helping to teach an elementary Sunday school class, inviting friends to an Entry Point program, visiting the elderly, or working in a soup kitchen. Some students will even have the leadership capacity to start their own ministry in the community.

Each of the spiritual development points leads to the next, and more often than not, students involved in the Leadership Points of the ministry draw more students to the Entry Points of the ministry (see fig. 14.1).

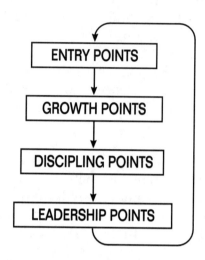

Figure 14.1. *Strategic Points of Ministry*

There are two assessment questions at this point. Do we have opportunities for each of these spiritual growth points in our ministry? And, do we have students engaged in each of these spiritual growth points? If a ministry is solely made up of Entry Points without any Growth, Discipling, or Leadership Points, students will never grow up in their faith. In fact, many students will never even find their faith. However, if a ministry is void of Entry Points and only focuses on Discipling Points, it will become ingrown, stagnant, and elitist. We need to have a full-cycle ministry that draws in students, leads them into a personal faith, disciples them as followers of Christ, and then allows them to develop their gifts and talents in leadership roles.

One simple way to make this assessment with your adult leaders is to divide a chalkboard into four quadrants, with each quadrant representing one of the four spiritual development points. At the top of each quadrant list the programs that meet the needs of that spiritual development point. Place the names of students at the bottom of the quadrant that best reflects their spiritual development. If some students do not seem to fit in just one quadrant, write their names in two quadrants. This is not meant to be judgmental, but rather to help us assess the spiritual needs of our students. (See fig. 14.2 for an example of a spiritual development points quadrant.)

CREATING INNOVATIONS

With all of these assessments in hand, it is time for some strategic decision making. By examining the school and community assessment you can easily observe what opportunities are available to become strategically involved in the lives of teenagers outside the youth ministry programs.

Karen found that the high school in her community was in need of an assistant drama director for the school's spring musical. Being a thespian herself she volunteered and spent ten hours a week from Christmas to Easter working at the school with teenagers who had never been a part of her youth ministry. As she developed relationships with these students (without proselytizing), many of the students began attending her ministry, and nearly the whole cast showed up for the youth ministry's Easter service. Accommodating our ministry to serve a need in the school or community can open numerous doors to reach teenagers we may never meet otherwise.

The reverse is also true. What resources did your assessment uncover within the community and schools that could meet the needs of some of your students or help you attain one of your ministry goals? John learned that many of the store owners in town needed part-time workers during the busy holiday seasons, but couldn't afford to pay teenagers very much for their time. John rounded up students who couldn't afford to pay for summer camp to work in the stores as volunteers. The students were paid nothing, the stores contributed to the ministry's camp scholarship fund, and the kids went to camp.

PLANNING FOR CHANGE

Changes in the ministry itself will be driven by a vision that clearly projects what the ministry should look like in the near and distant future. Some programs may need to be

ENTRY POINTS

Club, ski club, fall retreat,
  basketball, starve-a-thon,
  mission trip, coffee houses,
  contact work

Bill, John, Gary, Beth, Karen,
  Amy, Nancy, John, Bob, Susie,
  Mary, Fred, Amanda, Robin,
  Charlie, Matt, Greg, Bill,
  Steve,Karen, Kristy, Chris,
  Elisabeth, Jenny, Marsha,
  Kevin, Ellen, Jerry, Josh, Amy

DISCIPLING POINTS

Bible studies, mentorships, prayer
  groups, quiet time challenges

John, Gary, Mike, Beth, Nancy,
  Susan, Brian, Paul, Mike,
  Sandy, Kerry, Kris, Heather,
  Rob, Janice, Ashley, Carrie

GROWTH POINTS

Starve-a-thon, mission trip,
  Sunday school

Rick, Bill, Amy, Kathy, Karen,
  Leslie, Sam, Dale, Christy, Laura,
  Rachel, Curtis, Ed, Mark, Craig,
  Robert, Kristen, Kevin, Allison,
  Shelly

LEADERSHIP POINTS

Sunday school assistants for
  grades 1–4, nursing home
  volunteer, invitational
  evangelism, school prayer
  fellowship

Bill, Lisa, adult SS teachers, Tina,
  Jenny, Katrina, Rich, Jason

Figure 14.2. *Spiritual Development Points Quadrants*

added, some programs may need to be deleted, and leadership almost always needs to be recruited and developed.

The first part of your plan is to develop a mission statement for the ministry. The mission statement (some call it a vision statement) is based on what you believe to be essential about your ministry. It should embrace the uniqueness of who you are, what you do, and whom you serve. Your mission statement should also be compatible with the mission statement of your church or parachurch organization. If these statements are not compatible, you may need to find a new venue for your ministry. The following are examples of some good, concise mission statements for youth ministries:

- Breakaway is a ministry of Ridgewood Community Church that exists to teach biblical truths and communicate the reality of these truths to middle school students.
- The youth ministry of Sunnyside Church exists for the purpose of introducing teenagers to the gospel of Christ and then discipling them into mature followers of Christ.
- Hope Community Church is committed to a youth ministry that joyfully shares the good news of God's sovereign love by calling teenagers to repentance, to a personal faith in Jesus Christ as Savior and Lord, to active membership in the church, and to obedient service in the world.

Notice that each of these mission statements is brief and concise. Every member of your ministry should have a clear understanding of the ministry's purpose and be able to state it clearly to anyone who inquires about the nature of the youth ministry.

With a mission statement in place you have a clear vision of where you need to go, and your ministry assessment reveals where you are now. Next you need some goals to move yourself from where you are to where you want to be.

Goals are long-range tasks that will be undertaken in response to a perceived need in the ministry. Goals tend to be general and may be broken down into specific objectives for implementation. You may set a goal for developing biblically literate students. This goal would primarily involve students at the Discipling Point, but the goal and the audience is not enough; you also need objectives for accomplishing your goal.

Objectives are the short-range accomplishments that will help you achieve your goals. A good objective has three elements:

1. *Performance:* States what is to be accomplished or "performed."
2. *Conditions:* States the conditions under which the objective will be accomplished.
3. *Criterion:* States a criterion for the performance that is realistic and acceptable for the ministry (realistic because it is what can reasonably be accomplished, even though we always strive for perfection).

An objective for developing biblically literate students could be outlined this way:

Objective: Ten to twelve Discipling Point students will be able to discuss at least five great themes of the Bible after completing a new ten-week Walk Through the Bible series.

Performance: Create a new Walk Through the Bible series.

Conditions: Ten to twelve Discipling Point students will participate in a ten-week series.

Criterion: Students will discuss five themes of the Bible.

After the objectives are set, programs must be developed to accomplish the objectives. Every program should consider five critical questions.

1. Who is the audience to be reached?
2. What point of Christian growth is being presented?
3. Why will the audience attend this program?
4. How long will this program last?
5. What is expected of the participants upon completion of the program?

KEY QUESTIONS FOR
A SCHOOL ASSESSMENT
MARK W. CANNISTER

❏ What are the names of all the middle/high schools in the area?

❏ Where are the schools located in the community?

❏ Who are the superintendents of each school system?

❏ Who is the principal of each school?

❏ What is the enrollment of each school?

❏ What is the sociocultural makeup of each school?

❏ What are the major strengths of each school?

❏ What are the major weaknesses of each school?

❏ What religious clubs exist in each school?

❏ How does each administration feel about religious clubs?

❏ In what ways can community members serve the school? (lunchroom monitors, library aides, teacher's aides, chaperons, coaches, drama assistants, and so on)

❏ What is the school traditionally known for? (academics, sports, drama, music, and so on)

❏ What do students like best/least about their school?

❏ What do parents like best/least about the school?

❏ What is the power structure of the school? Who are the key teachers, students, coaches, custodians, administrators, and staff?

❏ What are the school's nickname, mascot, and colors, and which schools are its rivals?

❏ What are the most important events in the life of the school?

❏ When are the major times of stress in the school? (exams, prom, SATs)

❏ What are the main nights for school sports, activities, practices, and rehearsals?

❏ Where do students hang out around school?

❏ What are the different subcultural groups within the school?

KEY QUESTIONS FOR
A COMMUNITY ASSESSMENT
MARK W. CANNISTER

❏ What is the sociocultural makeup of the community? Is it the same or different from the school's?

❏ What is the center of community activity, and what is its significance?

❏ What community groups serve the needs of teenagers?

❏ What are the adult perceptions of teenagers in the community?

❏ How do organizations and businesses interact with teenagers?

❏ Where do teenagers socialize after school, evenings, weekends, and during the summer?

❏ Where do teenagers work after school, evenings, weekends, and during the summer?

❏ What resources are available in the community for troubled teenagers? (for example, counselors, abuse programs, intervention programs, teen pregnancy centers)

KEY QUESTIONS FOR
A MINISTRY ASSESSMENT
MARK W. CANNISTER

- ❐ How long has this youth ministry been in place?
- ❐ What was the philosophy of the previous youth minister?
- ❐ What are the perceptions of students and parents about the past youth ministry?
- ❐ Who are the students on the mailing list?
- ❐ Who are the students who attend youth ministry programs?
- ❐ Which students have dropped out of the ministry in the past year?
- ❐ Who has joined the ministry in the past year?
- ❐ What is the church involvement of these students?
- ❐ Do these students attend any other youth ministries in the area?
- ❐ What have been the primary programs of the ministry over the past two years?
- ❐ What is the history of the volunteer leadership of the ministry?
- ❐ What talents/gifts has each volunteer brought to the ministry?
- ❐ What were/are the goals of the ministry?
- ❐ How does the Sunday school program relate to the youth ministry program?
- ❐ What is the philosophy/theology of church membership for teenagers?
- ❐ How are teenagers integrated into the whole life of the church?
- ❐ How does the worship service reflect the needs of teenagers?
- ❐ How are teenagers represented on church committees?

❏   What are the pastor's and the parents' philosophies of youth ministry?

❏   What do the pastor and the parents believe are the responsibilities of a youth minister?

❏   What does the church value about teenagers and youth ministry?

❏   How does the church feel about cooperative programs with other ministries in the area?

❏   How does the church feel about the youth minister working with teenagers who are not members of the church?

❏   What types of activities for young people are encouraged/discouraged?

Although many of the above questions are appropriate for parachurch youth ministers, the following questions may be particularly useful for parachurch ministries:

❏   Is there a single ministry methodology that the organization promotes, or is the youth minister free to experiment with innovative methods?

❏   What is the relationship of the ministry with the local community, local congregations, and schools?

❏   What support for innovations can be expected from the regional director?

❏   What are the goals of the regional director?

❏   What kind of support system will be provided to the youth minister?

❏   What is the extent of parental involvement in the ministry?

❏   How do students view the ministry in relation to the church?

❏   How does the ministry feed students into local churches?

A program proposal for this Walk Through the Bible series should state that the audience will consist of Discipling Point students; the program will present Discipling Point content; students will participate in the program because adult volunteer leaders will personally recruit them; the program will last ten weeks, and upon completion of the program, students will be expected to take on some Leadership Point responsibilities.

BRINGING ABOUT CHANGES

The following is an example of how your philosophy of ministry, mission statement, goals, objectives, and programs all fit together to bring about changes in your youth ministries. Notice that all the programs are directly related to goals and objectives that reflect the beliefs stated in the philosophy and mission statements. There is no limit to the number of goals, objectives, or programs a ministry may develop. What is important is that all of this reflects the innovations gleaned from the initial assessments.

EXCERPT FROM
A PHILOSOPHY OF YOUTH MINISTRY

I believe that people come to know God through the proclamation of the gospel and that proclamation is preceded by a relational presence. Christian maturity is developed through study and implementation of God's Word.

Mission

The Westside youth ministry exists for the primary purpose of proclaiming the gospel to teenagers and discipling them in a new life in Christ.

Goal I

Adults and leadership people will meet and befriend secular high school students.

Objective A

Leadership people will meet secular students by playing basketball with kids, half of whom will be unchurched, during the summer months.

Program Proposal 1

Summer Basketball League: The league will be made up of four teams and will last eight weeks. Christian students will invite unbelieving friends to play. The games will be played in a good moral atmosphere and the gospel will be shared through our actions only. No verbal presentations will be planned until the awards banquet at the end of the season. Following a good Entry Point experience in this program we expect that unchurched students will be open to attending our Wednesday Night Fellowship Group.

Objective B

Adult leaders will meet new students by attending all home high school football games this fall.

Program Proposal 2

Home Football Games: At each game adult leaders will sit in the student section and attempt to meet new students. To help break into the unchurched crowd and to help Leadership Point students do some invitational evangelism, adults will arrange to attend the games with at least one student from the ministry who is willing to reach out to unchurched students. The gospel will be shared through our actions, and we expect that as students get to know us they will be open to attending our Wednesday Night Fellowship Group.

Goal II

Students will experience the importance of servanthood.

Objective A

Ten to fifteen students will be able to explain what they learned about the importance of servanthood after they experience poverty within the local and the global community.

Program 1

Thirty-Hour Starve-a-Thon: This is a lock-in at the church. Students will be invited by their Bible study leader. The time will include recreation, Bible studies on poverty, prayer, and a guest speaker from the local soup kitchen. The money we would have spent on food we will give to the soup kitchen. Through this one-time event, we expect students to be open to volunteering at the soup kitchen project.

Program 2

Men's Shelter Dinner: One Sunday evening we will prepare a dinner at the church for forty people and take it to the men's shelter, where we will serve it and clean up. Students will be invited by their Bible study leader. Through this one-time event, students will be interested enough in poverty to attend the Compassion Project.

Program 3

Compassion Project: This is a six-week study on poverty in Third-World countries. Students will choose to do this project as a follow-up to the starve-a-thon and the men's shelter dinner. The conclusion to this project will be to commit as a group to support a Third-World child for one year. Students at this point should be taking responsibility for their own growth as servants.

Goal III

Christian students will demonstrate their knowledge of Bible basics.

Objective A

Students will name all the books of the Bible when quizzed.

Objective B

Students will memorize one verse each week for twelve weeks.

Objective C

Students will describe the basic contents of each book of the New Testament after twelve weeks of instruction.

Program 1

A twelve-week Walk Through the New Testament course will be held for two hours once a week at the church on Sunday afternoon. This program is for Christian students who desire to grow in their understanding of Scripture. A number of students have requested that this program be implemented, and each has agreed to recruit one person to attend the initial meeting. Upon completion of this program, we expect that students will want to learn even more about the Scriptures through another Walk Through the Old Testament or a walk through a specific book of the Bible. We also expect students at this point to begin taking on the responsibility for the spiritual growth of other younger Christians.

When changes are made through this type of strategic plan, there tends to be less resistance from parents, pastors, and teenagers because they can see the method behind what often looks like madness. Innovations that are well thought-out before they are implemented also tend to last longer because ownership in them has been created. Developing a strategic plan of innovation should not be done by the youth minister behind closed doors. Instead, it should involve a vast cross section of the ministry, including volunteers, parents, and teenagers at appropriate times in the planning process.

Innovation is not an event; it is an ongoing process that should be constantly evaluated as the ministry progresses. Changes large and small should be constantly occurring based on a yearly assessment of the ministry. Through proper assessment, planning, and implementation, innovations can keep our ministries fresh and alive with the Spirit of Christ without being offensive or threatening to those associated with our ministry.

FOR FURTHER READING

Anderson, Leith. 1992. *A Church for the Twenty-first Century.* Minneapolis: Bethany House.

_____. 1990. *Dying for Change.* Minneapolis: Bethany House.

Drucker, Peter. 1984. *Innovation and Entrepreneurship*. New York: Harper & Row.

Ford, Leighton. 1991. *Transforming Leadership*. Downers Grove, Ill.: InterVarsity.

Mead, Loren. 1993. *The Once and Future Church*. Washington, D.C.: Alban Institute.

Robbins, Duffy. 1990. *Youth Ministry Nuts & Bolts*. Grand Rapids: Zondervan.

Roehlkepartain, Eugene. 1993. *The Teaching Church: Moving Christian Education to Center Stage*. Nashville: Abingdon.

Schutz, Thomas, and Joani Schutz. 1993. *Why Nobody Learns Anything at Church: And How to Fix It*. Loveland, Colo.: Group.

Towns, Elmer. 1993. *Ten Sunday Schools That Dared to Change*. Ventura, Calif.: Regal.

Warren, Rick. 1995. *The Purpose-Driven Church*. Grand Rapids: Zondervan.

15

OUTREACH:
HOW CAN WE RENEW
TRADITIONAL CHURCH
YOUTH MINISTRIES?

Chuck Rosemeyer

Collinsville is a city of 35,000. It would be plausible to estimate that there are 5,000 students in grades seven through twelve in Collinsville. Fifteen would be a reasonable, perhaps even generous, estimation of the number of Christian churches in Collinsville and its surrounding unincorporated areas. Probably most churches have under 100 members. Two churches are rather large, both having around 750 members. Although the two larger churches each have youth ministry programs, with just over one hundred students actively involved, most churches have very small youth groups—in some cases fewer than five members. The resulting average number of teenage participants per church in this community is about twenty-three, if one includes both junior high and senior high.

What is a realistic portrait of youth ministry in Collinsville? If an adult attended one of the two larger churches, he might be tempted to conclude that churches were exerting a broad influence in the local schools. However, 23 multiplied by 15 yields 345. Add to this number two campus ministries that reach a total of 50 students not already being counted among the local church statistics. The number now climbs to 395. Of a pool of 5,000 students in the community, fewer than 400 are being ministered to by youth ministry leaders. That is less than 10 percent! The imbalance is dramatic and sobering.

Collinsville is a fictional illustration. Consider the factual results of *Effective Christian Education,* a study done for five mainline denominations by the Search Institute. The researchers found that only about 30 percent of the teenage *members* of most churches are still active by the tenth grade (Benson 1990, 3–4, 50). Popular wisdom suggests that 80 percent of the *resources* of most church youth ministries are going into efforts to effect spiritual change in that 30 percent. Only 20 percent of church resources are spent on the 70 percent of the kids that they have lost.

The representative example of Collinsville and the statistical findings of the Search Institute suggest an urgent need to rethink youth ministry in traditional church settings. Too much of the local churches' precious youth ministry resources are being turned inward, whereas little or no attention is being given to the masses of unchurched youth in the local schools. The time for the renewal has come.

But how does one turn a youth ministry that faces inward, dealing with the 30 percent of the teenage population in the church, into one that also faces outward, focusing on both the 30 percent who are in the church and the 70 percent who are not? Beyond this, how does the church refocus itself toward reaching the broader population of unchurched youth illustrated in the Collinsville scenario? Four steps are suggested for the leader who is hearing the call for an "about-face" ministry perspective.

STEP ONE: AN OUTREACH MIND-SET

Step one is not under the direct control of the youth leader, for it involves the whole church and its leadership. The fact is that a youth ministry can only move in the direction that the church is going. If the whole church is not focused on outreach, the youth ministry *cannot* be. Youth ministry absolutely cannot go it alone. Therefore, step one consists of making sure that the *whole* church is interested in reaching out beyond itself and will welcome new people.

STEP TWO: INTENTIONAL DESIGN

A program must be designed so that it consistently reflects the church's commitment to outreach. A program for those who have been born and reared in the church is very different from a program for students who have never opened a Bible or been exposed to a worship service. Music, drama, skits, entertainment, talks, audiovisual material, Bible studies, recreation, camping, and retreats must be developed with awareness and appreciation for where the kids are—spiritually, physically, and emotionally.

STEP THREE: OWNERSHIP AND LEADERSHIP

Vision casting and leadership development are necessary if the program is to get off the ground and become a ministry. Vision casting consists of articulating the new direction of the ministry. A word of caution is necessary for all church youth ministry leaders: changing things in the church must be done with patience, care, and good communication. Without wise, humble, and sensitive leadership even the best program will fail. It will fail because the people will not "own" what the leadership already values.

Gaining the personal investment of the people in the church is only the beginning. New programs of outreach must be led by trained leaders. Leading an outreach-oriented ministry requires understanding, attitudes, and skills that may have to be learned by staff and lay leaders alike. Shortcuts must not be taken at this point. Many great ideas have been "sold" to the people in the congregation but have failed to materialize because no one knew quite what to do in order to make the ideas work.

Change takes time. Building that foundation in a logical progression will help assure success.

ON SUNDAY MORNING
SCOTT W. BENSON

Let's face it. Sunday morning ministry can be challenging. Students often shuffle in exhausted from the festivities of Saturday night with brain cells that are not fully functional. A 9:00 A.M. Sunday school class is not exactly the place they want to be. Mentally, they've often checked out before they even check in. And it's tough to grab students' attention when they're thinking about the pile of homework they've still got to tackle before Monday morning rolls around. Spiritually and emotionally? They might have just come from a heavy-duty argument with a parent or sibling in the family car on the way to church. Sometimes their only motivation for showing up is to catch up with a few friends and to go along with a parental order to be there.

So what do you do? Here are ten hot tips to help you facilitate the teaching-learning process on Sunday mornings.

1. Lose the name "Sunday school." Kids don't need a reminder of that dreaded academic experience they face during the week. How about something like "A.M. Stretch," "Cross Training," or "The Edge"? Avoid names like "B.O.B." (Big Outrageous Blast), which can create unrealistic expectations that will be hard to meet on a Sunday morning.

2. Create an environment conducive to learning. Most church classrooms don't provide the comfortable ambiance students are looking for. So, what if you were to deck out the room with a few couches, Ping-Pong tables, and posters on the wall—along with a Christian music video for kids to check out while they're munching on some tasty edibles when they walk in?

3. Begin with the end in mind. Clearly defined teaching objectives will enable you to stay on target. Before launching into the lesson, ask yourself what you want your kids to know, feel, and do by the time you've wrapped up the class. Application is the key in helping kids to internalize and own their faith. Here's the operative question: How would the lives of your kids be different if they were to live out the reality of the truth that you are communicating?

4. Know the scoop on curriculum. There is a ton of quality stuff that you can either use as designed or reformat to meet the needs of your kids. Contact curriculum companies that will provide some of their free samples. One word of caution: Make sure that it is up-to-date. With our rapidly changing youth culture, curriculum must have a contemporary edge. Also, be sure to get feedback from your kids about the issues they want to cover. Give them a survey with lots of options under such categories as Bible content, spiritual growth, hot topics, and life skills. You will probably want to focus on the specific needs and struggles of your students.

5. Always keep 'em guessing. Predictability is bad news. So why not surprise your kids with a quick road trip? Toss them into vans and explore new "on-location" sites, such as a cemetery, a greenhouse, a construction site, or an athletic track. Any of those can provide an innovative environment for learning. Or if you need to jumpstart that early morning teaching-learning process with a hefty dose of caffeine, roll into your local Starbucks Coffee.

6. *Get their gray matter in gear.* Involvement-based, active learning activities, such as role plays, simulation games, interviews, panel discussions, and agree/disagree debates can help the students' understanding and retention levels to soar off the charts. Plug in to creative resources like "Tension Getters" that provide detailed descriptions of real-life situations that challenge kids to think through various cutting-edge choices. Videos like "Edge TV," episodes of popular TV shows, and clips from movies can be terrific catalysts for group interaction.

7. *Get a grip on the four basic learning styles.* Most students learn in more than one style but have a tendency to interact with content in one primary style. Experiential learners ("feeling") grasp truth intuitively through relationships and creative expression. Analytic learners ("watching and listening") are reflective observers. Common sense learners ("thinking") process information through such strategies as discussion, debate, and personal study. Dynamic learners ("doing") are active experimenters. The teaching-learning process is radically enhanced when you become skilled in communicating truth by using strategies in each of the four styles.

8. *Stay on the growing edge as a teacher.* Read books like *Teaching the Bible Creatively* (Bill McNabb and Steven Mabry) or *Secrets of Dynamic Communication* (Ken Davis). Get honest feedback from students and your ministry colleagues whenever you teach. Listen to effective communicators who grab students' attention and help them wrestle with biblical truth.

9. *Focus on the friendship factor.* Kids need to feel a sense of belonging where they know they are

cared about in the group. So how can you build a greater feeling of community where your kids learn to connect with one another? Crowd breakers, small groups, and team-building activities help facilitate those warm interpersonal dynamics.

10. *Hold on to the truth of 1 Corinthians 2:1–5.* Paul was an honest man. He realized that without "the Spirit's power," there could be no eternal impact for the kingdom. The "Difference-Maker" in kids' lives is not us, it's the living God. When we walk into our Sunday morning class with a firm grip on that reality, that's when our ministry will begin to make a significant difference in the lives of students.

STEP FOUR: PROGRAM IMPLEMENTATION

With trained leadership in place and the prayerful spiritual support of the congregation, a program shift toward outreach can be implemented. Leaders would be wise to begin with small successes, building both enthusiasm and motivation for future endeavors. Starting with a program of multimedia combined with a live Christian band and a dynamic speaker—all of which cost one-third of the annual youth budget—may be an exciting idea. In fact, it may draw a crowd. But what will happen next week? How can such energy be maintained?

The case study below illustrates the process of moving from vision to implementation. It is the true story of a church in a traditional, mainline denomination that moved from an inward-focused youth ministry to an outward one. Chris Smith, the youth pastor in the story, actually lived this experience. The change in mind-set Chris and the congregation of Pleasant Hills Community Presbyterian Church achieved serves as a model for what can happen when people come together with a heart for renewal.

PLEASANT HILLS
COMMUNITY PRESBYTERIAN CHURCH

Pleasant Hills Community Presbyterian Church had been typical of many mainline churches in the Pittsburgh area. Most of its programs, including its youth ministry, had been established many years ago. The focus was inwardly oriented, weighted toward maintenance. The church had 1,540 members. Its new senior pastor, Dr. Stanley Ott, had written material on church growth (Ott 1989), and his application of his study and knowledge was beginning to pay off. The church was growing numerically and starting to look outward. The key to this revitalization was shifting the thinking of the church from program maintenance to a principle-based concept of ministry. A significant part of this shift was introducing "The Seven Vital Signs" of ministry and putting them into practice in every facet of the congregation's ministry (11–24).

However, the youth ministry was small and still focused on maintenance. Volunteer leadership was minimal. About fifty junior and fifty senior high students were members of the church, but few people were directly involved with teenagers and there was little participation by teens in the life of the congregation. So after Dr. Ott had been at the church five years, the church hired a full-time youth director who could shift the approach of the youth ministry from maintenance to a principle-based initiative. The new youth director was just out of college. He had little training in youth ministry but did have good experience from his own church and a university ministry.

In eighteen months the youth ministry went from a struggling youth group focused on the twenty-five students of the church who came each week to a youth group that had a growing ministry that reached out into the community and presented the gospel to upwards of fifty students a week. How did this happen?

It happened in part because the youth group applied the four steps to renewal, enabling them to reach those who were outside the traditional church youth ministry program. This outreach extended to those who had previously been a part of the church and extended to the larger unchurched populations of the local schools.

Step One: Outreach, the Goal of the Entire Church

Fortunately, the senior pastor and the leadership of the church had already determined on an outward focus for the church. They saw the church's ministry as one of reaching out to the unchurched in the area. In fact, that was why Dr. Ott had been hired. The new focus of the youth ministry would be the same as the focus of the church.

The church and the youth ministry must be going in the same direction for the youth ministry to survive. If the church and the youth ministry do not have the same general focus, tension will begin to build and eventually the church will stop the youth ministry from going in the direction it desires, which will eventually kill it. This is often done in subtle, indirect ways, such as reducing the budget for the youth ministry, giving the ministry reduced access to church facilities, increasing rules and regulations, and finally letting go of the youth ministry staff ("because we need to cut back").

Step Two: An Intentionally Designed Program

Once the goals of the youth ministry were established, the "how" had to be figured out. Chris Smith, the new youth minister, took a year to get the lay of the land and determine what kind of program to run. When Chris arrived, the senior high program consisted of a youth group that met each Sunday night at 7:00 P.M. and a Sunday school class that met at 9:30 A.M. before the worship service. Someone else ran the Sunday school class. The youth group format consisted of a discussion on current topics, with perhaps a game or two at the beginning. Because Chris was not sure what to put in its place, he continued this format for a time. About fifteen to twenty-five teenagers were involved.

Although Chris and the teens enjoyed being together, they found the youth group meetings boring. And no *new* students came, largely because of the style of the meeting. The new stated mission of the youth program was outreach and discipleship, but both the Sunday school class and the youth group meetings were run in a nurture format.

A nurture format consists of activities and content suitable for kids who have grown up in the church. It assumes that those involved are already committed and growing in their personal faith; they just need to be consistently fed. Bible study and discussions of issues of the Christian faith intended to help teens grow in their faith are the usual content.

How a youth ministry is designed, the number of adult leaders, and the number of core teenage leaders in a program are very important to the overall focus, size, and success of a youth ministry program. The *how* of the objectives produces the *what* of the goals.

During this first year of youth ministry, Chris learned from other youth leaders that successful outreach youth ministry is based on a three-layer format. (Success here is defined by a national study that indicated that most churches reach 35 percent of their senior high students. Anyone reaching more than 35 percent is considered successful [Benson 1990, 50]). The first layer is discipleship, developing more mature Christian teens into peer leaders. The peer leaders discipled in this layer can later be given responsibility for new teens in the program (the third layer). The second layer is nurture, an introductory Bible study and discussion of issues of the Christian faith. The final, or third, layer is strictly evangelism and outreach.

Chris quickly recognized that his mature Christian teens (first layer) could be a major component in helping a youth ministry grow. Studies of youth ministries consistently show that there is a 1 to 5 ratio of leaders to teenagers in successful youth ministries. This 1 to 5 ratio is the same, no matter what the size of the program. In a successful youth ministry, if a church has two leaders, ten teens will come to a meeting; three leaders would mean an average of fifteen teenagers will come to meetings. Youth ministry is driven by relationship *first* and program *second*.

Chris had four adult leaders plus himself and was reaching about twenty-five kids each week in his senior high program. He realized that as he began to develop the first layer of ministry—the core Christian kids—the number of kids in the third layer (outreach) would grow proportionally.

What was true in other youth ministries in the city proved to be true for Chris. The size of his youth ministry depended on how well he discipled kids. Two adult leaders could be running an outreach meeting with fifty and sixty teens attending regularly. The leaders did it by each discipling five kids and those in turn reaching five others. In a mathematical sense it looked like this:

$$2 \times 5 = 10 \times 5 = 50 + 10 = 60$$

Chris's church had been no different from many others; it was difficult to identify teens that were being discipled. The church had assumed that its Sunday school class, which was run by a different department, was discipling teens. However, when Chris asked, "Who attends the Sunday school class?" the answer was "anyone," no matter where he was in his spiritual development. The Sunday school class was not intentionally discipling. Instead, it was offering a little bit of everything for everyone.

That is the clear difference between most church youth groups and the ones that use a three-layer model. The youth groups and the Sunday school classes are generic. They both offer a little evangelism, a little nurture, and a little discipleship for everyone. They are not focused enough to be truly effective. Core teenagers are not being developed into leaders who can then help to reproduce themselves. The result is that kids often drop out because their needs are not being met. Even though the ratio of kids to adult leaders is still 1 to 5, the number of teens who might be called leaders has little or no effect on the size of the youth program.

Step Three: Ownership and Training

After reviewing these issues, Chris established a six-month plan to change the program from nurturing only to the three-layer combination of discipleship, nurture, and evangelism. The six months were needed to plan and train for the new program elements, develop leadership (both adult and teen), and to allow the whole church to develop ownership of the new direction.

One reality of the teenage years is that *everything* is changing. Too quickly changing youth ministry programs teens have depended on—even if they are not good programs—can produce anxiety and anger in teens and be the kiss of death for a youth leader. It is better to develop a solid, understandable program format and give people a chance to buy into it. If possible, add program elements first. Then change or replace what has been ineffective. Once the new operation is established, major changes should be few and far between. However, evaluation should be done on a regular basis and small improvements and adjustments made constantly.

THE DISCIPLING PROCESS
CHUCK ROSEMEYER

Figure 15.1 (below) helps to show how the discipling process works. The chart and discussion are adapted from Laurent A. Daloz, *Effective Teaching and Mentoring: Realizing the Transforming Power of Adult Learning*, 212–14. Copyright 1986 Jossey-Bass, Inc., Publishers. Used by permission.

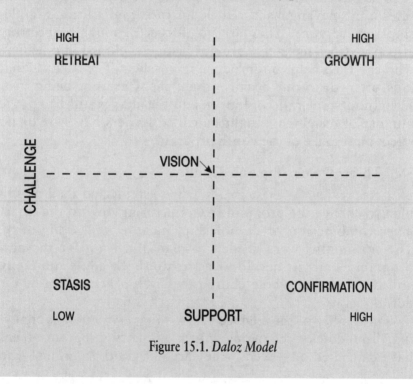

Figure 15.1. *Daloz Model*

> *Support*, through empathy and encouragement, lets a person know he or she is understood. This in turn builds trust; it brings boundaries together.
>
> *Challenge*, on the other hand, peels boundaries apart. It "opens a gap between the student and the environment, a gap that creates tension in the student, calling out for closure" (214).
>
> *Vision* is provided by mentors (or leaders). By "'hanging around' through transitions, a foot on either side of the gulf, [mentors] offer a hand to help us swing across. By their very existence, mentors provide proof that the journey can be made, the leap taken" (212–13).
>
> By providing both challenge and support, the mentor enables a person to grow and develop a vision for his life. Daloz points out that when a person is not supported or challenged, little if any growth occurs in his life. When a person is supported, he may feel good about himself and some growth may occur, but often it is not as great as it could be. When a person is both challenged and supported he can often reach levels of maturity he never thought himself capable of (214).

Step Four: Implementing the New Program

Chris then added two new layers to the existing youth ministry program. The first layer he added was discipleship. Two major events, one planned and the other an act of God's grace, set up that change. The first event was taking teens and leaders to the Pittsburgh Project, a week-long Christian service camp in the inner city of Pittsburgh. It opened everyone's eyes to how much bigger and more exciting the Christian faith really could be. The second "event" was having one of the new teens in the group make a commitment to Christ as his Lord and Savior. For students who had grown up in the church, this was a new experience that again exposed them to a new and vital aspect of their faith.

After these experiences, a new leadership training study was set up for students that really wanted to grow in their faith. Some students were not ready for leadership but likewise needed and wanted to grow in faith. The second layer was added for them. Several nurture-level Bible studies were established. These were held in leaders' homes: one at 5:30 A.M., two at 6:00 A.M., and a couple in the evenings. Because they were run by the volunteer leaders, the result was that meaningful relationships developed between the leaders and the students.

The next layer to be added was outreach and evangelism. The old youth group time slot was replaced with a ministry program that targeted those who did not yet know Christ.

On the last week of October there were twenty-five teenagers at the old youth group meeting. The next week a new format—music with a small band, some skits, and a felt-needs-related Bible message on the basics of the Christian faith—was introduced, along with a new name. It was no longer to be called the "Pleasant Hills Community Presbyterian Church Youth Group" but "Cross Over" (based on John 5:24). The name was changed primarily to help non-Presbyterian students feel open to coming. At the first meeting of Cross Over in November, thirty teenagers showed up. By the end of the month, forty came; and by the end of January, one hundred teenagers were on the roll, with some forty to forty-five attending each week. A year later, the numbers had gone to more than fifty attending each week. The next year, a junior high program was being started along the same lines.

More Than a Program

There was more to Chris's success than just a new program format. From the very beginning, Chris had been doing the basics of outreach ministry.

Relevant, Christ-Centered Youth Talks

Chris's talks at Cross Over were specifically focused on presenting the person and work of Christ and how Christ fits into our everyday lives. Rather than being boring, his talks quickly became very popular because he was able to combine basic theology with relevant issues kids were dealing with. For many students, it was the first time they had ever heard the Christian faith presented in a relevant, contemporary format.

Meaningful Friendships with Unchurched Students

Chris developed friendships with many new students from the school, even though they did not come to his church or youth group. He went to games and school events with church students or alone and began to build friendships. He even began an optional chapel for football players before football games. He knew that to do evangelism with teens means going into their culture and winning the right to be heard. Doing outreach ministry meant spending 25 percent of his time just hanging out with kids, building relationships. This became a model for the volunteer leaders, who were the focus of another 25 percent of Chris's time.

Quality Investment in Lay Volunteers

Chris discovered that if he wanted volunteers to be effective and enjoy the ministry, he had to spend time with them helping them to be the best they could be. He found out who was running the best youth ministry in the city, then went to those people and talked with them. Denomination was not important; experience and quality were. He learned that a good way to get volunteer leaders started in building relationships with kids was to take an audit of what leaders really enjoyed doing. Then together they looked at how they could do that with kids. One leader fished and set aside time to take kids with him fishing. The times alone with just one or two kids were a great way to build relationships. Another played guitar, and so he and his wife developed a band they could use in the new Cross Over program.

Wise Time Management

Chris learned to balance his limited time. His ministry investment had to be appropriately divided between planning the program so it was effective and helping to run the program. Good, basic administration and communication with

kids, parents, and the whole church were not Chris's strengths.
Yet he knew these elements were very important, and they are
areas he is growing into. Many youth ministers look like they
are shooting from the hip with no real plan—even if they have
one—and this hurts their programs. Students and parents both
like things that are well planned and well communicated.

WHAT ARE THE VALUES
OF CHRISTIAN SCHOOL EDUCATION?
DAVID L. ROTH

Role Modeling

Dr. Luke quotes Jesus as saying that "a student
. . . will be like his teacher" (Luke 6:40). The
primary way we as Christian school educators can
minister to church kids in Christian schools is by
being godly role models before them. Students
"hear" what we do much more quickly than they
hear what we say. Our teaching and our ministry
take on meaning and become worthy of emula-
tion in the eyes of a student when the fruits of the
Spirit—such as love, kindness, and gentleness—
are seen during times of stress and crisis in our
lives.

Integration

There is an axiom in Christian circles that one
can't preach beyond one's experience. If teaching
how to integrate faith and learning is a way to
minister to church kids in Christian schools, the
teacher must himself be integrated before he can
ever hope to understand and effectively teach
integration. Students need to be *shown* how their
faith will affect their daily lives.

Truth

In a world where everybody seems to be saying
truth is relative, we can forcefully say that there is

such a thing as absolute truth. The late headmaster of Stony Brook School, Frank Gaebelein, was fond of quoting the maxim "All truth is God's truth." Some people express concern that kids in Christian schools are sheltered. One response to that concern is to note that in fact students in the public school are the ones who are sheltered from truth —truth about man's sinful nature and truth about who God is. The key textbook in the Christian school is the Bible, in which we can study the life of the One who said, "I am truth." It is exciting to be able to teach students that there are absolutes.

Teaching Students to Think

A primary ministry in the Christian school is to teach young people to think—not give pat answers, but really think and then respond. Unlike the Sunday school teacher who interacts with a student one hour a week, Christian school teachers have six hours a day, five days a week to nurture growth. A primary goal of the Christian schoolteacher is to help students grow deeper into the Word. We focus on the head and the heart—on the practical and the theological. In the context of the Christian school, one has the opportunity to teach and to challenge students daily. Ministry in a Christian school is not a hit-and-run type of activity.

Accountability Partners

It is not uncommon in a Christian school for students to have an accountability partner. Seniors disciple freshmen. Classmates hold each other accountable through prayer and Bible reading. This can and does happen in Christian schools where there is a vision for impacting students' lives.

Journaling

Joshua, the Old Testament leader, didn't ask the Israelites to keep journals, but he did ask them to pile up stones of remembrance. When future generations asked, "What do these stones mean?" (Joshua 4:21), the people were prepared to tell their children of God's power and love. Likewise, we can help students in our Christian school learn the values of keeping prayer journals. Journals can help a young person to remember God's greatness and His faithfulness.

Freedom

There is great freedom to minister in a Christian school. Prayer and the Bible are not directly or indirectly excluded from the curriculum. When studying Hemingway or Camus in a Christian school, the English teacher can put God's Word alongside the works of these great authors and compare their conclusions with the words of Jesus. In science classes, the Christian schoolteacher will explain the theory of evolution, but definitively point students to the Creator.

Christian Worldview

Some people are annoyed by people who insist on regularly using the phrase "What would Jesus do?" Annoying or not, one of the biggest tasks of a Christian teacher or a Christian parent is to help a child develop a Christian worldview. The incredible exposure young people have to every technological development, societal trend, and political upheaval demands a response from the thinking Christian. We minister to young people in Christian schools by teaching them how to think Christianly.

Partnership with Parents

The bottom-line responsibility for the spiritual growth of children lies with parents. As Christian teachers we serve *in loco parentis,* in place of the parent. The Christian teacher and Christian parent work in partnership; together they work in partnership with the youth pastor, the Sunday school teacher, and the church. Nothing reinforces the teachings of God's Word more in the mind of the student than the consistency of the message among parents, pastors, and teachers, i.e., home, church, and school.

Servant Leaders

The goal of the Christian school is to produce servant leaders (Matthew 20:25–28). We minister to Christian students in Christian schools to help them develop into leaders in the youth ministries of our churches. Our objective is to give students the skills and tools to minister. Our Christian school students need to know Scripture well enough to lead biblically.

Temptation

Josh McDowell's famous survey of young people indicated that moral choices made by Christian young people aren't as upright as many Christians would like to think. The fact of the matter is that Christian school students face the same temptations young people in public schools face. We minister to church kids in the Christian school by directing our attention to matters of the heart. We focus on character issues that equip young people to make good choices when faced with temptation.

Service

The Christian school student is given opportunities to serve locally and internationally. The importance of going on short-term missions trips while in high school is stressed. We don't want robots in our Christian schools just saying, "Jesus loves me." We encourage our students to have a passion for outreach and for missions. The Christian school has a mandate to put its students into situations where they can minister. We minister to kids in Christian schools by teaching them to minister.

The Christian school provides a unique boot camp experience under the instruction of godly role models for students. The goal of ministry to students in the Christian school is to produce authentic servant-leaders who are well equipped to impact the world for Christ and His kingdom.

TOTAL CHURCH FOCUS: FIRST AND FOREMOST

From the initial stages of step two to the ongoing process of lay leadership development, Chris was aided by the outreach focus of the whole church. The average church in the United States only has about 30 percent of its adult members involved in attending Sunday school and other training programs. As a result there are never enough trained, mature leaders in the church. Since youth ministry demands many leaders, a church like Pleasant Hills makes the job a lot easier by developing a good adult Christian education program and encouraging all of its members to participate.

In response to perceived needs, the leadership in Pleasant Hills also developed a blended worship format of contemporary and traditional music. Parents of teens in the youth program who were not church members were encouraged to attend church along with their kids. Classes and small groups for the parents were added to the overall program of the church. Renewal had occurred, not because the church had hired Chris to take care of the youth, but because the church was in partnership with Chris to reach students for Jesus Christ.

May the renewal of Pleasant Hills provide inspiration and instruction for all the "Collinsville" churches that remain inwardly focused in youth ministry.

FOR FURTHER READING

Benson, Peter L., and Carolyn H. Eklin. 1990. *Effective Christian Education*. Minneapolis: Search Institute.

Bertolini, Dewey M. 1994. *Back to the Heart of Youth Work*. Wheaton, Ill.: Victor.

Burns, Jim. 1988. *The Youth Builder*. Eugene, Oreg.: Harvest House.

Coleman, Robert E. 1963. *The Master Plan of Evangelism*. Old Tappan, N.J.: Revell.

Mueller, Walt. 1994. *Understanding Today's Youth Culture*. Wheaton, Ill.: Tyndale.

Ott, Stanley. 1989. *The Vibrant Church: A People-Building Plan for Congregation Health*, edited by Carol Lacey. Ventura, Calif.: Regal.

Robbins, Duffy. 1990. *The Ministry of Nurture*. Grand Rapids: Zondervan.

Veerman, David R. 1988. *Youth Evangelism*. Wheaton, Ill.: Victor.

16

OUTREACH: HOW DO WE REACH IRRELIGIOUS STUDENTS?

Bo Boshers

Derrick is a typical seventeen-year-old American high school student. He has a B average, is a member of the junior varsity soccer team, and works fifteen hours each weekend at a local hardware store. Derrick dreams of one day owning his own business. With the work ethic his family has instilled in him and his natural relational skills, he seems destined to realize those dreams. Derrick has a younger sister, Tina, an eighth grader. His mom, Martha, has a part-time business she runs out of their home, and his dad, Tim, works in sales.

Derrick is by all accounts an average teenager. He is even average in his religious life. He is what has been termed "unchurched." When he was preschool age, his parents were nominally involved in a local church, and they still attend the annual Christmas Eve service. He has no true affiliations, however, with a particular church body or religious group.

Derrick is not without an awareness of God; he simply does not actively pursue any relationship with Him. Like the majority of his peers, he is outside the bounds of the influence of any Christian youth ministry leaders in the community. He is not antireligious, but he is decidedly irreligious in his daily personal life.

It has been suggested that only 25 percent of the populations of local high schools are being reached by the traditional church and parachurch youth groups. The other 75 percent, the "Derrick's," are left without a clear witness to Jesus Christ. If it is true that the majority of youth ministry resources is going into efforts to effect spiritual change in only 25 percent of the high school population today, it is time to take a serious look at how we can minister to the other 75 percent.

REACHING IRRELIGIOUS STUDENTS

How can a youth ministry earn the right to be heard by nontraditional high school students? How can we connect relationally with the Derricks in the local high school? What is the best language for communicating with today's high school culture? And how can we keep the vital balance in youth ministry between discipleship and evangelism so that we continue to care for our own in the process of reaching out to the other 75 percent?

Seeking answers to these questions fuels the ministry of Student Impact, the high school ministry of Willow Creek Community Church in South Barrington, Illinois. Our mission statement is "to turn irreligious students into fully developed followers of Christ." Within our mission, we define a "fully developed follower" as a student who

- personally understands the grace of God, and has trusted Christ as Savior;
- is committed to spiritual growth and demonstrates a pattern of life change;
- is committed to a small group of fellow believers to pursue maturity and community;
- is learning to express his or her God-given gifts as a servant of Christ; and

• is practicing good stewardship to the church by taking responsibility to own a part of God's work in the church.

With this vision as a backdrop, we have taken a close look at what makes a student ministry effective in reaching irreligious high school students (see also Boshers 1996). At the core of our approach to reaching students is our commitment to be a *student ministry* rather than merely being a *youth group*.

TRADITIONAL YOUTH GROUPS

The traditional youth group tends to be characterized by the following traits.

1. It is activity driven.
2. It sticks with tradition and forgets to ask the question Why?
3. It lacks vision and direction.
4. It has a tendency to focus inward, which can lead to stagnation and minimum growth.

What effect do these traits have on the ministry? Before answering this question, it will be helpful to describe briefly each of the four characteristics.

Activity Driven

What does it mean to be activity driven? Simply this: The youth group revolves around whatever event is on the calendar. Sure, the event may be fun (and that can be good), but no one asks if the activity fits into the mission and vision of the ministry. Does the event serve a purpose in the ministry year? Or is it simply an item on the schedule, because every week the youth group needs to get together to satisfy the kids and their parents? Purposeless activities do not move your ministry closer to the goal of doing effective outreach.

Traditionalism

A youth group that does things the same way it always has or one that is afraid to challenge the norm is in danger. The danger is that growth will not occur because today's youth culture does not fit with yesterday's youth group ideas. To be effective, you must be relevant.

Lack of Vision and Direction

If there is no vision or direction, what motivates students (or anyone, for that matter) to continue to participate and grow? Challenge and guidance are important factors. In their absence, students will find little or no reason to participate— especially long term—in the church. Their experiences as students can shape their motivation to be involved in the church as adults.

Inward Focus

Inward focus. Stagnation. Minimum growth. If your values are to reach the lost, an inward focus will never get you there. Your ministry as a youth leader must help students to look outward to the lost and confused. Jesus had great compassion for the multitudes "because they were like sheep without a shepherd" (Mark 6:34). How will multitudes ever find the shepherd without assistance?

Summary

The picture looks bleak for the lost 75 percent if youth leaders operate with a youth group mentality. The traits identified above prevent ministries not only from doing outreach but from experiencing internal growth. How can we take a fresh look at youth ministry? What if we establish some new principles for operating a youth ministry? The next section takes a look at some values that we have incorporated into Student Impact.

STUDENT MINISTRIES

A student ministry differs from a youth group in significant ways. Here are some of the basic principles.

- It is purpose driven.
- Its leaders communicate the vision.
- It has compassion for the lost and is excited about evangelism.

- It values prayer and worship.
- It meets students' needs for acceptance and accountability.

Purpose Driven

In contrast to a youth group, a student ministry has a purpose behind each activity that takes place. Leaders ask "Why?" every time an event or activity is proposed. The event must fit into the vision and mission of the ministry. Then it can meet the need for some aspect of the ministry goal—in this case, reaching the unconnected. Students can understand and own that. Their understanding means that they can focus on making good use of the purpose of the event—perhaps by bringing a friend, having a significant conversation, or building a relational bridge with someone they do not know.

Vision

True leaders do not just lead. They launch a visionary movement that a certain number of people can resonate with. Martin Luther King certainly knew how to attract, organize, inspire, and lead people, but what earned him a place in history is that he cast a vision. Likewise, Jesus combined His leadership skills with the overpowering vision of redeeming the world and establishing the church.

Vision must be clearly defined if it is going to be caught by others. Part of the success of Student Impact is not just the fact that we have a vision for reaching lost high school students but that we have that vision clearly defined in our Seven-Step Strategy.

The Seven-Step Strategy

Step 1. Integrity Friendship

The process begins as we challenge our core students to build relational bridges to their non-Christian friends.

Step 2. Verbal Witness

After they build relationships with non-Christian friends, we teach our core students to look for opportunities, in various ways, to explain and discuss their relationship with Christ.

Step 3. Student Impact: Providing a service for seekers

The Student Impact program is designed to nurture a student's spiritual interest by introducing him or her to the message of Christ in a contemporary and relevant way. Impact is intended to be used as a tool by our core students to reach their non-Christian friends and to be a supplement to their ongoing witness.

We believe that every high school student can be challenged by and exposed to God's truth in a relevant, practical way through Student Impact's program and messages. The purpose is achieved through the program elements by moving students emotionally to see God's love by exposing God's truth in a relevant, practical way through the communicative arts. The purpose is also achieved during the message section of the event through the teaching of God's truth from His Word. The message ends with a question to spiritually challenge students, which in turn can lead to significant conversations with friends or leaders.

Step 4. Spiritual Challenge

At this stage of their friendship, we teach our core students to ask pointed questions that intentionally challenge their friends to consider the claims of Christ. We believe that once a seeker has spent time listening to God's Word and observing fully devoted Christian students, he or she will discover through the conviction of the Holy Spirit his or her need for a personal relationship with Jesus Christ.

Step 5. Student Insight: Integration into the body

The Student Insight evening is designed to mature the new believer on the trek toward full devotion to Christ. Insight provides believers with an opportunity to participate in corporate worship and to listen to expository Bible teaching. We believe that each student can be deepened spiritually by studying God's Word and living out four aspects of the Christian life: a personal relationship with Christ, relationships with friends, building the church, and impacting the world. This stage will be achieved through the Insight program by moving students emotionally to challenge them to become fully devoted followers of Christ by exposing God's truth in a relevant, practical way through the communicative arts, worship, the Word, communion, and community.

Step 6. Discipleship "D-Teams"

D-Teams (small groups) provide a discipleship small group atmosphere that is triggered by a quality adult leader, an apprentice leader, and four to six student members. From this small group comes accountability, encouragement, and support, as well as biblical teaching through learning experiences. The following are our values within and the reasons for creating and supporting D-Teams:

- D-Teams are an essential element in the strategy of Student Impact.
- D-Teams are instrumental to a balanced and biblical process of spiritual growth, including evangelism and discipleship.
- D-Team leadership is reserved for spiritually mature high school seniors or adults.
- D-Team learning is maximized by student involvement within the context of a meaningful environment.
- D-Teams will study the Student Impact curriculum, but at a pace and level appropriate for the D-Team.
- D-Team leaders use the CLEAR method (discussed later in this chapter) when preparing the D-Teams to stay focused on the ministry purposes.
- D-Team leaders are led by their campus directors to receive shepherding and accountability.

Step 7. Ownership

At this stage of a student's spiritual development, he or she is taking an active role in service in the church. Through opportunities such as tithing or participating in our annual fund-raiser, STRIVE (a one-day work-a-thon during which we raise our entire yearly youth ministry budget), as well as through using their spiritual gifts in various other serving opportunities, thus owning their part of the Lord's work. A student now steps forward and takes the role of evangelist within his or her own circle of influence, and in turn begins a third spiritual generation. This stage occurs as the student takes non-Christian friends through the same seven steps he or she initially traveled.

Vision Casting

Students become excited about a vision they can grasp and own. The Seven-Step Strategy demonstrates how a vision can be specific, defined, and measurable. The vision must also be powerfully articulated—and rearticulated—so that everyone stays on track. That requires constant attention and continual restatement. But it is what our students need—constant reminders of why we do what we do, and of what the vision is. For purposes of application, students are asked to think about the questions below and their value in making sure that vision is happening, with the end result of reaching lost students.

- Does the person you are leading know where you are trying to take him or her?
- Does he know what the vision is? Specifically?
- Could he or she articulate it from memory?

Never underestimate the importance of vision casting in keeping student ministry evangelism clearly focused.

Compassion for the Lost and Excitement About Evangelism

How are these crucial elements developed in a student ministry? Be patient in positioning these key building blocks. First build a core of committed students within your ministry. Building a core means you must identify the "players." Christ did the same thing when He called His disciples. God uses ordinary people to do extraordinary things. Choose those who are ready, available, willing, and coachable. Once they are chosen, motivate them by giving them something to believe in. Paint the vision for what can be. Then draw the line. Give students the choice to follow, but clearly lay out what it means to be committed.

At this point, you are ready to go deeper. Invest in those who are committed. We are reminded in 2 Timothy 2:2, "The things you have heard me say in the presence of many witnesses entrust to reliable men who will also be qualified to teach others."

Finally, give these students opportunities to make a difference by entrusting them with teaching, and encouraging them in their evangelistic efforts. When students are given the chance to take ownership, you will be surprised at the ways they can make a difference.

What does building a core have to do with reaching unconnected high school students? Think about this: Once you have taken care of a small group of students and have focused on shepherding each individual into a growing relationship with Christ, compassion and evangelism will happen naturally for them. Those heart conditions are contagious—but they must be nurtured. At Willow Creek we believe strongly that reaching those outside the church happens most powerfully and effectively through relationships. If that is true, those who are reaching out need to have a solid relationship with the Lord Jesus Christ.

Prayer and Worship

The prayer and worship element is the thermometer of student ministry. How can we do anything for the lost if we are not connected fully to our Creator? Prayer connects us. Worship reminds us of who we are in Christ. Again, when we are in this position, we are poised for making a difference outside our Christian circles because we can't help but want to share what God is doing in our lives.

Acceptance and Accountability

Students face incredible peer pressure and find the world to be a cold, unrelational, uncaring place. What will make you and your church any different? What could possibly attract those who feel unwelcome or uncared for elsewhere? Acceptance is a priceless gift for those who feel judged or distanced in the world. And those are the unconnected 75 percent our hearts long to be connected to Christ. Accountability can provide the challenge that students need to keep them motivated to change and grow.

BALANCING THE SCALES
OF EVANGELISM AND DISCIPLESHIP

Much of what has been thus far developed has focused on methods for reaching the unconnected 75 percent. But in the midst of that battle, we can never lose sight of caring for our own. Consider the following statistics that occur each day in the United States:

1,000	unwed teenage girls become mothers.
1,106	teenagers get abortions.
4,219	teenagers contract sexually transmitted diseases.
500	adolescents begin using drugs.
1,000	adolescents experiment with alcohol.
6	teens commit suicide.
2,200	teens are assaulted; 80 are raped.
135,000	adolescents bring guns or other weapons to school.

(Dobson 1994, 6)

Given this sad picture of youth culture, it is obvious that caring for our own is crucial. They are not unscathed by the pain and confusion of the world.

Student Impact's leadership believes it is possible and right to shepherd our own, even in the midst of reaching those who are not familiar with church. By balancing the scales of discipleship and evangelism and adding the vital element of small groups, our own students in the church can be drawn closer to Christ.

The Value of Small Groups

Small groups build community within a student ministry. And community is something we all long for. It is an avenue for providing the acceptance and accountability that is so essential for your core students to have before they can extend it to the unconnected. Small groups can provide a place for prayer, honesty, encouragement, confrontation, teaching, for-giveness, and fun!

Beyond this, small groups make significant contributions to the overall effectiveness of the student ministry.

Small groups prevent program-driven ministry. Small groups remind students to take ownership in the ministry instead of just attending. If a student merely attends your ministry but never participates, he or she will likely not develop the skills to share Christ with others, let alone face the pressures of man and the world after graduation.

Small groups disciple students and leaders. Without bibli-cally based small group study, there is very little control of the discipleship and growth elements of a ministry. Every student needs a shepherd if he is to experience a place of safety, rest, and care. Small groups provide a place not only for that to happen, but also for student and leader investment in the lives of others to occur.

Life change happens best in the context of small groups. Life-on-life daily accountability and experience allow us to remind each other of what it means to be Christlike in the big and small things. Each of us desires to have someone with whom we can talk through life's issues and sort out daily experiences. If we provide a Christ-honoring place in which that can happen, we are honoring God's plan for the disciple-ship and growth process.

Small groups allow a growing ministry to stay small. Stu-dents and leaders will always have a "home" within the larger ministry, since they will always have a place to connect with friends.

The Process of Starting Small Groups

Finding a small group structure that will work well within your ministry is worth the investment of time. Much of Stu-dent Impact is modeled after the small group concept present-ed in Carl George's book *Prepare Your Church for the Future*

(1992). George's philosophy of small group life is about care: "The most significant church ministry manifests itself as changed lives in the context of a small community of believers who use their gifts to serve their group and their world. Only on the cell level can man's deeply felt care needs be met" (57).

We have chosen to monitor and inspect what is happening in group life is through what we call the CLEAR method. In addition to our staff visiting various small groups on a regular basis, each leader is given freedom to be creative in his leadership of the group but has a core curriculum and method on which to base the group. Our CLEAR method upholds these essential values:

C — Teaching *Christ,* using passages from His life
L — *Listening* to students; meeting their need to be heard
E — Placing value on and praying for the *Empty* chair . . . the sudent who has yet to connect to the ministry.
A — *Affirming* students, both in what they are learning and in how Christ is changing their lives
R — *Reading* and praying; the Bible is opened and read; prayer is included

In addition to following these guidelines, which assist in preparation as well as group interaction, each leader submits a CLEAR report after his or her group meeting, evaluating what happened based on these criteria. This allows us to take the pulse of the ministry and get a feel for the life-changing experiences happening ministry-wide.

The Impact of Effective Small Groups

What happens when small groups are working well?

First, the desire for accountability for all students and leaders is met and the value of integrity is raised.

Second, care is provided for the small group leaders. Instead of one main youth director providing training, information, care, and leadership for each person, he or she can care for a group of leaders who care for others. Our goal in this structure is to prevent burnout and enable leaders to serve long term. We clearly define what the expectations of the position are, allow for an appropriate amount of care for each leader, and provide training and development opportunities. When those three essentials are in place, our leaders' needs are met and they can focus on shepherding their students, who in turn cannot help but reach out to others who need care.

Third, when your core feels cared for and their needs are being met, they will bring new life into your ministry—both through their relationships with Christ as well as through bringing in new group participants. Suddenly, recruiting and growth happen naturally. Growth happens through multiplication, for all groups are experiencing growth as they bring in new participants. Cliques are avoided, and the new participants prevent stagnation.

Not only are the students encouraged to bring friends, but leaders are constantly on the lookout for a young person they can bring into the group to serve as an apprentice. This apprentice will find a caring environment and will be in a position to serve as the group grows and needs to "birth" a new small group. Potentially, the original leader could take half of the group, and the apprentice leader the other half. The cycle of growth through multiplication would begin again, all within the context of healthy discipleship and evangelism, serving both core students and those outside the church.

SUMMARY

We have discussed what a youth group is and why that school of thought will minister to the connected 25 percent. We've also discussed what a student ministry is and why it has great potential to reach the unconnected 75 percent. Within the vision aspect of student ministry, we have defined what Student Impact is and does and what has developed as a strategy for impacting the lost. For the 25 percent, we've discussed the value of balancing the scales of discipleship and evangelism. Within that balance, we have discussed the importance of small group life. But what have we really said and learned about the lost 75 percent and the connected 25 percent? And why is it truly important?

To answer those questions, we must go to two familiar passages of Scripture. The first is Matthew 28:19: "Therefore go and make disciples of all nations, baptizing them in the name of the Father and of the Son and of the Holy Spirit." It is clear that God has called us not only to think about the "75 percent" but to *seek* them out and *draw* them toward God, using the gifts and opportunities He provides. We must be about evangelism—reaching the lost.

The second is Matthew 22:37–39, which records Christ's words about love: "'Love the Lord your God with all your heart and with all your soul and with all your mind.' This is the first and greatest commandment. And the second is like it: 'Love your neighbor as yourself.'" If we apply these principles we cannot miss the fact that Christ is calling us to discipleship —to love Him, and, out of obedience, to love others. Small groups are prime places for discipleship to happen. Of course, small groups can never replace the individual relationships we must have with Christ. But they can supplement and complement that in ways we may not have previously imagined.

Evangelism and discipleship: two things God has clearly laid out for us to be about. We encourage you to use the thoughts in this chapter to help you develop your own student ministry philosophy for accomplishing both elements. They are equally important and worth the investment of prayer and thought in hearing what God is calling you to do as you potentially take on the high calling of student ministry leadership.

WORKS CITED

Boshers, Bo. 1996. *Youth Group Versus Student Ministry.* Grand Rapids: Zondervan.

Dobson, James. 1994. *Right from Wrong.* Waco, Tex.: Word.

George, Carl. 1992. *Prepare Your Church for the Future.* Tarrytown, N.Y.: Revell.

17

HOW SHOULD
WE TEACH
BIBLICAL TRUTH?

Ronald T. Habermas

Teaching is scary. Teaching God's Word is even scarier. Teaching God's Word to twenty apparently uninterested, constantly moving junior high students may be the scariest of all.

Most teachers of the Word are aware of James's warning to teachers (James 3:1), but few realize that this apostle's concern was heightened by his insight into the comprehensive dimensions of pedagogy. For example, teaching certainly includes content, for James refers to what a person "says" (v. 2). But godly instruction is much more than verbally imparting truth. That is why James also identifies the "many ways" that teachers fail, along with the need a person has to "keep his whole body in check" (v. 2).

So when it comes to asking the critical question, "How should youth leaders teach Scripture?" teachers must never avoid the tension between valuing the big picture and seeking specific strategies. Maintaining that tension enables a youth minister leading the junior high Bible study consistently to see the forest as well as the trees.

THE "FOREST":
PEDAGOGICAL PRINCIPLES FOR TEACHERS

When the poet Alexander Pope said, "A little knowledge is a dangerous thing," he was commenting on the errors people make when they know only a little bit about a subject and do not have a comprehensive picture. What he said surely applies to the novice youth instructor who naively thinks that teaching means telling a couple of jokes and sharing a few good ideas now and then. Without a disciplined understanding of the teaching-learning process, teachers of youth may fail to evaluate themselves along the lines of foundational educational questions. Leaders need to be prepared to ask critical questions: "What are the implications of what I am teaching students about what it means to be a Christian disciple?" "What does the particular methodology I have selected say about my view of students as people?" "Are there any inconsistencies with what I purport to believe about the learning process and what I am teaching or how I am teaching it?"

When teachers of junior high and high school students prepare for teaching God's Word, they need to think through their philosophy of ministry. This process of surveying the "forest" begins with such questions as these: "How do I view myself and my calling?" "How is God presently working in my life?" and "What do I need to do to personally prepare myself for this awesome task of shaping youth?"

The following guidelines for teaching are not an exhaustive list, but they are drawn predominantly from Christ's example and will be useful to any youth worker. These principles will help teachers improve the quality of their teaching by focusing on the leader's role in the process of teaching and learning.

Be a Lifelong Learner

Whereas ample evidence abounds to demonstrate Christ's supernatural knowledge (for example, Luke 6:8 testifies that when the Lord confronted the Pharisees, He "knew what they were thinking"), for the most part, Jesus learned just as all humanity does. He memorized Hebrew as a young lad, He studied Jewish culture, and, more than likely, He was even reminded to do His homework. Luke 2:52 summarizes that the Son "grew in wisdom."

The mystery of Jesus, as the God-man, is that He voluntarily chose to temporarily set aside His ability to know everything. Therefore, in Hebrews 5:8, the Bible states, "Although he was a son, he learned obedience." Furthermore, Christ's own testimony regarding His knowledge of His second coming to earth is that He was uncertain; only God the Father knew the exact time, He said (Matthew 24:36).

Perhaps the best single lesson we can glean from the Master Teacher's cognitive example surfaces in John 15:15. There, Jesus makes a case for lifelong learning. How relevant for contemporary youth educators! In the final discourse to the disciples, He reviews His ministry while disclosing signs of cognitive maturity—both personally and interpersonally—testifying: "I no longer call you servants, because a servant does not know his master's business. Instead, I have called you friends, for everything that I learned from my Father I have made known to you."

Doubt Boldly

Revising a phrase from Reformer Martin Luther, successful youth workers must doubt boldly. Leaders must learn to be comfortable in the naturally uncomfortable places of doubt in the teaching-learning process.

Ted Ward is recognized as a proponent of the conception that humans are whole beings and quite complex. He offers a useful analogy to this end. Employing the picture of a person's hand, Ward suggests that everyone is comprised of six distinct categories. The thumb and finger represent the physical, mental, emotional, social, and moral domains; the palm represents the sixth domain, the spiritual (Ward 1979, 18). Each domain influences and is influenced by the other five. Consider, for example, the correlation between the mental and spiritual domains. Anytime someone does not know everything, doubts may arise.

MORAL CONVICTIONS/
PERSONAL CONVICTIONS
KEVIN E. LAWSON

I had been talking with a sixth grader about problems she was having with some friendships. As we finished I told her that I would be praying, asking God to help her. She began to cry, saying, "I'm not sure I believe in God." Up to this point our conversation had been fairly calm, but now she sobbed that she was scared about her doubts and what they might mean.

Here was a girl who grew up attending church and actively participating in the children's choir, club programs, Sunday school, and VBS. Her parents were Christians, as were many of her friends. She had professed faith in Christ at six and was baptized at nine. In spite of this supportive environment and personal faith-experience, growing inside of her was a collection of nagging doubts and questions about what she had been taught all her life, and it scared her to death! What would her friends and family think if she didn't believe as they did? What would they do?

Not only was *she* scared, but I found the cold grip of fear growing in *me*. I loved this girl—wasn't there something I could do to make her doubts go away? Couldn't I protect her from the questions that scared her? I reluctantly concluded that I could not. I could only help her through the process.

Using Westerhoff's model of faith development, I talked with her about how when she was little God had given her parents who loved Him and wanted to know and follow Him. She had grown up in that family, experiencing the faith of her parents, and through that had come to know and believe certain things about God.

Then when she was a little older, I said, she had attended church, where others modeled their faith and taught her about God from His Word. She had joined in the events and life of the church, accepting what she was taught without a lot of questioning. The questions she was wrestling with were good ones that needed to be answered, I said. God wasn't angry with her, and neither was I.

Some of the concepts of Christianity she had held as a child needed to be corrected, I told her, and this would only come as she found answers to her questions. This time of "searching" was God's way of strengthening her faith, making it her own, not just something handed down by her parents. It was a bit scary, but it was an important step to an "owned faith" that would be strong. I told her that God loved her, and so did I, and we wanted to listen to her questions and help her find good answers.

She listened intently and her tears subsided. Over the next few years she remained involved in the church. Her doubts and questioning continued, and she had her ups and downs, but her faith grew clearer and stronger. With the support of teachers and friends she began to resolve the doubts and "own" her faith. She continues to work through what she believes and its implications, and she is trying to live by those new convictions. Instead of being a leaf blown about by the wind, she is becoming a tree with strong roots.

At least three key followers of Christ exhibited this healthy form of doubts in the New Testament: the father of the demon-possessed boy; John the Baptist; and Thomas, the disciple. The case of the father of the demon-possessed boy (see Mark 9:21–27) expresses a curious, yet liberating, testimony. When Jesus asked this man if he had faith in Christ for his son's healing, the father replied, "I do believe; help me overcome my unbelief!" (v. 24). By subsequently healing the boy, Jesus implicitly confirms that doubt and question marks of faith can coexist simultaneously within the same person. Moreover, this miracle shows that, even when people are in this state of spiritual turmoil, heavenly blessings are not withheld. (Note that these types of doubt are not to be confused with the rejection and disbelief of the Pharisees.)

What application of these facts can be made to youth work? Doubts are as natural as breathing. When we substitute the term *dissonance* for doubt (from Piaget's theory), we realize that doubts are not only natural, but are necessary for growth and are essential for moving from one cognitive stage to another, and from one spiritual plane to the next. They are part of life *and* faith.

Never link doubts with stubborn disbelief. They are not synonymous. The former represents honest struggles, the all-too-transparent ebbs and flows of growing cognition and faith. The latter represents the Pharisee's "don't confuse me with the facts; my mind is made up" attitude. Its disposition is unteachable. Its people are untouchable.

Fully Face Agonies of Spirit

We must never forget Christ's own turmoil and despair, a mental and spiritual anguish, which included these struggles:

- (John 13:21) "After he had said this, Jesus was troubled in spirit and testified, 'I tell you the truth, one of you is going to betray me.'"
- (Mark 14:34) In the Garden of Gethsemane, He told His followers: "My soul is overwhelmed with sorrow to the point of death."

Jesus knew what was to come, and He grieved over it. Jesus' fullest agony is revealed when He cried out in a loud voice on the cross: "My God, my God, why have you forsaken me?" (Mark 15:34). Theologians have never completely understood this mystery. Rather than dismiss Jesus' humanity, however, we should celebrate His experiences. For as we do, we authenticate our own struggles and those of our students.

Connect Head, Heart, and Hand

When the people heard Peter's convicting sermon on the Day of Pentecost, Luke records, "They were cut to the heart and said to Peter and the other apostles, 'Brothers, what shall we do?'" (Acts 2:37). Any noteworthy youth education will ultimately contain three components, often identified as: (1) the cognitive/intellectual ("the people heard"); (2) the affective/emotional ("cut to the heart"); and (3) the skill/behavioral ("what shall we do").

Jesus constantly used His head and challenged others to do the same (see Matthew 17:24–27 and Luke 21:14–15). When asked what the greatest commandment was, Jesus added the word "mind" to the Old Testament *Shema,* commanding that people are to love God totally (Mark 12:28–31). Also, the Master Teacher expressly concluded that believers cannot become disciples without first attending to a rigorous plan of intentional, rational assessment (see Luke 14:25–33).

Certainly the affective domain was also at the fore of Jesus' instruction. In his book *Why I Am Not a Christian,* atheist Bertrand Russell confessed that although he believed Jesus to be no more than a humanistic moral prophet, modern progressivism owes its debt to Christ's influential concept of compassion. Youth workers need to be consciously in touch with God, for the affective domain features the value-laden treasures of our faith in Him and our passion for Him.

Add to these two domains the numerous references to Jesus' condemnation of the Pharisees for not practicing what they preached, and the third domain of behavior is highlighted. In several instances, Jesus deftly plied the skills of sharp wit and tongue to corner His opponents for their inconsistencies. In Matthew the Teacher doggedly challenged the religious leaders concerning such topics as

- keeping the Sabbath (12:3–8)
- divorce (19:4–12)
- the insights of children (21:16)

- His own rejection (21:42)
- the coming resurrection of the dead (22:29–32)

Repeatedly Jesus confronted the religious teachers with the statement, "Have you not read?" What an embarrassment! For these leaders had not only read the verse in question, they had memorized it! Jesus was mocking the authorities' ineptness at understanding and obeying what they had put to memory. He was leveling the worst criticism of all: When it came to following God's Word, the religious leaders' lives didn't match up.

THE "TREES": INSIGHTS THAT CONNECT TEACHERS WITH STUDENTS

When we picture Christ's instructional design holistically—both the "what" and the "how" of teaching—His model for youth ministry is at its best. It is more realistic, responsible, and dynamic. His noble pattern enables us to envision the "forest" and clearly see the "trees," the practical aspects of effective instruction. For example, in contrast to the verbal battles that are often waged today in youth work, why is it that the masses who heard Jesus never once accused Him of either irreverence or irrelevance? Because He was the Great Teacher who lived out what He taught. He balanced the truth of God's Word with the needs of the world. Here are a few ways He achieved that hybrid goal that youth ministry leaders must follow.

Be Sensitive to Learner-Initiated Comments

Of the more than one hundred teaching situations found in the Gospels, more than half were initiated by the people Jesus encountered. In light of such a curious approach to teaching, there must have been something quite important to Jesus about patiently waiting for and even encouraging learner response. At a minimum, youth leaders who follow a student-sensitive approach will begin to comprehend a student's thoughts. That benefit, alone, is worth it.

SUNDAY SCHOOL
DEWEY BERTOLINI

To paraphrase that master of the metaphor, Mark Twain, "The reports of Sunday school's death have been greatly exaggerated."

Contrary to popular belief, the Sunday school is *not* dead. It isn't even sick. Oh, sure, there may be some old-time traditions that the church of the twenty-first century will have to jettison in order to remain culturally contemporary. But the Sunday school is not one of them.

In my humble opinion, the Sunday school hour is the single most significant hour in the lives of Christian young people today. Let me tell you why.

A young person will spend an average of six hours per day in school, five days per week. That works out to a whopping thirty hours a week of formal training in a number of disciplines, ranging from how to calculate the length of the hypotenuse in a right triangle to how to properly put on a condom. When we factor in a typical student's daily devotion to the television set, we don't need a Pentium-equipped PC to tell us that today's teenagers are bombarded with a plethora of mixed messages. In light of this reality, we dare not disband the Sunday school. We do not have that luxury.

The Sunday school hour, like none other during the week, allows the skilled youth worker to do many things that are urgent and unique. There is no better time for us to

- focus our students' thinking on biblical principles

- apply God's Word in a compelling and relevant manner to our students' lives
- present our students with a healthy balance of topical, theological, and Bible-book studies
- teach the Bible in ways appropriate to the age group
- guide our students in spirited discussions about a whole host of issues that impact their lives daily
- highlight the incomparable importance and privilege of personal Bible study
- exercise our spiritual gifts in a life-changing context
- call our students to a commitment in the biblical sense of the term
- create an environment in which vital, wholesome, and, in some cases, lifelong relationships can begin and flourish
- inspire our students to see a vision and dream a dream about what God can do in and through their lives
- build men and women of character and conviction

Without a doubt, the time has come for youth workers across the land to trumpet a vision of, enthusiasm for, and commitment to the Sunday school. Let's shout together, in unison please, three heartfelt cheers for the Sunday school. *Hip hip hooray! Hip hip hooray! Hip hip hooray!*

Join me in fanning the flame and keeping the bright light of the Sunday school torch burning brilliantly for the sake of the next generation of Christian leaders. They will rise up and call us blessed for refusing to allow that flame to flicker and die.

Know the Neighborhood

In addition to picking up on learner feedback, the prudent youth worker will keep herself aware of changing circumstances inside and outside the classroom. Woe to the leader who is ignorant of shifts in the adolescent environment!

Jesus intentionally studied His subculture before, during, and after He encountered it. Technically, this is known as the discipline of ethnography, a practical application of anthropology and sociology. The gospel of Mark records that Jesus purposefully "sat down opposite the place where the offerings were put and watched the crowd putting their money into the temple treasury" (Mark 12:41). The Lord carefully observed that many wealthy people tossed in "large amounts" of money; meanwhile, a poor widow gave only two insignificant copper coins. Those who would emulate Jesus will intentionally study their own classroom—including nonverbal behavior, visual cues, and social interaction—and they will investigate teen behavior in malls, McDonald's, and other local hangouts in order to stay current on jargon, fashion, individual needs, "who's going with whom" news, music and movie items, and other updates.

Consume God's Word (and Let It Consume You)

Know Scripture, forward and back. Jesus used Holy Writ to fend off the devil in the wilderness, to correct errant teaching of His day (see Matthew 5:21–44, where five times the Lord used the formula "You have heard that it was said . . . But I tell you . . ."), to make people think, and to connect the natural world with the supernatural. Do not forget to stay in love with Jesus—in the process sometimes a task that is easier said than done. Read the Lord's only criticism of the church in Ephesus, to this end (Revelation 2:4). That historical congregation, like many today, had all the right doctrine but no heart commitment.

Create Heartburn in Teens

Luke 24:13–32 identifies one of the greatest earthly rewards of godly instruction. There, two disciples eventually recognized the risen Lord, after their day-long walk to

Emmaus with Him, exclaiming in retrospect: "Were not our hearts burning within us while he talked with us on the road and opened the Scriptures to us?" (v. 32). In particular, this duo notes how their superb instruction by Jesus emerged from (1) a focus on pertinent, value-laden themes ("hearts burning"); (2) social interaction ("with us"); and (3) an informal setting ("on the road").

If the context of this "heartburn" is read (vv. 13–31), we see that the Scriptures finally make sense to these two previously disillusioned followers when Jesus purposefully asked open-ended questions, patiently listened to their interpretations of what had happened (even though many of their views were in error), and then—and only then—taught them what the Bible truly predicted about Him as the risen Savior.

Superior instruction to teens occurs when all of these intentionally dialectical modes of teaching are used. Put another way, superior instruction occurs when praxis—personal reflection on experience and beliefs—is upheld. That is when heartburn comes.

Involve Students in Their Own Learning

Repeatedly, the Master Teacher sought active involvement from His pupils. Contrary to the superficial version of this strategy ("activity for the sake of activity") Jesus' participatory strategies were consistent, even to the end, when He elicited feedback from learner experiences. From Luke's gospel alone, some of these hands-on instances included the following lessons:

- To illustrate both to His followers and to the Pharisees that He was the Lord of the Sabbath, Jesus intentionally allowed His disciples to participate in a forbidden exercise on the Sabbath. As they walked through grain fields, His followers picked the grain and ate the kernels, purposefully setting up a subsequent confrontation with the religious leaders on this topic (6:1–5).
- To demonstrate to John the Baptist's two disciples that He was truly the Messiah, Jesus performed several miracles in their presence. Then, to include them, He turned

and said to them, "Go back and report to John what you have seen and heard" (7:18–23).

- To let the disciples practice what they had learned, Jesus sent His twelve followers out "to preach the kingdom of God and to heal the sick" (9:2). On another occasion, seventy-two followers were commissioned to perform the same tasks (10:1–16); Luke then carefully recorded the debriefing that followed (vv. 17–24).

- To convince His enemies of the truth, even they became involved in their own learning by satisfying Jesus' request to "show me a denarius" (20:24). In so doing, those who were attempting to trap Jesus in the controversy of paying taxes to the Roman government were "astonished by his answer" (v. 26).

Help Only Those Who Desire Help

"God helps those who help themselves" is an oft-quoted phrase, errantly attributed to the Bible. What would be a fair representation of Scripture is to say that Jesus never assisted anybody who did not want it. Frequently this One who worked mighty miracles would ask unusual questions of those He met, inquiries that seemed to have obvious answers—or did they? In John 5, Jesus heard about a lame man who had lain by the pool of Bethesda for thirty-eight years. When Jesus met the man, His first words to him were, "Do you want to get well?" (v. 6). Similarly, when Jesus encountered two blind men in Matthew 9, His initial response to their plea for mercy was to ask, "Do you believe that I am able to do this?" To which they answered, "Yes, Lord" (v. 28).

Why did the Master Teacher take what appears to be a reticent posture, a don't-get-involved-too-quickly attitude? Experienced youth instructors know the answer. They have had their hands figuratively tied by a learner who dismisses their assistance, expertise, and counsel. Students can only be helped once they decide they want to be helped. No passage of Scripture expresses this fact better than the time Jesus Himself registered surprise when the people of His hometown refused His help in Mark 6:1–6. And besides, coercion or manipulation is never Christian. That moral code must never be violated.

THOUGHTS ON
YOUTH SUNDAY SCHOOL
ED ROBINSON

I believe in youth Sunday school. The consistent, relevant look at the intersection of the Bible and life that characterizes a quality Sunday school class is a vital part of any comprehensive, church-based youth ministry. I believe in youth Sunday school enough that, even as a youth ministry professor in a graduate seminary setting, I've taught youth Sunday school in my local church for the past ten years. Three primary factors contribute to the significance of Sunday school for me.

1. Sunday school is the most consistent, systematic, comprehensive approach to Bible study for many teens. With the emergence of high-energy, midweek ministries designed to attract non-Christian teens to an exciting youth group, many youth ministries don't have a holistic approach to Bible study, except for Sunday school and, perhaps, the "core group" Bible studies that meet at other times during the week.

The midweek devotional is often a relevant, biblically based youth talk that focuses on a current hot topic. The target audience varies from non-Christian to nominally Christian. Most midweek programs don't require teens to study God's Word. They are only asked to listen and consider its truths. I'm not knocking the approach. In fact, I encourage my seminary students to develop the skills to present their midweek devotionals well. I'm only saying that midweek ministry isn't usually a systematic, comprehensive Bible study.

As much as we'd like to think otherwise, the "core group" Bible study reaches a very small percentage of any youth group. The Sunday school provides the best opportunity to reach the largest number of teens with a consistent (every week), systematic (challenging teens to discover for themselves the intersection of life and the Word), comprehensive (looking at the whole, not simply our favorite parts) approach to Bible study.

2. *Sunday school is the best chance many teens have for establishing continuity at church between childhood and adulthood.* Sunday school is the most continuous church activity for most persons. Youth activities like youth group meetings, retreats, lock-ins, wacky parties, camps, and mission trips are fairly unique to the six or seven years teens stay in the youth group. These events require a heavy commitment of time and energy. The youth group and its agenda defines to a large degree a "Christian" teen's identity. Most churches don't, nor should they, match the intensity of the youth ministry at the children's or adult levels. Children shouldn't have the same intensity of activity too early in life (some things are worth waiting for), and many adults are too busy for that level of involvement. In this way youth ministry is unique.

Sunday school, however, provides the continuous bridge between the activities of children's ministries and adult ministries—it is most like what takes place on either side. Same time, same place, same focus, different level.

3. *Sunday school provides many teens the best opportunity to develop a relationship with a significant Christian adult other than their parents (or youth pastors).* Let's face it, for many churches Sunday school is the backbone of the youth ministry program, and the Sunday school teacher is often the primary adult Christian influence in a teenager's life (other than parents, in most cases). Most churches don't have the luxury of a profes-

sional youth minister. Whatever youth ministry is accomplished is done by quality, committed lay persons who spend significant time with teens, sharing faith and life together. In most instances, this is a Sunday school teacher. If a youth Sunday school teacher takes the task of building relationships with teens seriously, he or she may have an impact that will last for eternity.

Even when a church can afford a full-time youth minister, that person cannot (and should not) be the primary adult spiritual influence on every teen in the group. Any good youth pastor will facilitate relationships between significant adults and teens and not reserve that influence for him or herself. Quality lay youth workers, most often Sunday school teachers, were there before the youth minister arrived and they'll be there when the youth minister has gone.

In the ten years I've been teaching the youth Sunday school class, I've worked with three youth pastors. They have each done well, but two of them aren't around anymore. I still am! I've had the privilege of influencing three distinct groups of high school students from their freshman to their senior years. Most of the first group have graduated from college, many have families of their own, and one served with me as a co-teacher while he was in college preparing for full-time youth ministry. Ten years have brought many great relationships and opportunities for ministry.

Press for Ownership of Ideas

There is nothing quite so irritating as the learner who never claims personal ownership of any idea. Such a person merely cites authorities ("So-and-so said") or traditions ("We've always done it this way"). For exceptional education to occur, the student will need to move from always relying on external authorities for his beliefs to holding positions on the basis of internal beliefs.

The Master Teacher demonstrated His insights here when He took the time to do some political polling among His followers. "Who do people say the Son of Man is?" (Matthew 16:13). It wasn't as though Jesus didn't know what others were calling Him; rather, the Rabbi was attempting to tabulate a list of public sentiments and opinions. No personal ownership was required of Jesus' followers to answer this first query, for they replied in third-person terms: "Some say John the Baptist; others say Elijah; and still others, Jeremiah or one of the prophets" (v. 14).

The Master Teacher's follow-up question quickly moved the discussion to the heart of the matter. It purposefully took the conversation to the necessary level of personal ownership: "But what about you?" Jesus asked. "Who do you say I am?" (v. 15).

It was Peter, the one who often spoke before he thought—except this time—who jumped in: "You are the Christ, the Son of the living God" (v. 16). Not only was Peter's insight correct and profound, but Bible experts unanimously say that this personal testimony marked the watershed of Jesus' life and ministry. With Peter's words, Christ's work shifted from public service to private focus upon His close disciples, all the way to the Cross.

The power of personal ownership helped to instigate this dramatic shift. And it will do the same for our youth, too.

"FOREST AND TREES": A SYNTHESIS

Ralph Waldo Emerson once said that a student learns more from the book under his or her desk than from the book on it. The disciple Peter experienced this kind of firsthand learning when Jesus used a practical activity (fishing) to teach Peter about God's provision, the believer's relationship to civil authority, and His own position as King. That lesson, found in Matthew 17:24–27, synthesized Jesus' unwavering commitment to both comprehensive education and practical education (the "forest" and the "trees") in four simple verses.

The Master Teacher balanced both kinds of education in Matthew 17 (see the sidebar "Sweet Sixteen: Strategies for Youth Education"). He taught theological truth at the same time He demonstrated a specific way to teach.

> After Jesus and his disciples arrived in Capernaum, the collectors of the two-drachma tax came to Peter and asked, "Doesn't your teacher pay the temple tax?"
>
> "Yes, he does," he replied.
>
> When Peter came into the house, Jesus was the first to speak. "What do you think, Simon?" he asked. "From whom do the kings of the earth collect duty and taxes—from their own sons or from others?"
>
> "From others," Peter answered.
>
> "Then the sons are exempt," Jesus said to him. "But so that we may not offend them, go to the lake and throw out your line. Take the first fish you catch; open its mouth and you will find a four-drachma coin. Take it and give it to them for my tax and yours."

SWEET SIXTEEN:
STRATEGIES FOR YOUTH EDUCATION
RONALD T. HABERMAS

At least sixteen practical strategies are documented in Matthew 17:24–27, which tells a creative method Jesus used to pay the temple tax and teach Peter a few lessons about Himself at the same time. These strategies represent pertinent concepts for twenty-first-century excellence in youth education.

1. Relational. Even though Jesus had compassion for the masses, it was the one-to-one tutoring that He actually preferred. Mark 3:14 notes, for instance, that Jesus intentionally appointed His apostles that "they might be with him." In particular, it was Peter's turn in this passage to meet Jesus face-to-face.

This first concept is nonnegotiable for teen instruction. For, whether it's confronted through formal counseling sessions or through informal encounters at a fast-food stop, youth leaders must regularly make concerted efforts to teach adolescents as individuals, or they will entertain the consequence of youth who perceive they are "just a face in the crowd."

2. *Conversational.* Matthew 17:25 states that "when Peter came into the house, Jesus was the first to speak." He initiated the ensuing dialogue about the required tax. And the Master was not someone who preferred superficial conversation, where the learner symbolically jumps through prescribed hoops for the instructor. The Master sought genuine feedback from Peter.

How can this second concept be implemented by teen leaders? It means that they cannot afford to raise absurd or insignificant issues. Nor can they frame their topics of study insincerely, for that would construct an impenetrable barrier to learning.

3. *Confrontational.* Occasionally teaching is pointed. Meant neither to be harsh nor cruel, it's sometimes aimed at a particular learner. Jesus' opening inquiry in Matthew 17:25, "What do you think?" before He had even posed the question immediately drew Peter into the discussion. That direct query called for serious private attention and individual involvement, yet another component of successful youth instruction.

4. *Rational.* By placing a different emphasis on Jesus' question—"What do you *think?*"—the importance of teen thought is stressed. The Master Teacher, like any skilled facilitator, expected His student's full mental reflection and cognitive commitment. Bill McNabb and Steven Mabry

warn about such no-brainer questions as: "Who do you think God would rather us be like—the apostle Paul or Jack the Ripper?" (McNabb and Mabry 1990, 13). They testify that being bombarded by such questions week in and week out when they were adolescents almost canceled the last bit of interest they had in the Bible. The same warning has always applied to productive teen ministry.

5. *Personal.* The Lord used His learner's original name, not the one He had given him. He called him Simon (Simeon in Hebrew). Peter, the Greek word for Rock (or Cephas in Aramaic), was the name we are more likely to know him by. Simon was his childhood name. It meant "hearing." By using it, it's as though Jesus invitingly said: "Hear this!" or "Listen up!" But He was also expressing His intimate knowledge of His pupil.

Do we know the secret titles that our kids are called "on the street" or in their neighborhoods?

6. *Meaningful.* Matthew 17 indicates that just prior to his instruction with Jesus, Peter had bumped into the tax collectors, who had implied that Jesus was shirking His duties. The apostle denied the charges. Jesus, either aware of Peter's recent conversation or knowledgeable of the season (it was the first-century version of April 15), proceeded to investigate this meaningful topic. His student was all ears.

If our teens were privately asked to rate the number of timely and relevant topics we teach them, what average percentage would they provide? Their standard of relevance is not the only criterion we should use, but it is still important.

7. *Controversial.* The subject of taxes was not solely a "meaningful" one; it also posed troublesome and complex problems. It was a hot topic, if

for nothing more than to reintroduce the controversy of who Jesus was supposed to be. Few believed the Messiah would be a spiritual leader, but most anticipated He would be a political revolutionary. Why would such a leader pay taxes?

What tough issues have we recently raised with our youth? Do they sense the freedom to initiate a controversial topic, if they want to?

8. *Transferable.* Technically called apperception, this educational strategy of Jesus skillfully links familiar ideas with unfamiliar. The Messiah takes the conversation to another level with Simon when He implicitly compares earthly kingdoms to heavenly ones. His lesson plan is straightforward: When Christ gets Peter to acknowledge that earthly kings' sons are obviously tax-exempt, Peter will also realize that the Son of the heavenly King must be exempt, as well.

What intentional connections do we attempt to make between twenty-first-century teens influenced by MTV and a two-thousand-year-old book?

9. *Moral.* The phrase "But so that we might not offend" well describes Jesus' honorable, ethical attitude. He had just told Peter that He did not have to pay taxes as the Son, but now He demonstrated yet another aspect of superior instruction: the teacher's exemplary model. He went beyond the call of duty, and He wanted Peter to know it. He would go ahead and pay taxes to refrain from any possible perception of moral offense.

Do our adolescents perceive us as morally sensitive? Identify three or four terms they might use to describe the moral character of their leaders.

10. *Practical.* The Lord gave Peter a pertinent assignment: "hands-on" homework. "I want you to go fishing," He tells the former fisherman. Wow! Jesus couldn't have selected a more familiar

task for this particular student. Peter could fish in his sleep (and he probably did).

This pragmatic teaching principle must not be lost by contemporary leaders, for we should always ask: "What are my youth able to do? What falls within their skill range?" Again, make no mistake about it, this concept demands specific knowledge of each learner. Jesus purposefully matched His student's talents to the task. Jesus planned for Peter's success.

11. Enjoyable. Whereas the previous point emphasizes the pupil's ability, this point has to do with the student's pleasure. It's the difference between being good at something and liking it. Fishing represented both for Peter.

What do our kids enjoy doing? Obviously, desires will vary among our skaters, cowboys, jocks, and music freaks. Is there any way to teach so as to incorporate several ideas from these diverse groups to produce a meaningful instructional form? Yes, there is. Do most of your teens like the aroma and taste of fresh pastries at a bakery? Take them there; then discuss the biblical concept of leaven. Do they enjoy the beach? Head for the sand; then reenact Christ's breakfast on the beach in John 21. Check out other tantalizing, hands-on ideas from Rick Bundschuh (1989).

12. Reasonable. Christ provided clear, specific directions for Peter's experiential assignment. As would any qualified teacher, He left no fuzziness in Peter's mind regarding the expected task. Peter was to go "to the lake" (not to the river); to "throw out [his] line" (not his customary net); to "take the first [as opposed to the third] fish" he caught; and to "open its mouth" (not to gut it). Precise instructions to our teens will likewise remove uncertainties. You won't hear excuses like "But I don't know what you want us to do."

13. Economical. Christ promised Simon that as he followed these guidelines he would find the resources he needed. Specifically, the "four-drachma coin" would be just enough—not too little or too much—to pay the two-drachma temple tax for both of them. Quality teaching is always mindful of all the necessary resources that are involved, including the peculiar demands of youth ministry.

14. Responsible. Jesus delegated the chore of taxes (for both Peter and Himself) to His student. The Bible never tells us what Simon did next, although it implies he complied with the Lord's request. But the fact remains that had Peter not acted responsibly, both teacher and pupil could have suffered serious consequences.

Teaching is risky business! Yet it's also rewarding. Think about a risky, yet rewarding instructional moment you've recently had with an adolescent.

15. Mutual. The Master Teacher told His follower to give the coin he would soon find to the collectors "for my tax and yours." What an exciting moment it must have been for Peter—to be purposefully associated with His mentor—even if it was simply for the purpose of paying taxes.

Successful youth workers recognize the invaluable reward of bonding through shared tasks. They invite connectedness for the common cause of Christ.

16. Memorable. There's no doubt about it, this educational moment was indelibly recorded in Peter's mind. The next time he went fishing or paid taxes (and we know he did both) he remembered this special encounter with the Master Teacher.

What productive memories will our teens recall long after they're gone? What legacy will we leave? How are we preparing our teens for the achievements they desire?

WORKS CITED

Bundschuh, Rick. 1989. *On-Site: 40 On-Location Youth Programs*. Grand Rapids: Zondervan.

McNabb, Bill, and Steven Mabry. 1990. *Teaching the Bible Creatively: How to Awaken Your Kids to Scripture*. Grand Rapids: Zondervan.

CONCLUSION

The story is told of a small boy who was put to bed one evening by his mother. Just a few moments had passed when the youngster was up and out of his room. At the top of the stairs, he shouted down, "Mom, I'm scared of the dark! Can you come back up 'til I fall asleep?"

"Go back to bed," the mother firmly replied. "Jesus is with you. He'll protect you."

The boy obeyed—at least for a minute or so.

"Mom!" he called again. "Could you send up Dad? I need someone with skin on!"

Leaders who teach adolescents must be absolutely clear about this one reality: The Jesus the teacher sets before them must be properly portrayed as "someone with skin on Him." After all, that is one of the best interpretations of His celebrated title Immanuel, "God with us." It is only as teachers attend to the full humanity of Jesus that they will begin to comprehend the mystery of the Christian faith—not just how to live, but how to live among students the way Jesus lived among men, as "God with skin on."

Nothing could be a more significant gift for students in their formative years of adolescence. Teaching Jesus in this way brings the story of Jesus to a place where its truth can touch the story of their lives. In this way they come to know and embrace the greatest story ever told.

WORK CITED

Ward, Ted. 1979. *Values Begin at Home.* 2d. ed. Wheaton, Ill.: Victor.

FOR FURTHER READING

Brookfield, Stephen D. 1990. *The Skillful Teacher.* San Francisco: Jossey-Bass.

Bundschuh, Rick. 1989. *On-Site: 40 On-Location Youth Programs.* Grand Rapids: Zondervan.

Ericksen, Stanford C. 1984. *The Essence of Good Teaching.* San Francisco: Jossey-Bass.

Habermas, Ronald, and Klaus Issler. 1992. *Teaching for Reconciliation.* Grand Rapids: Baker.

Issler, Klaus, and Ronald Habermas. 1994. *How We Learn.* Grand Rapids: Baker.

Lowman, Joseph. 1984. *Mastering the Techniques of Teaching.* San Francisco: Jossey-Bass.

McNabb, Bill, and Steven Mabry. 1990. *Teaching the Bible Creatively: How to Awaken Your Kids to Scripture.* Grand Rapids: Zondervan.

Richards, Lawrence O. 1970. *Creative Bible Teaching.* Chicago: Moody.

Wilhoit, Jim, and Leland Ryken. 1988. *Effective Bible Teaching.* Grand Rapids: Baker.

18

How Do We Minister to Youth in Ethnic Communities?

Ron Powell, Marta Elena Alvarado,
Wayne Mitchell, and Richard R. Dunn

INTRODUCTION
RICHARD R. DUNN

I remember the first time I saw it. I had walked up the three sets of steps outside the college's administration building, storing up images that as a prospective student I could take home with me for further reflection. Then I passed through double glass doors and ascended yet another set of steps. As I neared the top, the painting came into view. First, I noticed the long, wavy hair cascading gently to the shoulders of the figure in the portrait. Then I fixed my gaze on the relaxed face turned heavenward, as if the subject were both absorbing and being absorbed by what the eyes were seeing. The eyes themselves were perhaps the most striking feature of the painting—clear, focused, intense, yet warm and inviting. Before me, looming much larger than life, was the largest portrait of Jesus I had ever seen. The impression was dramatic, the memory lasting.

Having had many years since that day of visitation to reflect upon the wall-sized picture of Jesus, I continue to be shaped by its image. What has survived as the most significant point of recollection all these years is not the artistry or even the sense of Jesus' humanity the painter was attempting to communicate. What remains the most memorable to me, rather, is that the Jesus of the portrait was Caucasian. He appeared more Anglo than Middle Eastern, more like someone who lived in my Caucasian neighborhood than one who lived in first-century Nazareth.

The authors of this chapter remind all of us that youth ministry should not be exclusively conceived in any particular culture's image. Youth ministry is alive and active in African-American, Asian, Hispanic, and many other ethnic communities. As youth ministry moves into the next millennium, it faces the challenge of experiencing and presenting a Jesus who transcends all cultures, races, and communities. To do this we will not only need each other's help, we need each other. Without listening to, learning from, and ministering with one another we will fail to give students an authentic understanding of what it means to belong to Jesus in the multicultural, diverse world they are encountering. Moreover, without each other, we and our students are left captive to our own limited cultural conceptions of what it means to belong to the One who is the unity in our diversity.

YOUTH MINISTRY IN
NORTH AMERICAN KOREAN CHURCHES
RON POWELL

To the outside observer the Korean youth group appears almost identical to its North American counterpart. Boisterous youth gather for Sunday school, youth services, retreats, rallies, and activities, exhibiting the classic characteristics of normal adolescents. Yet, however similar the outward appearance, Korean youth ministry in North America is unique with regard to the pressures Korean youth face, the challenges of the youth leader, and the emerging models of ministry. Effective youth ministers in the Korean church pay serious attention to these differences and program accordingly rather than blindly mimicking successful youth ministries.

UNIQUE PRESSURES UPON KOREAN YOUTH

For second-generation Korean youth and the so-called 1.5 generation (youth who are immigrants from Korea) adaptation to the popular youth culture presents unique challenges, particularly in the areas of identity and relationships.

IDENTITY FORMATION

Korean children face an identity problem foreign to most other youth in North America: to adopt an English name, John, for example, that their teachers can pronounce, or stick with the given name, Huk Soo, that may draw unwanted attention every time attendance is taken. Instances such as this complicate the already confusing process the adolescent has of developing an integrated self-concept.

Research indicates that the process of identity formation in ethnic youth is dependent on the ethnic peer group (Rosenthall 1987). The youth group in the Korean church becomes an oasis for teens who feel isolated in their part of the city. In the youth group they have the freedom to experiment with other roles and develop an identity apart from being just the "Korean kid." The danger is that those youth, who are over-anxious to assimilate, may resist identification with the cultural group, rejecting, in some cases, both the ethnic church and Christ.

Another tension youth workers have noticed is the rejection of recent immigrants by the second-generation youth. As one sixteen-year-old Korean Canadian youth explained, "I don't want to hang out with those *Korean* kids because people might think that I'm an FOB" (fresh off the boat). Effective youth ministries have made successful attempts to help the second-generation youth become more inclusive, taking a positive role in assisting newcomers to adapt to the new culture.

RELATIONSHIPS

Having sacrificed to leave their homeland to give their children the very best, Korean parents are anxious for their offspring to excel. Unfortunately, this parental expectation of the brilliant Asian student is beyond the reach of many Korean youth.

Conflict also arises from a linguistic, cultural, and generation gap between parents and their Americanized youth "reared on Sesame Street and Big Macs" (Moul 1989, 56). This conflict is most intense in the area of values. Ethnocentrism can cause parents to be critical of their children's choices in areas ranging from music to marriage partners. The danger is that teens will totally reject Christian parents' guidance as culturally irrelevant.

For the 1.5 generation an added stress is acting as family interpreter. Korean teens find themselves dealing with English-speaking adults on behalf of their parents. This kind of role reversal places a heavy burden upon youths, who are often fearful of authority figures.

LEADERSHIP

For the most part, youth ministries in Korean churches are led by *jundosa,* or interns. The expectation is that the *jundosa* will become a senior pastor of another church upon graduation from seminary. Often these theological students are not studying youth ministry. The youth gap is then a training ground, not a vocational aspiration. The result is a high turnover rate for youth "pastors" and a lack of a long-term vision or a well-developed philosophy of youth ministry. A further complication of the leadership dilemma is that fully bilingual *jundosas* are rare. Frequently they are recent immigrants— culturally quite different from the second-generation youth, making relating to them difficult.

A solution some Korean churches have opted for to cope with this problem is less than ideal. Caucasian youth pastors lead Korean youth, because it is supposed that they understand the dominant culture and are fluent in English. These youth pastors face a myriad of obstacles ranging from lack of acceptance by youth to resistance from parents. Limited by the language barrier, they are not very effective with recent immigrants and are at a severe disadvantage when working with families. Without a reliable liaison between them and the

Korean-speaking adult congregation, the English-speaking youth pastor will be confused, frustrated, and ineffective.

The ideal situation, Moul argues, "is bicultural leadership that can bridge the gap" (56). Second-generation Korean professional youth pastors, fully bilingual and bicultural and able to promote understanding between parents and youth, are in high demand. They are uniquely equipped to meet the challenges of contemporary Korean youth ministry in North America.

MODELS OF MINISTRY

Most Korean churches have less than one hundred members and meet in rented facilities. There are rarely enough youth to establish a junior high ministry, although age-graded Sunday school classes are often led by college or university students. The main youth ministry is the Hi C, *Hak sang hwae,* which stands for "high school Christians." They meet on Sunday and often, for many churches, again on Friday night. The adults follow a similar schedule.

There are differences, however. Although the adults will normally be involved in cell group ministry at least once a month and a daily dawn prayer service at the church, this has not carried over into the standard youth program. The leadership structure is based on the executive model, with yearly elections of a president, vice president, secretary, and treasurer (although some churches are experimenting with the ministry team approach). One serious difficulty is finding Korean adult sponsors with whom the youth are comfortable.

Korean churches are at a point in their development where there are growing numbers of second-generation young adults who are not fluent in Korean and do not feel comfortable in the Korean language service. A second, normally more contemporary, Sunday service, conducted in English, meets the needs of the second-generation congregation. This also provides an outreach vehicle to other Asians and the non-Korean friends of the church members. A full-time youth or assistant pastor normally oversees the entire English ministry of the church. Some issues that the emerging English congregations must face are these: Who is responsible for the recent immigrant youth? How can the church minister to them effectively and help them assimilate with the second-generation teens?

As the next generation of Korean churches emerges, it will be fascinating to watch what new models of ministry develop and what new, creative solutions are found for some of the unique challenges of Korean youth ministry in North America.

RESPONSE TO RON POWELL'S ARTICLE ON KOREAN YOUTH MINISTRY
JACOB KWON TAE JOO

A new immigrant faces bipolar tension between segregation and assimilation to the mainstream of the society. The ideal is to become bicultural and bilingual so that he or she not only understands and holds onto the heritage of the ethnic culture, but also is fully integrated into the dominant culture. The reality, however, is far from the ideal. It is typical for most Korean youth to feel ashamed of Korean values and traditions during their teen years. As Powell says, youth who are overanxious to assimilate tend to reject and resist identification with the cultural group. It is a natural process of identity formation for ethnic youth in North America to move from desire for assimilation to integration as they grow older.

Estrangement in the relationship between Korean parents and youth is quite common. As Powell says, Korean parents are very ethnocentric. Ethnocentrism is a way to protect themselves from assimilation. Sadly, the result can be a severe tension between youths' desire for assimilation and their parents' determination for segregation. The problem can be intensified when the parents do not speak English and are in need of their children's help for interpretation. Parents can lose authority and control over their children and children do not pay much respect to their parents.

Many Korean youth leave their church upon graduation from college or university. It is a struggle for many Korean churches to keep their young people. However, unless their needs are being met, this exodus is likely to continue. Even though it is rare to find, bicultural and bilingual leadership should assist and guide youth in the process of identity formation. The ethnic church is unique in that youth do not become a part of the adult congregation, but form and maintain a separate congregation. The ideal is to build an interdependent relationship between the two congregations. The youth leader should function as a bridge not only between the dominant and ethnic cultures, but also between Korean-speaking adults and the English-speaking youth congregation—between parents and their children.

Ownership is very important. Unless youth are convinced that they play an important role in the church they will not stay. The church must provide philosophy, long-term vision, and organizational structure to instill the idea that it is not just the parents' church but very much their own church. I believe that the long-term vision of the "three self movement"—self-supporting, self-governing, and self-propagating—is ideal youth ministry in an ethnic church.

HISPANIC YOUTH MINISTRY
Marta Elena Alvarado

A familiar children's chorus sung in our churches has the words "Red and yellow, black and white, they are precious in his sight." These words characterize the Hispanic youth in America. Because of the diversity of cultural and racial backgrounds comprising the Hispanics, one can find an adolescent that typifies each racial group within the same congregation, and in some cases even within the same extended family as Hispanics intermarry. All of them, no matter what the physical characteristics, are precious to God and to us, His people.

A YOUNG POPULATION

The Hispanic population in America is a fairly young population, with 38 percent of it being below the age of nineteen years. Approximately 17 percent of the total Hispanic population is between the ages of ten and nineteen (Bureau of the Census 1991). Those involved in youth ministry will need not only to develop programs for those who are currently adolescents, but will also have to work closely with those involved in children's ministries so that important youth leadership is developed early.

A DIVERSE POPULATION

The 1990 census report indicates that the current U.S. Hispanic population numbers 22,354,059, or nearly 9 percent of the total population (Bureau of the Census 1992b). Mexicans constitute 14.1 million, or approximately 63.6 percent, of the Hispanic population; Puerto Ricans constitute 2.4 million, or 10.6 percent; Cubans 1.0 million, or 4.7 percent; and all other groups total 4.7 million, or 21.1 percent (Bureau of the Census 1993b). Because of this diversity of cultures, it is important to become familiar with the distinctive norms, attitudes, and behaviors that characterize the particular group the individual youth worker will be ministering to.

HISPANIC YOUTH:
MULTIDIMENSIONAL ETHNICITY

James A. Banks identifies variables within a multidimensional concept of ethnicity that can be used to determine ethnic distinctives. These are: language and dialect, ethnic values, perspectives and worldviews, behavioral styles and nuances, nonverbal communication, cultural elements, methods of reasoning and validating knowledge, and ethnic identification (Banks 1981).

Language and Dialect

For the immigrant Hispanic, Spanish is the primary language of communication. One cannot assume, however, that the adolescent's preferred language of communication will be Spanish, even in the case where the congregation is a Spanish-speaking one. Hispanic youth will have varying degrees of Spanish and English proficiency. Those whose entire schooling experience has been in the United States may not feel comfortable speaking Spanish, even if that is the language spoken at home. Youth activities may need to be bilingual. To insist on only one or the other language may alienate youth.

Values

Perhaps the strongest value among Hispanics is the importance of the family, with the father being the center of authority. Although Americanization of the Hispanic family is beginning to break down the traditional family structure, 67 percent of Hispanic families are two-parent households. Over the past several years there has been a rise in female-head-of-household families, now at 29 percent of the Hispanic population (Bureau of the Census 1992a). In spite of this change, it will be important to take into consideration the strong commitment to family when planning activities. Home responsibilities may take precedence over outside activities. Youth meetings may be cross-age meetings, as older youth frequently have responsibility for caring for younger siblings. Parents will want to be included in planning.

Hispanic churches and Hispanic families tend to be somewhat more conservative than Anglo families—that is to say, behaviors that are considered perfectly respectable normally may not be tolerated in the Hispanic congregation. Some families may not allow their youth to go on overnight or week-long retreats. Physical signs of affection between "couples" are often considered taboo. Mixed-sex athletic games may not be considered appropriate. There tends to be more delineation between the sexes in terms of expected roles and behaviors.

Most Hispanic youth are drawn to the arts. Their tastes in art and music are a mixture of both of their cultural worlds, the Hispanic culture and the American one. Music used in the youth program should incorporate both types of music. Many Hispanic youth—even those youth living in the inner city—are talented artists and love to express themselves in the visual arts.

Ethnic Identification

Ethnic identification refers to the extent to which an individual chooses to identify with his ethnic group—its values, culture, language, behavior, religious beliefs, and problems. The majority of Hispanics in the United States live in Hispanic communities, yet this does not necessarily mean that the youth will identify themselves with that culture.

Sometimes the youth identify more with the urban, inner-city culture than with the ethnic culture. This is not surprising, since the majority of the Hispanic population lives in urban areas. For example, in 1990, New York City's Hispanic population was 23.7 percent; Los Angeles's, 39.3 percent; and Chicago's, 19.2 percent. Fifteen percent of cities in the United States with a population of 100,000 inhabitants or more have a more than 20 percent Hispanic population (Bureau of the Census 1993a). The youth worker will need to be aware of the problems facing urban youth and know how to deal with them. One danger is to assume that all Hispanic youth are members of urban gangs. Although this is a prevalent problem, gang membership of itself should not be the focal point of ministry. The roots of the problem must be dealt with—self-esteem, identity, and belonging.

Hispanic youth often feel caught between two worlds, their parents' ethnic world and the "American" world. They may feel that they do not entirely belong to either world. The problems of being a member of an ethnic minority, and often one that is easily recognizable because of physical characteristics, are numerous. Some youth may be influenced by militant groups who instill in them a hatred for what they term the oppressors—the Anglo majority culture.

Others adopt a downtrodden mentality and lose hope of being able to change themselves or their circumstances. Whatever the case, it is important that the church deal with both of these extremes. Youth must be taught to accept themselves and others with all their strengths and weaknesses, and they need to be helped in breaking down the walls that separate the races. Most important, they need to recognize and act upon their identity in Christ and grasp that in Christ we are reconciled with God and with each other and are no longer at enmity with God and people.

MINISTRY RESPONSES

Ministry responses to Hispanic youth must be holistic and realistic if leaders desire to serve the students meaningfully. Examples of these two ministry emphases are provided herein.

Holistic Responses

Not only should the church help youth deal with the aforementioned problems, but it should also help them with the educational challenges Hispanic youth face. A 1991 government report indicates that only 59.4 percent of Hispanics nineteen to twenty-nine years of age have completed twelve or more years of school. High school dropout rates in some urban areas reach 90 percent for Hispanic youth (Department of Education 1991). In 1992, the *Chronicle of Higher Education* reported that only 3.3 percent of college freshmen were Hispanic ("Fact File" 1992). The church may need to provide educational support services for students who are at risk. At the very least, the youth worker must be aware of how educational deficiencies will affect programming. A heavy emphasis on reading and writing may intimidate the very youth the church is trying to reach. Yet because of these educational deficiencies there is also the danger of concentrating too much on sports and athletic programs. That is a mistake. Hispanic youth need to be challenged to give their lives for something of importance—and what is more important than giving their lives for Christ? They need to be challenged to service and ministry.

The church can also help by encouraging students and providing career counseling that opens their vision to the types of vocational and career options available. More than anything, the church must excite students about vocations within the church. One of the greatest needs in Hispanic churches today is trained leadership. Talented Hispanic youth who do go to college are encouraged to enter the more prestigious vocations such as medicine, law, and education where Hispanic professionals are in short supply. Very few youth ever consider full-time religious vocations.

Realistic Responses

Finally, the youth worker must be cognizant of the limitations on resources in many Hispanic churches. These tend to be small churches, and financial resources are not great. Often the pastor of the church is a bi-vocational pastor. Few Hispanic churches have paid staff other than the pastor. Youth workers are usually volunteers. The youth worker must be especially creative in the use of limited material and scarce human resources. Yet those who have been called to ministry with Hispanic youth will find that although the challenges are many, the rewards of seeing youth grow into responsible, self-assured, godly men and women with a passion for God and a love for each other are great.

AFRICAN-AMERICAN YOUTH MINISTRY
WAYNE MITCHELL AND RICHARD R. DUNN

You are all sons of God through faith in Christ Jesus.
For all of you who were baptized into Christ
have clothed yourselves with Christ.
There is neither Jew nor Greek, . . . slave nor free,
. . . for you are all one in Christ Jesus.
Galatians 3:26–28

The spiritual unity of God's people transcends all ethnic, social, and gender barriers. Translating that spiritual reality into a social reality, however, requires much prayer, wisdom, and effort. Throughout the book of Acts God reveals how the early church encountered significant challenges in actualizing the equality and unity of Jews and Greeks who belonged to Christ. Even Peter, an apostle of Jesus, struggled with how to live out the authenticity of the gospel in a situation where sociocultural barriers blocked harmonious Jewish and Greek relationships (Galatians 2:11–21).

African-American Christians have an acute awareness of the gap that can exist between what God has declared to be truth and what is actually demonstrated among His people. Having been denied access in previous generations to worship in churches, enrollment in Christian schools, and opportunities for service because of their ethnicity, African-Americans were historically excluded from the broader scope of the Christian church experience in America. Exclusion has been characteristic of the total African-American social experience. In *What Color Is Your God?* James and Lillian Breckenridge write:

> Immigrants from many different countries have come to the United States in search of the "American Dream." African Americans differed from all other ethnic groups in that they did not willingly come to North America, nor was the "American Dream" made available to them. The predominant distinguishing factor for African Americans is the history of social, economic, and political oppression experienced because of color discrimination. This factor pervades every aspect of social institutions within which they participate. No aspect of the life of African Americans can be understood without giving consideration to the issue of racism that they have experienced. (1995, 217)

Youth ministry to African-Americans individually and to African-American communities corporately must be developed with respect to these social realities. Youth ministry leaders in African-American communities, therefore, must commit to ministering the spiritual realities of the gospel of Jesus in such a way that students can develop biblical perspectives on God's calling for their lives in the midst of their socio-cultural contexts.

Having demonstrated the importance race plays in the African-American experience, it is essential to move to a view of youth ministry that is broader than race. The root of all racial and social problems is human sin, not human skin. The focal point of youth ministry for all races and ethnic groups must be the work of Jesus Christ in redeeming humanity from its fatal sinful condition. Therefore, African-American youth ministry is not "about race" but rather is "about humanity," which is, of course, inclusive of the issues of race, social context, and cultural experiences.

DISTINCTIVES FOR
AFRICAN-AMERICAN YOUTH MINISTRY

Reaching African-American youth with Jesus' gospel of hope, freedom, and reconciliation begins with identifying the distinctive characteristics and challenges facing youth ministry leaders who minister to these youth. These distinctives apply whether a leader is also African-American or is different in ethnicity. (As demonstrated in the history of international missions, it is possible for persons of different color and culture to minister the gospel effectively among an ethnic group. However, missions' history also indicates the significance of raising up role models and leaders from among a group's own culture if the ministry is to flourish over a number of generations. Ultimately, African-American leadership is important as a part of any team that would seek to impact a community of African-American youth.)

Affirming Unique Characteristics

African-American youth have inherited a reservoir of spiritual and cultural experiences from which to draw their sense of identity as God's people. The informed youth ministry leader will recognize, affirm, and build upon that inheritance as he seeks to build ministry relationships with African-American teenagers.

Cultural heritage

Colleen Birchett observes that "the African American culture is the context in which Christian education must take place" (Birchett 1991, 374). Values such as faith, community, family, cooperative work, and creativity are evident throughout the African and African-American experiences of the ancestors of contemporary youth. These values, which are consistent with the heart of God's will for His people, have historically been a significant part of the fabric of African-American community.

Spiritual heritage

African-American theologians have lamented the Eurocentric interpretive perspectives on the Bible and Christianity. Leaders need to be aware of the presence of Africans in the Bible and the experiences of Africans in the early church as martyrs, leaders, and theologians. Without informed teaching by leaders, students may be confused by the often propagated but totally erroneous conception that slavery was the context for the introduction of Christianity to Africans (Birchett, 370).

American church heritage

Although African-Americans have been historically excluded from the churches of the majority Caucasian culture, this should not be misunderstood as an absence of Christian church heritage. The Breckenridges emphasize this point:

> The fact remains that the single institution that has had the greatest effect in maintaining cohesion in African-American society has been the black church. Religion is viewed as an integral part of the African-American family life and is not limited to just a Sunday morning service. The African-American church has served as a very important socializing institution for individuals and as a means of leadership in the community. (1995, 218)

From the time of slavery, through Reconstruction, in the midst of the civil rights movement and beyond, the local churches provided a center for spirituality, personal ownership, participation, socialization, and education. The church provided the African-American community with a place for developing these essential human experiences.

Family/kinship values heritage

"It takes a whole village to raise a child." The truth and depth of this simple phrase has become a rallying cry for those concerned with the educational, spiritual, moral, and social needs of American children. The African proverb reflects the collective relational consciousness often found in African-American families and communities. Grandparents, extended

family members, and neighbors have been historically significant in the lives of African-American families.

Creative expression heritage

The language, dress, music, dance, and art of African and
African-American culture are rich in creativity and beauty.
Creativity can be discovered throughout African-American
youth cultural expressions and can become a wonderful place
for the affirmation of persons.

Addressing Unique Challenges

Much of what is seen in the media, both on the evening
news and in popular television, has focused on the difficult
challenges facing African-Americans. Statistics on lack of
employment, criminal activity, unmarried teenage mother-
hood, and single parent families deliver messages of discouragement concerning the future for African-American youth.
While youth ministry leaders must not surrender to this discouragement or accept the media's often stereotypical por-
trayal of the black experience, caring leaders must
acknowledge and address the challenges facing African-American youth.

Demonstrating social reality

The gospel must be communicated and demonstrated as
viable, relevant, and personally meaningful for the lives of
adolescent African-Americans. Islam has gained a stronghold
among some African-American communities because of its
public message of dignity and integrity. The truth of Christianity must be expressed in ways that offer hope and demonstrate a commitment to persons.

Youth leaders must spend time getting to know students,
understanding who they are, and finding ways to support
them in their development of an identity that is truly African-
American and truly Christian. Youth leaders must also
demonstrate a commitment to relationships and reconciliation in their lives in the community and in the broader church
of Jesus Christ.

AFRICAN-AMERICAN YOUTH
RUSS KNIGHT

In one sense, all youth are alike. However, there are ways in which African-American youth differ from those of the majority culture. Those working in African-American communities must recognize those differences and find ways to be effective.

Fewer African-American youth are involved in church than ever before. It would appear that this generation has rejected the church, the Bible, and even God Himself. Their negative images of the church have forced them to dismiss it as not relevant. A great percentage of today's young people have never even visited a church. Unless the church comes up with ways of reaching young people who don't attend church, most of them are to be classified as "without hope." I believe that today's church youth workers must learn creative ways of taking the church to them.

As we reach beyond the four walls, we will discover a generation of parents desperate for help in raising today's youth. Out of their frustration or lack of parenting skills, they can generally be easily convinced to partner with those from local churches who care about young people. This will not only provide a context for working with the teenagers, but it will also provide some hope of reaching whole families.

The traditional methods of working with teens will often be of limited value in working with African-American youth. We must learn that instead of reaching them in large groups as a primary style, small group interaction and one-on-one contacts accomplish much more. This will allow us to get close enough to "know" them as never before.

Although it is important to recognize young people when they do well, it is also important to set limits and discipline when necessary. We must not show favoritism, and we absolutely must follow through on whatever we promise. All of this is possible through the strong relationships we build with youth who are often in need of warmth and friendship.

It is unusual to find African-American teens who know who they are spiritually and culturally. As we try to help them become confident and self-assured, we discover that these are best accomplished when helping them appreciate who they are in Christ and who they are as African-Americans. Don't assume that they know or understand either.

Those who work with African-American youth must expect them to do well—especially academically. Education is often the key to escaping their negative environment, and unless they do well in school today, they will not be able to take advantage of tomorrow's opportunities. Show them examples of how hard work pays off and how the "breaks" seem to favor those who are prepared.

However, many of the important lessons that young people must learn are not found in textbooks. The church must develop programs that teach survival skills and prepare them to think both long term and short term. Such things as conflict resolution, communicating, financial management, and home economics are just a few things we must offer.

If the church is ever again going to be considered relevant, it must get involved in helping young people with job preparation and finding meaningful work. The church is an ever-ready network that ought to also work for its youth. Being aware of the economic difficulties faced by many families, the church should be prepared to supplement the cost of program involvement by many African-American youth without "giving" them everything. They must learn to do their part. Don't deny them the opportunities of paying their own way whenever possible.

Under everything that we must do, we must get the job done. As much as African-American youth themselves have changed, and how much their environment and their needs have changed as well, they still must be brought into the kingdom and transformed into ambassadors who are skilled in reaching their own generation. Unfortunately, in the midst of so much change, the church has not adjusted. So, many churches will need to employ someone who has been trained and has the time, skills, and know-how to help us accomplish the bottom line—ministering effectively to African-American youth.

Developing economic stability

Many African-Americans experience economic dysfunction in their communities. The businesses and banks found in many urban settings are making money for the suburbs, not for the persons—often African-American or another minority —who are spending their money for goods and services. Economic factors restrict opportunities, drown hopes, and contribute to social ills such as crime and gangs.

Youth leaders need to demonstrate a commitment to the development of the local community in every facet. Social justice, economic empowerment, and job training are among the ways churches can show the "practicality" of Christian spirituality.

In a portion of an essay in *Christian Education: Foundations for the Future,* Birchett observes:

Academically, many African Americans feel like failures because they have not had the same educational opportunities as whites. They should not be regarded as persons with low IQs or who are ignorant, but they need to feel accepted and successful and be given opportunities for constructive learning. Because of the inequities in distribution of resources in public school systems, many blacks lack in basic knowledge concerning things whites often take for granted. (1991, 375)

Beyond the problem of lack of resources is the fact that the African-American child's style of language and modes of expression of feelings are often misunderstood and discouraged by the teachers in their public schools. Feeling that "something must be wrong with me," students lose their enthusiasm for learning and, consequently, their hopes of learning.

Supplemental tutoring programs, involvement in local schools and school boards, and giving parents/families assistance in their role in the educational process are among the ways youth ministry programs can contribute to the educational growth of the students in the church.

Healing family dysfunction

Statistics aside, the African-American family is in crisis. The lack of fathers in the home, the lack of parenting preparation for young mothers, and the lack of available role models in the community have left young African-Americans without the nurturing resources needed to become mature adults themselves. Young males have been particularly devastated by these problems.

Youth ministry leaders must begin by being role models. Of highest priority is that married youth leaders be husbands and fathers, wives and mothers who demonstrate Jesus in their homes. Furthermore, the church needs to join local agencies in providing parenting classes and counseling.

Providing age-group programs

Involvement in age-group sports activities, Boys Club, Boy and Girl Scouts, and extracurricular activities such as drama, music, and art is essential for building a community's socialization of its children. Without such opportunities, children and youth are not able to develop an adequate sense of themselves. Too often federally or locally funded programs have been started only to see them deteriorate.

Past failures from well-meaning church groups have also contributed to many communities' memories of dashed hopes.

Programs are important, but the people leading the programs are the most important. They need long-term commitments to the students and the communities. Youth leaders may find that the best way to help in this area is to become involved in existing programs and help them work rather than find the resources necessary to begin new programs.

Teaching Truth Meaningfully: A Personal Perspective

I (Wayne) have a goal: to present young people to God (Colossians 1:28). Ultimately I desire to see them become an example to everyone in their character and obedience (1 Timothy 4:12).

African-American students, however, have often developed stereotypical ideas about the Bible, the church, Christianity, and preachers. As an African-American youth pastor, I am committed to moving students past those inherited concepts and into the light of the truth. If they are to mature in the ways I pray for, they need to encounter God's truth in a way that is meaningful to them. By affirming them in the midst of their cultural heritage and addressing their social challenges I help them to see Jesus in their worlds. Furthermore, by teaching God's Word as the drama that it is, I enable students to see the Bible as God's inspired Truth, given to them in a way that makes sense in their lives as adolescents, as African-Americans, and as God's children created in His image.

WORKS CITED AND FURTHER READING

Korean-American Youth Ministry

Choy, Bong-young. 1979. *Koreans in America.* Chicago: Nelson Hill.

Lingenfelter, Sherwood G., and Marvin K. Mayers. 1986. *Ministering Cross Culturally: An Incarnational Model for Personal Relationship.* Grand Rapids: Baker.

Moul, Dan. 1989. "For Koreans in America: Growth and Growing Pains." *Christianity Today,* 3 May.

Ng, Donald, ed. 1988. *Asian Pacific American Youth Ministry: Planning Helps and Programs.* Valley Forge, Pa.: Judson.

Roehlkepartain, Eugene C. 1989. *Youth Ministry in City Churches.* Loveland, Colo.: Group.

Rosenthall, Doreen A. 1987. "Ethnic Identity Development in Adolescents." In *Children's Ethnic Socialization: Pluralism and Development,* edited by Jean S. Phinney and Mary Jane Rotheram. Newbury Park, Calif.: Sage.

Hispanic Youth Ministry

Banks, James A. 1981. "The Multiethnic Curriculum: Goals and Characteristics." In *Education in the 80's: Multiethnic Education,* edited by James A. Bank (Washington, D.C.: National Education Association of the U.S.), 109–10.

"Fact File: This Year's College Freshmen: Attitudes and Characteristics." 1992. *Chronicle of Higher Education,* 22 January.

U.S. Bureau of the Census. 1991. *The Hispanic Population in the United States: March 1991.* Current Population Reports, Series P-20, No. 455. Bureau of the Census. Washington, D.C.

_____. 1992a. *Household and Family Characteristics: 1991.* Current Population Reports, Series P-20, No. 458. Bureau of the Census. Washington, D.C.

_____. 1992b. *1990 Census of Population: General Population Characteristics.* Bureau of the Census. Washington, D.C.

_____. 1993a. *1990 Census of Population: Social and Economic Characteristics.* United States: 1990 CP-2-1. Bureau of the Census. Washington, D.C.

_____. 1993b. *Population Profile of the United States: 1993.* Current Population Report, Special Studies Series P23-185. Bureau of the Census. Washington, D.C.

U.S. Department of Education. 1991. *Postsecondary Education*. Vol. 2 of The Condition of Education. National Center for Education Statistics, Washington, D.C.

African-American Youth Ministry

Birchett, Colleen. 1991. "African Americans." In "Ministering to Major Cultural Groups," *Christian Education: Foundations for the Future,* edited by Robert E. Clark, Lin Johnson, and Allyn K. Sloat. Chicago: Moody.

Breckenridge, James, and Lillian Breckenridge. 1995. *What Color Is Your God? Multi-Cultural Education in the Church*. Wheaton, Ill.: Scripture Press, Bridgepoint.

Carney, Glandion. 1984. *Creative Urban Youth Ministry*. Elgin, Ill.: David C. Cook.

Foster, Charles R., and Grant S. Shockley, eds. 1989. *Working with Black Youth*. Nashville: Abingdon.

Myers, William. 1991. *Black and White Styles of Youth Ministry*. New York: Pilgrim.

19

HOW DO YOU COMMUNICATE TO GROUPS OF YOUTH?

Dan Webster

When Jesus had finished saying these things, the crowds were amazed at his teaching, because he taught as one who had authority, and not as their teachers of the law. (Matthew 7:28–29)

The teaching of the wise is a fountain of life, turning a man from the snares of death. (Proverbs 13:14)

He appointed twelve—designating them apostles—that they might be with him and that he might send them out to preach. (Mark 3:14)

✝ ✝ ✝

It's Monday morning and you are sitting at your desk quietly reading your Bible and attempting to recover from a busy weekend of ministry. You are enjoying a few moments with the Lord when suddenly your solitude is interrupted by a phone call from Mrs. Finklemier, a humanities teacher from one of the local high schools. She mentions that she is beginning her unit on religion and wonders if you would be interested in coming to her school and addressing her college prep humanities class on the issue of religion and society. You tell her that the issue of religion has never really excited you. You state that it's your opinion that "religion" causes more problems than it solves. To you, religion doesn't get the job done because it is man's feeble attempt to reach God.

Being clever and evangelistically opportunistic, you offer her an alternative theme for the lecture and suggest that the class might be more interested in a lesson on how Jesus Christ can transform human life and relationships. You mention that Christianity is all about God attempting to seek us rather than us working to find Him. Mrs. Finklemier is delighted with the option and tells you that you can talk about anything under the heading of Christianity and how it touches real life. She mentions that the class is fifty minutes long and she'd like about half lecture and half question and answer. It's a great opportunity and you agree to do it.

What will you talk about? How will you approach this opportunity to influence forty of the brightest students in your local high school? You begin to do a little research and find out that one of the students in your ministry is in the class and she recommended you to the teacher. In a brief conversation with her you discover that only five of the students in the class attend a church and all of them have questions about God and life. Your student briefs you on the discussions the class has had concerning the issues of God, morals, sex, right and wrong, and politics. What will you do? What process will you go through to develop a talk that will make a difference in this class and present Christianity in a good light?

Over the years I've received many such invitations to speak in high school classrooms, assemblies, graduations, conferences, and camps. It can be both intimidating and thrilling to stand before forty to more than a thousand students who do not know you and realize that God has entrusted you with the responsibility to communicate clearly and compellingly the good news of Jesus Christ.

How can we do this well? How can we improve our communication skills so that we make the biggest impact possible? I'd like to give you a list of guidelines that I have developed over the years and use when preparing messages for non-churched groups. These are things that I think about intentionally. After a while they become second nature, but I go back to this list often and run my message through it as a filter for effectiveness.

These thoughts are in the form of eight questions that specifically focus my attention on the principles of dynamic communication. They ensure that I'll be prepared to make an impact when I open my mouth to speak. Some of the questions are original; others are thoughts that my mentors have graciously taught me through the years. If you will seriously think about and apply these questions in your message preparation you will become an ever more effective communicator to students.

Eight questions to consider:

1. Am I being relevant to the needs of my audience?
2. Will my first two minutes grab their attention?
3. Am I illustrating connectively with their world?
4. Am I being authentic or "religious" and "fake" in my presentation?
5. Am I being brief or long-winded?
6. Am I being biblically centered or opinion centered?
7. Am I showing students how this applies to their lives in the real world?
8. Am I satisfied that I prepared faithfully?

AM I BEING RELEVANT TO THE NEEDS OF MY AUDIENCE?

Being relevant is saying something that matters to those we are addressing. The last thing we should want to do is bore our audience. When I consider what to speak about I list the needs of my audience. What are their problems, stresses, and challenges? Where do they hurt? What interests them? What captures their attention? I must remind myself that kids rarely sit around and talk about theology. But they do talk about life a lot. What about life captures their energy and attention?

This is so important because if students do not sense that we understand their world they will not listen. Conversely, if they recognize that we do understand their world, where they live, and how they struggle, they just might believe that we have something to say to that world.

How do we know what is relevant to students? What's relevant is what's important to them. How can we know what's important to them? Talk to them, read what they read, listen to their music, see the movies they attend, and watch the TV programs they enjoy. Be friends with them. I guarantee that your best communication will come out of the relationships you have with students. Knowing kids and what they think about is the place to start. As you live in the real world relating to students, allow all the input from the above sources to fill your mind. Out of this experience and diligent thought flow the right topics to address.

This discipline will ensure that you are in the ball park when choosing your topic. If I can't convince myself that what I have to say is both important and life changing for my audience, I won't say it. Every time I get up to speak to kids I focus on why this issue must be considered and taught on. This ensures both relevance to my audience and passion inside of me as a communicator.

WILL MY FIRST TWO MINUTES GRAB THEIR ATTENTION?

Every good communicator knows that the first fifty words of his message are the most important words he will speak. The speaker must grab the audience's attention from the very first. Coming out of the gate strong means we give students a reason to leave their world and enter our world. If we are not excited about what we have to say, students might be cold and uninterested. We must remember that kids come from a variety of life experiences. Some have had good days, some have experienced terrible days. A good introduction takes them from their world into your world. The opening of our messages must connect with the students' world and be highly interesting to them.

How do we do this? I have found that opening with a statement or question that creates interest or curiosity usually does the trick. My first few statements will almost always precede a story or illustration that introduces the topic.

Here are a few opening lines that I've used in the past.

"Next Sunday Ken Norton, Jr., will play in his first Super Bowl but his father refuses to watch the game. Do you know why? . . ."

"Last Sunday morning John snuck out of his house at 1 A.M. without his parents knowing he'd left. He had no idea that his life would be over by 4 A.M. . . ."

"I've always been amazed at the difference one person can make. One person can totally change a team, a family, a student ministry, a classroom . . ."

"My son said something to me last week that broke my heart. He looked at me and said . . ."

"How would you feel if the person you trusted the most lied to you?"

"She was five feet, five inches tall, had blue eyes and blonde hair and the body of an aerobics instructor and she wanted to go out with me . . ."

"It was the most humiliating thing that ever happened to her, and three guys were responsible for it . . ."

"If I was to ask you what Oral Roberts (the famous evangelist/healer) and Charles Manson (convicted mass murderer) have in common, what might you say? . . ."

Each of these opening remarks drew students into my topic and allowed me to move right into a story that led into the body of the talk. Come up with creative ways to get into messages.

Whatever I can do to gain the attention of the audience, I'll do. Sometimes props work well. Students love anything visual. I once brought on stage a brown bag filled with high school memorabilia and used it to introduce my talk "Living with a Full Heart." I told the students that everything that mattered to me in high school was in the bag. One by one I pulled out the things that I thought would fill my heart in high school. There was the picture of my high school girlfriend, then a picture of my VW bug, my basketball trophies, etc.

The point of the message was that there is a big difference between living with a full life (which relationships, accomplishments, and dates can bring) and living with a full heart (which only a relationship with God can bring). Many people's lives are full of accomplishments and relationships, but their hearts are empty. The bag of memories worked as an attention grabber.

A friend of mine often introduces his messages by using short video clips out of classic movies that apply to the topic of the message. Whatever you do, don't blow the first two minutes. And once you have their attention, don't lose it.

If you do lose them remember that at every new point you can grab their attention again. If you are giving a message with two major points, work hard to introduce each point just as you did at the opening of your message. I used to think that a good message had only one introduction. Now I realize that every point has an introduction. I must give students a reason to listen to every point. That reason is laid down in the first few lines under each new message point. Look at the transition between points as an opportunity to reintroduce why they should listen to what you have to say. Every point must be compelling to hear, and in reality, every point is its own message.

AM I ILLUSTRATING
CONNECTIVELY WITH THEIR WORLD?

Theologian and communicator R. C. Sproul has three rules to effective communication. They are *illustrate, illus-*

trate, and *illustrate.* Sproul is not far from the truth. Illustrating your talk well gives it life. It enables us to move from the factual to the visual, from the conceptual to the practical, from the abstract to the concrete. It's the main way we bring truth into the real world.

A good illustration practically explains the truth we are attempting to teach. It shows the idea in real life and displays the truth in action. Illustrations help your listeners remember the points we are trying to make. Occasionally I'll meet a student who attended a conference I spoke at years ago. I'm fascinated by students' ability to recount a story I told. They can rarely remember the topic I addressed, but they can often remember a story.

Stories and illustrations can touch the heart, the center of a person's emotional being. Principles that we teach touch the mind; stories we tell touch the heart. I believe that storytelling is the most powerful form of communication to the younger generation today. The media communicates just about everything to students in the form of stories. They love to see how lives connect and touch each other. Their lives connect and touch other lives. If we can help them see how their life can touch and connect with the person of God, we are doing something!

This entire area opens the door for us to both use stories to illustrate and to communicate the gospel as the greatest story ever told. Study good storytellers. I study Paul Harvey (famous for his newscasts that tell us the rest of the story) and Garrison Keillor (the great storyteller of Lake Wobegon). I want to tell the story of God to kids with the same impact that Keillor has when he touches me with the lives of people in Lake Wobegon.

We must remember that for us the goal of telling stories is not to simply entertain, touch students emotionally, or hold their attention. We must work to use stories to hammer biblical truth home. Most of the time I will build a point of a message around a logical flow of thought.

Each point will have
• an introduction to the point,

- a statement of the point,
- the biblical truth behind the point stated,
- a brief comment about the truth,
- a story to illustrate the truth, and then
- my attempt to hammer the truth home by applying it to real life.

Any time that I can help people "feel" the principle being taught, I will. If I can think *connectively* with the students' world, I will be able to get the audience to a place of experience.

Sometimes it's easier to take a real life experience and build a message around it, teaching the biblical principles that apply to the real life situation. Jesus did this all the time. Read the gospel of John and notice how often Jesus taught out of real life experiences.

Let me give you an illustration of using the things that happen in a student's world as an opportunity to teach. One of the lessons that I found myself constantly teaching our students was the importance of respecting and honoring each other. Kids can be so cruel and hurtful to each other.

I heard about a girl in a neighboring city who was manipulated by a water polo player on her campus into doing something she didn't want to do. At the beginning of the school year this great athlete, the captain of the water polo team, made a bet with his friends that he could get this girl into the school pool skinny-dipping. His friends laughed and said that they would give him fifty dollars if he could pull it off.

The water polo team captain loved the challenge and so he pursued the girl through flirting and attention. He asked her out on one date and while driving home he suggested that they stop by the school pool for a midnight dip. She agreed and they secretly snuck in. The coach had given the kid a key so that he could open the pool for early morning workouts.

She naively followed the guy into the pool area and before long found herself peeling her clothes in front of him and hoping into the pool. There was very little light around the pool. She never saw his two buddies sitting in the dark at the other end of the pool. At least she didn't see them until they turned on the underwater pool light. It's a horrible moment when a person discovers that he's been used.

The two guys walked up to the water polo captain laughing, gave him a high five and the fifty dollars. The girl felt embarrassed, humiliated, and taken advantage of when she saw what was really going on. When she asked the guy why he did it, he simply said that it was no big deal; he just did it as a bet. "No big deal!?!" No big deal to him, that is. It's always a big deal to the person who is hurt.

When I heard this story I knew that it revealed how life is when we ignore God's principles concerning human relationships. I was able to share the story and how God knows that it's a big deal to the person who is hurt. That's why the Bible tells us in Philippians 2:3–4 to "do nothing from selfishness or empty conceit, but with humility of mind regard one another as more important than yourselves; do not merely look out for your own personal interests, but also for the interests of others" (NASB).

It's horrible to live in a world where people use each other for fifty dollars. God hates the kind of insensitive pride that would motivate us to do something like that. God's way of living is much better; His ideas are true and protective. Each of us should be careful when feeling tempted to manipulate or use another person. We should be humble and honoring of each other.

I'm sure you see how real life is a great teacher. This experience illustrates so well the opposite of love and respect. I used it when it was appropriate. Work hard at illustrating. Don't let the real incidents of life on the high school campus blow by. They can be some of the best illustrating material you will ever have.

People often ask me where I get my illustrations. Here's a list of locations my illustrations come from: newspaper articles, magazines, personal experiences, books, other people's messages, commercials, movies, newsletters, record lyrics, and Bible stories, to name just a few. I encourage you to keep an illustration notebook. I have folders full of illustrations that I draw from.

THE DIVINE ALCHEMY OF
TURNING MISTAKES INTO MINISTRY
RIDGE BURNS

Have you ever made a really stupid mistake in ministry? The kind where you know better, but for some reason you stumble into it anyway?

My most recent blunder occurred while I was participating in Azusa Pacific University's Mexicali Program. For the last eighteen years I've been a base-camp speaker for this program that takes five thousand kids across the border. I provide spiritual leadership to the thousand kids in my camp and model for them what it means to walk with God. Each night the students come back from their villages or ministry sites excited about what God has done that day. My job is to use instruction from the Word to assist them to process their cross-cultural missions experiences.

One night in the middle of their six-day event, most of the kids came back jumping up and down and high-fiving each other. Our song leader capitalized on their enthusiasm and pumped up the whole crowd to frenzy level as they praised God for what He had done in their lives throughout that day. In my enjoyment of the ricocheting energy, I didn't realize that half the students were physically dragging from a very trying day.

"JUST AS I AM" WOULD'VE BEEN FINE, BUT . . .

So after my message—but still unaware of the whole situation—I asked our song leader to lead the most up, the most crankin', the most rippin' worship song he knew. Sure enough, throughout the duration of "King Jesus Is All," kids literally raised a dust cloud dancing on the bare ground in the outdoor meeting area. As the last hoots and cheers faded with the reverberating final guitar chord, I made a final, fatal error: I sent them to their small groups without bringing them down from their energetic max. Needless to say, the sponsors responsible for getting them to bed by camp curfew had a horrible night.

During the next morning's leaders meeting, these poor souls confronted me with my insensitivity. I felt defensive, but I knew their evaluation was right on. I'd looked right past the 50 percent of the kids who needed something other than the hype I had given them, and I had failed to see how my leadership would affect the other leaders.

But instead of admitting my mistake at that point (I'm embarrassed to even write this), I only compounded it by trying to vindicate myself and legitimize the way I handled the meeting.

"If you ask me to do that again," the song leader broke in, "I'm not going to do it. I won't follow that kind of leadership."

It was a direct challenge, and I bristled—but (thankfully) that slap in the face shocked me out of my defensive mode. I recognized what my friend was actually saying: "I'm not going to follow you out of the Spirit and into the flesh again."

You probably know what I felt that day in Mexicali—insecurity, defensiveness, an inability to function properly, and uncertainty about where I stood with about four hundred people in the camp. To put things right, I needed to admit that I was wrong—which I did before the morning was past. In doing that I (finally) modeled true spirituality.

You can let even mistakes turn a profit for you by exchanging *defense* for *confession*. Acknowledging bad decisions helps others understand that God uses people who make mistakes. Refusing to admit that you blew it, on the other hand, gives

Satan an opportunity to waste valuable time by stirring you up to defend your imperfections.

Messing up is part of ministry. Just look at the disciples of Jesus. They were accomplished at making mistakes; they were also quick learners at recognizing that God rectifies confessed errors. Provided we don't "sin that grace may abound," God is OK with the reality of our imperfection.

SINGLED OUT FOR GRACE

Maybe that's why on Resurrection Sunday morning the angel said to the women at the tomb, "But go, tell his disciples and Peter, 'He is going ahead of you into Galilee.'"

Why would the angel mention Peter? Maybe because the last thing Peter did was deny Christ. I bet Peter felt like a failure, felt that his mistakes would prevent him from being used by God. By singling Peter out, God reassured him that he was still in God's thoughts and plans.

Mistakes, whether Peter's or ours, are part of ministry—and another part of ministry is laying down our defensiveness, which only keeps God from using our mistakes to do good things.

AM I BEING AUTHENTIC OR "RELIGIOUS" AND "FAKE" IN MY PRESENTATION?

I learned years ago that my best presentations happen when I don't try to be someone that I'm not. It's tempting to try to mimic Tony Campolo or Bill Hybels. It will take a while to develop your own style, but being you is always your best strategy. Students don't like it when we try to be someone we aren't. They want us to be *us*. When we are personal and genuine, it is powerful.

Occasionally I teach a class in evangelistic communication to youth at Trinity Evangelical Divinity School in Deerfield, Illinois. In one of my classes a young man totally changed his natural speaking voice when he delivered his first message. When he got behind the podium he transformed himself into a bass speaking "preacher." It was hysterical.

I asked him why he felt compelled to become someone different than who he was when delivering a message. He said that was how the ministers spoke in his denomination when they entered the pulpit. I told him to knock it off. My counsel to him was to trust that who God had made him to be naturally was good enough. I encouraged him to simply be himself when he gave his next message. Next time up he trusted my instruction and did a great job. It was 100 percent better and more effective.

Stop and think for a moment. What type of communication turns you off? For me it's mindless, unprepared, opinionated, insincere, long-winded, arrogant, overly emotional, reactionary, or crude. So guess what? I avoid all that.

Now consider what type of communication is disarming and inviting? For me it's honest, vulnerable, gentle, well prepared, truthful, and respectful of my ability to make my own decision. This type of communication happens when the speaker talks to me as though I have a brain and respects my ability to make up my mind on the issue he or she is presenting.

It's a great challenge to be real, to be authentic as a communicator. How can we practice this more in our messages? Besides attempting to be genuinely ourselves, we can do it three ways. First, we can share our struggles and weaknesses whenever we can. Good communication is dropping one's guard and sharing deeply felt emotions.

We make a mistake when we assume that students want us to be perfect living examples of the truth we teach. They just want honesty from us. I've always been confessional in my speaking. I get a lot of positive feedback for doing this, not primarily from Christian listeners, but from non-Christian listeners. They have told me that my willingness to be real creates a safe environment within which they feel open to hear the truth. People want to hear how we struggle with the truth. They want to see someone live the truth before them honestly.

Second, share the truth of your spiritual journey. Where are you growing? Please remember that the minister is, to a large degree, the message. I always wrestle with the truth of a message as it relates to me and my world before I deliver it. This is risky business if you talk about temptation, suffering, truth telling, your thought life, living with joy, family life, hope, or faith. We must think about how the truth we're teaching fleshes itself out in our lives. If we are courageous enough to deal with that question and share the answer, students will be drawn to us.

Third, share what you are learning. There is a sense of the authentic when a person teaches out of his own growth. Let me ask you, how have you changed recently? We can never be agents of change in students' lives if God isn't changing us. We must continue to grow. Spiritual impact can only happen through spiritual people! Having integrity as a teacher is inviting people to live as we live. In our messages we invite students to come close to us and see how truth looks when lived out. Do students sense growth in you? Does your life have spiritual direction that can be offered to another? If we share our journey and what we are learning as we struggle with the truth, students will see firsthand what their lives will look like as they submit themselves to the truth of the Bible.

AM I BEING BRIEF OR LONG-WINDED?

One of my speaking mentors, Bill Hybels, used to say to me more often than I would like to admit, "Dan, that was a good thirty-five-minute message. It could have been a great twenty-eight-minute message." I hated it when he said that. But his point was well taken. He told me that one should not diesel when speaking. *Dieseling* is a term Bill uses for staying on a point longer than you should. In other words, don't say it, then say it again, and then say it again—just say it and move on!

Do you realize that last Sunday more than 55 million people heard over 1 billion words in sermons and when all was said and done, a lot more was said than done. The Lord's Prayer has only 56 words in it; the Gettysburg Address is made up of only 267 words; the Beatitudes are 122 words; and the entire Declaration of Independence has a total of only 1,322 words.

What am I saying here? Some very profound statements have been made in relatively brief statements. Students tell me, "just give me the goods and let me deal with it." How long you can speak without putting students to sleep depends upon the interest level of the topic and your skill as a communicator. Be aware of both. Don't go longer than you need to. Students will appreciate it.

AM I BEING BIBLICALLY CENTERED OR OPINION CENTERED?

I have a seeking friend who had an interesting response to a sermon he heard recently. This man is a senior vice president of a multibillion-dollar-a-year company. He's not a high school student, but his insight is priceless. He commented that the pastor told those listening, "I was in the shower the other day and I thought . . ." My friend's reaction to that was, "Listen, I don't want to hear shower thoughts. Why are his shower thoughts any better than my shower thoughts?"

When we begin our messages we should almost always launch at the point of students' needs. We begin with what they are interested in. This is not sin; it's how Jesus taught. But we must be clear about where our truth comes from, and we must remind everybody what our truth source is. The heart of our message is not shower thoughts—it is the truth of the Bible! Truth comes from the Bible, and any way that the Bible can be seen and read is important. "The word of God is living and active. Sharper than any double-edged sword, it penetrates even to dividing soul and spirit, joints and marrow; it judges the thoughts and attitudes of the heart" (Hebrews 4:12).

When preparing messages, thoroughly research what the Bible has to say about your topic. Build every point upon a biblical principle. If you can project verses on a screen so that everyone can read them, so much the better. If you give outlines to kids, put the Scripture on them.

Let us never forget that the Bible and the gospel have power. "All Scripture is God-breathed and is useful for teaching, rebuking, correcting and training in righteousness" (2 Timothy 3:16). I love psychology and sociology. I enjoy reading the insights of secular thinkers. But I always go over my message and ask myself whether I'm giving students psycho-babble or the truth of the Scriptures. We must be careful in this New Age era that we don't fudge on the Bible. Our challenge is to find new and interesting ways to say old truths. Don't ever forget that the gospel in its simplicity had the power to trans- form your life and mine. It's got enough power to transform your students' lives too.

AM I SHOWING STUDENTS HOW THIS APPLIES TO THEIR LIVES IN THE REAL WORLD?

The goal of our communication is life change. When we stand up to speak we should want God to impact students' lives. This means that we must clearly apply the truth that we teach. At the end of every point we must show how it lives out in the real world. I do this by carefully answering the ques- tion, "What difference will this make tomorrow on their cam- pus, in their relationships, in their private lives, or in their family life?" If I don't have a good answer to that question I back up and do some more thinking. We must work hard to help students see how truth can be lived out.

I have also found it helpful to apply the message based upon what type of message it is. There are many different types of messages. There are evangelistic messages that have as their purpose to lead students to saving grace in Christ. There are encouraging messages that attempt to lift students and motivate them to appropriate God's power in daily life. There are corrective messages that reprove and refine. There are shop-talks that address a specific issue that your ministry is facing. And there are instructive messages that simply teach what God has to say about an issue.

Make your applications based upon the type of message you are giving. I don't give an evangelistic call when I'm doing a shop-talk type of message. When I am giving an evangelistic message I focus directly on challenging students to trust Christ personally. That is the proper application for that spe- cific message. Make the application fit the purpose of your talk.

AM I SATISFIED THAT I PREPARED FAITHFULLY?

We live in a world of shortcutting. Very few people are willing to do what it takes to become effective as a communicator. I ask myself if I did my best in the preparation process and whether the message will be usable in God's hands. Let me plead with you to take this issue seriously. Many of you are in frustrating circumstances. You wish you could change your budget, church politics, or other circumstances. But all of us can do one thing this week that can make a difference in our ministries and that's to work hard at the task of preparing and delivering relevant, biblical messages. And if we do that we are making a difference.

Remember that you are a prophet for today. Truth needs a voice and a life to live through. Allow God to change you and then take yourself along with His truth before students and speak with confidence. As you prepare, pay attention to the eight questions and you'll be a difference maker in students' lives.

FOR FURTHER READING

Barna, George. 1994. *Baby Busters: The Disillusioned Generation*. Chicago: Northfield.

Briscoe, Stuart, Bill Hybels, and Haddon Robinson. 1990. *Mastering Contemporary Preaching*. Portland, Oreg.: Questar.

Davis, Ken. 1991. *Secrets of Dynamic Communications*. Grand Rapids: Zondervan.

Hendricks, Howard. 1988. *Teaching to Change Lives*. Portland, Oreg.: Multnomah.

Strobel, Lee. 1993. *Inside the Mind of Unchurched Harry*. Grand Rapids: Zondervan.

Webster, Dan. 1987. "Speaking to High School Students." In *The Complete Book of Youth Ministry,* edited by Warren S. Benson and Mark H. Senter III. Chicago: Moody.

PART FIVE

CHALLENGES IN YOUTH MINISTRY

20

✝

HOW SHOULD WE
RESPOND TO
POPULAR CULTURE?

Quentin J. Schultze

Not long ago I attended a professional basketball game in the southern United States. I expected sports with a regional flavor. Instead I witnessed a culturally homogenous, multimedia extravaganza aimed at young fans raised on MTV, teen movies, rock concerts, fast food, and kids' television.

As I entered the hallways around the arena, I saw one video monitor after another loudly playing commercials, team promos, and sports videos. Every few yards took me past more brand-name pizza counters, hot-dog stands, and hamburger kiosks. Then I walked into the brightly lit amphitheater, filled with adolescents watching the big-screen monitor flash rapid-fire video images from the court, where athletes practiced their pre-game moves. Soon the arena darkened and the spotlight focused on a spinning metal ball hanging from the ceiling, throwing shimmering, dancing lights around the stands and across the faces.

As I grew dizzy, thunderous music began pumping stacca-
to bass notes into my ears and through my skin. Young, scant-
ily clad girls danced rhythmically across the court, eliciting
the cheers of male fans. Advertisements flashed from bill-
boards ringing the court. The team mascot, a cross between
Barney and the Loch Ness monster, jiggled his rubber cos-
tume, taunting the visiting team. Fans screamed, cheered,
hooted, and hollered.

I felt like an overaged alien in an adolescent world, an old-
fashioned American from another era. Who were these young
folks? Where was I? What did all of this have to do with basketball? How could I get my cultural bearings in this multimedia extravaganza that defied region, ethnicity, race, and
religion?

Youth ministry is caught in a whirlwind of change. If youth
workers ever could have ignored popular culture, they no
longer have that luxury. Professional and lay youth leaders
find themselves trying to communicate with people from an
alien culture. Youth ministry has become a missionary activity
to an adolescent subculture shaped by the media and other
popular culture.

It's not easy for youth leaders to see the anthropological
significance of their own youth's culture. Today's young people are influenced by soap operas, teen pics, and MTV. They
are inundated with teen magazines and romance novels, seemingly endless varieties of rock and roll, CDs and CD-ROMs,
personal televisions and monster car radios, musical concerts
and the Internet. They live in the culture of the *particular* fashion, food, and fun, the culture of the *particular* car and hair-
style. This culture is a swirling tornado of media and
messages, moving so quickly youth leaders can never quite get
it entirely in focus.

Some observers label this reality postmodernism. According to this view, youth culture simply reflects a larger societal
shift away from stable, absolute values toward a virtual truth
and virtual reality. The media, in particular, create multiple
interpretations of everything—what to believe, what to think,
what to value—leaving youth with no transcendent pegs on
which to hang their hearts and souls.

In one sense, this diagnosis is indeed accurate. The belief in absolutes—any absolutes—is simply not fashionable in postmodern society. But the postmodern label is a simple diagnosis for a complex case of culturally induced soul sickness. Youth are not mixed up only about absolutes or even just about "the truth." They are confused about who they are and how to be a human being. In Walker Percy's words, they are "lost in the cosmos." Ironically, they are lost in a cultural whirlwind of abundance; youth face more pop culture messages than ever, a seemingly unlimited array of personal identities just waiting to be selected.

THE SCOPE OF POPULAR CULTURE

Popular culture is not limited to the highest-rated television shows, the biggest box-office movies, or the most widespread fashion. In the simplest of terms, popular culture includes all cultural products created by industry for mass consumption. It is not the same as the "elite culture" enjoyed primarily by a select group of people with higher incomes and greater education—the "art" of most museums, operatic performances and classical recordings, haute cuisine, handmade designer fashions and the like. Nor is it the "folk culture" of a particular ethnic or localized group—traditional dances, ceremonial costumes, well-known music by unknown writers (for example, folk ballads), ethnic food, and all the rest. Popular culture is commercially driven culture produced for transient, mass appeal.

As a commodity, popular culture is not the work of one artisan, but of an industry. Fast-food restaurants thrive on the "sameness" of their cuisine across geography; each hamburger is essentially identical to every other one throughout the chain. Similarly, most teen flicks are largely indistinguishable from other teen flicks (in fact, many of them are mere copies of already-popular movies). So it is throughout the range of popular culture, from jeans to music. Much popular culture is highly conventional and not particularly innovative. When it loses all creative individuality, popular culture is often called "mass culture."

Frequently, however, the most popular forms of culture do

reflect important individual styles of expression and sometimes even special themes or messages. Particular movie directors, musical groups, and television producers sometimes
create their own, distinct kinds of popular art. This kind of
individuality often appeals to certain youth, who find a "common bond" in the message and sensibility of the expressions
of rock-music celebrities, for instance. Popular culture can
create this sense of "community" among the producers and
consumers, often as a kind of substitute for ethnic, geograph-
ic, religious, and other bases for community.

Finally, popular culture includes not just the products
themselves, but also the way youth use them. It includes the
dances created to go with certain styles of music as well as the
clothing worn particular ways. These actions, together with
the products, create powerful systems of meaning appropriately called subcultures. T. S. Eliot once defined "culture" as the
"entire way of life of a people." Youth-oriented popular culture is nothing less than the way of life of youth—all of it
increasingly organized around the industry of popular culture.

THE ROOTS OF POP CULTURE

Popular culture is largely a product of ninteenth- and
twentieth-century industrialized society. It reflects both the
movement toward mass industrialization and the weakening
of traditional sources of cultural authority anchored in home,
school, neighborhood, ethnic group, and religious faith.

Popular culture reorganized the modes and channels of
communication among people. It replaced many kinds of
local, person-to-person communication with distant, mass
communication. Not surprisingly, the major purveyors of
popular culture are the media, including periodicals, books,
broadcasting, and electronic recording and playing devices,
such as phonographs, videocassette recorders, and, more
recently, CDs and CD-ROMs. These media are not used primarily to enhance family life or to build stronger communities
or more active church congregations, although these are certainly possible goals. Instead, popular media create channels
of communication within generations and across geography,
producing similar popular culture among youth simultane-

ously around the world. North America, especially the United States, produces most of the world's popular culture.

Although popular culture has always been far more than media, the mass media generally have the greatest impact on youth values and beliefs. Media-related popular culture has the most meaning to people because it expresses values and beliefs in the potent forms of story, music, and image. In fact, more and more contemporary popular culture is multimedia, combining sound and sight in narratives such as movies and music videos.

If popular culture initially expressed itself in rudimentary products, such as comic books and magazine advertisements, it has become a fully orbed, cross-media extravaganza linking together a diverse array of companies. One popular artist, "owned" by a multinational corporation, suddenly appears in musical recordings, stage performances, movies, CD-ROMs, books, magazines, electronic games, and even on "online" (via computer modem) entertainment services. This kind of diversification turns popular culture into a "world," not just a commodity.

CHURCHES' RESPONSES

Generally speaking, churches have responded to the growth of popular culture in one of two ways. Either they have tried to deflect the impact by closing off the channels of communication into the homes and hearts of their youth, or they have tried to use popular culture to create a hospitable climate for their youth and to attract new youth and their parents to the church.

Neither strategy has worked very effectively. The "head-in-the-sand" defense ignores the fact that youth have increasingly easy access to popular culture via portable media technologies. It is virtually impossible to fully "protect" youth from popular culture. The second approach typically has failed because there is often a fine line between using popular culture and being used by it. Indeed, some church youth groups seem to do a much better job of introducing youth to "Christianized" versions of secular popular culture than of creating discernment about that culture.

Both of these responses are represented in much of the Christian popular-culture industry. Contemporary Christian music (CCM), for instance, largely imitates its secular counterparts while creating a "safe" musical haven for some believers. The vast majority of Christian youth, however, prefer mainstream music partly because it's more widely available and partly because their friends and peer groups are anchored in mainstream popular culture. To a large extent, CCM "preaches to the choir" of existing fans of such music.

Also, there are few CCM artists with distinctive musical styles. They and their fans define "Christian music" by the lyrics alone. When these Christian artists try to "secularize" their lyrics to get the music played on mainstream radio stations, they often face considerable criticism from the Christian community. By staying in the CCM arena, however, they reach few non-believers.

Christian youth often are extremely sensitive to these dynamics. If they like Christian music, typically they are critical of mainstream fare. Similarly, if they like mainstream music, they are often highly critical of Christian music for being formulaic and predictable. The truth is that formulas and predictability are just as prevalent in mainstream music, and there are quite a few highly talented Christian music artists who create music just as fine as the best mainstream fare. In other words, both sides stereotype the other side to the detriment of both Christian and mainstream music.

If nothing else, the history of popular culture suggests two essential lessons for youth ministry. First, the most effective weapon against sinful forms of popular culture is a strong, healthy family life integrated into a loving community of faith. "Christian" popular culture is never an adequate substitute for in-the-flesh nurturing.

Second, popular culture itself is not evil, but it easily takes on evil forms as it tries to please a fallen world. Youth leaders who too easily or glibly praise or condemn one form of popular culture or another can easily lose respect from the youth who hold different, sometimes very intelligent opinions. Similarly, it can be tough dealing with parents who are absolutely convinced that they know more about popular culture than do their children. Since the church typically has sought simple, neat categories of "Christian" and "secular" popular culture, it has not produced a great many people who have spiritual discernment about culture.

COMMUNICATION AND IDENTITY

Discernment starts with biblical understanding. We can begin to understand the significance of contemporary popular culture by contextualizing it biblically. The media, in particular, are understood best in the context of Creation and the Fall. God created humankind as distinct communicators—different from all other creatures. Already in the first few chapters of Genesis, human beings use symbols (messages) to create interpretations of reality. Adam's first task, naming the creatures, reflects this fundamentally important but often overlooked truth. Whatever name Adam gave the creatures, that's what they were called, that was their identification. Naming is nothing less than symbolic communication. Communication, in turn, is nothing short of creating human identity through the use of symbols.

The Fall radically shifts the role of human naming from godly identification to purely human, selfish naming. Adam and Eve don't call their own sin what it really was—willful disobedience of God. They try to hide from each other (clothing) and from God, who tracks them down to set them straight. Our first parents rejected God's absolutes for their own interpretation of the truth. In one sense, Adam and Eve were the first postmodernists, creating their own, new interpretations of reality. They were also the first "media moguls," spinning symbols into cultural webs of meaning.

Human communication essentially plays this role of "naming"—forming identity—in all popular culture. Speech, writing, and film, for instance, are all media used by human beings to create a sense of who they are. This is precisely why parents are right to care about the peer groups of their offspring; peer groups are communication groups and, therefore, identity groups. In short, the media are not primarily in the entertainment or information business, but, biblically speaking, in the identity business.

MEDIA AND INTIMACY

Popular culture also plays a crucial role in shaping how and why youth achieve intimacy—emotionally deep relationships. Youth learn especially from the media how to become intimate with another person. Teen movies, for instance, provide the images and language of intimacy grounded largely in sexuality. These movies implicitly if not explicitly instruct young women on how to dress to attract the attention of males. They similarly teach young men how to conquer women.

Far more subtly, the media shape youth's basic conception of intimacy. Young people learn, for instance, that intimacy is not "normal" between parents and their children. In popular culture, youth are typically alienated from most adults, and almost certainly from their parents, teachers, and pastors. Moreover, youth learn (wrongly) that intimacy is nearly equivalent to physical or sexual intimacy. There are very few displays of non-sexual intimacy in youth-oriented media. When non-sexual intimacy does emerge in the media, as in the film *The Breakfast Club,* it nearly explodes with emotional power, creating for many viewers a kind of cathartic experience.

The prevalence of sexual language and portrayals in youth culture undoubtedly reflects a deep yearning for intimacy. Research suggests that this is particularly true for women, who are more likely than young men to use media content to learn about intimacy. Nevertheless, for both genders the media are often the most influential depictions of adult versions of intimacy. This would not be true if parents and other adults spent adequate time modeling non-sexual intimacy for their youth and being mentors on this subject. At a minimum, youth leaders must recognize that media sexuality is far more than entertainment in the lives of youth; such messages are the "textbook" that many youth use to learn about identity and intimacy.

THE GENERATION GAP

Decades ago the concept of a "generation gap" between youth and adults was all the rage. Since then the term has largely disappeared because such a gap is assumed to be normal. The explosion in youth-oriented media, coupled with many young people's increased spendable income, has transformed the generation gap into a society-wide phenomenon and parental expectation. Youth-oriented popular culture both accelerates the gap and gains from it.

The generation gap is really a communication gap. Adults and youth use vastly different media for information and entertainment. Adult men, for instance, often read a daily newspaper and watch television news. Young men and women, on the other hand, are largely uninterested in most news content. Adults and youth similarly tend to like very different films and television programs—to say nothing of the obvious gaps in musical taste. Youth live largely in their own media worlds of music, film, radio, and television. In fact, it is increasingly true that youth even from the same family inhabit different subcultures; a difference in age of three or four years typically makes a vast difference in media likes and dislikes.

This type of media-oriented, age-based cultural segmentation makes it difficult for leaders to communicate effectively with youth. More than ever, youth leaders have to take time to enter the various youth cultures. Like anthropologists, they must learn the meaning of the language and activities of the people they hope to understand. Youth ministry must be highly empathetic or it will either miss the cultural mark or, worse yet, implicitly communicate cultural arrogance. Such arrogance is evident in the "good ol' days" syndrome, where adults romanticize the past and expect youth to live up to romantic ideals that never quite existed in the first place.

THE CONSUMERIST TRAP

Popular culture does far more than shape youth's notions of gender and sexuality. The media, in particular, convey to youth a deeply consumerist vision of life—both in the cost of the media themselves and in what the media say about the rest of life.

First, the mass media are largely commercial enterprises that charge directly or indirectly for the values and beliefs that they peddle. Youth learn early in life that the media are not free, that at least the technology (for example, radios and TVs) requires considerable financial resources. As a result, youth's entrée to media products about identity and intimacy becomes a matter of price, not a matter of morality or spiritual discernment. Personal popularity, success, happiness, and the like are all linked to the cost of an unending series of "tickets" to the popular culture.

Second, and far more devastating, the media's "answers" to intimacy and identity issues are nearly always another price tag. Youth media are absolutely loaded with all of the "requirements" for a happy life: the right fashion, the hottest cars, the essential foods, the necessary personal hygiene products, and on and on. It's important to recognize that advertising itself is just the tip of this consumerist iceberg. In fact, there is considerable evidence that the media content that appears to be the least persuasive is often the most effective at changing values and beliefs. Movies and television dramas that depict youth, for example, are one grand commercial for the content of the stories and the dramas of the characters' lives.

The overriding message of youth media, then, is simply "you are what you consume." Identity itself depends on the stuff that a young man or woman can purchase and display. In biblical terms, we could say that contemporary youth culture inverts the biblical expression of identity; the media champion the external "look" and "sound" of a person, whereas the Scriptures focus on a person's heart. If popular culture encourages youth to focus on the externals, the Bible captures the essence of a person in his or her "inside"—the soul itself, as the embodiment of what people truly value and believe.

TWO CHALLENGES FOR YOUTH LEADERS

Youth leaders work in this dynamic whirlwind of cultural change. Their task is not only to befriend youth and their parents, but to help youth find their own way through the storm. In short, youth need help discerning the winds of popular culture. Two crucial problems have to be solved before this can be done effectively—involving many lay adults in every church in youth ministry, and enfranchising youth as producers of godly culture.

First, youth leaders can't do this on their own. They can't be parents, teachers, pastors, and friends of all youth. Instead, their job increasingly will have to be facilitating the involvement of other adults in the whole process of teaching, mentoring, discipling, and befriending youth. Historically speaking, all forces seem to be working against this process: parents want to be left alone to enjoy their own consumer toys; congregations are increasingly fragmented and without a sense of community and mutual "ownership" of raising youth in the Lord; individual adult members of churches are less and less likely to feel that they have or even should have any authority over other peoples' children; youth themselves often do not seem to want the church group to be the focus of their spiritual lives. Nevertheless, unless other adults share with youth leaders the trials and tribulations of leading youth, the task will become increasingly difficult and youth-leader burnout will be even more severe.

The challenge is persuading other adults to join the work and play of youth leadership. My own experience, as well as my own professional research, suggests that this might be easier than we think. For one thing, there is a growing sense among adults over fifty-five years of age that they have given too much of their lives to things that do not seem very important in the long run—things such as work and individual hobbies or leisure pursuits. Many of these adults wish they had spent more time with their own families. In short, there is a growing population of baby boomers that might really enjoy and appreciate volunteer work with youth, especially if the "work" is in line with their talents and taps some of their abilities. Here is where the youth leader becomes a creative enabler of other leaders in youth ministry: helping others use their God-given abilities for the good of the youth. This can include everything from organizing volunteer work groups in the community to mentoring individual young people in an occupational interest.

For another thing, there is considerable evidence that youth do indeed want to have better, deeper relationships

with adults, including their parents. Youth say in surveys that
they don't spend more time with their parents primarily
because their parents are too busy or because they don't think
their parents really care about them! Obviously parents usually don't view their children through the same lens. Also, on
college campuses and even at high schools the "service learning" phenomenon is really growing. Youth are paired with
other youth and often with adults to volunteer in community
service. The fact is that youth not only like to do this, but
often they say that it is among the most rewarding parts of
their lives.

The benefits of getting more than one adult involved in
youth leadership are considerable. It provides additional role
models. It gives youth more experience with the range of adult
gifts and talents. It breaks down age segregation and reduces
the generation gap. It teaches youth the value of volunteering
for service. It helps youth see their own value as reflected in
the deeds and words of adults with whom they work and fellowship. It provides additional voices for building discernment and teaching wisdom in natural settings.

The second, related problem is how youth leaders can
break the consumerist cycle of identity-formation. As a media
scholar, I admit that my thoughts on this issue are rather radical. I believe that the days of straight, formal, doctrinal
instruction are numbered. Nearly all of culture says to youth
that their value depends on what they can consume. Similarly,
in church life we expect youth to "consume" religious instruction and doctrinal teaching, not to "produce" it. They are
expected to be passive consumers of the culture of the church.
No wonder so many youth in many Christian traditions find
church life boring and suffer from poor self-esteem.

Youth leadership will necessarily have to shift from purely
formal instruction, on the one hand, and largely consumerist
strategies (watching Christian videos or attending Christian
music concerts), on the other hand, to bold initiatives that
enfranchise youth in their own futures. In short, youth ministry
will have to be youth ministering to themselves and especially
ministering to others, not just other people ministering to
youth. If not, today's youth will become even more like many of

today's parents who are indifferent to real church involvement and largely preoccupied with their own toys and projects.

One way of thinking about this shift is to view it as turning youth into producers of Christian culture. Rather than merely consuming other people's popular culture, youth are given the opportunity to use their gifts and talents to produce works of art that can be enjoyed by others. In the language of Scripture, youth can be encouraged to accept their God-given role as caretakers of the Creation, as stewards of God's world both inside and outside the church. Or in the language of Ephesians 2:10, youth are helped to see and respond to the "good works" that God has prepared in advance for them. In short, their value is already given by God; they don't need to prove their value by being hip consumers of the latest popular culture.

In the context of the Bible, this approach to youth ministry becomes fairly obvious. It rests on the assumption that God both gives gifts and talents to people and sees to it that there are places for them to use those gifts and talents.

The real beauty of this approach to youth ministry, however, is its thoroughgoing challenge to the consumerist mentality that robs youth of even the desire to be discerning of popular culture. Only after youth begin to realize their inherent value as caretakers in God's kingdom can they turn from trying to receive their identities from a worldly culture created by industry to accepting their worth in God's sight and becoming participants in a godly culture created by others and themselves.

All aspects of church and community life are potentially open to youth service. This includes church planning, weekly duties related to church building and grounds, publicity and promotion, worship music, neighborhood canvassing, and on and on. Even more, it includes reaching out to the neighborhood through volunteer service, helping the deacons with assistance to the poor and needy, and so forth. I believe it also includes special youth activities designed to replace consumerist binges such as expensive spring break trips to exotic locations. I've seen again and again that the happiest young people are not those with the grandest spring-break getaways, but those who come back renewed and refreshed because of what they have done for others. Again, service-oriented learning, combining study with worship and work, is highly effective for most youth. More than that, it can be the springboard for involving other adults in mentoring other young people—without the formality and even the phoniness that are often projected through purely formal education.

A VISION OF THE FUTURE

Since the future of the church rests in the hands of youth, youth leaders have one of *the* most important—if not the most important—jobs in the church. Without a fairly broad and deep vision of the future for youth, youth ministry can easily become baby-sitting or crisis management. I believe that the vision of the future of youth leadership has to be informed by the darkness in popular culture. Today that darkness includes youth's badly confused notions of gender and sexuality, consumer-based identities, insufficient cross-generational communication, and preoccupation with "externals" instead of the heart. Youth need to be reborn from all of this.

To a large extent this darkness presses in on the work of the youth leader, limiting what he or she can accomplish. Let's face it, popular culture defines much of what youth believe and value in life. There's no way we can fully control or regulate youth access to popular culture. But we can help youth to see who they really are as God's children redeemed by the blood of the Cross. In so doing we can reorient youth to the surrounding culture, teaching discernment as we work along with them, together serving others. This is nothing short of loving others as we would like to be loved. Christ loved us. Now we reach out in love, helping youth to love others. It's a powerful vision that turns even some of the best popular culture into an empty commodity.

FOR FURTHER READING

Carter, Steven L. 1993. *The Culture of Disbelief.* New York: Basic Books.

DeMoss, Robert G., Jr. *Learn to Discern.* Grand Rapids: Zondervan.

Ekstrom, Reynolds R. 1989. *Access Guide to Popular Culture*. New Rochelle, N.Y.: Don Bosco Multimedia.

Medved, Michael. 1992. *Hollywood vs. America*. Grand Rapids: Zondervan.

Meyers, Kenneth A. 1989. *All God's Children and Blue Suede Shoes: Christians and Popular Culture*. Westchester, Ill.: Crossway.

Schaeffer, Francis A. 1973. *Art and the Bible*. Downers Grove, Ill.: InterVarsity.

Schultz, J. Quentin. 1991. *Dancing in the Dark*. Grand Rapids: Eerdmans.

_____. 1995. *Televangelism and American Culture: The Business of Popular Religion*. Grand Rapids: Baker.

21

How Should We Use Music in Youth Ministry?

David S. Hart

"Did I ever need this!" I whispered with a sigh of relief. A beautiful sunny day, warm sand underneath my bare feet, the cool splash of ocean spray as the waves crashed just off shore. *I must be dreaming,* was the next thought that came to mind. Oh well, even if it was a dream, it was the most relaxed I had been in weeks.

I strolled over to where a group of teenagers was playing beach volleyball. They were laughing and kiddingly taunting one another about who was to be the victor. A fairly large crowd had gathered, so I remained in the back, not wanting to be the intrusive adult. I knew that the students had come here to be together, to play, joke, flirt, and listen to their . . . *Wait a second!* I thought so loudly that I was sure someone heard me. There was no music. No loud pulsating beats to drive the adrenaline, no boom box blaring sounds easily discernible to all passersby.

Even the refreshment stand twenty yards back from the volleyball pit had the same eerie lack of sound.

"What's happening? Have I stumbled onto the set of a new 'Twilight Zone' series? Is this some sociology department's weird experiment? Or could I be . . ."

Just then my radio alarm cried out to me with a "blast from the past" on the local oldies station. "I knew it was just a dream." Or was it a nightmare?

✞ ✞ ✞

Trying to imagine students in contemporary youth culture without the sounds, sights, and styles of their music is an almost impossible task. They listen to their music, they talk about it, they study it. It often shapes their appearance, their attitudes, even their identities. Yet, there are still adults whose response to this modern cultural icon is to ignore it, condemn it, ban it, or burn it. Youth workers cannot afford to choose any such tactics, however. Many students identify with their music so closely that ignoring and condemning the music is tantamount to ignoring and condemning the students themselves!

Dealing with music has never been an easy task; it is growing more complex all the time. Music is an emotional medium, and the debate on the proper use of music has been one of the most emotional debates in the history of the church. But youth workers have to find practical solutions to two basic questions: What *kind* of music works best with youth? and, What is the best *way* to use that music?

Issues regarding the kind of music begin with an understanding of the kinds of music that comprise the youth culture. Issues regarding methodology will naturally flow out of a grasp of contemporary music and its relationship to youth culture.

TYPES OF SECULAR MUSIC

When the parents of today's youth were growing up, there were basically two kinds of music: rock and roll and that stuff their parents listened to. Students were characterized as listening to one type of music, while adults listened to another.

Over time, students were caught up in pop rock, which drifted into psychedelic acid rock, and then evolved into the ponderous productions of album-oriented rock (AOR) or the plastic pleasures of disco. Disgusted with dinosaur rock *and* disco, young rebels began to slam to the revolting sounds of punk rock. The next British invasion brought us heavy metal, which degenerated into grunge rock. By the mid-nineties, everybody was listening to alternative rock—whatever that is!

However, somewhere along the line, something changed. Rock music could no longer be identified with just one style of music. The rock crowd grew apart from the pop crowd who thought the metal crowd was weird for making fun of the new wave crowd. As the culture became more self-centered and narcissistic, everyone seemed to be latching onto one brand of music, and there were dozens to choose from. It gets pretty confusing, even to the savvy youth worker with his/her ear to the ground (and the radio). Sorting through this confusing maze of musical styles can be helped by identifying some of the types of music that are characteristic of youth culture these days.

Rock and Roll

There are as many definitions of rock and roll as there are rock critics. There's not even a consensus on when it began. Some trace it to a song called "Rocket 88" in 1951, others to Bill Haley's "Rock Around the Clock" in 1954, and others insist it really began with Elvis. Like the Cajun term *jazz,* "rock and roll" was originally a euphemism for sexual intercourse. Musically, it is the gradual fusion of boogie woogie and rhythm and blues (R&B) by black artists, with up-tempo country swing and folk sounds (derived from Irish jigs) by white artists.

In the fifties, rock and roll was carried by piano (Little Richard), guitar (Elvis), or saxophone (the Coasters). By the sixties, it had become the exclusive property of electric guitars, with some help from loud vocals and pounding drums. At this point, it was just called rock. Although it was popular, it was not pop music, which was generally based on piano or orchestra arrangements. Since then, every new nuance in the music has gotten its own term and title as a separate style of music. Perhaps you (and Billy Joel) think "it's all rock and roll to me," but to youth today, the distinctions are crucial.

Heavy Metal

It is not completely clear where the term "heavy metal" originated. Some suggest it came from William Burroughs's novel *The Naked Lunch* (1959). Others say it refers to uranium 18, the original heavy metal used in the A-bomb. It is often connected to Steppenwolf's hit "Born to Be Wild" (1968). In that song, "heavy metal thunder" refers to a motorcycle, but rock critic Lester Bangs used the term to refer to hard rock music. It differs from regular rock only by degree: bombastic power chords, screaming lead guitars, throat-wrenching vocals, and a demolition-derby approach to drumming—all going on at a volume guaranteed to make your ears bleed—music to melt your face off!

The fans (metalheads) shake their heads and hair vigorously to the beat (headbanging). Many reel and careen into each other in a wild frenzy called moshing (or slam dancing) while people are passed overhead (floating, or body surfing) and others jump off the stage into the crowd (stage diving). The "axe" (the electric guitar) is still the most revered icon in the heavy metal ceremony. The faithful often live by the creed "sex, drugs, and rock-n-roll!" If rock music has become the religion of today's youth, then heavy metal is a cult of loyal and feverishly devoted fan(atic)s. And it has evolved and multiplied over the years, creating more than just one kind of havoc.

Alternative

Like the term "new wave," alternative rock has become so broad, it is almost meaningless. It is a catchall phrase for any modern music group that was not already established in the mainstream by the mid-eighties. Alternative tends to identify up-and-coming bands and college-radio favorites. The dramatic range of styles includes punk as well as piano ballads. Some of the styles that have been called alternative rock include modern/college radio (the softer side of alternative)

POPULAR MUSIC STYLES
DAVID S. HART

Here are some of the music styles popular with teenagers today.

GLAM METAL

Glam (short for glamorous) metal is also known as pop metal or party metal. It's a festive, colorful style that originally got its looks from the likes of Gary Glitter, David Bowie, and the New York Dolls. It's sort of a gay pirate look, with spandex, hair spray, and makeup. The chief proponents of this style were originally bands like Ratt, Mötley Crüe, Poison, and Bon Jovi. As bands grew less theatrical, the look toned down to blue jeans, T-shirts, and motorcycle boots by bands like Guns N' Roses and Skid Row. The concept here is "party," which can mean a lot of things to the fans: drugs, alcohol, sex, music, fun, dressing up, excitement, acceptance, belonging, romance, and/or escape from boredom. These bands preach hedonism with a capital *H*.

GOTHIC

This music started in an English dance club known as the Bat Cave in the late seventies. It was called death rock in America. It originated with bands like Bauhaus, Sisters of Mercy, and the queen of goth, Siouxsie and the Banshees. The most popular English imports were the Cure, Depeche Mode, and Morrissey of the Smiths. The sound is mournful and hollow, like it was recorded in a shower stall. The message is generally painfully sad and nihilistic. The dress is black and Victorian. Step into one of these clubs or concerts and you'll think you're at a Morticia Addams (from the "Addams Family" on television) convention. But the kids are generally sensitive, artistic, and intelligent, if a bit introspective and withdrawn.

INDUSTRIAL

This style combines the bleakness of gothic music with the anger of punk rock to scream about what soulless robots we've all become. At first, the music was an attempt to imitate the heartless factory, with a cold, clanging metal sound. Today, the use of synthesizers projects the cold whirring of the heartless computer. The theme here is pain and anger, with no way out. The dress is black. An early example is Einsturzende Neubauten (German for "knocking down buildings"), which used cement mixers and jackhammers as part of the music. Popular bands on this side of the Atlantic are Ministry and Skinny Puppy, although the most popular is probably Nine Inch Nails.

BLACK METAL

This is not a racial term. It is a dramatic, theatrical approach to celebrating the dark side, including black magic, satanism, and the occult. Inspired by KISS and Alice Cooper's brand of "shock rock," these groups use horror movie imagery with rock and roll for the ultimate in bloodcurdling entertainment. Groups vary in their stage shows, from throwing a little fake blood on the fans to fully-produced rock-opera horror shows. They also vary in their actual involvement in the occult. There are self-styled occultists like Danzig and dedicated satanists like King Diamond. Some, like Slayer, have confessed that it's just a marketing gimmick. Nevertheless, their dramatic stage shows can still get kids pretty excited about exploring the occult.

THRASH/SPEED METAL

This is a fusion of punk rhythms and lightning guitar leads for a heavier metal than glam. The look was basically borrowed from punk, dressed down in torn jeans, torn T-shirts, and Doc Marten boots—a direct rejection of the hair-sprayed hoopla going on in the glam movement. Thrashers see glam metal fans as "poseurs"—weak, effeminate, and safe. They like their music dangerous. Thrash shows are often a riot of seething fury, flailing bodies, and angry confusion—a living portrait of chaos and anarchy. As underground heroes like Metallica, Megadeth, and Anthrax found their way into the mainstream, metalheads moved on looking for something newer and heavier.

DEATH METAL/GRINDCORE

Metalheads looking for something deeper and darker found it here. Death metal, like Obituary and Cannibal Corpse, dives into detailed descriptions of death and dismemberment, while Morbid Angel and Deicide celebrate satanism and the dark side. Meanwhile in England, Napalm Death, Carcass, and Godflesh began to fuse metal with industrial music to produce grindcore (because of the heavy, grinding bass in the mix). If there's any distinction to be heard between the two styles, it might be that death metal vocals approximate the anguish of the damned, whereas grindcore vocals reflect the demands of the demons themselves. Although these groups may never become popular in the mainstream, they satisfy a loyal underground of angry kids looking for power and revenge for their abused and neglected lives.

GRUNGE METAL

Grunge is the bridge between the metal of the eighties and the alternative music of the nineties. Grunge features overdriven guitars and dripping-with-lithium vocals, which make the music hard, yet muddy (that's why it's sometimes called heavy muddle). This style originated with Seattle-based bands like Alice in Chains, Nirvana, and Pearl Jam. Grunge was also a fashion statement with its plaid shirts, baggy shorts, and grungy army boots. But it's mainly known for its manic-depressive themes and the high percentage of suicides and drug overdoses among its musicians.

HYBRID HARD ROCK

Metal music is basically blues-based, but some acts began to fuse it with rap, jazz, funk, punk, and psychedelic sounds, creating a hard-to-classify hybrid hard rock. The more notable of these avant-garde acts are Jane's Addiction (later renamed Porno for Pyros), Faith No More, Red Hot Chili Peppers, and Primus. These groups offer a more sophisticated cynicism than the overblown anger of most metal, and the psychedelic chaos adds an edge of madness as they explore insanity and question reality.

HARDCORE

Punk never really died; it just got absorbed into thrash metal. When punk bands like Bad Religion made a comeback, newer bands like Green Day and Offspring quickly followed in their bootsteps. The look here is dressed-down simplicity: baggy shorts and jeans, T-shirts, and shaved heads. The music is pounding and abrupt, with as much focus on the drums as on the guitar.

The theme is usually anger at a messed-up world. There's also some political and social commentary here, as many of these guys are college graduates. Not that anyone should confuse education with wisdom. Fans will talk about Old School and New School punk, but the unschooled won't be able to hear the difference. An interesting offshoot of the movement is the Riot Grrrls: all-female punk bands like L-7, Hole, Babes in Toyland, and Bikini Kill.

POSTMODERN ROCK

Also called post-punk or garage rock, it falls somewhere between punk and the Rolling Stones. It features a big guitar sound and cryptic lyrics about feeling lost in a big world. Early bands include Husker Dü and the Replacements. Bands like Dinosaur Jr. and Soul Asylum offer music that is less angry, but more aimless, than punk or industrial music.

COLLEGE RADIO

Although this is not an easily defined term, it generally describes the softer side of modern rock. It includes the more playful, jangly rock sounds of groups like the Breeders and Weezer, as well as the mournful ballads of groups like Belly or the Cranberries. Quirky female artists like Tori Amos, Sam Phillips, and Kate Bush also fall in this category.

RAVE

Originally, a rave was a spontaneous dance/happening—a kind of gypsy circus, set to music. Today's raves include music from every dance style: hip-hop, gothic, industrial, and especially house and techno. *House music* is basically disco, dance, and hip-hop sounds updated with modern instrumentation (drum machines and synthesizers). Although it originated in Detroit, European groups are often the biggest house favorites. Techno (technical disco) is a danceable style of electronic music, which originated with bands like Kraftwerk and Cabaret Voltaire. Dance rhythms over 130–150 bpm (beats per minute) are usually considered techno, whereas slower sounds are called house music. Other rave styles include: acid house (with '70s flashbacks like day-glo colors and the ubiquitous happy face), ambient, tribal (jungle), trance, hardcore, and progressive. A large part of a rave's appeal is sensory overload: pounding rhythms, multicolored lights, and smoky rooms with TVs, DJs, and several records going at once. To complete the sensory experience, dancers may use psychotropic drugs like Ecstacy or Euphoria.

and postmodern/post-punk/garage rock (somewhere between punk and the Rolling Stones, featuring a hard guitar sound and cryptic lyrics about feeling lost in a big world).

Urban Sounds

The heading of "Urban Sounds" encompasses a variety of music ranging from gospel to rap/hip-hop. *Gospel,* in the broadest sense, is used to describe music with a Christian theme. In the strictest sense, however, gospel music refers to African-American church music. *R&B (rhythm and blues)* describes the pop music produced by black artists from the forties to the sixties. Formerly called "race music," it provided the bridge between Big Band jump blues and early rock and roll. It later evolved into soul, funk, disco, and early forms of hip-hop and house music. The term is still used today to describe ballads and light dance tunes of melodic African-American music. *Rap* evolved from the street-corner doo-wop of the 1950s. The first true rap song is said to be "Rapper's

Delight" by the Sugarhill Gang in 1979, but it was "The Message" by Grandmaster Flash in 1982 that got the music industry interested. It took heavy metal, however, to bring rap to the white audience. Aerosmith's version of "Walk This Way" with Run-D.M.C. in 1986 put rap on MTV and on the map. The danger factor went up several (gun-belt) notches when West Coast rappers like Ice-T and N.W.A. started revealing the dark underbelly of the ghettos with what came to be known as Gangsta Rap. Some critics saw this as a great awakening for the general public; others saw it as a graphic ploy to use shock value to boost sales. After a decade of controversy, rap held its popularity and contributed to the new hybrid hard rock produced by white groups like the Beastie Boys, House of Pain, and the Red Hot Chili Peppers.

HOW TO REACH YOUTH WITH THEIR MUSIC

In the seventies, just about any guitar-based Christian band could draw a crowd of church youth who were disenchanted with organ music. Such is no longer the case. Music styles and tastes have become so diverse that it is no longer possible to draw all the kids in the neighborhood with any single concert act. Yet they remain fiercely loyal to their music and continue to be fascinated by most aspects of the music scene.

Contemporary music is, therefore, still one of the best tools to build bridges with Christian kids and one of the best hooks to go fishing for the unsaved. Given these conditions, what is the best way to reach students with today's music? There are no surefire, guaranteed strategies, but here are some ideas to build on:

Student Surveys

Survey students about their music preferences. Youth workers tend to stay on top of this, but many parents and pastors are unaware that most students in the church today listen predominantly to secular music. Periodically, it is important to survey the youth group to see where the students' tastes in music lie. Start with the more general and work toward the specific. What are their favorite styles of music? their favorite radio stations?

their favorite bands? their favorite albums? Every six months or so, every youth worker ought to compile a list of five to ten of his youth group's favorite artists and bands.

This information is a valuable springboard for opening up communication with students, and it will provide clues about how to minister to them more deeply. Why are musical tastes so significant? Students tend to choose secular music that relates to their emotional needs. Knowing this will allow you to offer them spiritual solutions, instead of just musical ones.

Discuss Their Favorites

Once or twice a year, it is important to discuss today's music with your youth group. Attempting to cover all the styles and topics in one sitting will not, however, be productive. Pick a specific area to focus on. Later in the year, focus on another area. The key is to be current. Unfortunately, much of the printed material on this topic is fifteen to twenty years out of date. (The most current information is available from Dr. Dobson's Focus on the Family or from Al Menconi Ministries.)

It is not crucial to know everything about today's music to have a successful youth night or retreat on this topic. The *very best source of information* is the students themselves. Listen and learn from them. They will know what is current and popular. As they identify their current crop of favorite songs, look for springboards for building discussions on topics that matter to them: sex, relationships, politics, parents, money, faith, life, death, and God.

No matter what topics or styles are selected, there are always two primary goals for group discussions. First, lead them in discovering what God has to say about any given topic. For example, compare what the artist says about sex to what Scripture says about it, or what the band says makes life successful to what the Bible teaches as the components of a successful life. Second, students are not primarily moved by the idea that music or lyrics might be evil; they are concerned about whether or not it could *affect* them. No matter how sinful a song might be, if it does not affect them, they conclude there is no harm in listening. But if it does affect their feelings, their attitudes, and their choices, then it will affect their ability to live the Christian life. It is important to guide them toward understanding how the experience of music can and does have a profound affect on their personal and spiritual lives.

Use Their Music

An interesting way to enhance discussions in a youth group setting is to use tunes that are currently popular with them. In the old days, songs like Pat Benatar's "Hell Is for Children" (which dealt with child abuse) or Billy Joel's "Honesty" or Poison's "Give Me Something to Believe In" provided a springboard for some valuable and energetic discussion on topics that are important to kids. You may want to make printed copies of the lyrics available for reference during the discussion. (A warning here. All song lyrics are under copyright. Be certain to check current copyright laws before distributing copies. One clearinghouse that processes requests to reprint the lyrics of secular songs is ASCAP, 1 Lincoln Plaza, New York 10003.)

Lyrics of popular songs provide an opportunity to point out the difference between the world's perspective and God's. Furthermore, if the leader is listening carefully, discussions around these lyrics will provide invaluable insights into the personal feelings and issues the students are currently struggling with. A bold move would be to invite students to bring their favorite albums or lyrics to their favorite songs to explain why this music is important to them. Such a risky move may not work for everyone, but along with the risk comes the great reward of hearing from the heart of students what is truly meaningful at this point in their personal journeys.

Use Contemporary Christian Music

Use contemporary Christian music for the above approaches as well. Pick a couple of songs that reflect a specific topic, pass out copies of the lyrics, play the tunes, and launch into a lively Bible study on that theme. (Studies like this are available through Interlinc; or contact Youth for Christ, Youth Specialties, or the National Network for suggestions.)

USING SECULAR MUSIC
IN YOUTH MINISTRY
JOHN FISCHER

Secular music is a window on culture. It reveals the values and attitudes that reflect a generation. The songs of the '60s were hopeful and involved; the '70s were tuning in and dropping out; the '80s escaped to disco; and the '90s are hopeless. Through it all, the love song is perennial.

Kids don't need to be encouraged to listen to secular music—most are already listening—they need to be challenged with *how* to listen. This can be modeled by bringing secular music into the group and addressing it head-on. Once every few weeks, try playing a few top ten songs and put the lyrics on an overhead. Then discuss them. One good way to pick appropriate songs would be to take a survey of their favorite groups and select songs from the most popular ones.

Use questions like:

What is the writer's perspective on life?

What does this song say about the value of human existence?

What does it say about love?

Is the song appealing to you? Why?

Is the song consistent with a life with God or outside of God?

Do they mean what they sing about, or are they just trying to make money or be popular?

Is the author searching for something?

Is the song good or bad? True or false? Is it mixed? If so, where does it go wrong? How far can you agree with it?

Remember, not all secular songs are all bad. Many can be a springboard to talk about truth. Paul went into Athens and found an idol to an unknown god to which he cleverly attached the message of the gospel. He also quoted a popular Athenian poet—someone probably comparable to a rock star today (Acts 17:16–28). Don't use all bad examples to try to make a personal point about music you don't like. Pick songs that are thoughtful as well. All truth is God's truth regardless of the source.

The important thing is to get kids thinking critically about their culture. Our role in society is not to reject culture or run away from it or judge it without compassion, but to be transformed by God's Word in the way we think and act toward it. Unfortunately, most kids are not thinking very critically when they entertain themselves.

Repeated practice at such critical thinking about their music can help get them into the habit of thinking Christianly about everything.

"The spiritual man makes judgments about all things" (1 Corinthians 2:15).

Identify "Testimony Songs"

Another way to use Christian music is to encourage your students to find a "testimony song." Specifically, a testimony song is a Christian song that inspires them and describes their walk with the Lord. Each student should have copies of the lyrics to pass out to the group. After the group has listened to the song, the student should be prepared to give a five-minute talk to answer the question: "Do you see why Jesus Christ is important to me?" This is not necessarily recommended as an exercise to fill up an entire youth night, but one or two of these testimonies every couple of weeks from various members of your group can be encouraging to everyone. This strategy can become ineffective if overused, but when sprinkled throughout the regular youth curriculum, the testimonies can create interest and excitement in your group, as well as some healthy bonding among your kids.

Expose Students to Contemporary Christian Music

Most youth groups have many music styles represented, and no single artist or band can satisfy all those musical tastes. Punks do not usually like country, and rap fans do not usually care for mainline pop/rock. So what is to be done?

Determine needs

The first thing is to identify *who* these particular students are and what they need. Are they especially savvy about music? If so, bring in or go to the most talented artists you can find. Do you want to encourage the Christian kids in your group? If so, choose artists who are especially good at relating to those who are already Christians.

Many churches hope to use music for youth evangelism. The hard truth is, however, that it is increasingly difficult to identify single groups that will draw a wide variety of kids. It is not advisable to mix two contrasting styles in one concert. Rather than such a concert drawing kids from both styles, many kids tend to stay away because they do not like the other style. The exception to this is the all-day festival, which offers a wide variety of groups covering all styles. Kids can come and go, getting ministered to by their favorite style at the right time.

Offer a concert series

In a concert series you can provide a different style of music each concert. This will broaden the outreach and ministry effect of the series. A concert series like this can be an enormous undertaking and can best be handled when several churches join forces in the neighborhood. One final suggestion is to use a little comedy. It is one style that reaches kids across the board. These "concert artists" of comedy can often touch a wider range of kids than a specialty rock group.

If a youth group does have a critical mass of students with similar musical interests, find Christian groups that are competent in that style. Effective Christian equivalents to secular musicians or groups can be identified through some of the Christian music magazines that are available in your local

Christian Bible bookstore, for example: CCM *(Contemporary Christian Music)*, HM *(Hard Music)*, or *True Tunes*.

WORSHIP AND THE ROLE OF MUSIC: IMPORTANT DIFFERENCES

Youth seem to have a hard time with the average worship service. If there is a universal stereotype about students and church, it is that they think the whole thing is boring. It is even difficult to get them to sing in their own youth group settings. There are probably a lot of reasons this is so, but three seem to stand out: a difference in *need,* a difference in *experience,* and a difference in *the definition of worship.*

A Different Experience

Students experience their music in an increasingly different way than previous generations. In the days of transistor radios, three or four channels on TV, and concerts that came to town once a year, kids had to really concentrate to find the music they loved. Today music is available twenty-four hours a day. It is on radio or TV and in all the shopping malls. Music simply accompanies other activities. It has become background music for work, play, parties, homework, driving around, shopping at the mall, talking on the phone, and socializing.

Students' immediate impulse is, therefore, to talk to their neighbor as soon as music starts to play. That fact is also why most students argue that they are not affected by the words— much of the time they are not actively listening to music. They do not sing along with the radio—unless they are alone—so they are not going to sing out loud with you. Singing aloud could be embarrassing, especially if the youth group is small. These youth cultural responses to music can be tough to overcome.

A Different Need

Contemporary young people need a point of identity, something they can relate to and claim as their own. Many older people in the church already have this. They have a relationship to God and a worship service that is familiar and reliable. Familiarity with the music and the order of worship, repeatedly positive worship experiences, good memories, and emotional attachments are all learned experiences.

Most students have never experienced this for themselves. The music is often strange and archaic, and the words are ancient and unrelated. Nothing is being described in the language of their everyday lives. The result is repeated Sunday after Sunday in churches everywhere: students sit around listless and bored waiting for something to relate to. After all, how many worship committees plan relevant worship experiences exclusively for students?

Youth groups need special moments of worship that are directly tied into their own present-day realities. That is why summer camp experiences can be so powerful to the youth group. Camp gives them a unique experience of fellowship and worship that is specifically their own. They will want to recall those special moments and feelings over and over by singing the songs that were so much a part of that experience.

A Different Definition of Worship

The popular conception of worship may be too narrow. Paul says, "Therefore I urge you, brethren, by the mercies of God, to present your bodies a living and holy sacrifice, acceptable [well pleasing] to God, which is your spiritual service of worship" (Romans 12:1, NASB). Worship is more than what is done on Sunday mornings or Wednesday nights. It is more than what takes place inside the church walls. It is certainly more than the music that may or may not give the participant spiritual goosebumps. It is what we do with people's lives that constitutes the ultimate in worship.

In limiting worship to music, adults may give students the idea that worship (and God Himself) is one-dimensional, antiquated, and boring. Worship does not relate to modern times; it is apathetic and dull. Such misconceptions of true worship are overcome, however, when young people start seeing missions or acts of mercy such as feeding the homeless as worshipful experiences. Fellowship can provide worshipful experience; activities such as helping friends or even doing homework can also be seen as opportunities to bring glory to

God with a worshipful heart. Recasting worship as more than Sunday morning services and hymns enables worship to be perceived as relevant and appealing and opens students to becoming more expressive, even in their music.

WORSHIP AND THE ROLE OF MUSIC:
IMPORTANT EMPHASES

Facing these challenging differences may be discouraging to church worship leaders. But just because kids are not responding at church does not mean they are not responding. If an adult wants to see the human worship impulse in action, then that adult should attend a rock concert. For many students rock and pop music has become the new religion, and concerts are the part where everyone gets to go to church. The faithful dress up in their best outfits and gather to give thanks for their rock-religion's benefits. There is fellowship and a feeling of unity, certain rituals to be performed, time and money sacrificed to be there, loyalty to and faith in the "priests" who lead the service, and worship of the "gods" that promise them fulfillment. They are often quite loyal to their favorite artists and will defend them with intense fervor—all the while claiming that the music does not affect them! (One way to measure young people's devotion is to determine what they do with their spare money and spare time. It will tell us a lot about where their true interest lies.)

The urge to worship is definitely present. But it is not always met in a church setting. What does the youth group offer to compete with the glitter of rock and roll? Can a swim party ever compete with a stadium full of lights and sound and screaming fans? What can be learned from the world of rock without compromising the gospel? How do leaders attract their attention long enough to get them to take a long, loving look at Christ? How are such efforts to be shaped by biblical guidelines? If that worship impulse is there—if it can be seen pulsing through the crowd of a worldly concert—then how can leaders redirect that worship to the One who is really worth our worth-ship?

WANTED: A DIFFERENT APPROACH TO WORSHIP

Making worship more exciting does not always make it more meaningful. True worship can be a powerful, wonderful experience, but it was never intended to be a circus. There are several keys to opening up the mystery of worship to youth.

Reestablish the foundation of true worship. A clearer picture of who we worship must be presented. Worship services reflect a picture of God. It is pretty hard to convince kids that believers serve an incredible, awesome, vital, infinite God, when even their parents are yawning in church.

Teach the group how to structure worship by using models already suggested in Scripture. The tabernacle, Isaiah's temple experience (Isaiah 6), and the Lord's Prayer are three of the best. Are there other passages that suggest a model for the structure or order of worship? What are the elements of worship described in these passages? What do celebration, confession, reflection, prayer, petition, thanksgiving, reverence, enlightenment, forgiveness, and revelation mean to students in their present realities? What place do they have in worship? How do they affect real, everyday lives? What part do they play in getting in touch with God?

Model a dynamic worship service. Ministry leadership must be prepared to be stretched toward a new, active meaning to worship by creating exercises that actively demonstrate forgiveness, confession, restoration, offering, etc. This can be done one topic at a time each week, or by several experiences of creative worship services.

Get students involved personally, not just in the planning, but in participating in worship. Create a youth band to lead the music. Get rhythm instruments (kazoos, egg shakers, tambourines, bongos, and so on) and pass them out to kids in the group. If they cannot sing, they can shake and bang things to celebrate. Have the more experienced youth group members explain why certain worship approaches are being used at youth group or in the church service. Get them to pray out loud! The key is this: just do not let them get the idea that church is simply religious TV for sitting back and watching. The church is a fellowship, a congregation of active believers, not an audience waiting to receive one-way communication.

As youth begin seeing the relevance of worship, encourage them to use their insights, talents, and lives to plan worship experiences for the group. More than filling roles, they can begin contributing content. They can write their own prayers, hymns, poems, dramatic readings, and skits. There are unlimited ideas for scenes that teach about who God is and how that relates to our lives today. Students can write memorials to a friend who recently died, or act out a last conversation they would have liked to have had with him. Sports can often become a parable for life, church, or the youth group. Who's the quarterback—Jesus? The youth worker? The most popular kid at school? The ideas of bringing real life into the elements are endless, once we know what some of those elements are and see creativity and relevance modeled in the worship service.

Most youth leaders are motivated in part by the belief that there is a God-shaped vacuum that needs to be filled in each teen. Participating in worshipful activities can be an expression of that void—not just a response to what they have, but the reflection that they are still seeking. As long as young people are looking for meaning in their lives, they have the potential to worship. At the very least, adults can recognize their capacity to celebrate. They have the quality of being devoted, even fanatical, to the music and experiences of their lives that seem to meet their immediate needs. They have already learned that there are certain places and situations, like concerts, that are appropriate to express their emotions in an effort to celebrate. They may have also learned that church is not the appropriate setting for this.

THE GOAL: MOVING STUDENTS TOWARD WORSHIP

The goal is not so much teaching students how to worship as it is redirecting their focus without resorting to manipulating them. The potential for worship can be redirected to a living, active God who is concerned about their lives, in the here and now as well as their future. Those ideas can be expressed in a way that is relevant, contemporary, personal, and meaningful. They can have hands-on experience at communicating the nature of their lives and what they seek from God. This

kind of worship will not always fit into the traditional structure of the church. It will not often express meaning in the
same terms that their parents find meaning. But it will be real
worship, an experience they can learn from and own.

SUMMARY

Music is one of the most powerful tools God has provided
to the youth leader who is committed to moving students
toward worship. Music provides entry points for hearing their
hearts and entry points for speaking to their hearts. Because it
is difficult to imagine teenagers without their music it is,
therefore, difficult to imagine teenagers at worship without
their music. Music can be used to provoke interest, provide
opportunities, and promote personal investment in worshp.
By using the strategies and paying close attention to the principles outlined above, the adult leader can be a catalyst for
leading students to the place where they could not imagine
their lives without worship as well as without music.

FOR FURTHER READING

Baker, Paul. 1985. *Contemporary Christian Music: Where It
Came From. What It Is. Where It's Going*. Westchester, Ill.:
Crossway.

Bill, J. Brent. 1984. *Rock and Roll: Proceed with Caution*.
Old Tappan, N.J.: Revell.

Erlewine, Michael, with Chris Woodstra and Vladimir Bog-
danov, eds. 1994. *All Music Guide*. San Francisco: Miller
Freeman.

Hart, David. 1966. *It's All Rock-n-Roll to Me*. San Diego:
New Song.

Key, Dana, with Steve Rabey. 1989. *Don't Stop the Music*.
Grand Rapids: Zondervan.

Lawhead, Steve. 1987. *Rock of This Age*. Downers Grove,
Ill.: InterVarsity.

Menconi, Al, with Dave Hart. 1966. *Staying in Tune: A
Rational Response to Your Child's Music*. Cincinnati, Ohio:
Standard.

Meyers, Kenneth A. 1989. *All God's Children and Blue Suede Shoes: Christians and Popular Culture*. Westchester, Ill.: Crossway.

Muncy, John. 1989. *The Role of Rock*. Campton, Ohio: Daring.

Pareles, John, and Patricia Romanowski, eds. 1989. *The Rolling Stone Encyclopedia of Rock-n-Roll*. New York: Summit.

Seay, Davin, with Mary Neely. 1986. *Stairway to Heaven: The Spiritual Roots of Rock-n-Roll*. New York: Ballantine.

22

WHAT IS YOUTH MINISTRY'S RELATIONSHIP TO THE FAMILY?

Mark DeVries

After five years of banging my head against what seemed like an immovable wall, I had become certain of at least one thing: The way we were doing youth ministry simply was not working. I was reading all the right books, attending all the right seminars, working long hours. But our youth ministry had settled into a comfortable stagnation, and I was very tired.

I had left seminary only five years earlier with a deep commitment to long-term youth ministry. I had plans of staying in this church for at least ten years. But the longer I stayed, the more convinced I became that, alarmist though his words may sound, Mike Yaconelli was on to something when he said,

> Kids today are unlike any other generation of kids we've ever had to work with in youth ministry. All the techniques, all the strategies, all the philosophies that we are all using and grew up with don't work any more. But if we don't wake up

in the church and begin to radically alter and change what we are doing with kids, we've lost them. (Yaconelli 1989)

And so I offered a rather startling proposal: cancel youth group—indefinitely.

No, I am not normally given to fits of mental instability. I was not acting out some "vocation relocation" fantasy. Surprisingly, I was neither in a state of panic or desperation at the time we made the decision.

However, I was, and still am, committed to taking whatever steps were necessary to accomplish the intended purpose of the student ministry of our church: to lead young people to mature Christian adulthood.

As the months went by, I recognized that our decision to cancel youth group was the most radically offensive (in every sense of the word) step we had ever taken in our ministry together at our church. And now, as I begin my eleventh year at this same church, I am convinced that this change marked the turning point in our work with students.

Leaders should be cautious not to misinterpret my experience—abandoning the existing youth group should not be seen as the silver bullet that can rescue every church struggling with its youth ministry. In fact, we have now gone back to having youth group most Sunday nights, but for an entirely different reason and with a radically different foundation. "Nuking the youth group" (as the change came to be affectionately called) was simply a catalyst that led us to a whole new model of ministry that we have grown to refer to as *Family-Based Youth Ministry*. The change has been as powerful in the lives of students as it was dramatic in the life of our congregation.

In order to understand accurately the *why* and the *how* of the emphases of Family-Based Youth Ministry, four important questions need to be addressed.

1. Why build a youth ministry on families?
2. A generation ago, youth ministries thrived without giving more than a tip of the hat to families. Why are families so important now?

3. Family-Based Youth Ministry sounds like a fine idea for kids who come from stable families, but what about the kids whose parents will do nothing for their children's Christian nurture?
4. How can a church begin a Family-Based Youth Ministry?

Not all Family-Based Youth Ministries will look the same, of course. Strategies and methods will naturally vary from one context to another. Yet the answers to the above four questions suggest that in a youth ministry based on the families in the church there are values and principles that are relevant to all contexts and models of youth ministry.

WHY FAMILIES?

I grew up as the son of a Presbyterian minister. My mother grew up with only one desire—to be a missionary. Her friends used to tease her by calling her "Mish" when she was young. During my teenage years, I pulled away from my parents' faith sharply. Strangely enough, I established my independence by seeking to be *more* spiritual than my parents. There were years when I was sure that my minister father and my missionary mother were not even Christians. But my movement away from my parents' faith, like that of most teenagers, was temporary. Like a rubber band, I pulled the farthest away from my parents' faith during my teenage years, only to return to many of their central faith commitments as an adult.

Based on my experiences, I find a lot of wisdom in Jay Kesler's advice to parents.

While you wait for your teenagers to grow up, you can take comfort in the fact that by the time young people reach their mid-twenties, their lines are almost always identical to the lines their parents drew. Even those who do not like certain attributes of their parents find themselves following their parents' patterns. So perhaps the point is not how can we get our kids to behave as we want them to, but how can we be the kind of parents we ought to be so that when our kids are like us, we'll like what they are. (Kesler 1990)

SUGGESTIONS FROM THE
NATIONAL CENTER FOR FATHERING
DAVID WARNICK

1 *Acquaint all dads, but particularly younger dads, with a fathering life course.* A father needs to think ahead about the combination of his own adult development issues and the new challenges he'll face as his oldest child matures.

Our research does provide hope: those dads who remain in close verbal communication with their teenagers show higher satisfaction. In addition, scores on *behavior* (as opposed to satisfaction) for dads of teenagers actually climb over dads whose oldest child is a grade-schooler. Their consistency is higher. They do more active listening. They are more committed to the task of being a father and show dramatic increases in how they see themselves expressing love (or for those who are separated, *respecting*) their children's mother. They do better at protecting and providing for their children.

Many dads will be going through a "mid-life crisis" during their children's adolescence. That can provide a point of connection, as both fathers and children focus on questions about the meaning of life. Dads at this age need to be in small groups with other men where they can be supported and encouraged—but they also may be least likely to pursue them.

2. *Assist and encourage dads to provide rites of passage for their children when they enter adolescence.* Encourage other ceremonies and celebrations as they move to adulthood.

Whether it's at age twelve or thirteen, as a father-son camp-out or a group ritual, there is a place for restoring a rite of passage. It should be more than simply an occasion to discuss sexuality and receive a pledge of purity; there are so many issues new adolescents want direction on—and this is a great time for dads to provide it.

3. Recognize your God-given calling to assist dads by confirming the messages they have imparted to their children. A father is described in 1 Thessalonians 2:11–12 as someone who encourages, comforts, and urges his children to live lives worthy of God. Interestingly, the first two words are two of the words the apostle Paul uses to describe the purpose of prophecy in 1 Corinthians 14:3. It is for strength, encouragement, and comfort. In other words: fathers have tasks similar to prophets.

But we also know the rejection our Lord experienced at Nazareth—there are times when prophets have no honor in their own hometowns. A child's adolescence can be one of those times. In the midst of teenagers' journey to be independent, people around teenagers are given another prophetic calling: It's described in Malachi 4:5-6—to turn the hearts of children to their fathers.

National Center for Fathering
10200 W. 75th Street, Suite 267
Shawnee Mission, KS 66204
Telephone: (913) 384-4661

Several years ago, I was leading a Family-Based Youth Ministry seminar with seventy-five or so youth leaders from around the country. I decided to test my own theories with a little informal one-question survey of my own. I asked, "How many of you come from families in which at least one of your parents is a committed Christian?" (I let people use their own definitions.) Their response? All but three of these youth leaders raised their hands. Parents have an incomparable effect on their children's faith development.

A study done of the transmission of religious values from parents to their teenage children by the Seventh-Day Adventist Church revealed, "Youth tend . . . to resemble their parents in religious values held . . . and even the independence of adolescence cannot usually obliterate these values completely" (Dudley and Dudley 1986).

Counselor Kevin Huggins's assessment reinforces the significance of the family role: "In the vast majority of cases parents remain the single most important influence in the development of an adolescent's personality" (Huggins 1989, 143). Jonathan Edwards's exhortation over two hundred years ago still holds true today.

> Every Christian family ought to be as it were a little church consecrated to Christ, and wholly influenced and governed by his rule. And family education and order are some of the chief means of grace. *If these fail, all other means are likely to prove ineffectual.* If these are maintained, all the means of grace will be likely to prosper and be successful. (Holbrook 1973, 83)

More recently, the Search Institute, in its broad-based 1990 study of Protestant congregations, determined that the level of "family religiousness" was the single strongest predictor of faith maturity in teenagers (Benson and Elkin 1990, 83). How active a young person is in a youth program is a much less reliable predictor of faith maturity than is the faith maturity of his family of origin.

A TALE OF TWO STUDENTS

Most long-term youth ministers have a busload of stories like Jenny's. Although her family was only nominally involved in the church, Jenny came to our youth group faithfully throughout her teenage years. She went on mission trips and attended Sunday school; she was a regular fixture in our program. We had been successful with Jenny, or so we thought.

Jimmy, on the other hand, never quite connected with our youth ministry. We really worked to get him involved with our youth programs. He had no interest in retreats or mission trips; Sunday school bored him; and youth group seemed a little on the silly side for his taste. He sometimes attended another church across town. On my mental scorecard of kids we had been effective with, Jimmy was on the "loss" side.

But Jimmy had one thing going for him—every Sunday, he was in worship—with his parents at our church or with his friends at another church. Jimmy didn't need our outrageous and creative youth ministry to lead him to faith maturity.

But for Jenny, our youth ministry was her *only* Christian connection. Unlike a real family, the youth group "family" forced her to resign when she was too old to fit the requirements. She now looks back on her youth group experience as she does on her high school Farrah Fawcett haircut—as a fun, even laughable part of her past, but as something that belonged exclusively in the realm of her teenage years.

There is something wrong with a standard of success that prematurely rates a leader's work with Jenny as the example of success and Jimmy as an example of failure.

"ORPHANING" STRUCTURES

Most traditional youth ministries are "orphaning" structures. They carry students to the doorway of adulthood but often leave them there. For many young adults who have grown up with the youth group (or the FCA or the Young Life group) as their primary faith community, their only hope frequently is to try to re-create their youth group experience as an adult (by becoming a youth leader or finding a church that is as much like their youth group as possible). This is at least one cause of the amazing phenomenon of new, short-lived, "hip" churches springing up across the country, where members over forty are as rare as a snowstorm in the Sahara. These churches may simply be the perpetuation of a traditional youth ministry.

The question is, "Are we connecting our kids to nurturing relationships that will last them after they complete their teenage years, or are we simply exploiting them as public relations tools to make our ministries appear successful?" I submit that unless we are making intentional, focused efforts at

PARENTS AS ALLIES,
NOT OBSTACLES, TO THE MINISTRY
DAVID OLSHINE

I have learned over nineteen years that without parental support, the likelihood of teens growing in their faith as an adult is significantly reduced. In many youth ministries today, parents are seen as an enemy or obstacle to the ministry. This stems from the model of youth ministry that was predominant in the sixties and seventies. This model focused exclusively on ministry to teens. The parents did not need to be involved in counseling with the youth minister and teen. The youth minister ministered only to teens. This old model neglected parents, ignoring the question of what was to be done with them. Many youth ministers and parents are intimidated by each other, even today.

The new approach is for ministers to be in partnership with parents. Parents are not seen as enemies; rather, the parents are part of the same team. Youth ministers or parents alone cannot fully get into the world of a teen; each needs the help of the other. The fact is, most parents, Christian or not, do want help in rearing their teens. The church needs to be on the cutting edge of finding creative ways to help parents become better equipped as parents. The church needs to help the parents deal with their own baggage and insecurity, the same issues the youth minister is also dealing with. "Parentnoia" (the fear of parents) needs to be erased. The parents are not the enemy.

Based on the model of parents as *partners in the ministry*, here are some practical suggestions for beginning to include parents:

1. *Parent information meetings*

   These meetings provide the opportunity for the youth minister to inform parents of upcoming events, such as missions trips, retreats, and fund-raising activities. This is also a great time to share the philosophy of ministry for the church and the youth ministry.

2. *Newsletters for parents*

   The newsletter should be sent out one to four times a year. The letter can focus on Sunday school teachers, students, and parents. This can also be an informative letter of upcoming events.

3. *Parent classes*

   One example of this is a four- to six-week class for parents on understanding their teens.

4. *Thank-you notes*

   Send a note to the parents of your students thanking them for their students. This is also a great time to encourage the parents.

5. *Parent advisory groups*

   Have the parents get involved in planning events for the ministry. (Many of these suggestions have been adapted from the book *Tag Team Youth Ministry: 50 Ways to Involve Parents and Other Caring Adults*, by David Olshine and Ron Habermas.)

We need parents to be involved in youth ministry. They can be great assets, not obstacles, to the ministry.

connecting kids with mature Christian adults in the church
(not just their youth leaders), we are more like the vultures
preying on kids at rock concerts and less like spiritual leaders
praying that their children's lives would be founded upon
eternal things.

Our teenagers' families of origin *will* have a huge impact
on those young people's faith development—for better or for
worse. Youth ministries that hope to have a lasting impact
with young people can no longer afford to ignore the incomparable power of the family in faith formation.

WHY FAMILIES NOW?

Most churches have their fair share of charter members of
The-Way-We-Used-to-Do-Things-When-I-Was-Doing-Youth-
Ministry Club. Some of the club members in our church have
raised an incredibly significant question that gets immediately
to the heart of why Family-Based Youth Ministry is so needed
at this particular time in our culture. They have asked, "We
had a very successful ministry with a church full of kids without ever considering the role their parents might play. Why
are families suddenly so important *now?*"

When I think back to the "good old days" of youth ministry, I think of the late sixties and early seventies with Youth
for Christ filling stadiums and Young Life clubs filling living
rooms. Those were also the years of "Leave It to Beaver" and
"Father Knows Best." For the most part, the kinds of ministries that worked a generation ago were silently undergirded
by a culture that understood stable families to be the norm,
not the exception.

In a youth culture undergirded by stable families and many
available adults, the old model of youth ministry (isolating
youth from the world of adults for an hour or two) worked
fine. But in the current environment where, in Allan Bloom's
words, "the dreariness of the family's spiritual landscape
passes belief," the old model for youth ministry is no longer
capable of carrying young people to Christian maturity.

In our church, I did a little poll of my own youth to see
what relation, if any, there was between kids who were active
in our church and kids who were living with both of their

original parents. I found that kids from traditional two-parent families were at least three times more likely to be active participants in our church than those who came from other family configurations.

But at the same time that our culture seems to be losing its moorings about what a healthy family is, there is an unprecedented interest among Christian parents to learn to be faithful and effective in helping their children grow as Christians. The mid-nineties' growth of the Promise Keepers movement among Christian fathers has been nothing short of amazing. And some of the best-selling Christian books are directed at Christian parents who are diligently seeking to break the old, negative patterns they grew up with.

In almost twenty years of working with teenagers, I have never seen the sort of genuine concern and determination of Christian parents that we are seeing today. Perhaps now more than ever, parents *want* to join us as partners in ministry and are simply waiting to be asked.

Another reason for drawing on the natural power of families at this particular time in our culture is that kids want to have better relationships with their parents and spend more time with them. With one in four teenagers now indicating that they have *never* had a meaningful conversation with their fathers (McDowell and Wakefield 1989, 13), is it any wonder that 76 percent of teenagers surveyed in *USA Today* actually *want* their parents to spend more time with them ("Parents of Teenagers" 1988, August/September, 8)? The common stereotype of teenagers who want nothing more than to avoid their parents' input and influence simply is not consistent with the research of families today.

THE CHURCH AS EXTENDED FAMILY

Many assume when they hear about Family-Based Youth Ministry that I am advocating a model that only works with kids whose parents are Christians. Actually, just the opposite is true. Family-Based Youth Ministry looks realistically at the tremendous obstacles young Christians growing up in non-Christian homes face and seeks to provide the kind of faith-nurturing extended family that can lead them to maturity.

THROUGH A TEENAGER'S EYES
SARAH KATHERINE MCDAVITT

*D*o parents and teenagers have to have a "communication gap"?

Can the church provide any help to youth and their parents struggling to do more than just "survive" the adolescent years?

At least one youth ministry has moved toward an intentional focus on linking parents and youth together. The following is a reflection of how Sarah McDavitt, tenth grader and youth group member, feels about a recent Sunday school class in which she and her parents participated.

When my parents first told me about a class that I would attend *with* them, I was really not too thrilled. I mean, having parents and teenagers in the same room—really! I don't have a problem being around adults. But discussing my faith? You've got to be joking! There was no way I was going to tell about my personal relationship with God right in front of my parents, let alone all the other families in there.

But as time went on, I found that I wasn't the only one uncomfortable. Talking about something personal was very hard for everyone to do. After a while, I found myself listening. I could not believe some of the feelings or thoughts these people had. They were so much like mine. Having teenagers in the class and listening to them talk made me realize I wasn't alone and made my parents realize they weren't alone. We learned to communicate. We felt for each other, and we understood, because at some point in our lives we all have been hurt. We all were striving for the same goal—to make our families stronger through Christ by communicating.

This class isn't easy. It isn't a class where you sit back and relax while someone tells you what is right and what is wrong. This class is about learning to give a little of yourself and learning to tell someone you care.

The hardest task I believe the members of my family had to overcome was to tell the group how they have grown in Christ, when it began, and how it has gone either up or down until now. Although that may sound easy, for a family who rarely talks about Christianity, it's hard. Watching my dad express himself and my mom cry as he did so made me realize what they have been through and how the power of God can change a person.

And I learned that it is OK to cry. As other families told their stories there were more tears and more laughter. But my point isn't about the tears or laughter but that adults and teenagers were actually communicating. There isn't much difference between adults and teenagers—they both hurt, cry, and feel the need for help. This class wouldn't work if the parents just came or if only the kids showed up—it takes both, and it also takes both sides trying in order to make a successful family.

Yes, my parents and I still argue, but now I know in my heart that when I hurt they hurt and that they have been through struggles the same or similar to the ones I face today. And by listening to their feelings and thoughts, I am able to relate, appreciate, and respect them, not only because I'm supposed to, but because I want to.

According to the "National Fathering Profile" published by Headfirst Ministries (Newsletter, Summer 1994, 4), only 10 percent of fathers were rated as "excellent," while 40 percent of fathers were classified as "dangerous." Gary Bauer raises a pointed question about the cost of the national neglect of our children: "What are we saying to our children if we allow them to spend more time watching television by the time they are 6 than they will spend talking with their fathers the rest of their lives?" (DeMoss 1992, 14).

What young Christians need is a lifelong structure to carry them to maturity. The church can become this sort of extended family for young people, but often the very success of our youth ministries keeps this sort of lifelong extended family from being built. I love Stuart Cummings-Bond's image for traditional youth ministries. He calls it the one-eared Mickey Mouse (Cummings-Bond 1989, 76).

Figure 22.1. *One-Eared Mickey Mouse*

I was fortunate enough to grow up in a church small enough that it could never sustain a "successful" youth ministry for more than a few months. We had moments when things went beautifully, but for the most part, we struggled along, year after year, with our ten to fifteen member youth group. We spent a lot of time reinventing the wheel, figuring things out by ourselves. And because our Presbyterian church had trouble hanging on to our part-time Baptist youth directors for very long (go figure), our pastor wound up spending a lot of time with the teenagers. He knew all of our names. He knew our parents. And he helped us as we muddled along together. Every teenager in that church knew that he belonged —not just to the youth group but to the church.

"Successful" youth ministries, on the other hand, are able to insulate themselves effectively from the larger church. In many ways, the successful youth ministry does not need the larger church. It has its own worship, its own discipleship groups, its own budget, its own offering, its own Sunday school classes, its own choir, its own council, its own mission programs, its own elders (a bit oxymoronic, don't you think?), its own service projects, and (my personal favorite) its own pastor! Ben Patterson argues that

> it is a sad fact of life that often the stronger the youth pro-gram in the church, and the more deeply the young people of the church identify with it, the weaker the chances are that those same young people will remain in the church when they grow too old for the youth program. Why? Because the youth program has become a substitute for participation in the church. . . . When the kids outgrow the youth program, they also outgrow what they have come to know of the church. (Patterson 1984, 60)

The Search Institute report (previously cited) also studied what factors were most likely to lead to faith maturity in adults. The study found that the strongest predictor of adult faith maturity was lifetime "Christian education involvement" (Benson and Elkin 1990, 40). In other words, those with the greatest faith maturity as adults are those who have made a lifelong connection with the extended family of the church.

The church's best hope for seeing young people grow to maturity in Christ is not to connect them to the orphaning structure of the youth group but to connect them to a lifetime nurturing structure of the larger community of the congrega-tion. The fact that more and more students are coming from openly dysfunctional homes is all the more reason that youth ministries must make a priority of connecting kids with a nur-turing extended family of adults in the church.

The U.S. Census Bureau confirms that the average American household is made up of 2.63 people. But in the Old Testament, the average Hebrew "family" was made up of fifty to one hundred persons. What modern Americans would call a nuclear family, the Israelites saw as part of a much larger fabric of a multigenerational extended family.

A connection to the extended family of the church is a helpful reminder to adults that hope is not to be found in some nostalgic return to the days of the pristine and protected nuclear family. Rodney Clapp asserts:

> We cannot affirm that the hope of the world rests in the bosom of the biological or nuclear family. . . . The hope of the world is in Jesus Christ, and the people called to bear witness to that hope is a people drawn from all families and all nations. It is the church. (Clapp 1993, 46)

Where do hurting students turn for their most significant long-term help? In her fascinating book, *Children of Fast-Track Parents,* Andree Alieon Brooks documents, "Studies of resiliency in children have shown time and again that the consistent emotional support of at least one loving adult can help [children] overcome all sorts of chaos and deprivation" (Brooks 1989, 68–69). Urie Bronfrenbrenner's declaration, "Somebody's got to be crazy about the kid," points to the heart of Family-Based Youth Ministry. Perhaps the best gift a youth ministry can give teenagers is not to impress them or attract them but to ensure that each young person in the church has someone who delights in him or her. The church family becomes the family-base for the adolescents.

WHAT IS YOUTH MINISTRY, ANYWAY?

A seven-year-old child went through his parents' devastating divorce. And for months after the divorce he was wetting his pants. His father tried everything to get his son to correct the problem. He read books. He took his son to the doctor. He sent off for programs. Nothing worked. Finally, the father sat his child down and said, "What is going on? Babies do this!"

The boy answered, ". . . and their daddies hold them."

Often teenagers do not have the clear insight of this seven-year-old boy. But most want the same thing—they want to be held in a family where the love is secure, where they know they belong, where there is someone older and stronger to carry some of the load. A harried, overworked youth minister under pressure to produce programs that bring in more and more kids has little time or energy to provide the consistent, ongoing emotional support that the youth in the church need.

I spoke with a frustrated pastor in Texas several years ago who was striving to get a youth ministry off the ground. The church had approximately fifteen youth on the rolls, and the pastor expressed a high degree of frustration that he could not seem to get the youth to come to any "youth programs." When I asked how many of his teenagers were involved in the life of the church on a weekly basis—not in youth programs but in other activities—he explained that fourteen out of the fifteen were doing something *every week!* They were singing in the choir, working in the nursery, or just sitting in worship with their parents.

But this pastor felt like a failure because he could not get kids to come to "youth" meetings! It is time to break out of the narrow perspective that assumes that youth ministry can be equated with only those programs planned for the youth. Often the greater, more significant ministry of connecting young people to adults in the church can most naturally take place when kids are not frantically running from one youth event to the next but when space is created for youth to do something in the church other than be involved in a youth program.

TOWARD FAMILY-BASED YOUTH MINISTRY

We canceled youth group. It was step one in our journey toward creating the space for students to be involved in programs other than those sponsored by our youth ministry. Clearly not every situation calls for this radical change. There exist, however, a few key strategies of implementation that are applicable for all leaders as they begin to embrace the values that have been presented as a rationale for Family-Based Youth Ministry.

HOW PARENTS HAVE CHANGED
KEVIN CONKLIN

When I first started out in ministry parents really intimidated me, but now I don't know what I'd do without them. In the beginning I was too young to appreciate them, too naive to counsel them. They were older and wiser and they had kids. I was young, inexperienced, and kid-less. Though I did have a better handle on the youth culture and I could relate to teens easier, I kept parents at arm's length for years before I realized that they see and influence their teens much more than I do—so why not work together? After having kids of my own I discovered in Deuteronomy that parents are to "disciple" their own kids throughout the day and night. In contrast, youth pastors/ministries are not mentioned anywhere in the Bible.

Today, I plan events for parents only, parents/teens only and even senior citizens/teens, senior citizens/parents only, or all together. I genuinely want to encourage, equip, and reach out to parents so that *together* we can help build the next generation of dynamic Christian leaders. Here are some of the ideas we have used over the years to make this partnership a reality. Do not add these ideas without subtracting some of your current "youth only" activities; you'll be too busy, and so will everyone else. Keep it simple.

Some things you can do include the following: Combine adult and teen Sunday school classes for a while, put them in triplets, or have each person lead the discussion according to the questions/topics. Publish a bimonthly newsletter for parents, updating them on what you are doing, giving details for events, introducing leaders, and copying an article to encourage/equip them.

Sports are a great way to take advantage of time with dads and sons. Divide the teams but don't pit dads against sons. Bring in speakers on specific topics that the parents have let you know they are interested in hearing. On a monthly basis ask the parents to give you prayer requests for themselves and for their teens.

We ask any adult in the church to "adopt" a student for prayer for the entire school year. A number of touching stories have occurred through these relationships.

The key in all of this is how sincerely we communicate our care and love for parents. We do not need to "lord it over them," implying that we know their teens better than they do (we don't). We do not need to segregate them, because partnering is so much more effective, and the real responsibility and privilege of discipling lie with the parents anyway. What we need to do is walk alongside them and ask how we can best assist them in raising their children for the kingdom.

Setting the Stage

Because Family-Based Youth Ministry represents, for some churches, a radical departure from the way youth ministry has been done for so long, youth leaders would be wise to make changes only as the congregation (particularly the parents) understand why the changes are imperative.

Some churches have begun study groups with parents, using the book *Family-Based Youth Ministry* (DeVries 1994) as a springboard for discussion. Other churches have created monthly roundtable groups for parents and leaders to find ways to harness the extensive power of the family and the extended family of the church for the Christian nurture of the youth in the church. Others have brought in consultants to facilitate the setting of a new direction. Some have begun the change with a parent/youth weekend retreat that allows the group to actually experience an extended Christian family before making specific plans. Still other youth leaders have called together the parents and summarized the principles of Family-Based Youth Ministry and asked for their understanding and support during the time of transition. The idea is not simply to rush into a grand unveiling of a "Family-Based Youth Ministry."

Minimizing the Program

A central component of realizing the ministry potential of parents and families involves freeing up the youth ministry calendar, so that slowly the center of gravity for the youth of the church is no longer exclusively youth programs but the programs that intentionally connect youth and adults.

I remember hearing Earl Palmer speak a few years ago about how to make a ministry grow. He explained that the first and most obvious way that things grow is if new things are planted. Most youth ministers are great at creating this kind of growth. We tend to thrive on more and more new programs and more and more exciting activities. But most of us forget an equally effective and necessary means of growth.

Earl explained that the second means of growth is not planting something new but *pruning* something that already exists. We chose to cancel our youth group as a pruning exercise—a way to create space for something else to grow. It is difficult to grow anything of any size or significance in a youth ministry choked by activity.

Build on Small Successes

Some have read *Family-Based Youth Ministry* and tried to launch multiple new family-based programs at the same time. Often this kind of approach is destined to bring frustration and failure.

The key is to create only what can be executed well, evaluated, and revised. Surely, after the first year's experience, there will be a great deal that has been learned about the church's unique needs and its level of receptivity to change. The biggest single mistake youth leaders make in moving toward a ministry that involves families is moving too quickly and creating a jungle of mediocre programs that are naturally (and appropriately) resisted by the parents and the kids alike.

During our first year of doing this type of ministry, we invited six families to join us for a one-year experiment. (Sarah McDavitt, pp. 490-91, describes that group.) During Sunday school that year, we met with those six families for lessons on communication, faith sharing, and family relationships. If the families had not made a year-long commitment to this experiment, I'm sure many of them would have dropped out of the group.

But the group hung with us, and by the end of the year, we had learned volumes about what we would do next. At an after-church luncheon, this group gave us candid, clear, and insightful feedback that moved us in a drastically different direction than we had expected to take when we started the course. This step builds in a natural feedback loop so that continuous revisions can be made.

Find out what works well, repeat it, and add one new parent/youth emphasis. For example, after our first year with the Sunday school class, we determined what would work in the Sunday school classes in an ongoing way, and then added a family kick-off event at the beginning of the year. Each year, we try to add one more dimension to our program that will help our youth build connections with Christian adults.

Be Creative

Leadership will need to be prepared to brainstorm on ideas that may be appropriate for realizing the values of family-based ministry in their own context. In addition to the 100-plus ideas for implementing this type of ministry that can be found in *Family-Based Youth Ministry,* here are a few of the most popular ideas for connecting youth and adults in the church.

- Develop a youth mentoring program in which each youth in the church is matched up with an adult in the church.

- Create a parent council to plan programs just for the parents.
- Establish a pattern in Sunday school of each grade dealing with a different hot topic each year in a multi-week, parent/youth class. (*Bridges,* by DeVries and Russell, InterVarsity Press, 1996, offers a series of fifteen studies designed for this kind of setting.)

PARADIGM SHIFT VS. PROGRAM ADDITION

The call for Family-Based Youth Ministry is a call to move away from the traditional orphaning structures of youth ministry toward an emphasis on connecting students to their extended family of God's people. The challenge is not simply to add family programs. The truth is that most youth ministers simply do not have time to create, implement, and develop family ministries *in addition to* their work with the youth.

Quite frankly, it is all most leaders can handle to do the work they think they are being paid to do—attend meetings; write newsletter articles; have compelling lessons for kids; hang out with kids in a relaxed, relational way; counsel kids who are in emotional and behavioral trouble; recruit volunteers; train volunteers; fill in for volunteers when they are not able to do their job; network with other youth ministers; attend meetings; be informed about current trends in youth culture, particularly the names and the messages of the most important groups; promote and execute impressive youth ministry events; lead young people to make decisions for Christ; read all the latest youth ministry books; attend meetings; and, of course, lead a balanced Christian life!

Therefore, when I advocate that youth ministers take a hard look at the family, I am not suggesting that they take family ministry and add it as number sixty-three on the "when I have time" priority list. What I am advocating is an entirely different paradigm for youth ministry—a paradigm based not on how many kids we can get to meetings but on how effective we can be in leading young people to mature Christian adulthood. After all, is this not the reason we all immersed ourselves in youth ministry in the first place? It is time to return to a vision for this purpose. The day has arrived when leadership must courageously, and sometimes radically, take steps toward embracing the nurturing roles of the students' nuclear biological family and spiritual extended family. The time has come for "parenting" rather than "orphaning" structures.

WORKS CITED

Benson, P. L., and C. H. Elkin. 1990. *Effective Christian Education: A National Study of Protestant Congregations: A Summary Report on Faith, Loyalty, and Congregational Life.* Minneapolis: Search Institute.

Brooks, A. A. 1989. *Children of Fast-Track Parents.* New York: Viking Penguin.

Clapp, R. 1993. *Families at the Crossroads.* Downers Grove, Ill.: InterVarsity.

Cummings-Bond, S. 1989. "The One-Eared Mickey Mouse." *Youthworker* (fall).

DeMoss, R. G. 1992. *Learn to Discern.* Grand Rapids: Zondervan.

DeVries, M. 1994. *Family-Based Youth Ministry: Reaching the Been-There, Done-That Generation.* Downers Grove, Ill.: InterVarsity.

DeVries, M., and N. Russell. 1996. *Bridges.* Downers Grove, Ill.: InterVarsity.

Dudley, R. L., and M. G. Dudley. 1986. "Transmission of Religious Values from Parents to Adolescents." *Review of Religious Research* (September).

Holbrook, C. A. 1973. *The Ethics of Jonathan Edwards: Morality and Aesthetics.* Ann Arbor: University of Michigan.

Huggins, Kevin. 1989. *Parenting Adolescents.* Colorado Springs: NavPress.

Kesler, Jay. 1990. *Energizing Your Teenager's Faith.* Loveland, Colo.: Group.

McDowell, J., and N. Wakefield. 1989. *The Dad Difference.* San Bernardino, Calif.: Here's Life.

Patterson, B. 1984. "The Plan for Youth Ministry Reformation." *Youthworker* (fall).

Yaconelli, M. 1989. *Youth Ministry to Kids in a Post-Christian World.* 1989 Youth Specialties Resource Seminar Video (El Cajon, Calif.: Youth Specialtes).

23

✦ ✝ ✦

HOW CAN WE
HELP HURTING
ADOLESCENTS?

Les Parrott III

3:17. The red numbers on the radio alarm clock are the only light available to Russell as he struggles, half asleep, to find his socks, belt, and shoes. Russell moves quietly, trying not to awaken his wife, Melanie. At least one of them needs to get enough sleep to be alert when the kids wake up in the morning.

Russell also moves quickly. He wants to join Mrs. Bergman at the police station as soon as possible. The rush of adrenaline that shot through his body when he answered the phone ten minutes ago is sustaining his efforts—at least for the time being.

If only this were the first time, Russell reflects silently, then sighs. *If only this were the last time,* he says to himself.

Johnny Bergman had been arrested for DUI just three months ago, the day after he turned seventeen. Since Russell came to the church five years ago, he had watched Johnny's attitude and behavior slowly deteriorate. He had suspected drug abuse, so the alcohol problems came as no surprise. In fact, nothing Johnny could do would surprise Russell. The product of a broken home with an absent father, an alcoholic mother, and an older brother who ran away two years ago, Johnny had enough hurt inside him for two lifetimes.

Russell climbs in the car, searching his dashboard for just enough change to buy a cup of coffee from the all-night donut shop. He begins to rehearse what the next few hours will be like. In what condition will he find Johnny? In what condition will he find Mrs. Bergman? What can he say to a kid whose life is a mess turning into a disaster? How can he help Mrs. Bergman be a part of the solution when she is one major source of the problem?

If only, he grieves silently, *Johnny were the only kid in the youth group with these problems.*

HOPING TO HELP

Teenagers have historically been judged by adults to be hostile, moody, withdrawn, whiny, narcissistic, aggressive, rebellious, and unpredictable. Even Anna Freud, who specialized in treating young people, considered adolescents to be "normal psychotics"! As a result, many adults simply do their best to stay out of the younger generation's way. Even among youth ministers, counselors, pastors, and other care givers, attitudes may vary as to how desirable it is to be in a relationship with a teenager. After all, coming alongside the life of a student like Johnny means experiencing a part of his painful, "messy" world.

Genuinely concerned adults, however, can no longer avoid the compelling need to get personally involved and provide help to hurting kids. The sheer number of hurting adolescents combined with the intensity of their life struggles means that the adult community can no longer sidestep their painful issues or simply refer them to someone "more qualified." *Their* problems must be seen as *our* problems.

But how can Russell be effective in helping Johnny? What hope can he have that his relationship will minister to Johnny's hurt? For all the men and women who share Russell's heart and concerns, welcome to the world of contemporary youth ministry, a world characterized by helping hurting teenagers.

THE NEW TEENS

Who are the teenagers of today's world? Consider the differences between these students and those of the recent past.

First, teenagers no longer marshal the demographic might they once did. Compared to earlier generations such as the baby boomers, there are much fewer among their number.

Second, not only has the adolescent demographic clout diminished, so has their social insurrection. The radical rebellion of young people in the 1960s and 1970s has given way to a resigned relinquishment. Today's students seem more interested in getting ahead in the world than in cleaning up its injustices. In a survey of high school seniors in forty Wisconsin communities, global concerns, including hunger, poverty, and pollution, emerged last on a list of teenage worries. First were personal goals: getting good grades and good jobs. Not quite the "revolution" of the Beatles' generation!

Psychology Today described the late twentieth-century teenagers as the "post-Yuppie, post boomer, baby buster" generation (May/June 1992). The article asserted that their first priority is themselves, and they want money, power, and status. Their career aspirations are charged with the electricity of financial reward and personal advancement, not with altruistic motivations needed for such professions as social work or teaching.

Third, the new teen generation is pessimistic. It sees its legacy as a polluted earth, a racially fractured society, and overwhelming social problems without probable solutions. It feels cheated and betrayed by the possibility that America's best years are over. The new generation of young people "bows to no one." It questions authority and has a visible disregard for hierarchy. In many ways it is restless, eager to grow up—but afraid of the consequences.

Fourth, research is discovering a new adolescent these days. A study reported in the *Journal of Research on Adolescence* indicates teenagers—at least white, middle-class teens—

BEING PROACTIVE
TERESA R. DUNN

It is important to be proactive when it comes to the emotional needs of your youth group. When Sara comes to you saying she has been bingeing and purging several times a day for the last three months or Jake reveals he's not sure he can take it anymore and just wants to die is not the time to try to discover who in your area is available and qualified to be of help.

Do Your Homework

Where Do I Go?
1. Ask around the church. Perhaps there are counselors within the body who know of a qualified adolescent therapist. (If you have an adolescent counselor within the church, by all means use him or her as a resource, but think critically about the potential boundary problems that may arise if the person provides the counseling.)
2. Call other youth pastors in the area. They may be aware of good counselors in the community.
3. If your area has a local Christian college or seminary, it may have a counseling center or be able to refer you to an appropriate resource.

What Do I Look For?
1. Ideally seek to find a counselor who has specific training in working with adolescents. Working with an adolescent is very different from working with an adult. If there are no adolescent counselors in your community, find someone who will look at the whole problem and not just symptoms of it.

2. There are some issues that require additional knowledge and experience, for example, eating disorders and substance abuse (alcohol, drugs). It is appropriate to ask about the counselor's training, years of experience, and expertise. A competent counselor will welcome such questions.

3. Working with a Christian counselor in the community is ideal. However, consulting a non-Christian counselor who has training and knowledgeable experience in the field is preferable to consulting a Christian counselor who has no experience in working with adolescents or the issue being referred. A competent counselor will be accepting of his clients' values and beliefs regardless of his own belief system.

Why Should I Plan Ahead?
1. Establishing a contact or resource ahead of time will be invaluable to you as a youth worker. There will be times when having a professional with whom you can consult will assist in clarifying your role.

2. Establishing a referral resource will give you a greater sense of confidence when you are dealing with a troubled, emotionally unstable, or suicidal youth. Knowing where to go in a crisis will diminish the likelihood that you will panic in a crisis situation.

3. Your connection to a professional in the counseling field will allow you access to his or her knowledge of and network with local treatment facilities, hospitals, and programs that specialize in the treatment of adolescents and their issues.

> Establishing a psychological referral resource will require some footwork and time in what may already seem to be an overcrowded work schedule, but it is energy well spent. The ability to be proactive in an emotional crisis can greatly speed the healing process for the youth and give confidence to an often overwhelmed and bewildered parent.

are far less rebellious than what we have previously assumed (1991). A current-state-of-knowledge list dispels four common myths about teenagers.

- First, G. Stanley Hall's *strum und drang* version of adolescence is rejected in the nineties after nearly a century of belief. Equating youth years with inevitable storminess is inaccurate.
- Second, the predictable disintegration of parent-teen relationships is also false. Most conflicts with mom or dad eventually yield to healthy adolescent autonomy.
- Third, a teenager's peer-group values are not always the opposite of the parents' values. Surprisingly, they are more likely to support parental values than to be in conflict with them.
- Finally, pubertal hormones affect behavior far less than first expected. Biological determinants are just one of several factors that affect behavior. Social and psychological factors are equally important.

Although research shows that traditional excuses for the attitudes and behavior of today's youth are no longer valid, there is no arguing that, as a generation, these students face more adult-strength stresses than any generation before them.

PRESSURES AND PROBLEMS

"Pressure," perhaps more than any other term, best describes contemporary adolescent struggles. Of course *peer* pressure is nothing new. Larry Dumont, author of *Surviving Adolescence*, calls it "the fad that never fades." What's new is that teens are feeling the heat from parents as well as peers. Parental egos are increasing the already boiling temperature of the pressure cooker where adolescents must survive. Well-meaning parents are promoting the "adultification" of teens, according to authors like David Walsh *(Designer Kids)* and David Elkind *(The Hurried Child)*. Parents today want their children to grow up quickly. They want them to have an edge. School performance has become a symbol for how a youngster will do in the future, and getting into the best college has become an obsession with many parents.

The stress level for teenagers in our society, tracked by the Fordham University Index of Social Health for Children and Youth, has been on a constant rise since 1967. The world is becoming increasingly more precarious and pressured for the young.

While a list of specific struggles (for example, suicide, eating disorders, abuse, inferiority, premarital sex, anger, shyness, depression, anxiety, loneliness, guilt, drugs) could fill several pages, the following are some of the most "in-your-face" problems for today's teens.

Violence

This generation has grown up with the TV on and they have consumed big doses of bad news. By age sixteen, students have been jaded witnesses to 33,000 murders on TV and in the movies. But the line between "entertainment" and reality is beginning to blur for this generation. During the thirty-year period between 1950 and 1980, there was a 300 percent increase in the number of homicides of teenagers in the United States. Between 1984 and 1988 the firearm death rate for teenagers aged fifteen to nineteen increased 43 percent—to 18,000 deaths. According to 1989 Department of Justice records, nearly 85,000 people under eighteen were arrested and charged with violent-crime offenses, an increase of 20,000 in five years. The estimate of violent crime is much higher than arrest records show, however, with more than 1.8 million youths age twelve to nineteen involved in violent crimes today (*Children and Stress Today* 1991).

WHEN SHOULD I REFER?
G. KEITH OLSON

The very reason you are in youth ministry, to help kids, can sometimes make it difficult to know when to refer. We usually think of helping as being able to fix the problem. Sometimes the best way to help is to get the teenager to the best source of help. Here are some counseling situations where it is advisable (and in some cases necessary) to make a referral to a professional therapist.

Emotional Symptoms
• Indications of depression lasting over a week, including depressed mood, discouragement, hopelessness, a sense of helplessness, and dejection.
• Low self-esteem, poor self-concept, feeling worthless, excessive and inappropriate guilt, and feeling inadequate also indicate depression.
• Anxiety; fears about multiple situations, objects, or people who do not normally trigger such fears; panic attacks; and frequent nightmares suggest a serious disturbance.

Symptoms Related to Thinking
• Delusional thinking, beliefs and thoughts that don't correlate with reality, and hallucinations (hearing voices, seeing insects that don't exist) are indicators of serious problems.
• Obsessions are unwanted thoughts that cause significant distress and seem uncontrollable. They usually represent repressed fears and impulses.
• A preoccupying fascination with the occult, satanism, witchcraft or fervent anti-Christianity usually indicates a psychological and/or spiritual disturbance.

- Suicidal thoughts, plans to commit suicide, and thoughts or plans to harm oneself or someone else should be taken seriously.

Behavioral Symptoms

- Suicidal behavior always indicates the need for referral.
- Substance abuse and behavior associated with substance abuse (driving while intoxicated) are reasons for making a referral.
- Eating disorders evidenced by obsession with eating, diet, exercise, or other weight management preoccupation requires referral.
- Sexually promiscuous behavior endangers teenagers psychologically and spiritually, as well as physically from sexually transmitted diseases.
- Repetitive violence or destructive acts against people, animals, and objects require referral. Violence includes making threats as well as violent acts themselves.
- A marked drop in academic or extracurricular performance indicates that something is wrong.
- Teenagers who isolate themselves are typically distraught or experiencing psychological pain.
- Self-mutilation occurs as cutting, burning, or biting one's own body.
- Compulsions are repetitive, uncontrolled behaviors (hand washing, re-checking locks) that are disruptive.
- Breaking the law indicates that the adolescent is struggling.
- Difficulty controlling impulses (aggression and sex) and concentration problems indicate the need for referral.

Dangerous Situations
- Suspicion of child abuse, including physical abuse, sexual abuse, and neglect, should be referred.
- Disruption within the teenager's household (marital separation, divorce, severe illness or death of a family member, violence and substance abuse by a family member) will create psychological pain.
- When a teenager or a young person's sexual partner becomes pregnant, it is time to refer.

Making an appropriate referral is not your confession of inadequacy or incompetence. It is an expression of the fact that you know the limits of your expertise and that you care enough about the teenagers in your group to make sure that they get the very best help available.

STDs

There was a time when the younger generation felt invincible. The prevailing attitude was, "We're young and it can't happen to us." Not so now. Teens today fear AIDS more than any other illness, and with good reason. The number of AIDS cases among teenagers is doubling every fourteen months. Sixty-three percent of all sexually transmitted disease cases occur among persons less than twenty-five years of age, and there are more than twenty different and dangerous STDs rampant among the young. To compound the problem, consider this fact: Since 1970 the government has spent $3 billion to promote contraception and "safe sex" ($450 million this past year alone)—but only $8 million was spent this past year for abstinence programs.

Parental Absence and Conflict

Many of today's teenagers are left to parent themselves. If they are not from the 40 percent of young people who come from broken homes, they most likely come from homes where both parents go to work. This makes for a home life that is often characterized by busy schedules, chronic fatigue, and weary battles of discord and dissension. Parent-adolescent conflict occurs in all families some of the time and in some families most of the time. Sadly, however, the latter category is growing.

Job Stress

Yes, *job* stress! Since 1940, there has been a sevenfold increase in the number of sixteen-year-old boys who work while in school and a sixteenfold increase in the number of girls who do (*Developmental Psychology* 1991). Nearly two-thirds of high school juniors hold jobs in the formal part-time labor force during the school year. The root causes of what motivates youth to work can be seen in the shallow soil of consumerism. Most do not work out of dire economic need. Researchers have shown that *a materialistic lifestyle is the number one driving force behind kids getting on the payroll.*

Young people once labored in the fields alongside their parents, motivated by the economic needs of the family. Most current adolescent work is done in fast-food chains and retail stores. This type of work has been labeled *luxury employment* —where adolescents themselves are the chief beneficiaries. Fewer than one in ten kids who hold a job during the school year contribute a portion of their paycheck to the support of their families. By the way, it's not the children of blue-collar or poor families who dominate the youth labor force. The earliest and most numerous entrants into the world of work are the children of the well-to-do *and* the well educated.

Teen Parenthood

More than 600,000 babies are born to adolescents every year. About 1 million teenagers in the United States have become pregnant every year since 1973. Put another way, one out of ten girls ages fifteen to nineteen gets pregnant every year. Forty percent end in abortion. Kids having kids has become an infectious epidemic. Half of all pregnant teens never complete school, and many of the dropouts end up on welfare. Given the stress in these "families," the little children become highly vulnerable for suffering abuse and being shuffled through foster care. In spite of the prospects, some male adolescents see fatherhood as a shortcut to adulthood. A 1995 issue of *Fortune* magazine quoted a teen father saying, "It looks like the Nineties are going to be the Pregnancy Hall of Fame."

Troubled youth are now obviously doing more than cutting class or smoking behind the garage. Other contemporary problems of this generation include date rape, racial tension, abortion—the list seems endless. They are coping with tougher troubles than any generation before them.

HELPING TEENAGERS AND THEIR PARENTS

Among the findings reported in a study by R. K. Tomlinson published in *Child and Adolescent Social Work* was the following disturbing fact: Parents of youth are expressing a widespread disappointment about the ineffectiveness, inaccessibility, and general shortage of persons who are in a giving relationship to their teens (Tomlinson 1991). Nearly 60 percent of the parents surveyed over a one-year period, who had sought help from professionals, declared that they were not satisfied with the help received. Parents described in painful detail how all too frequently the helping process turned out to be non-helpful and quite often seemed to make matters worse. The most frequent complaint was that helping professionals did not *understand* what was happening to them as parents, to their families, and to their acting-up teen.

There is a charge to all who strive to help young people: We must become collaborators with parents as well as their teens. We must "encourage the timid, help the weak, be patient with everyone" (1 Thessalonians 5:14). Competent professionals, however, cannot replace an adolescent's family as the single most important factor in helping young people today. Mom and Dad rank higher than peers, relatives, pastors, teachers, or counselors as resources for advice and help.

Parents are increasingly in need of support for themselves in their roles. One study of parents and teens found that about half of the 10,467 parents surveyed thought they were not as good a parent as they should be. Of the parental worries listed in their survey, the top-ranking worry was "the job I am doing raising this child" (Stommen and Stommen 1985).

However, there is good news for hurting parents. A growing body of evidence indicates that parents, with a little guidance from people like you, can successfully help resolve a number of struggles for their adolescents. Often, it is enough for parents to realize that their feelings are normal for what they are going through, that they are not alone, that someone understands and can articulate their troubles, that God has not forsaken them, that they are not failures, and that there is hope.

THE "GOOD ENOUGH" MYTH

Youth ministry leaders often feel unequipped to help this unique generation of adolescents, let alone their parents. These leaders are not alone in their sense of inadequacy. Many of us in the helping profession do not feel competent to counsel. Leaders must not wait until they feel "good enough" to make a difference. Accepting this myth may prevent leaders from fulfilling the very role that students need most: loving them and being there with them.

The most important instrument of healing a leader can have is herself. Why? Because *who* a person is in relationship to hurting teenagers is more important than *what* a person can do in terms of professional competence. Furthermore, the leader's attitude and behavior either help or hinder what work the Holy Spirit, the real Healer, can do through her ministry to hurting youth.

Many researchers have attempted to identify the qualities that contribute to successful helping. They have discovered the importance of sensitivity, hope, compassion, awareness, knowledge—the list could go on and on. However, a four-year study done more than two decades ago seemed to cut to the bone. The findings are unequivocal: People are more likely to find help when they are with someone who is warm, genuine, and empathic. Without these traits in a helper, a teenager's condition can actually worsen, regardless of other skills a parent or other adult may possess.

FIRST STEPS IN CRISIS SITUATIONS
STEPHEN P. GREGGO

A crisis successfully overcome can become a foundational faith experience, whereas prolonged pain may produce a festering bitterness toward God. Use these principles, generic to most personal crisis resolution, to get recovery started.

FOCUS THE HELPER

The helper needs to prepare himself or herself to enter the world of the adolescent in crisis by praying for a clear mission and a heart to help the traumatized teen. Since there is little time to ponder when responding to a crisis, I hold the words of Jesus regarding "whoever welcomes a little child in My name, welcomes Me" as my mission focus. The adolescent in need may not physically appear as a "little one," but when overwhelmed due to crisis, a teen may resort to impulsive, regressive, or aggressive behavior patterns or express raging emotions that can seem almost childlike.

A biblical "welcome" implies an embrace, and I guide my approach using the prayerful query, "Lord, how can I best be Your arms and hands as You reach out with a divine hug?" *A focused helper can be the person used by God as a stable resource to soothe pain.*

FACILITATE DEFUSING

The initial shock of a tragic event may produce instantaneous disbelief and denial, which is typically followed by an intense emotional release. The helper in the first contact attempts to facilitate *defusing,* which is an interpersonal healing process involving the ventilation of rapid-fire thoughts and emotions immediately following a crisis. This stabilizing embrace communicates through empathetic listening that expressing the inner turmoil is acceptable and that someone cares.

There is no need to immediately answer, correct, or judge. In this early recovery stage, a safe and supportive listener is exactly what is needed. The teen ascertains that the intensity of these moments filled with fear, anger, and uncertainty can be tolerated and that real help is available from real people. During defusing discussions, the youth leader is wise to take refreshment breaks, provide any available information on what might happen next, and not make any attempt to probe for details or feelings, but just let the teen lead. Prepare the teen for personal "aftershocks" such as anxious feelings, nightmares, crying, shaking, nausea, etc. *Defusing discussions help the teen gain a sense of control.*

FOSTER DEBRIEFING

When the critical period is over and the crisis is managed, the teen will need help in *debriefing*. This is a dialogue dedicated to developing understanding and finding meaning in the midst of tragic events. The youth leader listens to the teen's thoughts and feelings while quietly and confidently providing support for discovery and integration. There may be no clear answer for the big "why" question, but hope may be found in "what does this mean for you?" When your hurting teen starts to look for meaning, gently take him or her to the *Wonderful Counselor* who does know the pain of crisis and who is willing to be an everlasting resource through troubled times. *The youth leader can indeed be the catalyst for dynamic debriefing.*

CLOSING THOUGHTS

Ministry to teens in crisis requires entering into chaotic situations and building a sensible help plan. I have found it useful to check my approach using an acrostic for the word "crisis" that aids in the development of a specific recovery strategy and keeps the Divine Embrace mission in view.

Constructive caring means being a good listener in defusing and debriefing conversations.

Receive the teen into a safe, identifiable care group prepared to do concrete help tasks.

Individual needs are the priority, so find out exactly what the needs are and respond accordingly.

Special moments are created when the crisis is recognized, memories are shared, and prayer is offered.

Involve peers and other adults in the help plan as a supportive network.

Strategic support plans, activated for several weeks, provide the necessary nurture needed during critical times.

Warmth

Paul Tournier, the renowned Swiss physician, said, "I have no methods. All I do is accept people." The key to personal warmth is acceptance. It is an attitude that does not evaluate or require change. It simply accepts the thoughts, feelings, and actions of the adolescent. This warmth allows a teenager to develop a base of self-worth: "If my parents accept me, maybe I *am* valuable."

Non-possessive warmth is not necessarily approving of *everything* a teenager does. Jesus showed warmth to the woman at the well, but He certainly never condoned her sinful behavior. Jesus respected the woman and treated her as a person of worth in spite of her lifestyle.

Through unconditional warmth we invite troubled youth to catch a glimpse of God's grace. *Grace is the bedrock of growth.* When adolescents feel sure they can never be condemned for who they are, that no judgment can hurt them, the power of God's grace begins to turn the wheels of change.

Unconditional warmth also frees adolescents from attempting to win approval. Young people no longer wonder whether they are loved for who they are or for what they do. Why does this matter? Because teenagers who feel they must perform to get approval hold a nagging uncertainty about whether they are genuinely accepted. In their relationship with God, for example, they will continually chase the carrot of divine approval.

Genuineness

Without honesty there is no way to touch hurting teenagers. Adolescents have a built-in radar that spots phoniness even at a distance. They are experts at detecting fabricated feelings and insincere intentions. They give every overture of help their own polygraph test. They also respond negatively to things that are overdone. Honest thoughts and authentic feelings are best expressed in subtle forms—in our eyes and posture, for example.

Genuineness cannot be faked. In other words, authenticity is something you *are,* not something you *do.* Genuineness has been described as a lure to the heart. Jesus said, "Blessed are the pure in heart." Or, to say it another way, "Consider the youth minister in whom there is no guile." When genuineness is present, a hesitant and skeptical adolescent is likely to invest energy in becoming responsible.

Empathy

The best way to avoid stepping on an adolescent's toes is to put oneself in her sneakers. Empathy lets struggling adolescents know the adult has heard their words, understood their thoughts, and sensed their feelings. Empathy says, "I understand why you feel the way you feel."

Two important distinctions about empathy are helpful. First, empathy is not identification. It is not necessary to present oneself as having the same experiences, thoughts, and feelings as an adolescent. In fact, teenagers want to be seen as unique and complex. They resent blatant attempts by adults to identify with them. Saying "I know exactly how you feel" to a struggling teenager is like telling a Vietnam vet that his post-traumatic stress is easy to understand.

Second, empathy is deeper and stronger than sympathy. Sympathy is standing on the shore and throwing out a lifeline, whereas empathy is jumping into the water and risking one's safety to help another. And the risk is real. In empathy you risk change. Understanding the aching heart of a struggling adolescent *will* change you. Yet, when we have the courage to enter the pain of a hurting teenager we begin to build a relationship in which healing can occur.

For struggling adolescents, the best conditions for growth occur when they (1) feel they are accepted unconditionally, (2) feel they are with someone who is trustworthy and real, and (3) are deeply understood.

ADDITIONAL HELPS FOR THE HELPING ADULT

Focusing on who you are as a person is at the heart of helping a hurting adolescent. Once you have incorporated personal warmth, authenticity, and empathy into your way of being, then you can supplement your helping efforts with further helps. Here are some additional suggestions and reminders.

- *Avoid acting like a teenager in order to relate to one.* It's a common mistake that goes nowhere fast. A youth minister or counselor does not always need to wear the clothes and shoes that are the latest fad or use the current slang to relate to a young person. Thank goodness!
- *Identify and make available resources for parents in pain.* Buddy Scott, author of *Relief for Hurting Parents,* founded and directs an agency for helping families with teenagers. His "Parenting Within Reason" support groups provide a national safety net for hurting parents and are an excellent resource for care givers. (For more

information, write: Parenting Within Reason, P.O. Box 804, Lake Jackson, TX 77566.)

- *Pinpoint the severity of a teen's trouble.* Rely on an easy-to-use collection of paper-and-pencil measures such as *Helping the Struggling Adolescent: A Counseling Guide* (Zondervan) or *Measures for Clinical Practice* (Free Press). These resources contain rapid assessments of such problems as depression, guilt, anxiety, grief, drug abuse, eating disorders, and dozens of other issues.
- *Work diligently to chip away at adolescents' irrational declarations.* Many adolescents define their life situation in global terms such as *"everything* is terrible," *"nothing* is going right," "dad is a *total* jerk." As long as they continue to see themselves or the world in generalized terms, they remain stuck.
- *Become comfortable with sticky and delicate subjects.* Today's teens need youth ministers who do not shy away from issues such as masturbation, drug use, divorce of parents, death of a friend, date rape, and other sexual issues. With or without help, teens *will* deal with these issues. The question is whether or not they will deal with them appropriately.
- *Remember to listen to teens with what Theodore Reik calls "the third ear."* Without hearing the heartfelt pain —the anxiety, the sadness, the embarrassment, the loneliness, the shame—behind a young person's seemingly inconsequential message, true counseling dies. "Be quick to listen, slow to speak" (James 1:19).
- *Know your limits.* If you are not experienced in working with a young person's particular problem, refer. Avoid the danger of believing that you can work with *every* struggling adolescent.

Unfortunately, there are no universal or simple formulas for resolving the complex problems of today's youth. But if we are to make a difference in the lives of contemporary adolescents it will be because we practice proven principles of contemporary psychology, rely on biblically based theology,

and seek the ultimate counsel of the Holy Spirit in our efforts
to help hurting adolescents and their parents.

WORKS CITED

Dumont, Larry. 1991. *Surviving Adolescence: Helping Your
Child Through the Struggle of Adulthood.* New York: Ran-
dom House.

Elkind, David. 1988. *The Hurried Child: Growing Up Too
Fast Too Soon.* Reading, Mass.: Addison-Wesley.

Scott, Buddy. 1994. *Relief for Hurting Parents: How to Fight
for the Lives of Teenagers, How to Prepare Younger Children for Less Dangerous Journeys Through Teenage Years.*
Lake Jackson, Tex.: Allon.

Stommen, Merton, and Irene Stommen. 1985. *Five Cries of
Youth.* San Francisco: Harper & Row.

Tomlinson, R. K. 1991. *Child and Adolescent Social Work* 8,
no. 1.

Walsh, David. 1990. *Designer Kids.* Minneapolis: Deaconess.

FOR FURTHER READING

Olson, G. K. 1984. *Counseling Teenagers: The Complete
Christian Guide to Understanding and Helping Adolescents.* Loveland, Colo.: Group.

Parrott, L. 1993a. *Helping the Struggling Adolescent: A
Counseling Guide with 40 Rapid Assessment Tests.* Grand
Rapids: Zondervan.

_____. 1993b. *Helping the Struggling Adolescent: A
Guide to Thirty Common Problems for Parents, Counselors, and Youth Workers.* Grand Rapids: Zondervan.

Rowatt, G. W. 1989. *Pastoral Care with Adolescents in Crisis.* Louisville: Westminster/John Knox.

Van Pelt, R. 1988. *Intensive Care: Helping Teenagers in Crisis.* Grand Rapids: Zondervan.

24

✦

HOW CAN
SMALL CHURCHES
HAVE HEALTHY
YOUTH MINISTRIES?

WHERE TWO OR THREE ARE GATHERED
(SOMEWHAT RELUCTANTLY?)

Pamela T. Campbell

But Lord, how can I save Israel? My clan is the weakest in Manasseh, and I am the least in my family (Gideon; Judges 6:15).

But am I not a Benjamite, from the smallest tribe of Israel, and is not my clan the least of all the clans of the tribe of Benjamin? Why do you say such a thing to me? (Saul; 1 Samuel 9:21).

I am the least of the apostles and do not even deserve to be called an apostle (Paul; 1 Corinthians 15:9).

Why don't we have more kids? No matter how much I pray for, prepare for, and give myself to these students—we still never have more than eight or ten show up. Why won't God give us twenty-five or at least twenty students in our youth

group? Is this too much to ask? Am I doing something wrong?
I mean, aren't youth groups supposed to get bigger? (Leader
of a small youth group, late 1990s).

✝ ✝ ✝

When God calls judges (Gideon), kings (Saul), apostles
(Paul), and youth leaders (you), He sets no limits and gives no
guarantees on the size or status of the groups with which they
are associated. Yet the unspoken rule in youth ministry (and
in churches in general) seems to be that large membership
reflects God's blessing. So what are we who serve in small
churches to think? If we are not careful, the concern with size
can become a priority that often escalates into an obsession.

Youth workers with small youth groups still question
God's wisdom as did the biblical heroes who were called from
"the least" of the bunch. Like them, we argue with God:

- But there are not enough kids in my group to have a
  choir or even play a volleyball game.
- But I have to work a second job to supplement my
  church salary.
- But I do not even have an office or access to a secretary.
- But I have to do everything myself because there aren't
  enough volunteers.
- But the facilities in our small church are inadequate for
  teenagers.
- But the kids in my group do not seem to welcome newcomers.
- But the seniors do not want to be in the same group with
  seventh and eighth graders.
- But I *must* be doing something wrong since the group is
  not growing.

And the trouble is, we may convince ourselves that our
arguments are true without opening our minds to other possibilities. After giving the call and *opportunity,* God does not
force us into service. Gideon and Paul managed to get past
their initial thinking to become shining examples of what "the

least of us" can do. King Saul, on the other hand, never really got beyond his limited thinking. He attempted to take upon himself too much of the responsibility that would have been God's if he had been more patient. Far too many youth workers develop the same mentality and give up before they give a fair chance to youth ministry at a small church.

TRAINING INDIVIDUALS, NOT GROUPS

If it is the youth ministry leader's philosophy to train *groups,* he is likely to get caught up in the focus (if not obsession) on numbers. But if the leader shifts the goal to training *individuals,* he is free to pour his time and himself into the few, but valuable, students in his group—a privilege not usually available in larger youth groups. (Later, when God is seeking out someone to serve Him in other special ways, such leaders will not be surprised if He selects from their close-knit groups of three rather than from the larger programs which have three hundred.)

A word of caution must be inserted. The benefits of a small youth group should not be taken as an indication that youth workers in small churches have easy jobs. Far from it! Several issues must be dealt with before the leaders and members of small youth groups can develop attitudes of confidence and self-worth.

Issue One: Comparisons to Large Youth Groups

My church is within easy driving distance of a well-known megachurch as well as a couple of other "big and famous" churches. Their attractions are numerous—services with live bands, basketball·leagues, elaborate dramatic and multimedia presentations, winter ski trips, week-long summer mission trips, living nativities at Christmas, and so forth.

My church, on the other hand, has no gym. In fact, there are no large open areas for other kinds of games. Until a couple of years ago, we did not even have air conditioning! Obviously, there is no way I can compete at a program level with the big churches, and my kids do not seem to expect me to. (Which is not to say that I don't feel a twinge of envy when big events are staged by larger churches.) But some of the parents and adults in the congregation are another story. Some church members have suggested that I should be doing everything the megachurches are doing and having similar results—even though our yearly youth budget is less than what many of these larger churches spend on a single night of youth ministry programming. I have learned to respond with a meaningful "I'll think about it" nod and then focus on what ministry opportunities I *can* provide.

One of my first temptations when I began working in a small church was to quickly try to build a large youth group. That was certainly what the parents wanted. A large group was what the students wanted as well. And it would sure make me look good! The goal was not a bad one, but it needed to be a *long-term* goal. It certainly should not have been the primary (or only) goal.

A new youth leader does herself no favors by going into a small church that has an existing youth group and immediately communicating the impression that it is not yet "adequate." Giving an initial impression that "bigger is better" can eradicate any fragments of positive morale that might exist. Later, if the leader fails to accomplish her goal of bringing in large numbers of students, it is too late to convince group members to be content with being few in number.

On the other hand, if a leader begins by announcing the goal of "making this the best small youth group possible," that is something the students (as well as parents and church leadership) should quickly support. If three students show up for a "big event" planned for a dozen, the youth leader can shower four times the fun and attention on those three.

As soon as the youth group becomes a place where students enjoy coming and being themselves, the word seems to spread quickly. That leader may never have a herd of a hundred, but he or she is likely to see growth in numbers *after* helping group members establish a firm commitment to each other and to improving the existing conditions. If students are not challenged and excited in a small group, it is not likely that they will be satisfied in a large group.

VOLUNTEER LEADERS CAN MEET THE CHALLENGE OF STUDENT MINISTRY
DAVID J. GARDA

Fewer than 10 percent of churches have paid leadership to assist youth to meet the challenges they face daily, but any church with a youth has a youth ministry—though not necessarily a good one.

I have observed volunteer-led student ministries that are among the best models available for a loving, caring, and discipling impact upon students. If your church can disciple two students into the character and priorities of Christ, then you have unleashed a significant force for kingdom impact within this generation. If your church sees one or two students a year being introduced to Christ and assimilated into the body of Christ, then every effort necessary to serve as a volunteer leader is more than worth the investment.

As a volunteer leader I encourage you to major on the majors—you don't have time to waste. Invest your precious time in the following priorities and you'll be taking the most significant steps toward following Jesus' model for student ministry:

- Pray for students.
- Pray with students.
- Love students where they are in their spiritual development.
- Spend more relational time than programming time with students.
- Assist students in their study of God's Word to discover firsthand who God is, what He has done (and can do), and who they are in Him.

A volunteer leader can be one of youth ministry's most precious resources. Sonlife Ministries, the ministry with which I work, is committed to helping you work with volunteers to create the type of loving, caring environment combined with the ability to minister to each student at their level of spiritual interest that will produce student disciples.

Sonlife Ministries
526 N. Main, Elburn, IL 60119

Issue Two: Inclusiveness and Diversity

In a small church, being different tends to stand out more than in a larger one. This is usually more of a challenge for teenagers than for adults. It's almost impossible for one African-American student in a group of European-Americans (no matter how small the group) not to feel self-conscious. If someone is a bit slower on an academic level, it tends to stand out in a small-group setting. If one student is having problems at home when other families seem relatively stable, he or she cannot help but feel out of place.

Students will sense such awkwardness, but they may not know how to handle it. It is the leader's responsibility to involve everyone. In addition, the leader must have ears that detect derogatory comments, eyes that note disapproving looks, and the essence of wisdom to know how to address conflicts without drawing undue attention to the minority member that would only make him or her feel even more uncomfortable.

In some cases the youth leader may also have to contend with not-entirely-pure attitudes of the church as a whole. But even if the church has a somewhat closed mind-set, it need not filter down to the youth programs. By cutting off potential problems among the youth group members and opening up programs to any and all kinds of people, a small youth group can learn to become homogenous in Christ even while being quite diverse in most other ways.

Issue Three: Limited Resources

Many times a small budget will do more to impair a youth group than will its small number of students. When the church itself may be struggling to pay the pastor's salary, it is not easy to approach board members about money for "more balloons." Students from larger churches often boast to my group members of their retreats, summer trips, outings to amusement parks and other "exotic" venues, and more. They put up posters and wear printed T-shirts and caps that advertise their next "big event." Meanwhile, my handful of faithful members wonder why *they* are not provided an opportunity to be involved in such great events.

This is where we youth leaders of small churches must get creative. The most obviously economical activities are not always appropriate for small youth groups. It seems unwise to schedule a "big game" of softball, knowing that a grand total of five people are going to be present at most events. Neither will it be a breathtaking event to have those five people stand in a circle tossing a Frisbee to one another.

To remedy this dilemma, small group leaders should expend some of their energy in the process of adapting what larger youth groups are doing to fit the context of their fewer numbers. Retreats, for example, are just as important to small youth groups as to larger ones for the purpose of developing community and creating more intimate levels of friendship. Maybe the students can pay their own way for a weekend outing at a camp. Maybe an individual in the church can loan a vacation home or cabin to the group. If nothing else, perhaps someone would be willing to open his home for a "lock-in" where kids can be themselves with each other. (Usually the lack of sleep helps reveal the real person behind the usual "mask.") But a lock-in just does not provide the same impact as a weekend getaway retreat with its spiritual focus and longer hours to think without the normal demands of school, family, jobs, and such.

Because small-youth-group leaders can only plan significant events once a year or so, these leaders must work to maximize their contributions to the students' spiritual and interpersonal lives. Creativity with ideas which have worked in larger groups and sensitivity to the particular needs of one's own smaller group are critical ingredients for this process.

Issue Four: Leader Isolation

Loneliness comes with the job of youth worker at many small churches. No one else has any idea exactly what I do, how much work (and prayer, concern, emotional energy, fear) is required of me, or how others could possibly assist me in ministry. Some people in the church do not know to what extent I am personally helping the students in the youth group. They evaluate my success by how frequently they see those shining young faces in church on Sunday mornings (which is not very often for many of my youth group members).

Usually the pastor has some idea of what the youth worker is going through. But in a small church, the pastor may have plenty to do, and will be more than happy to let someone else "run with" the youth program. The job of a youth worker has the intensity of an air traffic controller, the pay of a Peace Corps volunteer, and the respect of an NBA referee. There is little if any instant gratification. So youth workers rapidly come and go—an unfortunate yet unnecessary reality in smaller youth groups.

I have been involved in some capacity for almost twenty-five years now—the past eighteen years at the same (still small) church. My husband and I work as a team with two other volunteer couples. Otherwise, I have a limited "network" with other youth workers. Such networks are extremely valuable for youth workers who need a peer group with whom to share trials and victories. As a part-time youth director, I have invested more of my time in students and staff than among my professional peers. Although some youth workers may occasionally feel the isolation of working without the support of professional associations, networking at conferences, denominational meetings, and community events can result in contacts that are only a phone call away.

SMALL, YET EFFECTIVE YOUTH GROUPS

Once a youth worker gets beyond the potential problems

and limitations that affect small youth groups, he or she may discover *opportunities* that are just as distinctive. Below are just a few of the benefits that can be identified among small youth groups; many of these benefits are not so readily available in the larger groups.

Community

When the days get short and the church basement offers little comfort or warmth from the gray winter, one group I know shifts its meetings to its leader's home. They take turns fixing simple meals (chili, soup and salad, pizza, burgers and chips). Then they sit down around the dining room table to eat *together*. It is no surprise by now to realize that this is no longer done in many families. Sharing a meal—even once a week—has probably done as much or more for the spiritual health of that youth group as the "regular" lessons that follow.

Mobility

A small group fits in a minivan. If the week's lesson focuses on the wonder of God's creation, it can be taught while driving through the autumn woods or beside a nearby lake or ocean. With a bit of planning, the lesson can be completed by the time you arrive at your destination—leaving more time for recreation and fellowship.

Or if the leader discovers at the last minute that a Christian musician happens to be in the area on an evening when a regular meeting has been scheduled, it is no big deal for a small group to pile in a car and go. Even if the special event runs longer than normal, all it takes is a couple of phone calls to let parents know their sons and daughters will be home a little later than usual.

A Sense of Belonging

The charm of the nineties' "Northern Exposure" and the success of the seventies' "Gilligan's Island" both reflected a desire for people to see small groups of quirky people succeed after being thrown together in somewhat stressful circumstances. (Sounds like a small church youth group!) Certainly, the challenge at first is to learn to interact and endure each other's idiosyncrasies. But if the leader can help them through this first stage, the group may also be on course for charm and success of its own.

So what if small youth groups cannot afford summer-long missions projects in Tierra del Fuego? Big deal! Small churches usually have plenty of work that needs doing right at home—lawn mowing, window cleaning, painting (inside and out), furniture moving, landscaping, major "spring cleaning" projects delayed for the past two decades, and much more. Many small groups can easily spend a week in true "home missions" without having to leave the church grounds. Such projects can be just as substantive and rewarding as foreign missions. (However, the youth worker should not be the only one to notice and comment on all the hard work. Others in the church need to commend the efforts of the young people as well.)

A sense of belonging can also be fostered by activities that pull students into the regular functions of the church. Some groups have done this by finding adults who will become "Secret Pals" of the young people. Adults correspond with students, and students with adults—and only the youth worker knows who is writing to whom. After several months, a party can be held where secret pals are revealed to each other and verbal communication replaces written correspondence.

Again, the success of a small youth group depends on the creativity of the leader. Writers and speakers have experience—but not with every kind of youth group. A youth leader shouldn't feel obliged to try anything just because it worked for someone else.

WANTED: LEADERSHIP FOR SMALL YOUTH GROUPS

For many churches, the biggest obstacle to having a growing, dynamic youth ministry is getting started. The biblical principle is clear: Seeds must be sown before reaping a harvest (Matthew 13:3–9). Only a mustard seed's worth of faith (13:31–32; Luke 17:6) is required as long as the youth group "branch" remains attached to the main vine (John 15:5–8). First develop some kind of vision as to the type of group to be established. Then, "go and do likewise" (to reapply Luke 10:30–37).

Beginning a youth ministry doesn't require a lot of up-front know-how as long as there is a lot of "want to" on the part of a willing volunteer. Resources abound to teach the leader all he or she needs to know—books, cassettes, videos, conferences, seminars, and so forth. But unless a definite call is felt by someone, the ministry is likely to come up empty in spite of all the available resources.

Following are five strategies for lay leaders who want to consider initiating youth ministry in a small church setting.

Strategy #1: Be Content with Starting Small

Jesus came to earth to save the world, yet He started His ministry by calling a group of twelve. Even twelve followers may have seemed too many to teach adequately, since He frequently drew three aside for more intense instruction. If you have three students, you have the same opportunity. Perhaps your three will become twelve. Perhaps those twelve will become fifty. But perhaps not. If the group remains at three, you need to make sure those three are convinced that they are every bit as special as any student in any youth group in the world.

But just a word of warning. The joke is told of a rural pastor whose scheduled church service was attended by just one rancher. When the pastor asked the rancher if he wanted to go back home, the man replied, "If I only had one cow to show up at feeding time, I'd surely feed her." The pastor was so excited that he launched into a powerful *(and powerfully long)* sermon. An hour later he noticed the rancher was asleep and felt quite hurt. He woke the man to ask how he had the nerve to fall asleep in light of his previous comments. The man replied, "I said I'd feed that one cow, pastor. But I wouldn't give her the whole load!"

Sometimes, in our enthusiasm, leaders try to make up for lack of numbers with extra intensity. That energy should be channeled into creating a variety of activities and options—not just teaching. It is a good idea not to scare away the few committed students you do have.

Strategy #2: Get Involved with Other Students

Even if a youth leader can resist the temptation to focus on numbers, sometimes the *students* in the youth group feel the need to lose themselves in a larger crowd. That is not an unrealistic desire. The few students who show up regularly are under considerable pressure. They have to answer all the questions, do all the activities, fill in all the gaps, and adapt as best they can. Occasionally, they need to let someone else take care of all that responsibility. We need to look for opportunities to involve our small group of students with other kids without losing our own identity as a group.

Student conferences are a good place to start. In fact, Christian conferences are some of the best places for students to see that life in a large group may not be everything it's imagined to be. Large percentages of students who couldn't care less about spiritual things are often part and parcel of larger youth groups. It is good for small youth groups to see other students like themselves—as well as those who are nothing like them.

In addition to major youth conferences, the youth worker can keep an eye open for the big events sponsored by larger area churches—picnics, concerts, game nights, and so forth. By planning to attend such activities as a group, students are made to feel more comfortable in those settings. Nor will it seem like a betrayal to their own youth group since the leader initiates their involvement. Many times a larger church will also be willing to loan out equipment or offer its facilities to smaller churches if a workable schedule can be arranged. This is one of those places where small church youth leaders can be creative and see what is available not only in their own churches, but in neighboring churches and the community at large.

Strategy #3: Get to Know Your Students

No matter how many books are read and conferences are attended, no one will be a better expert on any particular youth group than its own leader. Every group has a unique personality, and no one knows it better than the person who shows up to work with the students every week. So read the books and go to the conferences. But remember this: good youth leaders learn to *adapt* what they read and hear to *their* groups.

Students need to know that the youth leader knows them well and genuinely cares about them. If a leader begins by trying to pound spiritual knowledge into their tiny teenage heads, not much is likely to soak in. But after they see that the leader is truly concerned about them, they will begin to open up to him or her. As a result, it soon becomes apparent how to best present spiritual truth.

For the past several years, my teenage Sunday school class has begun with everyone (students *and* teacher) telling the best thing and the worst thing that has happened to them during the previous week. On a particularly good or bad week, that may be all we get around to doing. But I think it is important to spend time ministering to kids on a relational level as well as an instructive one. The theological lessons will be learned over a period of time. Unless kids feel they are genuinely cared for, many will not stick around long enough to absorb much of a spiritual understanding.

Strategy #4: Learn the Culture

If I were going to Siberia to work among the native people, I would want to learn as much as I could about the culture before going. I would want the natives to be comfortable with me, and know that I respect who they are. I would want to communicate (as best I could) at their level. I would try to learn as much from them as possible and in return offer any knowledge that I could.

Yet it amazes me that so many people enter youth work with a know-it-all attitude. They try to establish themselves as *the* authority. They "complete their assignment" a couple of years later, feeling rather proud that they endured. Yet they do not know any more about young people than they did going in. (And they would be shocked to realize how little the students learned during that time as well.)

Youth work is most satisfying when it becomes a mutual learning experience. Good leaders first listen. They absorb. They empathize. They are patient. Perhaps they get around to imparting deep spiritual knowledge right away. If not, they should not feel overly concerned. They will in time. Teenagers will not be ready to respond to deep spiritual knowledge if they don't first feel that someone is listening to and understanding them.

We hold up as models Christian missionaries who go to foreign countries and faithfully proclaim the gospel—even if no results are ever observed. It is a sad comment on the narrowness of others' perspectives, however, when youth workers who do not get dramatic and immediate results are usually branded as "ineffective."

Strategy #5: Address Developmental Needs

One of the hazards of a small church is the popularity of combining junior and senior high students into one youth group. Although the emotional, physical, and spiritual needs are quite varied between a seventh grader and a twelfth grader, many of us are required to work at meeting those needs.

I have found that "intergenerational" ministry is not so bad—in spite of its negative reviews. I encourage older students to build the qualities of patience, encouragement, and leadership into their interaction with younger students. On the other hand, I suggest that younger students look to the wisdom and maturity of the older students.

In programming, I have found it helpful to divide into smaller groups by grade. In this way, Bible study, questions, discussions, and activities can be more age-appropriate. In addition, it is helpful to regularly plan high-school only or junior-high only events. These activities strengthen relationships between the youth leader and students as well as between the students themselves.

Concluding Remarks

We in small churches may never get the glory that some youth leaders in larger churches get. We may never have enough students to play a football game or conduct a church service. We may be called from "the least" to minister to "the least of these." But I am convinced that if God has called us, and we have the opportunity to lead even two or three into a closer relationship with our heavenly Father, it is the least (and maybe the most!) we can do for His kingdom.

For Further Reading

Bierly, S. R. 1995. *Help for the Small-Church Pastor.* Grand Rapids: Zondervan.

Burns, R., and P. Campbell. 1986, 1994. *Create in Me a Youth Ministry.* Wheaton, Ill.: Victor.

_____. 1992. *No Youth Worker Is an Island.* Wheaton, Ill.: Victor.

Plueddemann, J., and C. Plueddemann. 1990. *Pilgrims in Progress: Growing Through Groups.* Wheaton, Ill.: Harold Shaw.

Rice, W. 1986. *Great Ideas for Small Youth Groups.* Grand Rapids: Youth Specialties, Zondervan.

_____. 1989. *Up Close and Personal: How to Build Community in Your Youth Group.* Grand Rapids: Youth Specialties, Zondervan.

Warden, M. 1994. *Small Church Youth Ministry Programming Ideas.* Loveland, Colo.: Group.

PART SIX

RESOURCES FOR YOUTH MINISTRY

25

WHERE CAN WE
TURN FOR HELP IN
YOUTH MINISTRY?

Paul Fleischmann

Coffee breaks, discussion times, and after-meeting talks are my favorite parts of a youth ministry conference. At first, youth leaders tend to talk only about their successes, their strengths, and what is going well. But then, when one secure person shares a failure, a weakness, or an area of struggle, the whole group seems to open up. Soon the conversation progresses beyond the superficial level and a wonderful ministry of encouraging one another begins.

Unfortunately, a youth leader's human nature leads him to want to hide behind an image of "having it all together." But nobody really has "arrived," no matter how experienced or gifted that person may be. An extensive survey conducted for the National Network of Youth Ministries revealed that leaders listed their top needs as the following: being mentored, having accountability, learning more about recruiting and training volunteers, building significant relationships to overcome loneliness, training for working with parents, training for counseling students, and developing better personal time management/planning. Focus groups further revealed that leaders would welcome help for: motivating disinterested kids and adults, equipping adults to do youth ministry, developing a vision and casting it to others, navigating through church politics, and dealing with the emotional drain of doing youth ministry. Every youth ministry leader, as evidenced by this survey, needs help in some way.

The degree to which an individual leader needs help is greatly influenced by the leader's motivation and objectives. If the leader's focus does not extend past what has to be done for next week's youth meeting, she may not feel she has any critical needs. But, if her goals include building mature disciples of Christ and reaching all the teenagers within her sphere of influence, then she will recognize more readily that she has many needs for additional resources and support.

Identifying specific personal and ministry needs is an essential first step toward getting help. However, getting help requires receptivity and openness on the part of the leader. By definition, "help" implies teamwork. Jesus demonstrated the design of teamwork personally through His partnerships with John the Baptist, His twelve disciples, and the seventy-two others sent out in pairs (Luke 10:1). Paul, in Romans 12 and 1 Corinthians 12, provides an explicit theology of the church as Christ's body. Christians are described in interdependent relationships with one another as a result of their dependent relationship with Christ, the Head. From these examples it is clear that God did not intend for any person to be a "ministry island."

But where does a youth ministry leader turn for help? To get the best possible answers to that question, I asked for help! I surveyed forty-three experienced youth workers with the goal to discover where they turned for help in youth ministry. I found that these leaders get help from three primary points of access: God, people in networking relationships, and youth ministry resources.

TURNING TO GOD FOR HELP

My life verse since childhood has been Jeremiah 33:3: "Call to me and I will answer you and tell you great and unsearchable things you do not know." From the beginning of time, God has chosen to work in partnership with people. He seems to reveal His guidance little by little as His children look to Him and develop a readiness to receive His guidance. As leaders honestly face their need for help and come humbly to God, His provision becomes a vital part of their growth process—and, through it, He receives glory and praise. "The eyes of all look to you," the psalmist says of God in Psalm 145:15–16. "You open your hand and satisfy the desires of every living thing."

Prayer: A Line to God

Personal time alone

Virtually every person surveyed indicated that prayer was a primary resource in finding help. One Oklahoma youth pastor said, "When I am in His presence, everything else seems to take care of itself." Isn't that the truth? Several youth pastors surveyed take every Monday morning to be alone with God—as one called it, a "fill my cup time." A youth pastor from Port Angeles, Washington, said, "I lock my door and hit the 'do not disturb' button on my phone—sometimes I even unplug it!"

There are so many times that a "to do" list drives youth ministers to sacrifice or diminish their time with God. This is unfortunate because it is through connecting with Him that leaders begin to see as God sees, rather than being limited by their nearsightedness. Furthermore, waiting on the Lord renews the youth ministry leader's strength (Isaiah 40:31). (What youth ministry leader do you know who does not need his strength renewed?) When leaders take refuge in Him, they find Him to be "an ever-present help" (Psalm 46:1). It should not be surprising that choosing to "get things done" at the expense of spending time with God will ultimately lead to a depletion of one's vision and passion for youth ministry.

Planning through prayer

Many youth workers find prayer to be a key ingredient in the planning process. One twenty-three-year youth ministry veteran from Memphis, Tennessee, said, "I must be careful not to just plan my program and ask the Lord to bless it—I want *His* program." A youth worker from Anderson, Indiana, said, "God helps me plan and create activities. When I pray, I make sure I have a pencil and paper." Another from Castro Valley, California, said, "When I take time alone to dream and seek wisdom from God, He gives me great ideas. He is an awesome youth pastor!"

Discerning needs

An important aspect of creating a powerful youth ministry is to build it according to the needs of your students. A youth worker from Colorado Springs said, "I take a 'day away' each month to pray, seek what the Lord wants to do here, and determine our needs as a youth group." A twenty-one-year veteran youth pastor said, "As I pray for my kids, I see their needs, and then feel led to base a lot of what we do on the needs I see." A youth worker from Maine said, "When I keep focused on what is happening in their environment, God will usually bring a verse, topic, or song to mind that gives me insight about what to do."

The prayer of others

Another avenue used by many experienced youth workers is the involvement of others in praying for their needs. In recent years, I have discovered the power of this incredible resource. One September, the school year started off particularly well. Record numbers of students were meeting around flagpoles to pray for their schools, and thousands of campus Christian clubs were being initiated. However, at the same time, the bottom had dropped out of our national office income, putting us well behind in paying bills. Donations to the salary accounts of our top leadership had dropped off so that some were not getting full salary. Then, all of a sudden, one of our most faithful staff members quit without notice while I was out of town.

I hurriedly sought the counsel of my trusted board members and advisers. In discouragement, I asked them to level with me about what they thought I was doing wrong. But they concluded that it was simply Satan resisting the progress we were making for the kingdom of God. They agreed unanimously that they should each pray for me personally every day for the next month.

I could not believe the impact those prayers had. Frankly, I did not put it all together until I did an inventory at the end of thirty days. At the beginning of the month we had $18,000 of past-due bills. At the end of the month we had paid all our bills and had a balance of $18,000! One staff member who had been short $1,500 per month held a banquet and—"coincidentally"—the total raised averaged out to $1,500 per month. The staff member who had quit got another job. But after two weeks she returned and asked for her old job back. God is awesome in His grace to do "immeasurably more than all we ask or imagine" (Ephesians 3:20)!

Ever since that month three years ago, I have not been without regular prayer support from others. Currently, I have eighty-eight men committed to praying regularly for my ministry. I send them prayer requests on the first of each month and report on answers to prayer from the previous month. It is the principle articulated by the apostle Paul in Colossians 4:3: "And pray for us, too, that God may open a door for our message." If the prayer of others was vital to the help he received, then it surely ought to be important to us as well.

Scripture: A Word from God

Second only to prayer, youth workers surveyed emphasized their dependence on the Word of God when needing help in youth ministry. Some find this through the continual flow of input from a daily study time. In the process, biblical principles and examples are logged into our memory banks. Quite a few are journaling their thoughts. A youth worker from Massachusetts finds the Old Testament particularly helpful, seeing how God dealt with the men of Israel and their leaders. Another from southern California loves to study how Jesus ministered. The wisdom of studying Jesus' life and ministry was brought home at a National Network of Youth Ministries gathering of youth organization presidents. The speaker, a respected national ministry leader, admonished, "If you want to be like Jesus, you must think what He thought, say what He said, and do what He did." It seems so logical.

Counsel: A Signpost for God

Confidence in God's Word leads the believer to pursue Scripture as the truth, the authoritative basis for life and practice. Every Christian will also need help in understanding more clearly how the truth discovered can be applied and appropriated. In these times of seeking, the counsel of others becomes a tool of God's grace in our lives.

Proverbs 15:22 says, "Plans fail for lack of counsel, but with many advisers they succeed." Many of the youth workers I surveyed mentioned that they found direction from God through the counsel of mature Christians, mentors, their pastors, and others in youth work. But another frequent response was that they drew on their staff teams. One youth pastor from Texas said, "I share my vision and pray it through with my fellow workers." Another from Glendale, Arizona, said, "I get direction from the Lord in areas of need by surrounding myself with a good volunteer staff team to get feedback on what I believe God is saying." Part of seeking God is seeking God in partnership with other members of His body. Perhaps this is why the leaders surveyed made so many references to the next section: networking relationships.

TURNING TO NETWORKING FOR HELP

When the National Network of Youth Ministries began in 1981, "networking" was a fresh concept in the Christian world. Today, it is much more familiar and maybe even taken for granted. Nevertheless, the concept should be no less valued as the next generation of youth ministry leaders emerges.

The Toshiba Company predicted that the nineties would be the decade of the "strategic alliance." Its prediction held true in the business world as evidenced in the unprecedented company mergers and buy-outs. Strategic alliances have become the norm for youth ministry as well. Many youth leaders have discovered that "the whole is greater than the sum of its parts" when ministry leaders have humbly and genuinely joined forces to serve the Lord.

A commitment to networking was a common thread among the forty-three youth ministers the Network surveyed. A veteran youth pastor and writer said, "It is a lifeline to me." A youth pastor of six years said that meeting regularly with the same group "has been my mainstay in youth ministry." A newcomer of six months said, "It keeps me both accountable and sane!"

Networking may be a modern term, but it is a trusted biblical principle. Solomon shared his advice about where to turn for help when he was inspired to write Ecclesiastes 4:9–12:

> Two are better than one, because they have a good return for their work: If one falls down, his friend can help him up. But pity the man who falls and has no one to help him up! . . . Though one may be overpowered, two can defend themselves. A cord of three strands is not quickly broken.

Relationships: The Key to Networking

Networking is about relationships. Solomon's advice explicitly describes relationships of trust, cooperation, and support. As mentioned earlier, a key requirement for getting help is simply recognizing one's need. Networking is important, not only to help meet that need in a practical way, but in the building of relationships en route. Two interpersonal dynamics that are central to fostering meaningful networking relationships are encouragement and accountability.

Encouragement

The "newcomer" I mentioned in the last section said, "It is encouraging just to talk to men who are pretty much in the same boat as me. Youth ministry is not for 'lone rangers'— networking is key to success." An Oklahoma youth pastor said, "It's encouraging to have someone else out of the church's hearing distance who understands my 'gripes.'" I interviewed a youth pastor friend of mine from California. He said, "True networking develops a shared intimacy. It's an atmosphere that makes me feel that I can share my heart and you're OK with that."

Networking is clearly much more than a tool to help us "do ministry." As one youth worker said, "It's a 'safe place' to run to and vent my frustrations, fears, and downfalls." "Safe places" result from building strong connections by working, playing, and praying together. Although these connections develop gradually over time, even starting to build relationships will bring encouragement to most of us.

Accountability

As relationships develop, more and more youth workers are finding help from a deeper level of commitment to one another. In a study by Howard Hendricks of Dallas Seminary, of 237 cases of moral failure in the ministry, not one person reported involvement in an accountability group. Happily, that trend is reversing in youth ministry. Of the youth workers sampled in my informal survey, 79 percent are involved in some kind of accountability relationship. Most of them feel strongly, as did the youth worker from Boston, that "accountability is the salvation of youth ministry."

Sharpening: A Benefit of Networking

Proverbs 27:17 says, "As iron sharpens iron, so one man sharpens another." That certainly is the case in finding help from others. One youth worker of eighteen years said, "Why reinvent the wheel? If others are doing something successfully, I want input from them!"

One youth worker said he uses his network as a place to "bounce ideas" off. Another says he "gleans" things that are of tremendous benefit to him. One youth worker who has just discovered the networking process said, "These men are invaluable! It's so good to talk with others in my same line of work and to find out what really works. As I compare notes with them, I find out what is going on outside my own little world."

Of course, this sharpening can happen at all levels— monthly Network meetings, casual conversation, or personal accountability. One youth pastor from British Columbia said that he meets weekly with a group of fellow workers for sharpening. They follow an outline in their meetings called "SOAP": Scripture Memory/Meditation, Outreach and Witnessing, Accountability Questions, and Prayer.

There are times when every leader finds himself "stuck." In the same way a driver may need someone's brief help to jump-start his car because of a weak battery, ministry leaders often need short-term assistance in order to continue on their ministry journeys. For instance, when I began to conceptualize this chapter, I realized that my work would be improved if I received the input of veteran youth workers. I wanted to reflect a broader perspective than just my own—one that might apply well into the future. So I used the networking principle by asking a group of youth workers from across the country to each give me a few minutes of input. Their responses helped stimulate my thinking and provide fresh perspective.

Synergy: A Distinctive of Networking

At one of the early Network meetings in San Diego, one youth pastor brought an idea to the table: For several years his church had done an annual outreach event called "Overtime," which followed the high school football games each of the four Friday nights in October. He said, "What if our local Network sponsored it this year? We could each take part of the responsibility, yet no one would have the whole load." The response was positive—and so was the result! Everyone did his part and the combined youth groups filled the stadium at Sea World with the five thousand kids who came!

Dan Webster of Authentic Leadership would probably define what happened at "Overtime" as synergy: the combined action that yields greater results than the sum of the individual parts. Or, as a youth pastor from Oklahoma said, "When you network to pull off a major event, you pool your time and resources and end up with a better product."

A youth pastor from the San Francisco Bay area said, "There are just some things we cannot do alone that we can do together." Consider these three examples: See You at the Pole started as a result of youth workers in the Dallas, Texas, area wanting to motivate kids with a burden to reach their campuses for Christ. True Love Waits started at one church that wanted to encourage its youth to wait for sex until marriage. Every Campus Strategy, a Network initiative, grew out of a desire to identify a ministry to every junior high and senior high school in America. Whether leaders are involved locally, regionally, nationally, or internationally, the synergy of gifts and passion always produces more than what could have been accomplished by isolated lone ranger ministry leaders.

If you are not part of an active local network to reach youth in your area, please do not wait any longer. Maybe there is no network in your area. Do not let that stop you. I was surprised to discover that about three-fourths of those surveyed found their network by either "seeking it out," or starting it themselves. In addition, our National Network office is set up to help you if you need it. See the information provided at the end of the chapter.

Turning to Resources for Help

Finding a resource is simple. Finding the best resource for a specific need is not. When the Network started back in the early eighties, resources were not nearly as prevalent as they have become in recent years. In fact, the challenge today is how to sort through the plethora of resource options available for the youth minister. Leaders may feel as if they are standing in the center of an information-age geyser. So many ideas, so little time. Where does a person begin?

Resources come in many forms: books, curricula, workbooks, magazines, newsletters, monographs, films, videos, tapes, compact discs, computer programs, on-line services, conferences, seminars, consulting, and mentoring to name a few. Even if I could name the top resources in each area, in a very short time the list would be outdated. I learned this in my first position as part-time youth pastor while I was going to college. When I was preparing for my first retreat I made up a song sheet and gave it to the high school senior who was going to play guitar. She looked at the songs and then quipped, "These may have been OK for your generation . . ."

I was only two years older than she was, but already I was feeling the swiftness of change!

Therefore, rather than suggesting what resources to choose, the content of this section will focus on how to discriminate among the options. Three ways of thinking about resources are essential in the process of choosing the best alternative for one's particular ministry need: the criteria to use in choosing them, the context in which they will be used, and the creativity by which they can be used most effectively.

DENOMINATIONAL RESOURCES
WESLEY BLACK

Denominational resources can make a dramatic impact on the effectiveness of your youth ministry. Youth activities sponsored by the larger body can offer a sense of community beyond your local group. Youth and youth leaders can sense the excitement, inspiration, and new vision of being part of a large crowd. A teenager in a stadium or an auditorium filled with other Christians can say, "I'm not the only Christian teenager around. There are a lot of others who believe like I do."

Youth leaders can benefit from training opportunities, curriculum resources, various media resources, and networks of other youth leaders. Two examples illustrate this point.

A group of youth ministers and volunteer youth directors meet regularly for lunch at a local restaurant. They are mostly from one denomination, but they include some leaders from other churches. They usually spend a lot of time talking about their churches, the victories and frustrations, the challenges, and their hopes and dreams. They agree for one person each month to review a new book or video on youth ministry. They plan for city-wide softball leagues, retreats, and back-to-school functions. They plan concerts together, pray together, and help each other in difficult situations.

Although this is not a nationally structured organization, it is an example of youth leaders with denominational ties working together in a regional setting. They often discuss with other denominational leaders the work of their group and receive affirmation and encouragement from them.

Another large group of youth ministers, mostly full-time or part-time paid staff members, meets every four to five years for a national meeting sponsored by their denomination. National speakers and entertainers share moments of training and inspiration. The bookstore area is packed with the latest in books, curricula, video, music, Bibles, and magazines. The youth leaders leave the week-long meeting with hearts full of new ideas, new energy, new friendships, and new vision for their youth ministry.

Although these are but two examples of meetings or events, other resources abound, including printed resources, audio and visual media, training books and conferences, resource magazines, dated and undated curriculum materials, and planning books. Many denominations have consultants and field service representatives who stand ready to help churches and youth leaders do their work better.

These processes can take place best by denominations being committed to effective, life-changing youth ministry. Youth leaders can benefit most by active participation, encouragement to denominational leadership, and personal willingness to serve on a national or regional scale.

Criteria: Standards for Excellence

In my survey of youth workers, I asked what criteria they used to sort out the resources they ultimately used. I have categorized their primary responses into several major areas. To help you remember the qualities to look for when choosing resources for yourself, just remember the acronym CRITERIA.

Compatibility

Is it compatible doctrinally and biblically with your beliefs? The highest number of responses from those surveyed emphasized the need to be sure the resources were biblically based, Christ-centered, and doctrinally in line with their church or organization.

Recommended

Do those you know and respect recommend it? The next highest number of responses came from those who said they seek the counsel of others in making their choices. Even one youth worker who has been in ministry for thirty-five years said, "I listen to what others have used and what has worked well for them."

In tune

Is it in tune with the needs of your students? Youth workers who addressed this on the survey felt very strongly about the importance of using materials that students feel are relevant. "We've got to reach our students where they are," said one veteran of twenty-three years. Resources need to be appropriate for the maturity of the group, the size of the group, and the personality of the group. They should be practical. Some youth workers are concerned that current resources do not go deep enough to be spiritually challenging. "I look for resources that respect teenagers," commented a youth pastor from southern California, "that treat them like they have a brain."

Targeted

Does it help you reach your ultimate target for ministry? One of the most important criteria in my view is to choose resources that are in line with the long-range goals you have for your youth. Of course, if one's goal is simply to get through a quarter of Sunday school lessons, it is much easier to plan, because the program is an end in itself. But, as we said in the beginning, if our goal is to turn out disciples of Christ and to reach all the teenagers within our sphere of influence, then we will want to choose the kind of resources that will be instrumental in helping us get to that target. Start with the end in view. From your long-range objectives develop objectives for each level of commitment. Then develop program objectives for each individual event.

Esteemed

Is the source well respected, qualified, and user-friendly? Many workers surveyed admitted that they were influenced by the reputation of a publishing house. Their confidence is based on past experience. This is often affected by how relevant the materials appear to be and how easy they are to use. When they trust the resource provider, then the promotion they receive is no longer "junk mail." Several surveyed said they look to see if people they know have written the material.

Reviewed

Have you reviewed it, compared it, or tested it? When all else fails, read and review! Quite a few admitted they didn't spend much time going over the material they chose. Others did a thorough job of studying, comparing, and testing. Several had topical filing systems they used when interesting materials or promotions came across their desk. At the very minimum, read the table of contents and scan the major sections.

Inviting

Is it attractive, affordable, and culturally relevant? Students will definitely be affected by the initial appearance of the materials presented to them. Whether or not the graphics and illustrations are relevant will make a big difference to our youth. "I am quick to discard material that looks dated (for example, out-of-date hairstyles)," said one midwestern youth pastor. Another frequently mentioned concern was, "How practical is it? Does it help the youth pastor achieve his objectives? Does it help motivate kids to action?"

A final criterion in this subheading is affordability. As stewards of limited resources (in some cases very limited resources), ministry leaders are careful to question not only the cost of a particular resource, but also whether it is worth giving up those things that cannot be afforded if this resource is purchased.

Adaptable

Can it be easily customized to fit your situation, if needed? As revealed in the survey, most youth workers do not use resources completely as is. No materials could fully anticipate our uniqueness, so most of us take liberties to adapt them to the needs and opportunities of our groups—as we should. But that makes it important that the chosen resources are flexible. It was also important to some that the materials are easily transferable so that laymen, staff, and students could be easily trained to use them.

Context: Surroundings That Enhance

In ministry, who you surround yourself with is just about as important as the resources you use. Look around and see the wealth of available helpers.

Mentors

My survey group said it best. Let me quote a few veteran youth workers. From North Carolina: "There are dozens of quality conferences, hundreds of videos, thousands of books, but I feel a Paul/Timothy relationship is the most beneficial." From Washington State: "A textbook on youth ministry can be helpful, but whatever is used should be in the context of working through it with someone who has been there. He will serve as a springboard, adding to and taking from according to his seasoned perspective." From Florida: "Every person needs a Paul, a Barnabas, and a Timothy at all times. Your mentor may not even know you view him that way, but have someone whose life and teaching you follow and learn from."

Parents

There is at least one group of people that cares a great deal about the individual students in the youth ministry—their parents! In fact, Deuteronomy 6 indicates that parents have the primary responsibility for educating their children. So, at the very least, leaders should be working in tandem with parents.

"Throw a parents' meeting and brainstorm!" says one enthusiastic youth pastor. To this suggestion should be added, "Get together with them personally, as well." Now that I have two adolescents, I know firsthand what a help it is to have other caring adults who show an interest in my children. They can communicate the same things we parents try to communicate, but in a different way—one that is heard!

Leaders must not be afraid to ask for parental assistance, advice, and counsel. Parents feel indebted to anyone who genuinely loves their kids, and the relationship can be mutually beneficial for everyone involved.

Other laymen

There are a host of other interested adults in local churches and communities that, like the parents, have a genuine concern for students' lives. They may be somebody's grandparents, aunts, or uncles. They may have no training or experience; they may not be potential youth staff; but they would love to pray for students or leaders, offer their homes for meetings, cook meals on a retreat, or help in any number of small ways. Leaders who fail to see this invaluable hidden resource are robbing themselves and their students of meaningful relationships.

Youth staff

The key to success in youth ministry is the kind of staff with which the leader surrounds herself. It does not matter how small the church, every youth ministry setting needs a team. Furthermore, all members of the team, whether paid or volunteer, should be considered "staff."

The ministry leader who has well invested in staff will receive the reward of having trusted persons to turn to in time of need. Youth staff members are a part of the "youth family" and should be empowered to contribute not only to the tasks of the ministry but to the lives of the leaders and the students. These committed men and women are the best resources any youth ministry could claim.

Church or organizational staff team

I was encouraged to see my survey reveal that a number of the youth pastors saw their senior pastor as a mentor. That is ideal. One such youth pastor said, "The times I have not had that 'mentoring friendship' with my senior pastor have affected my ministry [negatively]." Youth ministry leaders will be blessed immeasurably by a close relationship with other staff members. With meaningful church or organizational staff relationships come encouragement and guidance for ministry as well as support and challenge for personal godliness.

Community facilities

It is easy to get lost in one's own boxlike world of relational contacts. Such narrowness is unfortunate in view of the many adults in every community who care greatly about youth. There are teachers, administrators, guidance counselors, tutors, coaches, athletic program directors, dance team and cheerleading clinic coaches, and psychologists. There are PTAs, inner-city ministries, the YMCA/YWCA, community centers, boys and girls clubs, 4-H clubs, crisis pregnancy centers, juvenile facilities, drug rehabilitation centers, health and disability groups, student political groups, colleges, seminaries, denominational offices—not to mention the local Network and similar youth programs in other campuses and churches. Much work is duplicated on the one hand and hindered on the other because the resources of these persons and agencies are not shared.

The leader's family

No one knows a person as well as his immediate family. The role of the family as a resource for youth ministry is often taken for granted. This should not be the case.

My wife's invaluable intuitive counsel or word of wisdom

has saved me on many an occasion. Or my children's innocent questions. Or my siblings' How-are-you-really-doing? probes. My parents have volunteered on a number of occasions just to help out. There is a very special connection that happens when these people are willing to come alongside, both in entirely personal contexts and in specific ministry contexts.

Creativity: Customizing to Empower

As mentioned earlier, youth workers typically adapt available resources, as opposed to using them exactly as suggested. Published materials, such as Sunday school curricula or small group Bible study guides, simply cannot be written to fit the context of every group of students. Therefore, a part of the leader's role is either creating curricula or creatively adapting published materials to the interests and needs of the group she serves. Leaders attempting to achieve the maximum "custom fit" will want to heed the principles listed below.

Develop purpose-driven programs

The ultimate goal of youth ministry is having students experience life-change for the glory of God. The goal is not about filling a time slot, but about teaching kids, through the power of Christ, to be prepared for life and to make a difference for eternity. Effective leaders know that they must consistently monitor their programs to be certain that their strategies and methods are being directed toward that final destination.

Before choosing curriculum materials, leaders must address several questions relevant to each program's purpose. For instance: Why does the Sunday school exist? What do we want to accomplish in the Sunday school class this year? How will what we do in Sunday school be related to the other components of the youth ministry of the church?

Questions that address the *why, what,* and *how* of Christian education are critical when the curriculum for a particular class is chosen. Creatively adapting that curriculum can then proceed along the lines of the purpose that has been set. It will be proactive in response to the purpose rather than reactive in response to what will "work."

Develop people-centered programs

One New Jersey youth pastor said it well: "There is no magic curriculum, sacred textbook, or wonder seminar. There are no perfect formulas or activities that will transform your group. You need to know your teenagers, your sponsors, and their needs." When resources meet needs, lives change. As with clothes, sometimes "one size fits all"; other times individuals need something altered or tailor-made. Given the purpose and the man, how can this curriculum contribute to the growth of the students?

One way to match the priorities of purpose and man in creating or creatively adapting resources is to use a system called NOPE: Needs, Objectives, Program, Evaluation. For each program, NOPE works from left to right, planning and implementing methods designed to respond to the needs of those for whom the ministry is designed. A leader may have one objective and program for each need, or several objectives and programs for each need. This approach can work for any activity, whether adapting or creating resources.

Proceed with caution

Leaders can ask themselves several evaluation questions before taking the time to radically change or personally create curriculum materials:

1. Will what I prepare really be that much better than what is available, given the limits of my time, manpower, and budget? (Most publishers have a lot more to work with than leaders do.)
2. Even if I can produce something more tailored to my group, will it be the best use of my time, in light of my long-range objectives? Will kids really care that much?
3. How much of a factor is it to have my name or our group name attached to it? This is a tough question, I know. But we all know of instances where different groups have created almost the exact same materials or programs just because of the need to "own" it. We must be sure we are not reinventing the wheel. We are all part of God's army, and we must use His resources wisely.

And more important, if our motives are wrong from the start, how can God bless it fully?

Build a leadership resource library

At the end of my survey, I asked, "What are the top resources that every youth worker should have?" I received 113 different responses from forty three different youth workers. Outside of the Bible, the most votes given to any one source was six! This further emphasizes the wealth of resources that is meeting needs of present-day youth ministry.

Once again, instead of giving a list of specific resources, which will soon be out of date or out of print, below are listed the categories of resources that were chosen, so that each leader can build a resource library suited to his needs.

- *The Bible:* a good study Bible for you and a youth Bible for your youth
- *Bible study helps:* lexicon, interlinear Bible, dictionaries, commentaries
- *Youth ministry philosophy:* an overview of how to build a youth ministry
- *Youth ministry skills and tools:* methodology, training, management, ideas
- *Personal growth:* spiritual nurture for the youth worker and general helps
- *Youth culture trends:* journals and newsletters to keep you current
- *Counseling:* references for working with teenagers
- *Parents:* helping you to help parents of teenagers
- *Contemporary Christian music:* current relevant music resources
- *Computer-related:* Bible study software, libraries, on-line services
- *Videos:* training tools, inspirational drama, outstanding communicators
- *Other aids:* network membership, camera, daily planner, filing system

Recharge personal batteries

My son got a remote control car for Christmas and he just loves it. It really goes fast, does some tricky maneuvers, and looks great. But on a regular basis it runs out of power. No matter how much fun he is having, he is forced to stop and recharge the battery. Likewise in ministry, despite how well it's going or how much needs to be done, we need an occasional stop for refreshment and rejuvenation. One veteran youth worker from Michigan said, "Be sure to make it a priority to take in one conference or training seminar each year. It's great for your development, but also gives you a breath of fresh air, a new perspective, and a renewed zeal for everyday ministry."

Creativity is a renewable resource. But it is not an endless well that never runs dry. Leaders need to be ministered to if they expect to keep the creative juices flowing. As one fellow youth worker from Colorado said, "Youth pastors are wearing out. We need resources that fill our spiritual cup. Refreshment from the Lord and from each other is vital if we are to continue." Conferences, retreats, personal days of renewal, regular recreational activities, and vacations that leave behind the demands of the ministry are all necessary if leaders hope to maintain their creative edge.

CONCLUSION

Youth ministry leaders have begun to realize two secrets geese have always known. With the same energy, geese fly 71 percent farther in their characteristic V formation than when they fly as individuals. Leadership discovery number one: leaders are always more effective when they are working together. Geese also are wise enough not to keep the same leader in front lest he tire and begin to slow the flock. Leadership discovery number two: Leaders need to step back occasionally and benefit from the leadership strength of others. In summary, everybody needs a little help, everybody has a little help to give.

Fortunately, this generation of youth ministry leaders has a vast array of help at their fingertips. Used strategically, outside resources will multiply a leader's ministry effectiveness exponentially. In business this is called "leveraging"—an ancient idea that one person can lift far more than his weight by properly positioning his resources. It is as Moses said in Deuteronomy 32:30: One person can "chase a thousand," but two can "put ten thousand to flight."

RESOURCES

National Network of Youth Ministries. For information about Network membership, contact:

National Network of Youth Ministries
12335 World Trade Drive
Suite 16
San Diego, CA 92128
Phone: 619-451-1111
FAX: 619-451-6900
E-Mail: NNetworkYM@aol.comPaul Fleischmann

26

✟

CHURCH/PARACHURCH: HOW CAN THEY WORK TOGETHER IN YOUTH MINISTRY?

Mark Moring

The question for Scott Benson was one that thousands of youth pastors ask all the time: "How can I best reach the students at the local high school?"

Benson knew that a straightforward approach—"Hey, come on out to the youth group meeting at our church next week! We'll have tons of free pizza!"—wouldn't necessarily produce terrific results. Benson knew he'd need more than sausage and pepperoni to get the local unchurched kids across that threshold.

"I wondered how we could be creative in reaching a stratum of kids we're not already reaching," Benson says. "If we're serious about the Great Commission, we've got to be serious about trying new things."

So Benson, youth pastor at Winnetka Bible Church in Illinois, considered other methods for reaching the students at nearby New Trier High School. He was discussing this one day with Rick Malnati, a volunteer leader at Winnetka Bible, when the two of them came up with this idea: "Why not use a parachurch ministry to reach those kids?"

Malnati already had a foot in the door as the assistant boys' basketball coach at New Trier.

"Why not the Fellowship of Christian Athletes?" Malnati said.

"Yeah," responded Benson. "Let's have a summer basketball camp under FCA's umbrella."

About thirty-five kids—some from the inner city, some from the 'burbs—showed up for that camp in the summer of 1991, including some who might otherwise never step into a church building.

The campers drilled, practiced, played—and heard the gospel. When the camp ended, Benson and Malnati wondered just how successful it had been.

They got their answer almost immediately. A few of the campers from New Trier High approached Benson and Malnati and asked, "Hey, why don't we keep something like this going during the school year?"

And just like that, the FCA huddle at New Trier High School was born. Today, some seventy-five students attend the biweekly meetings in Malnati's basement. (Malnati remodeled the place just for the meetings; now it's affectionately known as "The FCA Room.")

Benson says, "Through FCA, we've tapped into a social level at New Trier that is jock oriented and leadership oriented. Now it's really the place to be for those kids on a Monday night."

The FCA meetings also give the students in Winnetka Bible's youth group an opportunity to reach out to their New Trier classmates.

Says Benson, "Because most of my kids at Winnetka Bible also participate in sports, this gives them an opportunity to invite non-Christian friends to FCA—friends who probably would never show up at a church youth-group meeting. That's how we help our church kids—and our church leaders and parents—see the rationale behind what we're doing with FCA."

Benson's primary responsibilities remain with the church; only 20 percent of his workweek involves FCA. But that 20 percent makes him a better leader.

"I love that front-line, cutting-edge evangelism," Benson says. "These kids [at FCA meetings] are hungry, and they're extremely verbal. They don't just want to be lectured; they want to talk about it. And that keeps me on my toes."

Malnati says the Winnetka Bible–FCA marriage is a match made in heaven: "If I was a church youth pastor with a great ministry, but maybe my outreach was kind of stagnant, finding a parachurch ministry such as FCA is a very good idea."

Ron Frank, FCA's Chicago-area director, is tickled pink with the growth of New Trier's huddle—which, he notes, is also an extension of Winnetka Bible Church, albeit subtly. After all, Benson gives the main talk at most meetings.

"The kids come, they feel welcome, and they have a great time," says Frank. "They're free to ask questions, and they hear the gospel in a nonthreatening, loving environment. The majority of these kids are unchurched. Scott and Rick are reaching the kids they've set out to target. And many of them have come to Christ. It's just an incredible story."

An incredible story, yes. And a great example of how church and parachurch ministries can work together effectively in spreading the good news.

Winnetka Bible Church and the New Trier FCA huddle certainly aren't the only church and parachurch groups to find one another with great results. Such "marriages" are happening everywhere.

There seems to be a more concerted effort on both sides to explore ways to put their heads—and resources—together to find methods to best reach students with the message of faith.

The bottom line: Both types of ministry—church and parachurch—seem to need each other to most effectively reach this generation's students for Christ.

This chapter examines the philosophies of three of the largest parachurch youth organizations—Youth For Christ, Young Life, and FCA—as well as provides some specific examples of how churches and parachurch ministries are working together.

YOUTH FOR CHRIST:
"WE'VE GOT TO PARTNER TOGETHER"

Youth For Christ president Roger Cross says YFC is trying to hook up with local churches in its effort to reach students. "Most of us in parachurch ministry have learned that this mission is bigger than one group," says Cross. "We've got to partner together to make that happen. That's a very clear focus for us. We're moving toward a time when we won't even start a ministry at a school unless we're partnering with a church. When we partner with churches, we have a much better chance of getting converts into the church."

Cross says that, traditionally, YFC would make contact with kids at schools, lead them to Christ, and then "we'd try to turn them over to the church. But that wasn't very successful, because the relationship (between the student and the church) just wasn't there. For too long we've asked the church to come in at the end of the process, rather than get in it from the beginning."

"After all," notes Cross, YFC's stated purpose is "to participate in the body of Christ in responsible evangelism of youth, presenting them with the person, work, and teachings of Jesus Christ and discipling them into the local church."

Sounds great in theory, but how do these church/parachurch partnerships come about? Who initiates the process? Says Cross, "I feel it's incumbent on the parachurch ministry to take the initiative, since we're kind of seen as the 'outsiders.' We need to tell the local church, 'We're not here to put a program on you, but we're here to serve as your partner and to help get something done.'

"Let's say we've got some YFC people concerned about the kids at Central High School in a certain community. Those YFC people should find churches close to that high school and try to build relationships with those churches. They should begin to pray and strategize together and begin to ask, 'Is there something we can do together to reach that high school?'"

Cross acknowledges that church and parachurch ministries have sometimes acted as if they were in competition with each other, but he says those walls are breaking down.

"I've seen a big shift," he says. "The needs of kids have driven that. We all realize we can't do this by ourselves."

YOUNG LIFE:
PARTNERSHIPS "BENEFIT BOTH PARTIES"

"Young Life historically has felt that close relationships with local churches are vital to the health and prosperity of the ministry," says Bob Lonac, vice president for Young Life's Western Division. "It's a benefit to both parties to work closely together. We bring expertise in relational, incarnational ministry, and the church brings to us spiritual strength, fellowship, and resources. That's been our posture all along."

Recently, Young Life has taken that philosophy a step further, developing its Church Partnership Program, a concerted effort to work more formally with the local church—and, specifically, with its youth leaders.

"We're trying to be more intentional about it," says Lonac. "Basically, it's a matter of Young Life getting together with a church and finding qualified people who are capable of youth ministry. We then negotiate an agreement whereby the person leads a local Young Life club and is supported through the church."

The specifics of the covenant vary from case to case, says Lonac. Sometimes the church pays the leader's entire salary, sometimes Young Life pays the entire salary, and sometimes the salary is split between the two, depending on the situation.

"Some smaller churches can't afford a full-time youth person, and sometimes Young Life can't afford a full-time staffer," says Lonac. "So the partnership program helps in this area. It's a pretty good win-win situation for the church and Young Life in fulfilling both their missions."

The job description of a "Young Life Church Partner" also varies from case to case. YL's suggested guideline is that the partner devote "a minimum of approximately 40 percent of his working time" to local Young Life ministry. Again, says Lonac, such specifics are negotiable between YL and the participating church.

"We have a standardized covenant that churches can use," he says, "but many times other agreements come out of that.

It's often tweaked one way or another. Every church has different needs."

Lonac says the Church Partnership Program is just a formal way in which Young Life and the local church can work together. Most working relationships between the two ministries are more informal, as they historically have been.

Lonac believes the relationship between church and parachurch ministries is at an all-time high. "I feel that the Holy Spirit is bringing down the barriers between church and parachurch ministries," he says. "There's much more of a spirit of cooperation between the groups."

Working together, says Lonac, can only mean one thing: more students hearing the good news.

"I don't think kids' fundamental needs have changed," he says. "They've always had a need for quality relationships with adults who care for them. Partnerships are one way of mustering our resources. We're just trying to put our heads together to strategically deploy those resources."

FELLOWSHIP OF CHRISTIAN ATHLETES:
"STRONG LINK TO THE CHURCH"

The Fellowship of Christian Athletes has traditionally had a "really good working relationship with the local church," says Kevin Harlan, FCA's senior vice president of programs. "That's a cornerstone that we were built on. Pastors were involved in the founding of FCA, so we've had a strong link to the local church from the beginning."

Harlan says FCA's success depends on the local church's expertise and administrative resources. "We're a volunteer-intensive organization," he says. "We have just three hundred field staff across the country and an estimated fifty-seven hundred huddles. Our paid staff is not what's running those huddles; it's volunteers."

Typically, those volunteers are coaches or teachers who don't have the time or resources to efficiently "run" a huddle group.

Says Harlan, "They're often overloaded to the point where they'll sponsor a huddle but need somebody to do the legwork, the administrative work. That's not something we've strategically laid out as part of our philosophy, but that's how it often works out—a marriage with the local youth pastor. That youth pastor not only connects with the kids but provides an area of service for the huddle leaders."

At the same time, Harlan says, the huddle provides an area of service for church youth leaders. "Often, youth pastors want some entrée into the public schools, and their role as youth pastor scares away some principals. But they can easily enter the campus as a volunteer representative of FCA."

FCA's mission statement emphasizes the need to bring unchurched students into the local church. Its mission is "to present to coaches and athletes, and all whom they influence, the challenge and adventure of receiving Jesus Christ as Savior and Lord, serving Him in their relationships and in the fellowship of the church."

While FCA wants very much to work *with* the church, it doesn't necessarily want to be publicized as an extension of the local church.

Says Harlan, "We don't want to be recognized as a church or denomination, because that could limit who might attend the huddle meetings."

For example, in the story at the beginning of this chapter, Winnetka Bible Church does not put its name on the New Trier huddle group. Nor does Benson identify himself as Winnetka Bible's youth pastor when he speaks at FCA meetings.

Harlan says, "We want to be cautious about being identified with a church in an area. We view ourselves as a bridge for kids to plug into the local church. That's how our success rate is measured."

All in all, Harlan sees the cooperative efforts between church and parachurch ministries on the rise. "People on both sides are taking a bigger kingdom mentality," he says. "They're not getting caught up so much in boundaries or competition anymore."

CHURCH/PARACHURCH:
CAN I WEAR *BOTH* HATS?

John Berlin knows the marriage between church and parachurch ministries can work. After all, he plays both roles. Full time.

Berlin at one time was the full-time youth pastor at Virginia's largest Methodist church, Springfield's thirty-six-hundred-member Messiah UM. When he's not on the job working with the 170 active members of Messiah's youth group, he's busy with his other full-time job as a Young Life area director, overseeing seven YL high school clubs.

Why wear both hats?

"I'm only doing it because of a strong vision that the church and parachurch need to work together," Berlin said. "Parachurch volunteers have traditionally been trying to do their work as 'outsiders' to church ministries. As a Young Life volunteer leader, I tried to work with local churches, and they were either wonderfully supportive or very suspicious and afraid we'd 'steal' their kids. The idea should be, how can we work together?"

Well, how?

"Synergy," says Berlin. "That's the hot new term for church/parachurch relationships. That just means that we in youth work—whether church or parachurch—are looking at kids from the kingdom perspective. We're always looking at kids and asking ourselves, 'How can he or she *best* be discipled?'

"Parachurch ministries," says Berlin, "do a good job of leading kids to Christ, but then what? Then we hand 'em over to the next line—the church—and they disciple them. But that's not happening as much as any of us thought. Maybe it needs to be done from a different angle.

"I think the concept of having parachurch leaders significantly involved in the local church is a good one."

Berlin has seen the benefits of just such an arrangement in northern Virginia. "For me," he says, "when kids meet Christ, I'm very well connected with churches. So in some cases we're handing these kids over to churches where our Young Life staff are already involved as youth leaders."

Additionally, such partnerships give the church the benefit of trained volunteer youth workers. Cooperative efforts can also be more broad-based, encompassing a variety of churches and parachurch ministries.

Berlin is one of many northern Virginia youth workers in Teen Leader Coalition (TLC), which includes church youth directors and parachurch leaders. TLC meets monthly to brainstorm ways to more effectively reach kids.

At the meetings, he says, there's a lot of "networking, fellowship, sharing of ideas, comparing calendars, coordinating events."

For instance, TLC organizes four big youth rallies a year, a huge cooperative effort that brings together students from all over northern Virginia. They'll typically rent a high school auditorium and bring in big-name Christian bands and/or speakers that an individual ministry couldn't afford alone.

"We'll also join together to get group rates and discount prices on things like ski trips," says Berlin.

He cites a study suggesting that small churches aren't doing as good a job of "transmitting faith" to kids as larger churches. "A lot of it boils down to their ability to afford stuff. TLC gives the small church the option to have essentially a year-long youth program.

"The key to TLC's success," he continues, "is that we're a loose coalition, not owned by any one group. We're not under any one umbrella. There's no competition. We're all in it together."

ONLY AS GOOD AS THE "TOTAL SYSTEM"

Chuck Rosemeyer, who trains both church and parachurch youth leaders in his role as director of the Pittsburgh Youth Network (PYN), says a church's youth ministry can only be as strong as the church is as a whole.

"Why do some youth ministries work and others never will?" Rosemeyer asks. "It has to do with the total church system. If you take a fairly mediocre youth leader and put him in a growing church, the youth program goes bananas. But if you take a gung-ho leader and put him in a reeling church, it won't. We've got to look at youth ministry as part of a whole system in the church."

To that end, Rosemeyer and his staff train leaders to think

systematically. Youth work is not merely a collateral movement in the work of expanding the kingdom. Likewise, church
and parachurch efforts are not merely separate but similar
campaigns, and they can be most effective when working
together.

Rosemeyer says Pittsburgh has a solid network of churches willing to work together and with parachurch organizations as well. Combined efforts result in about seven weekend
camps a year, serving a total of some two thousand students.

While the leaders minister to the students at those camps,
Rosemeyer and PYN minister to the leaders. "Camps are the
method we use to get churches and leaders involved in the
training process," he says. "I spend my time consulting with
churches, helping them to do their youth ministry as effectively as possible. I do contact work with churches, just as Young
Life does contact work with kids. My ministry is to the fifty to
sixty leaders we take to the camps."

Rosemeyer, who started in ministry with Young Life, says
he used to believe parachurch efforts were more effective at
reaching kids than church efforts. "For years, we parachurch
guys thought we could show churches what to do and how to
do it," he says. "But we just alienated them, because we
thought we had the answer, and our attitude was 'If you guys
would just wake up and let us show you how to do it . . .'

"The big 'Aha!' came for me when I ended up working for
a church for eight years. The place was alive, and I realized
the church *can* do youth ministry well."

And a good church youth ministry, he adds, can only be
enhanced through cooperative efforts with parachurch ministries.

"By sharing major events that one church by itself can't
do, you can build a broad Christian community," Rosemeyer
states. "As far as the kids in a church youth group know,
they're the only Christians in the world. But when you can
broaden that, they see that other kids in their school are
believers too. And all of a sudden you begin to create a Christian subculture within a school, which really helps kids."

Finally, Rosemeyer offers this piece of advice: "Many parachurch leaders do youth ministry very well, but they don't

understand the church. They need to understand from whence they come. Parachurch people need to hang out in the church, to really know and understand what the church needs.

"The 'us-versus-them' mentality still exists, but it's got to go. The time is right for parachurch people to sidle up to denominational leaders and say, 'Is there anything I can do to help you?'"

FOR FURTHER READING

Allen, Roland. 1962. *Missionary Methods: St. Paul's or Ours?* Grand Rapids: Eerdmans.

Board, Stephen. 1979. "The Great Evangelical Power Shift." *Eternity* (June).

Cailliet, Emile. 1963. *Young Life.* New York: Harper & Row.

DeJong, James A. 1979. "Parachurch Groups: A Reformed Framework." *The Banner* (July 8).

Hollis, Harry. 1979. "Parachurch Groups: Some Implications for Southern Baptists." *College* 9 (January).

Hunt, Keith, and Gladys Hunt. 1991. *For Christ and the University: The Story of InterVarsity Christian Fellowship of the U.S.A., 1940–1990.* Downers Grove, Ill.: InterVarsity.

Jason, Noel. 1986. "The Relationship Between Church and Para-Church: Biblical Principles." In *The Church: God's Agent for Change,* edited by Bruce J. Nicholls. Greenwood, S.C.: Attic, Paternoster (U.K.).

Lausanne Committee for World Evangelism. 1983. *Co-Operating in World Evangelization: A Handbook on Church/Parachurch Relations.* Lausanne Committee for World Evangelization, Lausanne Occasional Papers, 24.

Perez, Pablo. 1986. "The Relationship Between Church and Para-Church: A Theological Reflection." In *The Church: God's Agent for Change,* edited by Bruce J. Nicholls. Greenwood, S.C.: Attic, Paternoster (U.K.).

Swamidoss, A. W. 1983. "The Biblical Basis of Para-Church Movements," *Evangelical Review of Theology* 7 (October).

Whallon, Doug. 1989. "Christ on Campus: Parachurch Ministries in College Life." *Youthworker* (Summer).

White, Jerry. 1983. *The Church and the Parachurch*. Portland, Oreg.: Multnomah.

27

How Should
We Use
Retreat Ministries?

Chap R. Clark

W hat are the five most essential programs in your annual youth ministry calendar?" Ask that question of one
hundred randomly chosen youth ministry leaders and
you will get one hundred different lists.

"What have been the most significant spiritual experiences
in your life?" Ask this question of one hundred randomly chosen students in those leaders' ministries and you would
receive equally diverse responses.

However, it is highly probable that all of the leaders' lists
and most of the students' responses would have at least one
theme in common: references to camps, conferences, and
weekend retreats. Why? Because these events are consistently
recognized as some of the most effective ministry settings for
bringing students into a deeper and more meaningful relationship with Jesus Christ. In fact, as youth ministry has come of
age in the last three decades, an ever-increasing emphasis has

been placed on providing students with these invaluable contexts for spiritual awakening and renewal.

In spite of the universality of the impact of such experiences, there is no single agreed-upon definition of the terms *camp* and *retreat*. To many, the idea of taking students to camp means anything from a ski trip to a week-long denominational conference. To others, a retreat happens during the school year, a conference is when the event is big and in a hotel, and a camp is out in the woods. No matter what such an event is called—and for the sake of clarity, in this chapter the term *retreat* will be used as a generic reference to all of these events—when leaders take students away from their daily, comfortable, and safe environment, and provide them the opportunity to experience life in new and fresh ways, they are helping to create an atmosphere in which the students can meet God in meaningful ways.

A PHILOSOPHY OF RETREAT MINISTRIES

There are varying philosophies as to what makes the most effective retreat programs for youth ministry. Some leaders think of stress and wilderness camping as the only "true" camping, because camping is not really "camping" if there is no touch with nature. Others have a "resort for kids" mentality that emphasizes the students' need to realize that God is the God of beauty, power, and excellence. Conference centers and parachurch camps, on the other hand, are built on the professionals' concept that these best provide an environment where students can grow spiritually. Finally, there are those who hold that the local church is the place where primary spiritual influence should lie, and they consequently stress that program, facility, and even setting are not particularly important; for them, simply being together is what matters.

Whatever your philosophy of retreat ministries, one vital question must be asked when it comes to programming: What is the primary purpose of the event? The answer to this should always be the driving force in any ministry program, especially one as loaded with long-term ministry potential as conferences, camps, and retreats. From this purpose one can begin to develop a philosophy of retreat ministries that (1) discerns the needs of the constituency, (2) identifies the availability of resources to meet those needs, and (3) programs in a manner consistent with the discerned needs and identified resources.

Discerning Needs

The first step, prior to any scheduling or planning of an event, is to determine the needs of your constituency, in this case the student participants. If you are not specifically seeking to address their needs, either felt or real but unknown to the students, the retreat will have little impact or long-term effect.

In every group there are three levels, or layers, of needs (fig. 27.1). Each layer is important in the formulation of your program. Asking whether a certain type of message or activity will miss a segment of your target group (or even do them damage) because of the students' varied needs will help to ensure an effective camp. If, for example, there has been a suicide in your community, you may want to choose a speaker who can talk about the value of life and the grace of God.

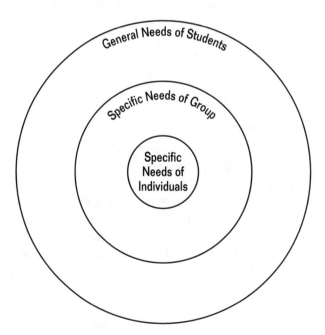

Figure 27.1. *Targeting Needs*

The *general* needs of students are broad-based ones that show up in every student, or nearly every student, whether he knows it or not. The *specific* needs of the group are those that are defined by general trends among your students (for example, in the group as a whole, a higher than average number of students whose parents are divorced, or a higher than average number who are experiencing self-image issues). The *individual* needs, represented by the bull's-eye of the chart, are the distinctive needs of individual students in your group. Obviously, you will never be able to meet every need, but being aware of these three levels will guide you toward proactively addressing those needs that you can intentionally serve.

The following five general needs of students are those that every student experiences, at least to some extent.

1. The need for an accepting community

In more than twenty years of youth ministry, the most drastic change I have seen in young people has been an ever-increasing sense of loneliness and isolation. Youth have always needed to belong, but in our Western, fast-moving, technological, relationally superficial society our children are being taught how to hide their true selves. This trend is destroying them, for God created them to know and to be known, to love and to be loved. Elaborate, high-tech programming will mean nothing to a lonely adolescent.

2. The need to feel like a "star"

Everywhere we turn there are heroes and experts, leaders and movers and shakers, but we have lost the value of the ordinary. Most students, if not the vast majority, are just that—ordinary. They will not win a competition, sing a solo, or present a sterling testimony. They sit, and they watch, and they wonder if they matter to God or anyone else. But everyone yearns for the spotlight. We all need to know that somehow we *do* matter and that God has ordained the ordinary to become extraordinary in Him.

3. The need for interaction and discussion

Many adults think that adolescents simply do not talk, but

they do, or at least they want to. Following the model of the Western church, youth ministry programmers, whether in weekly meetings or at massive conferences, seem to assume that students are best reached by sitting and listening to others sing and talk about God. The problem with this view is that our young people are often simply consumers of Christian teaching rather than individual, dynamic followers of Jesus Christ. For the gospel to mean anything to an adolescent, he must have the chance to talk about what *he* feels and discover what *he* thinks.

4. The need for quiet and rest

A healthy trend in youth ministry says that students should have more say in what goes on at a retreat or camp. The downside of this is that, because students are living in the middle of a pressure-cooker world, they often overlook what they need most—time to sit and think, time to wonder and breathe, time to rest. For some reason, youth workers, hearing students plead for late nights and wild activity, still must get them up at 7:30 A.M. when they went to bed at 1:00 A.M., in order to get in all the seminars and messages and small groups and Bible studies and games and fun that can be packed into a single day. But where is there time for reflection, for quiet conversation with a new friend, or for a walk in the woods?

5. The need to (re)discover Jesus

Because today's adolescents need so much moral direction and ethical teaching, youth ministries have given in to focusing almost exclusively on issues. The writer of Hebrews tells us, however, "Fix your thoughts on Jesus, the apostle and high priest whom we confess" (Hebrews 3:1). Biblically, behavioral change occurs when we are connected to the vine (John 15:1–8), and the fruit of the Spirit (Galatians 5:22–24) is described as a consequential fact for those who are in Christ Jesus (see Galatians 5:5–6). Teaching on issues is important so that students are guided in what it means to put faith into practice. But the overriding need of us all is a deep, rich, ongoing love relationship with Jesus Christ.

COMMUNICATING WITH PARENTS
CHAP R. CLARK

Parents need to know all the details of the planned event with as much advance notice as possible. Parent meetings, calls, or letters are much more effective than relying on students to communicate details. Poor student participation, angry parental confrontations, and damaged relationships can all be avoided with time set aside to be sure parents are clear concerning the places, times, types of activities, cost, and items required for each event. In this day of litigation, every time you take a student off site for any kind of church-sponsored event, you *must* have in your possession a signed medical release form in case of emergency. For a retreat experience you have no option. Keep in mind these two things when planning your trip:

1. *Mail the parental consent form well in advance of the trip (or attach it to the brochure).* Even sending a self-addressed envelope with a due date a few weeks prior to the trip will save you time in the long run. (See fig. 27.2 for a sample information and release form.)

2. *Keep the forms with you at all times*—in the van or bus on the way, in your room (or with a camp nurse or doctor) while at the event. Be sure to get them back from the conference or camp before you leave—this is the most frequently violated rule.

SOURCE FOR FIGURE 27.2:
Materials from *Play It Safe,* Chariot Victor Publishing, Copyright 1993. Used by permission of Chariot Victor Publishing.

Figure 27.2
Parent Information and Release Form
(Name of Church or Youth Ministry)
Parent/Guardian Information and Permission Form
Name of Activity and Dates

(Please Print)
Name of Student _____ Date of Birth _____
Address _____ Age _____
Town _____ State ____ Zip _____
Phone # (____) _____ Sex _____

Student Information and Code of Behavior
Agreement

Description of the activity/event and dates
> What you will be doing
> Departure and return times/locations
> Supervision and free-time activities
> Accommodations and curfew times
> How you can be reached by phone

Listed below are some of the activities we have planned to offer to the students during the trip. Initial your approval for your child's involvement in specific activities listed below:

____ horseback riding ____ playing in sports
____ rock climbing ____ swimming in a lake
____ canoeing ____ taking the ropes course
____ participating in program

Rules of Behavior Expected of Each Student
> 1. No alcohol or drugs permitted
> 2. Attendance at meetings mandatory
> 3. No guys in girls' sleeping quarters
>   (and vice versa)
> 4. Follow curfew
> 5. No smoking
> 6. (as necessary)

Parent Information and Release Form—Page 2

Parent and Student Release Statement:
As parent/legal guardian of *(name of student)*, I have reviewed the information about the youth ministry activity/event and give my permission for the subject of this release to be involved in the overall activities and in the specific activities that I have initialed above.

I/We have reviewed the rules of the activity and agree that the subject of this release will abide by them. I/We also acknowledge that if the subject of the release has to return home early for discipline violations, it will be at my/our expense.

I/We consent to the use of any video images, photographs, audio recordings, or any other visual or audio reproduction that may be taken of the subject of this release during the activity/event to be used, distributed, or shown as *(name of the church or organization)* sees fit.

I/We understand all reasonable safety precautions will be taken at all times by *(name of the church or organization)* and its agents during the events and activities. I/We understand the possibility of unforeseen hazards and know the inherent possibility of risk. I/We agree not to hold *(name of church or organization)*, its leaders, employees, and volunteer staff liable for damages, losses, diseases, or injuries incurred by the subject of this form.

Parent/Guardian Signature _____
Student Signature _____
Date _____   Notarized

Identifying Resources

A step often overlooked in youth ministry programming, and especially with major events such as camps and retreats, is the leadership's failure to accurately and honestly assess the resources that will affect the program. "Resources" are defined as any element, issue, or information that makes a difference when it comes to the program. Resources can be assets, liabilities, or factors that can be either assets or liabilities.

Assets are, for example, a solid history and tradition, strong financial assistance, supportive parents, and the students' enthusiasm. By reflecting on and taking seriously these positive resources, a camp or conference leadership team can greatly enhance the effectiveness of the program.

Liabilities are elements that can hurt a program's effectiveness: lack of vision in the church, the parents, or the students; a lack of drivers to get you to a given conference; the lack of sufficient funding for a specific program; or a lack of spiritually mature leadership. When these and other potentially negative elements are not taken into account, a camp, retreat, or conference that looks great on paper as a way of meeting the needs of the constituency will ultimately fall flat.

Neutral elements that must be considered as resources are those things over which you have no control but will still affect your program. For example, if you are in a denomination that expects its youth to attend the denominational camp, you probably have no choice. You will be attending that camp. But that does *not* mean that you have to ignore the needs of your students and the other resources available to you. Use these neutral resources to your advantage. For example, offer to help out with the planning of the required conference as a way of increasing the chance that the retreat will be a product about which you can be excited.

Programming Consistently

A summer camp, weekend retreat, or annual conference should be planned like any other program. First, the needs must be assessed and taken seriously. Second, the resources that can affect the program—both the positive and potentially negative ones—must be listed and taken seriously also. With these two sets of data, retreat experiences can be successfully refined or even created from the ground up, greatly enhancing the chances of an effective program.

FOUR TYPES OF RETREAT EXPERIENCES

Four types of retreat experiences are most commonly used in youth ministry programming. They are (1) weekend retreats, (2) conferences, (3) parachurch camping, and (4) stress or wilderness camping.

Weekend Retreats

John Dettoni, the author of *Introduction to Youth Ministry,* defines weekend retreats as "minicamps, two to four days in duration"(Dettoni 1993). A more generic definition is: "a time away from the normal environment with (usually) a single ministry entity for the purpose of building community and renewing faith." Weekend retreats are often the least complicated and most free-flowing of Christian camping programs. If there is a program, it is usually flexible, fluid, and guided by the feel of the group. Outside resources such as a speaker or musician are often utilized in a role that is dictated by the needs of the group.

Positive aspects of weekend retreats include:

1. They are inexpensive.
2. They are intimate.
3. They are good for enhancing relationships and building community.
4. They are easily programmed and led, allowing for maximum flexibility for meeting the needs of the group.

Denominational Conferences

Conferences are large gatherings sponsored by denominational organizations or committees. A conference usually includes a speaker (at least one), musicians (again, at least one), seminars, and programmed activities. Groups who attend have placed their trust in the planning team and conference organization, and they (generally) are asked to flow

ENVIRONMENTAL AWARENESS
TIMOTHY VOSS

Recreational activity will impact the environment. We need to think through and practice good stewardship and consequent limitation of some activities. One would do well to learn "no impact" camping skills. This means leaving an environmental setting virtually untouched after our use. It entails not scarring the earth by ground fires and not moving earth, rocks, and dead wood. Everything brought into the setting is packed out, including human waste. Can a youth group really enjoy an outdoor adventure and afterward show that they have not adversely affected the various ecosystems? This is a maturation process.

Even outdoor games must be considered from an environmental reference point. As an example, should Christians "T.P." (toilet paper) a house? Is it good stewardship? What are the outcomes? Why is this kind of activity "fun"? Does the Bible give us a blueprint for playing in relationship to others and with the earth? I believe so. Your local library or bookstore offers practical guidelines for environmental care. You may also find college courses specifically designed for addressing environmental issues.

with the direction of the conference. Numerous conference centers regularly host such events, and many organizations utilize hotels or college campuses for their events.

Positive aspects of the Christian conference include:

1. They are often relatively inexpensive (for the quality and setting).
2. They are of high quality in terms of speaking, music, and program.

3. They give students the chance to join with many peers who also desire to follow Christ.
4. They enable students to build networking that can be renewed and built upon annually.
5. They allow church adult leaders—who are free of most program responsibilities—to spend time with students.
6. They can be effective in building denominational loyalty and momentum.

Parachurch Camping

Parachurch camps are developed and operated by specific organizations with a single mission purpose. They are not connected to any one denomination or to a particular branch of a church but are solely dedicated to the purpose of the parachurch organization. Parachurch camps range from youth-outreach organizations (Young Life, InterVarsity, and the YMCA have properties all across North America) to Christian sports camps (Kanakuk in Missouri is an example of this) to smaller, more focused facilities and organizations. Included in this latter category are Christian conference centers that put on camps for individual students to participate on their own without coming with a church group.

Positive aspects of parachurch camping include:

1. They have the potential to offer high-quality programs because their purposes are specific and the sponsoring organizations have held many such camps.
2. The centrality of a defined mission statement enables the program to single-mindedly achieve the desired goals of the camp.
3. The staff is usually highly trained and therefore highly competent to build meaningful relationships with campers.

Stress or Wilderness Camping

Getting students away from the rapid pace of everyday life—the phone, the car, the CD player, the TV, the videos—is vital in providing a setting where they can experience God. Anyone who has spent a night outdoors with a group of students, or who has sat around a campfire after a white-knuckle white-water adventure, or who has stood with a group on a mountain peak looking down at the world, knows the power of getting away from the hustle of this technological and superficial lifestyle.

When we offer students the chance to be stripped of comfort, to at times encounter an element of healthy risk, or to be forced into cramped sleeping quarters in the pouring rain, they are divested of pretense. As John and Ruth Ensign said thirty-five years ago, "The church camp should provide an experience in Christian living which makes full use of the natural resources of the environment; helping campers to encounter God at work in the processes of creation in the world about them" (Ensign and Ensign 1958, 8).

Character cannot be camouflaged in a wilderness or stress camping adventure, and this is the starting point of authentic, life-changing ministry. There is, in fact, nothing in youth ministry that is comparable.

Positive aspects of a commitment to regular stress and wilderness camping experiences include:

1. By its very nature the setting encourages worship.
2. Creation thrusts God to the forefront where He is impossible to miss. The psalmist sings, "The heavens declare the glory of God; the skies proclaim the work of his hands. Day after day they pour forth speech; night after night they display knowledge" (Psalm 19:1–2).
3. Wilderness experiences are effective in preparing people for God's service. Moses, Israel, David, John the Baptist, and even Jesus all encountered God in the wilderness.

VITAL INGREDIENTS FOR EFFECTIVE RETREAT MINISTRIES

Planning retreat ministry experiences for next year's calendar requires thoughtful, purposeful attention to needs, resources, and opportunities. Even more will be required, however, if the planned event is to be effective in encouraging and facilitating life-change for students. Considerable energy will also be necessary for training the counselors, scheduling, budgeting, communicating with parents, and planning specific activities. If these areas are not adequately addressed, the best of intentions may fail.

Before these vital concerns are addressed more specifically, it should be noted that the most effective retreat experiences will be those that are committed to a *counselor-centered* approach. For decades, parachurch organizations have been committed to a philosophy of camping that uses the experience to deepen relationships between students and the adult leadership. The basic tenet of counselor-centered philosophy is that the most important person in the life of a camper is his or her counselor. The speaker, the music, the seminars—all that goes on in a retreat or conference setting—are tools in the hands of the counselors, who live out mature, committed Christian lives in front of the students. They are the ones who connect the content of the message with the individual life of a camper.

Churches have begun to pick up on the importance of bringing their own counselors, especially those volunteers who are so critical to the regular program at home, to camps and conferences. For several reasons, many youth leaders will organize their camps only in this way.

1. The adult leaders already know the students. Get-acquainted time is, therefore, unnecessary. The campers already know and trust their leaders, so they do not have to waste valuable hours or even days "winning the right to be heard."
2. The group comes to camp with built-in unity and direction. The camp is not simply an opportunity for individual reflection and growth but a time of corporate community building.
3. The leader who was a part of the experience is able to go home with the students, so that after God has moved in their lives the leader can continue to remind them of what God has done and is doing in them. This is the most solid antidote for the typical "mountaintop high and ultimate valley low" syndrome so common in Christian camping.

RETREATS CAN MAKE A DIFFERENCE:
JUST ASK JILL
CHUCK NEDER

Beautiful, full of life, popular at school, with lots of friends, and in all the right groups; on the outside Jill had it all together. However, turmoil, confusion, fear, and doubt would best characterize Jill on the inside. Her parents did not talk to her or to each other. Though they never talked about it, Jill feared divorce. She longed for quality time with her mom and dad, but she felt as if her whole family were like "passing ships in the night."

At school, things were not much better. School was hard, she struggled academically, and she never seemed to have time to study. The "in" group that she was part of was getting involved in more and more things that scared her and challenged her sense of right and wrong. She felt she needed the group for identity and self-image, but she questioned just how far she should go with them.

Then there was Bob, her boyfriend, who said he would love her forever; but now "forever" meant she would have to sleep with him. It seemed that their relationship had deteriorated to nothing more than physical involvement, and she just didn't know how far she could go to keep Bob. Deep down, she knew she needed help, but she did not know where to turn.

Mary sat next to Jill at lunch. They were friends but not very close ones. Mary stayed away from the things that Jill thought were important. There was something strange about her, but also something appealing. Mary wanted to know what Jill would be doing in three weeks. Jill had no plans. Mary invited her to a retreat.

"What is a retreat?" Jill asked. Mary explained it was a time when a bunch of kids got together, had fun, and talked about what was going on in their lives. Jill, for reasons she could not explain, said she would go. She had a lot to think about; maybe this would be the time.

Mary then dropped the bomb when she said, "I'll pick you up at four, and we'll meet everyone at the church at four-thirty."

The church, Jill thought; *I've been tricked!* But she could think of no excuse to get out of going. She decided that she would tell no one about going on a church retreat.

After a two-hour bus ride to a retreat outside of town, Jill was still unsure. The kids on the bus seemed normal. Mary had introduced her to many of them, and it seemed as if they had something that she didn't have. She didn't know what it was, but it seemed like a joy she could not explain.

"A church camp at this resort?" Jill asked when they arrived. She thought all church retreats took place at mosquito-infested camps that had lousy food, bunk beds, and bathrooms 100 yards away. She was even more surprised at the first meeting. The music was great, and the skits, though corny, were funny. But the biggest surprise was the speaker. He talked of a personal relationship with Jesus in words she could understand. She had never heard of a personal relationship with Jesus. He spoke of the unconditional love of Jesus and how that love could be the basis for our identity, security, and self-image. All of these thoughts raised many questions.

Then she met Susan, her counselor for the weekend. The first night, she and Susan talked a lot about Jill's life and how Christ could make a difference in her life. Susan listened in such a way that Jill knew she understood; it was as if Susan listened with her heart.

Saturday night, the speaker spoke about the Cross and what Jesus suffered that we might live. This touched Jill very deeply. She had to talk to Susan about what it all meant. That night, under the stars, Jill gave her life to Christ. From that moment on, Jill began to fall in love with Jesus. She still had problems at home and at school, but Jesus, her new Friend, and the Scriptures would now guide her life.

✝ ✝ ✝

WHAT CAN WE LEARN ABOUT RETREATS FROM THE ABOVE STORY?

- Kids may look like they have it all together, but they don't.
- Christian kids, like Mary, need a place where they can invite their friends.
- Once kids like Mary invite their friends, it is important that the program not be an embarrassment to them.
- Getting away from one's normal environment and schedule is important to life-changing situations.
- A good location, good music, and a speaker who can present the gospel are all crucial to effective retreats.
- Most important, a retreat should be counselor-centered with counselors who know how to listen and offer scriptural advice.
- Follow-up is important. It is not only what happens at a retreat that's significant but what happens after a retreat. Jill is going on in Christ because Susan, Mary, and others stayed close to her.
- What are some more benefits of retreats that you can think of from the above story?

Given that adults who have invested in students' lives are available to multiply that investment as retreat counselors, the following areas become the most important focal points for ministry preparation.

Training the Counselors

Every counselor may not want to be trained, but every counselor wants to be successful, so counselor training is a must for every adult who wears the "counselor" mantle. Whether the youth leader conducts a lengthy, one-night training session, or spreads the information and training over a few nights, is not as important as how prepared these adults are to spend time in close quarters with the students as ambassadors of Christ. The following three elements are important to communicate in any counselor training course:

The importance of the counselor

How counselors talk to, act toward, and communicate love for the campers speaks volumes more to the student about the veracity of the Bible than anything that they hear from the front.

The qualifications of the counselor

Perhaps the best summary of the qualifications of a counselor is found in the gospel of Matthew, where Jesus tells us that the greatest commandments are to love God and to love others as we love ourselves (Matthew 22:37–40). The most effective counselors are those whose love for God is genuine and who really love and, yes, like students.

The responsibilities of the counselor

The kind of event planned will dictate most of the counselor's responsibilities, but there are some basic expectations for any adult called upon to counsel teenagers:

1. *To the director and staff:* Loyalty, even when needing to confront and/or criticize, is essential.
2. *To the speaker:* Almost every speaker feels insecure about his message in a camp or conference setting. Pray

for the person, offering the speaker encouragement and feedback on how students are doing.

3. *To the campers:* This is the primary responsibility of every counselor. Knowing the campers and their family backgrounds, being a listener, being available to them, and displaying appropriate authenticity in order to build a friendship with each one is the ultimate task of the counselor. In addition, the counselor is usually called upon to lead small groups. This is not a natural skill for many people, so they must be trained.

Scheduling

For most camps, and even some weekend retreats, the schedule is a crucial contract for those responsible. When the schedule is not taken seriously—especially the larger the numbers get—the entire program can suffer.

For example, if a morning musician decides to take an extra fifteen minutes, the speaker goes over by another fifteen, and the seminar leaders maintain their right to their entire allotment of time, lunch gets set back thirty minutes. At a retreat this may or may not be a problem, depending on who is doing the cooking. But the larger the event, the more likely that innocent fudging can turn into a massive headache for everyone. Deciding on a schedule, asking the parties involved to do their best to stay on time, and everyone's being willing to flex when the need arises will make for a successful camp.

Some believe that the schedule should be made public, even for the students. But there are problems with this philosophy. First, when adolescents see in print something they do not want to do, they will often complain and even create discord among other students who started off neutral. Many a program has been sabotaged by one or two campers, who allowed their preconceived negative feelings to spoil the entire camp.

Second, when the need arises to change something—the hay got wet for the hayride, or the kitchen needs an extra hour, or the counselors suggest a needed adjustment in the schedule—the students have to be thoroughly and quickly brought up to speed. This has caused many a headache for camp directors. The best policy is to provide campers with a skeleton schedule and let the weekend or week unfold from there.

Budgeting

One of the more difficult tasks in putting together retreats of any size is trying to come up with a workable financial plan that fulfills the goals of the event without destroying the youth budget. Unless you were an accounting major at school, the issue of budgets and money may trigger legitimate fear. With advance planning and a little homework, however, you can avoid the "final bill blues."

All camps, conferences, and weekend retreats have certain fixed costs. Most of these are per person costs, and a few are one-time payments. Where most budgets are likely to get into trouble is with a second category, what most call the "program budget"—speakers, musicians, program necessities. The best way to handle both kinds of costs is to work backward. The reverse process looks like the following:

1. Decide which kind of experience the students need.
2. Decide the maximum dollar amount the students can afford, factoring in scholarships and subsidies from the church.
3. Determine the fixed costs of the trip, including transportation (always leave a little room here for a few empty seats), lodging, and meals.
4. Subtract the fixed costs per minimum number of students you anticipate from the maximum per student cost you can afford to charge. This is the amount available for miscellaneous program expenses, including those for speakers and music.

An important note: Be certain to complete this process *before* contacting speakers and musicians and before planning any expensive program item.

One way to fund a program is to contact potential donors who could underwrite the program budget, so that you only have to charge the campers the fixed costs. Such contributions

QUESTIONS TO ASK IN CHOOSING A RESIDENTIAL CAMP
GWYN BELDAN BAKER

1. What is the philosophy of this summer program? (Why are you doing what you're doing?)
2. What is the ratio of campers to staff? How old are the staff members? How are they trained? What qualifications do you look for when hiring staff?
3. What first-aid training or background does your staff have?
4. What is your waterfront program like? Who is in charge?
5. What are the camping facilities like?
6. How do you handle an emergency?
7. What is a typical day at camp like?
8. Can parents visit? What is the parental involvement in the program?
9. Who does the planning of the program of a particular camp? Who does the teaching, and what teaching methods are used?
10. Is evaluation used to improve the program and better meet the needs of the participants? Will the young people and parents have the opportunity to critique the camping experience?

can enable the leadership to produce high-quality results at a reasonable cost.

Planning Specific Activities

A central part of almost any camp or retreat is activities and program. After all, youth ministry is still youth ministry, and adventure is an important need of students. Games, humor, fun, and activities are all components of a well-rounded program. There is one piece of the program where we need to be very careful—competition.

Tony Campolo, in his book *Growing Up in America,* states: "The competitive lifestyle engendered by American society creates tremendous fear and self-doubt in the psyche of young people" (1989). Campolo suggests that we avoid competition in youth ministry. Whether or not we agree with his conclusions, we should take pause at his warning. If what we do programmatically causes a student to be hurt at the point of his or her basic need, we have undone everything we have been trying to do in the camp setting.

Here are three suggestions for effectively planning activities:

1. Make sure that everything done is an attempt to somehow address both the general and specific needs of your students.
2. Carefully think through and evaluate every aspect of the program that has been planned. Do not go with the first set of ideas that emerge from a brainstorming session or simply repeat something that has worked in the past.
3. Strive to achieve a good balance between activity that creates an atmosphere of warmth and community and leisure, and activity that allows relationships to deepen.

SUMMARY

Retreat events are essential ingredients of a comprehensive, effective youth ministry program. By its very nature retreat programming requires advance planning and strategic thinking. Many youth ministers believe that a balanced youth ministry program should have as a minimum the following camping programs: two weekend retreats during the school year, each having a significantly different purpose (that is, one discipleship and one outreach); a missions or service project; a summer camp or conference; and a wilderness or stress adventure.

These represent a minimum program. Many churches and youth ministry programs also include in their retreat experience strategies several short-term service and missions trips, a leadership planning and nurturing weekend, and a few smaller creative experiences.

A well-planned, creative, and comprehensive camping program will do more in one year to provide an environment where evangelism and discipleship can flourish than will a decade's worth of Sunday school and youth group curriculum.

WORKS CITED

Campolo, Anthony. 1989. *Growing Up in America.* Grand Rapids: Youth Specialties/Zondervan.

Dettoni, John. 1993. *Introduction to Youth Ministry.* Grand Rapids: Academie, Zondervan.

Ensign, John, and Ruth Ensign. 1958. *Camping Together as Christians.* Richmond: John Knox.

FOR FURTHER READING

Blest, Steve. 1988. "Taking the Church Beyond Its Walls." *Journal of Christian Camping* (March).

Cagle, Bob. 1989. *Youth Ministry Camping.* Loveland, Colo.: Group.

Cannon, Chris. 1994. *Great Retreats for Youth Groups.* Grand Rapids: Youth Specialties/Zondervan.

Clark, Chap. 1990. *Youth Specialties Handbook for Great Camps and Retreats.* Grand Rapids: Youth Specialties/Zondervan.

Cowan, Rebecca. 1985. "The Street Camping Experience." *Youthworker* (summer).

Crabtree, Jack. 1993. *Play It Safe.* Wheaton, Ill.: Victor.

Mattson, Lloyd. 1984. *Building Your Church Through Camping.* Duluth: Camping Guideposts.

Wright, Norman. 1968. *Help, I'm a Camp Counselor.* Ventura, Calif.: Regal.

28

HOW CAN PHYSICAL ACTIVITY AND SPORTS BE USED IN YOUTH MINISTRIES?

Timothy Voss

Raymond was always chosen last. It did not matter where the game was played—neighborhood, school, park, even church—it was always the same. Sometimes it was even worse, like the time when one team promised to bat left-handed if the other team would only take Raymond on their side.

What confused the Forrest Gump–like junior higher was the fact that church was supposed to be different. It was supposed to be a place where people accepted you for what you were, not for what you weren't. Yet it seemed the youth pastor was just as bad as the kids. He always seemed to make heroes out of the athletic kids and tolerate the awkward ones.

It was not that Raymond wanted to become a great athlete—he just wanted to have fun without having to feel dumb. Actually he would prefer enjoying a good game of chess, but he did want to hang out with his friends and have the opportunity to participate as an equal at least once in a while.

Where do the Raymonds of the world fit in youth ministries where winning is more important than being?

Unfortunately, Raymond's problem is standard fare for many youth ministry programs. Outreach events, retreats, and fellowships often structure "movement" as a part of bringing students together to enjoy and to experience being a part of a group. Yet the movement components of youth ministry programming are often not understood in their fullest dimensions. Whether the activity is building a pyramid during youth group or playing basketball in a church-sponsored league, physical activities can be powerful tools when planned, administered, and evaluated well—or they can be devastating to a developing adolescent.

In order to effectively use the ministry of movement, several questions must be addressed. First, what is the role of physical activity and team play in the development of the person? Second, how can movement strategies be implemented in such a way as to promote personal and spiritual growth? Third, how can competitive activities remain cooperative in nature? Fourth, what types of activities should leaders consider when planning the annual calendar?

ORGANIC SANCTIFICATION

Being thoroughly Christian involves recreation and play. Understanding this idea enables youth ministers to approach life with enjoyment and a sense of adventure. Many Christians have a hard time understanding and acknowledging God's ownership of the recreational side of life. Consequently, it becomes difficult for students to exercise an appropriate stewardship of their bodies and free time. They compartmentalize. God may be given their schoolwork, relationships, and even money. But the final frontier in personal sanctification, the last bastion of selfism for many Christians, turns out to be physical. When God has lordship over a student's physiology, including free time, well . . . there's nothing left! Sanctification is well under way. The student is beginning to change at the applied level!

Sports and recreation can again be approached as a key to spiritual recreation, or "organic sanctification"—to coin a phrase. Playing games as Christians may be the best test of adolescent faith. The discipline of sports when played as Christians sets the stage for living out a lifetime of adventure. Being thoroughly Christian usually involves recreation and play.

Playing Leads to Joy

Play can be defined as any activity approached voluntarily and with a free spirit (Holmes 1981). This definition reflects the very character of our God. God's actions are voluntary and free-spirited. Joy and pleasure are integral to His nature. He redeemed people for His own glory and pleasure and His pleasure leads to the pleasure of His children. The psalmist writes, "You have made known to me the path of life; you will fill me with joy in your presence, with eternal pleasures at your right hand" (Psalm 16:11). The Westminster Shorter Confession states that the chief end of man is to glorify God and enjoy Him forever. A key question the youth minister should face in attempting to understand this idea is, how is God's pleasure fleshed out in everyday relationships? The Christian's body belongs to the Creator. One important context for answering the question in the lives of young people is made possible when the church fosters healthy play and sport in this fallen world.

The free-spirited Christian is one who has integrated not only his body and free time with his faith but has allowed this attitude to pervade all of life. His is a life that ultimately depends on God and not on his success in the classroom or on the playing field. Celebration, joyful expression, and playfulness are appropriate responses to God. The key feature of the Christian's life is not that he serve; it is that he serve *joyfully*. This orientation offers balance and grace as the young person learns to practice the spiritual service and physical disciplines called for in Scripture. That is truly a winning attitude. Through play, recreational activities, and sports the church can help cultivate this attitude.

Play Leads to Integrated Lives

Integrated people can "work out" spiritually and physically at the same time. Their play is celebration and discipline together. This synergism can turn games upside down. It changes the perspective of competitors at a fundamental level. The opposing team is no longer viewed as the adversary— Satan remains the foe.

Actually, competition invites individuals and teams to be *guests* brought together for the purpose of bringing out the best in everyone. Sparks may fly in the heat of competition. Intensity can refine character. "As iron sharpens iron, so one man sharpens another" (Proverbs 27:17). Cheap shots—physical, verbal, or psychological—are not part of these games. Spectators can applaud great effort and plays on both sides. There is no place for negative cheering. Such active, dynamic competition stretches the whole person in relationship to God, others, and self. Young people experience firsthand what it means to be a temple-keeper, a person-keeper, and a body-keeper in the midst of challenge.

At the end of the nineteenth century, people working with the YMCA created two games to help young men develop traits of Christian character. The idea was described as "muscular Christianity." But as the games—basketball and volleyball—became more competitive, YMCA officials began to observe some unintended results. The sinful nature, rather than free-spirited play, was driving the competition. In response, Luther Gulick wrote and circulated among YMCA participants what he called a "Clean Sport Roll" for the competitors. Though first published in 1896, the principles are equally important today.

1. The rules of games are to be regarded as mutual agreements, the spirit or letter of which one should no sooner try to evade or break than one would any other agreement between gentlemen. The stealing of advantage in sport is to be regarded as stealing of any other kind.
2. Visiting teams are the honored guests of the home team, and the mutual relationships in all particulars [are] to be governed by the spirit which is supposed to guide in such relationships.
3. No action is to be done, nor course of conduct is to be

pursued, which would seem ungentlemanly or dishonorable if known to one's opponents or the public.

4. No advantage is to be sought over others except those in which the game is supposed to show superiority.

5. Advantages which the laxity of the officials may allow in regard to the interpretation and enforcement of the rules are not to be taken.

6. Officers and opponents are to be regarded and treated as honest in intention. When opponents are evidently not gentlemen, and officers manifestly dishonest or incompetent, it is perfectly simple to avoid future relationships with them.

7. Decisions of the officials, even when they seem unfair, are to be abided by.

8. Ungentlemanly or unfair means are not to be used even when they are used by the opponents.

9. Good points in others should be appreciated and suitable recognition given. (Hopkins 1951, 266)

This kind of winning attitude cannot always be seen by others. After all, it is first and foremost a conditioning of the heart. From the perspective of an observer, two people can be working out in a weight room with the same vigor and intensity. But one participant may have the goal of promoting vainglory, personal ambition, and drawing attention to himself by seeking that "cut" look. He may be one of the most skilled on the playing field—but also the most selfishly motivated.

The other athlete may have more selfless reasons for working out. He is actually dying to himself, being a good steward of his body, and becoming physically equipped for a lifetime of service and ministry. This is first and foremost a presentation of himself to God, a living sacrifice. He is being transformed into the likeness of God, and physical discipline is playing an important role in that transformation. This person is the true winning athlete. Like the first athlete, he may enjoy sweating salty drops in the weight room and on the playing field. But this pilgrim's sweat has a spiritual component that flows deep into the activity setting with the intention of changing lives all the way to the spiritual core, including his own life.

USING PROFESSIONAL
ATHLETES TO MINISTER
MARK MORING

Long before Michael "Air" Jordan soared into the NBA record books, Julius Erving was doing his high-wire act. Doctor J was the original His Airness; MJ was only the Air Apparent.

And, in my eyes, the good Doctor could do no wrong. If Julius Erving had told me, as a high school student, to go jump in the lake, I'd have probably done it. And if he had told me I needed to turn to Jesus, well, I'd have done that too. If it was good enough for the Doctor, a godly man, it was good enough for me too.

Such is the potential clout the professional Christian athlete has with high school students. But how do we best tap this valuable resource and use this "clout" as a viable witness to youth?

First, decide on an athlete you'd like to have address your group. Don't necessarily settle on a big-name pro; he or she may be difficult to land for a speaking gig. Lesser-known athletes (even bench sitters) often have testimonies that are as strong, if not stronger, than the headliners. (And don't rule out former pro athletes, or even college athletes, as potential guest speakers.)

Second, do your research. Just because a guy kneels for prayer after a touchdown doesn't mean he's a solid believer. Ask somebody about the athlete's daily walk. You don't know who to ask? Start networking: you know somebody who knows somebody who knows a pro athlete. One place to start: your area or state Fellowship of Christian Athletes leader. Another good source: *Sports Spectrum* magazine, which features dozens of Christian athletes every month.

Third, invite the athlete. Again, it's best to use networking here. Get someone who knows the pro to extend the invitation as a favor to you. Try to avoid the athlete's agent or his team's publicity department; you're likely to get some runaround by going that route. And don't ask the team chaplain, either; that puts him in a conflict-of-interest bind.

Fourth, once you land your speaker, exercise some control. Don't just invite an athlete to talk about Jesus; some speeches are so "canned" they lack vitality—or they're just not appropriate for your group. Give the athlete some direction—tell him or her about your students, what they're struggling with, what they're looking for, etc. Most athletes can "tweak" their talks to fit your group.

Finally, arrange for an after-speech question and answer period with the athlete. Your students will be itching to ask questions, and if they see the athlete is willing to take the time to give thoughtful answers, revealing a more down-to-earth "human" side, his or her message will pack that much more punch.

With a little work, you can land a winner for your group. It's worth the effort.

A GAME PLAN FOR PURPOSEFUL PLAYING

How can youth leaders learn to incorporate physical disciplines along with recreational play in their personal lives to prepare for the awesome responsibility of leading youth in sports and physical activities? Three steps come to mind: learn the plays, hang out with veteran players, and get lots of practice.

Learn the plays

For many youth workers, their own experience as a high

school or college athlete has prepared them for leadership.
Other youth pastors may choose to learn the plays by seeking
formal training in recreation and sports. They could do this
by adding an undergraduate minor or major in physical education or recreation. Another route would be to attend recreational education workshops offered by community schools
or agencies. Recreation that leads to re-creation and meets the
needs of growing adolescents is both an art and a science. The
science component is learning techniques for leading particular games or learning guidelines for explaining and monitoring rules in competitive events. The art of leading recreation
comes only through practice.

Hang out with veteran players

Locate and build a relationship with veteran players who
have integrated sport into their ministry. Excellent resources
are those persons in the community or at a Christian camp
who are involved in full-time "movement ministries." These
are professional physical education instructors and recreation
leaders. Next are certified coaches, outdoor enthusiasts, and,
sometimes, athletes who have trained under quality coaches
that established character development as a priority in their
programs. (Sport does not automatically build character. That
happens only if the coach *intends* to build character through
the arena of sport.) Watch these individuals at work. Develop
a trained eye. Raid their files. Ask them to critique your work
whenever possible.

Practice the plays

Only after playing a game, leading a game, and evaluating
the results of the game does the leader begin to have a feel for
how a game can create enthusiasm in all the participants.
There is a vast difference between declaring the winner of a
game and having everyone walk away with a sense of being a
winner personally for having participated in the event.

Learn to approach play from the spiritual point of view.
Study, pray, memorize, observe, mentally rehearse the most
excellent ways to play and lead. Consider your own attitude
and responses. What are you modeling through your leader-

ship? Consider the attitude and responses of the participants. What are they learning through their play—about themselves? about being one of God's children? about enjoying life? The outcomes will be unmistakable: lovely, true, noble, right, pure, and admirable.

PLAYING IT SAFE(LY)

It is essential that youth leaders know as much as physical education teachers regarding health and safety precautions. Injuries are going to happen! Therefore, the youth leader must *anticipate.* Youth (and parents) need to be forewarned of potential hazards and risks.

Proper equipment is essential. Maintain equipment regularly. Walk the playing field before a game to identify and communicate potential hazards. Remove glass, rocks, and other obstacles. Provide liquids on hot days. It may be wise not to require youth to participate in a game or activity they do not feel comfortable doing. Match people up by size and ability. Know proper skill progressions. Train students to respond immediately to a certain command to freeze action in the event of a potentially hazardous situation. Realize that the higher the level of competition is raised, the more chance there will be for injury.

Whenever you are preparing for physical activities, take appropriate precautions to minimize the chance for injury, and then be ready to act if an injury does occur. Is ice available? Is the first-aid kit at hand? Do you have emergency telephone numbers? Do you have the proper forms to document what happened and how you responded? Proper follow-up is also important.

Know the participants. Know the proper progressions regarding skill learning. If you have doubts, try the activity with your leaders beforehand. Establish procedures and practice them with other staff members. Earning certification in coaching, first aid and CPR (cardiopulmonary resuscitation), and lifeguard training is a good first step for everyone planning to work with youth.

Having a trained leader on the site is the most effective way to avoid mistakes that cause needless injuries and to avert possible liability suits. Wrong play stifles growth. I know one youth leader who planned a gunnysack race on the grass using plastic garbage bags because he could not find burlap sacks at the time. This may have been safe. However, because rain was feared, the activities were moved indoors to a hardwood surface.

During the race, a number of the players slipped on the floor and fell hard. However, the leader wanted everyone to complete the activity. A girl fell and shattered her elbow. The youth leader was caught completely unprepared, and the ministry was sued. The question raised in court was, "Was this accident foreseeable?" To a layperson, maybe not. To a trained individual, the answer was yes. Youth workers must realize that they will be compared to other professional leaders who deal with youth in the community. Peers will establish if the actions taken were reasonable and prudent.

EFFECTIVE STRATEGIES
FOR "MOVEMENT MINISTRY"

What kinds of activities and sports should you consider as you plan purposeful play in the coming months? Three strategies are suggested as beginning points for future program development. The strategies are *outdoor activities, sports,* and *cooperative games.* Although leaders may want to continue to use games that have been enjoyed by students in the past, consider how these three types of events could enrich your students' enjoyment of and experience of being God's people.

Outdoor Activities

Outdoor adventure activities are rich in opportunities for spiritual awakening and growth. Day trips are a good way to start. Cycling, hiking, canoeing, and orienteering are worthwhile skills to develop. Team-building and trust-building leadership skills are also a must. Advancing to overnight trips and extended excursions in the out-of-doors requires more training. The risks are greater. But so are the growth factors. One week on an outdoor adventure can sometimes accomplish more in the life of a youth than what can be internalized throughout the rest of the year. It takes the students out of the comfort zones of their everyday lives and forces them to become resourceful and reflective.

Leading groups in outdoor activities requires careful planning. Done right, the actual event looks effortless and seamless to the participant. It's fun! However, leaders know better. It takes hours of planning and preparation to make a trip safe and enriching. Christian camps offer ideal opportunities for outdoor leadership skills training and working with various age groups. Many camps have staff who are certified in leading rock climbing, rappelling, and various other challenge courses as well as having seasoned wilderness-camping skills. Some camps will offer counselors free room and board and a small stipend each week for the summer. The gain of experience is well worth the investment of time.

Sports

Sports in youth ministry consists of everything from a pickup basketball game after youth group gathering, to students against leaders in volleyball, to an official community softball league sponsored by a church for local youth and adults. Because sporting events, sports celebrities, and team logo clothing are an integral part of the youth culture, many students thrive on the enthusiasm built from playing the games. But the spiritual and character-building benefits come from using sports as living object lessons. Youth pastors can readily move in and out of spiritual topics surrounding the playing of sports. Teachable moments during and after game play are numerous as leaders informally interact with participants.

A word of caution should be sounded to all who use sports events on a routine basis. Remember that sports in our culture is already a natural religion—an end in itself. To make it distinctively Christian is neither obvious nor easy. Some very destructive things can happen in the midst of competition among Christians. Leadership must be prepared to respond to this and be purposeful in the way it handles sports activities if playing is to accomplish spiritual goals.

SPORTS AND THE CHRISTIAN:
IS IT JUST A GAME?
TONY LADD

Sports hold a significant place in American society, and many Christians enjoy them as much as anyone else does. While such attachment is not necessarily unusual, the degree to which Christians are embedded in a social structure that has become increasingly secularized and anti-Christian is a cause for concern. Should the values of participation, the ethics of play, or the way one views sports be different for the Christian? If so, how?

One elder from an evangelical church who has all the "right" answers on abortion, child abuse, and Sunday evening services indicated that an All-American basketball player was justified in taking extra money from alumni (under the table) since he was simply playing a game. According to the elder's thinking, the sports experience is outside the realm of real life and therefore beyond conventional laws of morality.

But wait a minute—by making such exceptions, aren't Christians forfeiting to non-Christians the ethos of sports? Especially since Christians value sports as an arena for character and value development, such neglect is potentially detrimental to living Christianly when the models for behavior emerge out of a philosophy of greed, selfishness, and ego supremacy.

Although educators and pastors testify about Christians providing a vital witness of their faith through sports, Christians have not heard nor have we listened to those outside the faith who claim that Christian behavior in sports is often no better and may be even worse than that of non-Christians. The stories of unsportsmanlike behavior in church league games and Christian colleges are legion. And in Christian colleges, for example, the giving of special, and often illegal, treatment to athletes in the areas of financial aid and academic performance occurs all too frequently. Yet Christians have remained silent while rules have been broken.

Solutions to problems in sports for Christians are difficult to define since the Bible does not give specific directives. With sports as with many aspects of life, the reader of the Bible must identify Christian action from general principles rather than from specific commands. What is needed within the Christian community is the development of a *philosophy of sports* for Christians. Such a philosophy would provide a theoretical framework to set forth the role of sports in society rather than a restatement of platitudes or testimonies about sports. If sports have meaning and value for the Christian, it should be "taught" rather than "caught."

By doing this the Christian can take the offensive and set the agenda for our culture. Christians should establish teaching models based on Christian ethics rather than secular values. Summer youth programs could teach ethical actions as well as fitness or sports skills. Sports clinics could combine Christian living strategies along with scientific study. In an era of social and cultural relativity such an emphasis is timely.

The time for action is now. At the present time sports are controlled by non-Christians who use the cultural frame to entice us into the arena. Although we think we are building God's kingdom through sports, we may be constructing a social/cultural frame that is molded after the world.

For example, a church may decide to join the local park or church youth basketball league. A plea goes out for participants through the youth group newsletter, announcements, and personal contacts. Twelve students sign up. The person in charge is excited. Some participants and spectators naturally have winning as the driving goal. They and their parents expect the best players to play and substitutions to be made based on a strategy for accumulating the most points. Practice is a must. Two players are even non-believers whose friends signed them up to improve the odds of winning.

Other students just want to be involved on a team. They may have never been asked to play for a team, and they join for fun and recreational play. They expect everyone to have equal opportunity to play and have a good time. For these players, winning, like practice, is fun but not necessary. Neither group has a bad motive for its interest. Lack of initial planning and communication, however, almost ensures that someone will be disappointed. Such disappointment may even translate into damaged relationships with the youth pastor in the future.

Whenever sports are being used for ministry, whether in an organized league or as a way to build enthusiasm for the group, be sure to consider the following:

1. The needs of the students
2. The purpose of the overall event that is the context of the particular sports activity
3. The level of skills required
4. The availability of leadership for monitoring and facilitating play
5. The long-term goals you have for the group that will be involved

All of these issues are important factors in determining how participants will be divided into teams, how the activity will be led, and to what level of intensity the competition will be allowed to escalate.

It is fitting to recall that the modern Olympics were begun with the goal of reducing hard feelings between countries and fostering unity between diverse cultures. Yet modern culture is losing the Olympic spirit in the race to win. Prime-time sports convey a society lost to selfism. Christians, however, need to have a passion to be all that God desires—in Christ. This is ultimately what youth should experience. Perhaps one of the greatest competencies students can learn is how to compete without having to put down, taunt, or consider less important those against whom they play.

Cooperative Games

Most games used by youth leaders are zero-sum competitions. This means that in order for someone to win, someone else has to lose. Even the practice of choosing sides for a competition can be a win-lose experience for some. The person picked last is the loser. The right fielder or blocker in pickup games is subtly reminded by his assignment that he has no talent. But there are many creative ways to pick teams that enhance the growth of *all* participants. The fastest way I ever saw a leader divide a group into two was with four commands: "Everyone find a partner and stand back-to-back." "One partner sit down." "Those standing are team A." "Those sitting are team B." No pecking order promoted in this youth group!

Beyond picking teams according to chance rather than skill, there are a number of ways to emphasize cooperation rather than competition. Games or activities that require teamwork to overcome a physical challenge and involve every participant may not produce the same wild cheering as a competitive volleyball game, but they may produce better results in personal self-esteem. For example, students can be challenged to move through an obstacle course or over some physical barrier such as a rope or wall. Students can be intentionally "disabled" for the game, using blindfolds or slings. The physical event becomes dependent on the problem-solving skills and cooperative attitude of all group members.

After playing cooperative games, debriefing sessions are important.

Problem-solving activities naturally provide opportunity for higher-level thinking. Spiritual connections can be made.

Youth become better connected with each other, themselves, and with God by the end of game time. Even the youth leader can demonstrate the importance of stepping out of the traditional command-centered style of leadership to a more nurturing leadership mode, helping youth learn how to plan and execute activities themselves.

Even sporting events such as basketball can become fun for all levels of skill by having everyone play with his "off hand." (In other words, if they are right-handed, they must only use their left.) Or consider using a beachball instead of a volleyball so that less skilled players can compete as well.

Other traditional contests, such as relays or strength events, can be altered to minimize skill and emphasize the fun of giving an enthusiastic best effort as a team. Students pick up on the attitude of the leaders that it really does matter how you play and not just if you win. Groups learn that, unlike in school and community activities, winners and losers are not determined by skill. Rather, everyone has a chance to make himself or herself a winner simply by getting involved and cooperating.

CONCLUSION

There is more to youth ministry in the area of physical activity and sports than is commonly assumed. The breadth of the field may be a bit overwhelming. It takes time and a team effort to attain competency in the broad field of movement. Some large churches are finding it desirable to hire full-time physical education and recreation leaders. Their jobs entail what is being called "life-span involvement." This means offering developmentally appropriate and scientifically sound activities for all age groups from preschool through old age. Some new churches are even designing their facilities so that the gymnasium becomes the feature space to be used throughout the week for a wide variety of programming. Other churches go so far as to offer midnight basketball to their communities, or a well-equipped weight training facility. Visiting these churches and talking to their leadership will prove a valued source of in-service training.

Recreation, games, sports, playing, activities, and competition provide a wonderful and challenging ministry with youth. Keep moving! "May God himself, the God of peace, sanctify you through and through. May your whole spirit, soul and body be kept blameless at the coming of our Lord Jesus Christ" (1 Thessalonians 5:23). When youth ministers can advance peace even in the midst of competitive sports and physical activity—while still maintaining quality—then the ministry promotes the Prince of Peace.

WORKS CITED

Holmes, A. 1981. "Towards a Christian Play Ethic." *Christian Scholars Review* 11 (2): 138–47.

Hopkins, Howard C. 1951. *History of the Y.M.C.A. in North America*. New York: Association.

FOR FURTHER READING

Bucher, Charles A., and March L. Krotee. 1993. *Management of Physical Education and Sport*. Chicago: Mosby Year Book.

Cagle, Bob. 1989. *Youth Ministry Camping*. Loveland, Colo.: Group.

Ford, Phillis, and Jim Blanchard. 1993. *Leadership and Administration of Outdoor Pursuits*. State College, Pa.: Venture.

Gillquist, Peter E. 1979. *The Physical Side of Being Spiritual*. Grand Rapids: Zondervan.

Glover, Donald R., and Daniel W. Midura. 1992. *Team Building Through Physical Challenges*. Champaign, Ill.: Human Kinetics.

Heintzman, Paul, Glen E. Van Andel, and Thomas L. Visker. 1994. *Christianity and Leisure*. Sioux City, Iowa: Dordt College Press.

Miles, John, and Simon Priest. 1990. *Adventure Education*. State College, Pa.: Venture.

Rohnke, Karl. 1991. *The Bottomless Bag*. Dubuque, Iowa: Kendall/Hunt.

Seaton, Don. 1992. *Physical Education Handbook*. Englewood Cliffs, N.J.: Prentice-Hall.

Walters, Albert M. 1985. *Creation Regained*. Grand Rapids: Eerdmans.

29

HOW CAN MISSION OUTREACHES BE EFFECTIVE IN YOUTH MINISTRY?

Paul Borthwick

Mission outreach for youth groups has taken its place with retreats and lock-ins as a normative and expected part of the youth program. Today's youth leader often needs to know how to be a travel agent, cross-cultural minister, and tropical health expert—in addition to the traditional roles of pastor, teacher, and counselor.

Unfortunately, the zeal to participate in these outreaches often carries with it little consideration of why one should pursue them. Youth leaders find themselves expected to take the teenagers to Mexico or Haiti, but the rationale provided ranges from "We've always done this on spring break" to "Every other youth group goes to Tijuana" to "It's even a better experience than wilderness camping!"

Corresponding with the youth mission trip trend is the reality that the terms *discipleship* and *youth ministry* are sometimes not linked. Some people (whether parents, church leaders, or students) see youth ministry as an intermediate phase, a sort of holding pattern in the spiritual growth of teenagers in which the goal is to keep them out of trouble and in the church until, at age eighteen and beyond, they can make an intelligent and intense commitment to Jesus Christ.

When this perspective persists, mission trips become just another experience, like taking the youth group to Disney World's Epcot Center for a virtual reality encounter with another culture—yet with few expectations of spiritual growth, challenge, or life change.

These concepts of youth ministry and youth mission teams miss the mark for two reasons. First, they cheat the youth leaders because the leaders get reduced to being baby-sitters or entertainers whose top objective is to keep the junior or senior highers busy. Second, they cheat the youth because they concentrate on the students' immaturity and perpetuate that immaturity rather than taking advantage of their vast potential for growth.

So how can youth be discipled? How can the leader go beyond the fun-and-games approach to youth ministry? How can the potential for growth be tapped in the teenagers with whom youth leaders work? Of the tools and programs developed for discipleship with youth, the outreach/mission project provides the greatest all-around context for growth.

MINISTRY CONTRIBUTIONS
OF YOUTH MISSION OUTREACHES

Cross-cultural outreaches—whether local or international —fuel youth ministry like gasoline on a fire. Spiritual vitality, social growth, leadership development, and evangelistic results all come as part of an effective youth outreach endeavor. Students return home talking about life change, altered goals, and deeper-than-ever commitment to servanthood.

Our experience teaches that short-term mission projects, properly executed and led, well trained for and followed up, provide the best opportunity in youth ministry for discipling and developing teenagers as leaders and as growing people.

We base this premise on eighteen years of intense involvement in our youth ministry with short-term summer mission teams. The results we have seen in students and in families have made our church so firm in its commitment to outreach teams that the idea has now infiltrated our young adult ministry, our singles program, and our senior adult programs. We have experimented with cross-generational teams, and we are presently considering sending out a team made up of families.

MISSION PROGRAMS IN YOUTH MINISTRY

Every church or youth organization needs to determine what form its mission outreach will take. One-day programs? Two-week summer teams? Teams sent over the school vacations? Large teams? Small teams? Teams with leaders functioning as disciplers (with a ratio of one leader to every four or five students) or teams with leaders serving as "chaperons" (dedicated to supervising larger groups)?

We send out teams on one- to four-week projects. The groups travel cross-culturally, ranging from our own country to Latin America, the Caribbean, Europe, Africa, and, on one occasion, Asia. Over the years, youth teams have built houses, painted buildings, dug wells, led backyard Bible clubs, preached at churches, led evangelistic campaigns, conducted sports camps, and participated in any number of other ministries.

Many of our projects have focused on physical labor (painting, building, simple construction, pouring cement). We keep the ratio of leaders to students consistent at about one to four. We initiate and set up most projects by contacting the mission agency or local host organization or church. Planning begins between nine and twelve months before the project, although some (such as a building project in Burkina Faso) can take two years to plan, while others (a trip to Trinidad after a coup in Haiti forced us to cancel our trip there two weeks before our intended departure) have been put together in a matter of weeks.

This has been our pattern, but every church or youth group can design its own plan. An evaluation of resources (funding, contacts, time available for leaders), church or organizational support of the idea, church or organizational history and experience with teams, and other competing programs help determine what is realistic.

Having observed our own experiences as well as the experiences of others, we would suggest that several general principles affect youth mission outreaches most positively:

1. Start small and build. Youth leaders sometimes want to start with a glamorous "Let's go to China and rebuild the Great Wall" project. Instead, start with a two-day trip. Take a small group to a cross-cultural setting nearby—an inner-city shelter for the homeless, repair work at a nursing home, or a service project at a Salvation Army camp for kids.

Youth groups that start with overly ambitious projects run the risk of either failing (building up expectations and then not being able to fulfill them) or of creating youth who will be unwilling to undertake less glamorous projects in subsequent years (after you go to the Great Wall, who wants to go to Chinatown?).

2. Get leadership and parental support. Youth leaders may find it easy to get students excited about mission service projects, but church leadership and parents need to be recruited as well—preferably eight months or more before the project team departs (see below for expanded ideas on this subject).

3. Plan ahead. The youth leader who calls in May asking for help in setting up a July trip scares me. The teams that are truly effective take six or seven months to recruit and train leaders, inform parents, raise money, set up the details with the hosts, and train students.

4. Integrate mission teams with the overall program. The most effective youth mission outreaches flow together with the overall youth ministry.

- Students from discipleship groups participate. Team members return as youth group leaders, thus making the team not only a mission outreach but also a defined part of the leadership development program.
- The summer calendar is modified so that mission outreach becomes an extension of rather than an addition to the youth program.
- Students who do not participate on teams offer prayer support, help raise finances, and serve as "senders."

5. *Recruit to cover your weak spots.* Youth leaders who build their ministry on being people-persons often need help with administrative details. The wisest and most effective youth leaders recruit the help of others early in the planning stages. The disorganized youth leader needs to recruit administrative planner-types. The younger youth leader recruits older volunteers to help build credibility with parents, and the inexperienced youth leader recruits leaders who may already have cross-cultural missions experience.

GETTING STARTED

If you are willing to consider a mission outreach team for your youth, what do you do next?

1. *Consult existing resources.* Several publications are helpful in the planning process and—more important—in understanding the philosophical basis for undertaking these outreaches. A list of resources is provided at the end of this chapter.

2. *Consult other youth workers or churches who have had experience.* Contacting churches that have sent youth teams works well because their feedback offers a reality check. Talking with others as to the details and practical outworking of a mission outreach may result in your modifying your own plans. These experienced people can explain how some of the principles in this chapter worked (or did not work) with their teams. By listening to others, you can learn from their mistakes, copy their successes, and send better prepared teams.

3. *Look for service opportunities.* "I want to do a missions outreach project, but where can I take my youth group?" That's the most common question I hear from youth leaders. Don't wait for an exotic chance to paint the Taj Mahal or build rafts in Tahiti. Look for practical, cross-cultural opportunities close to home—a home for the elderly, a neighborhood church serving people of a different ethnicity than your own, a shelter for the homeless.

As the youth group grows accustomed to local ministry, look for other challenges. Make contact with a church-supported missionary or a youth leader from another country.

These personal contacts provide the best platform for enlarged projects across cultures.

4. *Look for hosts who believe in the vision.* The greatest results on mission teams come when the hosts believe that they also are part of the discipleship process. Hosts who see the youth team as a form of cheap labor will have a neutral or negative impact on the young people. But hosts who believe that the *primary* purpose of the team is to change the lives of the participants will contribute greatly to the growth of all involved.

COMMON QUESTIONS

What are the most important ingredients of an effective youth outreach team?

The most important ingredients fall into three categories: effective leadership, effective training, and effective follow-up.

Leadership

The premise is carefully worded: *properly executed and led.* The reason for this is obvious. When projects are sloppily executed or led by those who are ill-equipped to work with teenagers, the results can be disastrous. To find those who will do best as leaders for such teams, we look for people with the following qualities and characteristics:

Administrative ability. At least one leader on a team must be a detail person. There will be a myriad details (especially on the international teams!), and if these are not cared for, the team will function poorly and opportunities for discipleship may be lost.

Rapport with teenagers. Some of our team leaders are in their twenties, and others are in their fifties; age neither guarantees nor negates success with youth. The key ingredient is the ability to listen to, understand, and enjoy teenagers. The person who has a great zeal for missions but who has a short temper with those who giggle, talk after "lights out," and turn their noses up at a sardine-spread sandwich will not fare well on a youth team.

Spirituality. We can only teach others that which we have learned ourselves; Jesus taught this in Luke 6:40. If youth mission projects are to maximize the potential of discipling the youth who are involved, the leaders must be spiritually established themselves. The marks of spirituality for which we usually look are consistency in quiet times, a solid understanding of Christian doctrine, commitment to discipling others through relationships, and leadership by example—modeling the Christian lifestyle.

Adventuresomeness. It is entirely possible for a leader to have all of the characteristics listed above without having any desire to venture out in cross-cultural service. A person may be a great administrator, a gifted leader of teenagers, and a man or woman of God, but if he or she will drop dead at the sight of a tarantula, it is probably better that he or she not lead a team to South America.

The leaders of a mission team can excite the students about the wonderful new things they will learn on a team experience. If the leaders take on the new experiences as an adventure from God, the students will most likely follow. If, however, the leader is unduly timid about new experiences, a substantial part of the students' learning process may be thwarted.

Cultural sensitivity. Though a team leader need not have a degree in anthropology, it is important that each leader be able to view the host culture with empathy and respect. Immature high school students see unfamiliar customs ranging from cute to weird. The adult leader must help students to step outside their biases and learn from other people.

One final observation about leadership. We have found that the best people to lead youth mission teams are those who have worked with our teenagers throughout the year. The adults who already have an established rapport with the youth are more likely to be able to make use of the intensity of a mission team to the fullest in terms of discipleship.

Training

Training is the most important variable in the preparation process. In general, we have seen that increased training yields increased growth as a result of the mission outreach. To maximize growth in our team members, we exhort students to begin praying about involvement as much as eight months before the project. In March (all of our teams operate in the summer), an official presentation of the project opportunities is made, and in April we begin to accept applications.

Then we oversee fulfillment of the requirements. The preliminary requirements for participating in a project include the following:

1. A written testimony
2. A financial deposit
3. Parental permission
4. A commitment to fulfill the team requirements

If a student meets these conditions, we accept that student onto the team with an "official" acceptance letter. If he/she cannot meet the requirements, then we investigate the reasons; we try to go out of our way to make it possible for a student to participate.

If the teenager cannot write the testimony, it is usually because of lack of assurance about personal faith or lack of understanding of what it means to be a Christian. In our experience, a number of students have made personal commitments to Jesus Christ through such investigations.

After initial acceptance, a student is then given the team requirements. These training essentials include the following:

1. Scripture memorization
2. A geographic/cultural report on the area/culture to which the team is going
3. Participation on our team training retreat (a three-day boot camp type of weekend)
4. Continued involvement at team meetings (at least four) in which details and plans are discussed, team unity is built, a spiritual foundation is laid, and some cross-cultural education takes place
5. An appearance before the church missions committee
6. Raising the remaining finances

7. Reading a missions-oriented book
8. Participation in a team commissioning service (in which they will recite the Scripture verses they have memorized and are sent out by the laying-on-of-hands by church leadership)
9. Completion of a number of assignments and readings in our team training manual
10. A commitment to report back to the youth group, church, and school about their mission experience

Additional requirements include recruiting prayer supporters, attending "how to paint" seminars (conducted by a painting contractor), and applying to our missions committee for financial aid (as needed). Other churches include fund-raising activities and local community outreach as part of the requirements.

We have been amazed to observe that student interest and participation in these projects have increased in proportion to the number of requirements. Our first team had fewer requirements, but as we have progressed, we have demanded much more of those who want to participate. Their zeal to serve has been in direct relation to the amount that has been demanded of them. If students are made to pay the price of fulfilling hard requirements, they tend to value the service project much more.

Follow-Up

Continuity of relationship between leader and student after the trip makes the difference between a life-changing experience and a "been there, done that" experience notched in the belt of an overstimulated generation. Follow-up involves taking the mission outreach experience and integrating it into "normal" life back home—whether at the church, in the youth group, at school, or at home.

Immediate follow-up can include:

1. A team debriefing where all gather to share their most profound experiences and their personal growth applications for life back home

2. A follow-up written evaluation by the leader, which asks questions about the team and encourages specific ways to respond to the experience
3. Various reports to the youth group and church—the theme being "Here's how we'd like to encourage you in your faith by sharing what we learned on our missions outreach"

Longer-term follow-up can include:

1. Involving students in a missions reading program
2. Recruiting missions-project students into weekly discipleship groups
3. Exposing the participants to visiting missionaries
4. Encouraging consistent prayer on behalf of the people served on the outreach
5. Getting the team together for a six-month reunion to discuss how their lives have been changed as a result of the service project

Whatever specific programs or ideas are pursued, follow-up focuses students on how they can grow long term as the result of a short-term experience.

What mission outreaches can be undertaken by a small church with a limited budget?

The best cross-cultural outreaches do not need to be overseas. When the church is limited in terms of financial resources or availability of leaders' time, local outreaches are less expensive and less time-consuming. Any experience of service outside one's own culture can provide the learning experience of missions. English-speakers serving in a Hispanic neighborhood, suburbanites serving in an urban or rural setting, or rich serving with poor all provide the context where students can learn that the body of Christ crosses racial, ethnic, and economic barriers.

Another related question pertains to youth group size. How small is too small? If your interest is in getting the maximum amount of work done, then size becomes significant, but if your priorities are seeing students' lives changed and building relationships with people of other cultures, then a team of one leader and one student can be highly effective, especially in teaching students that one life can make a difference!

What are the most important issues to consider when choosing a group to partner with?

We ask the following questions:

1. Do the hosts really believe in seeing our students' lives changed through their exposure to serving others in another culture (see above)?
2. Will there be opportunity to befriend people in the culture, or will we be assigned to a work location where we are isolated? Our goals include helping our students develop friendships across cultures, worshiping with the local church, and experiencing the food, lifestyle, and family structures of other cultures.
3. Will our hosts train us with regard to the culture we are serving in so that our team gets a true sense of being missionaries adapting to someone else's world? We would rather be trained by those who live there than run the risk of making cultural blunders.
4. Do we agree with the basic theological tenets of our potential hosts? We do not want to spend time arguing theology during a brief service project.
5. If our hosts are missionaries from our culture to another, do they exemplify missionary work by serving the people of the local culture? If our hosts are dedicated to serving and empowering others, then they model the kind of missionary service we want our students to imitate.
6. Will there be opportunity for spiritual ministry, or will it be physical labor only? Sharing music, testimonies, or even an evangelistic opportunity gives our students a stronger sense of being God's agents in another culture.
7. Do our hosts have experience in working with USA teenagers? If they do not, we feel compelled to give our hosts a cultural briefing themselves so that they understand the culture that we bring with us.

How can you get the local church behind you—mobilizing the
church to support and encourage youth mission outreaches?

Objectively, the youth leader can point church leaders to
some of the existing resources on short-term missions (see
above). These often contain the convincing anecdotes that
will help church leaders say, "This is an idea for us!" The
same result can be achieved by putting the pastor or church
leadership in touch with other pastors or church leaders who
believe in the vision. In this respect the ACMC (Advancing
Churches in Missions Commitment) organization (P.O. Box
ACMC, Wheaton, IL 60189) can provide a valuable network
of churches dedicated to youth mission outreaches.

Subjectively, the most convincing proof of the effectiveness of mission outreaches is the returning students. In the
first summer of our involvement, church leaders were either
ambivalent or opposed to the idea of teenagers on cross-cultural mission projects. After the teams returned that summer,
student growth was so pronounced that the church leadership
gave its full support to youth mission outreach—to the point
now that it is one of the church's most celebrated summer
programs.

What information and preparation do we need to provide for
parents?

Obviously, parents should know as many details of the
project—cost, dates, destination, leaders, mission—as early as
possible. In addition, leaders can convince parents of the serious nature of the outreach project by reviewing with them the
requirements and training for students.

We seek to establish credibility by listening to the parents'
concerns. We try to find answers to the questions they have
about health and safety as quickly as possible, but we also see
the mission outreach as an opportunity to train parents in
their faith. Inevitably the project will involve some danger
and therefore some risk, and we invite parents to grow in
their own faith by challenging them: "We're inviting you to
grow with us in your faith this summer—as we trust God to
take care of us, and as you trust us to God's care." A gentle
challenge like this reminds parents that while we as leaders

will do our best to plan and prepare, we are all ultimately entrusting ourselves to God.

What growth are we looking for in students?

The preparation of both students and leaders for mission outreach yields the best results of any aspect of our youth ministry in terms of discipling and building Christian qualities in young people. Leaders have grown out of students who, at first impression, would have been written off as dormant in their spiritual lives. Many parents have commented, "We sent our teenager off as an immature youth and received him back as a growing young adult."

Where has the growth come from? We have seen measurable growth in our summer team participants in the following areas. (We initially discovered these growth areas by accident; now we factor them into our planning for teams so that we create a maximum growth environment.)

Quiet Times

The idea of a personal, daily devotional time is familiar to many church youth, but few would claim much success in this area. Two-week projects have enabled us to create a controlled environment where there is a set time each day for this devotional exercise. Students have learned how to make entries in a daily journal (a requirement on many of our teams), and they have experienced an increased degree of consistency in prayer and Bible study. One student commented in an evaluation that the most valuable aspect of his team was that "I got into the habit of either memorizing a verse or having a quiet time every morning."

In other evaluations (we have conducted post-project evaluations since 1979), when asked, "How did you grow spiritually?" most students list the habit of daily quiet times as the primary way that they grew.

Character Development

The intensity of these work projects has enabled us to see the students grow in depth of character. Because of stress, a new environment, and exposure to people who live much differently than we, the students have grown in endurance, flexibility, and thankfulness. We teach them the difference between Western values and Christian values by letting them see that not all Christians are the same, look the same, or worship the same. This cross-cultural education has helped students develop personal priorities. One said, "I see how much time I spend shopping; when I saw how poor some people are, I began to rethink my habits. Owning a lot of 'things' just isn't as important to me anymore." Another student, in response to the freedom he experienced on a mission team, came home and sold his television set because "I saw how much time I was wasting watching TV."

It should be noted that many parents have noticed growth in the diligence of their youth as a result of mission teams. Most teenagers, especially those under age sixteen, have never experienced a forty-hour workweek. When we work on these projects, we work at least that much, and many students are stretched into realizing their potential as workers.

Personal Responsibility

Perhaps the best maturity factor that has come as a result of mission teams is the way students have grown in being responsible for themselves. From the preparatory requirements to the close of the project, students are reminded that they are both members of a team and responsible for themselves. They learn that their behavior directly affects the success of others. If they fulfill their requirements, the team benefits. If they are lazy in their work, the team suffers. Although some would disagree with this, we have allowed students to go on shopping trips in groups of two or three in foreign countries. Our underlying philosophy has been "If we treat students like adults and give them responsibility, they are more likely to respond as adults."

Leadership

The responsibilities learned and the experiences of youth missions projects have had a wonderful effect on our youth group. Of the more than one hundred students who have gone out on teams in the past, more than 50 percent are involved in some sort of leadership in our youth group today. As a result of seeing the success of their teams on mission projects, they have returned with a deeper commitment to serve in the leadership of the youth ministry. Serving on a mission team has given students a feeling of responsibility. This sense that "we fulfilled our responsibility there" seemingly has led to increased willingness to undertake responsibilities here. The positive effect of working on service teams has assured students that God wants to use their lives, and this assurance has given many of them courage to be used by Him in our youth group.

Witness at School

It is sometimes stated that those who want to be missionaries abroad should first be witnesses at home. This is true, but we have found that the opposite has also been true: those who go out on teams (many of whom would never speak about their faith before they went) come back with a new zeal to share Christ with friends at school. The reason? Perhaps the deeper commitment a project requires has had a corresponding effect on their boldness in witness. Perhaps the exposure to missionaries has given students more understanding of the need to proclaim Christ. Whatever the cause, the effect has been more students who are sharing the love of Christ with others.

The project requirements ask that when the participants return home they talk with their peers about what they have learned. This reporting-back mechanism has taken on various forms. One student did a report in a geology class on erosion in the Yukon. As a result, he was asked why he went to that area, and he told the class about the basis for missionary service. Another student produced a slide show for her sociology class based on her "missionary" experience in Newark, New Jersey. As a result, she had an opportunity to share her testimony. She was then invited to show the production to two other sociology classes!

Servanthood

As a result of mission teams, many of our students have gained a deeper sense of what it means to serve others. The team emphasis on our projects has taught them how to care for each other. It has been a beautiful experience to watch our students care for those who get sick, and through the course of a project, everyone gets an opportunity to serve as an encouragement to others.

The lessons of servanthood have been transferred to our home environment as well. Students have learned the importance of serving the members of their own families through the team "family" experience. The work they have accomplished on the teams has been of the behind-the-scenes variety, and this has taught them the importance of all the work done in Christian ministry that goes unnoticed and unappreciated. There has been marked increase in our students' willingness to take on obscure tasks in ministry, a factor we attribute to the mission teams.

Worldwide Perspective

Those who work with youth may find it easy to be frustrated with the shortsightedness of teenagers. Today's crisis—whether it be an exam or a new pimple—tends to dominate their thinking. We have been refreshed to find that those who have gone on team projects have gained a healthier perspective of the world and of their individual lives. Their perspective of God has enlarged as they have seen new lands, new people, and new ways to serve Him. As a result, the everyday problems they confront have seemed less significant.

This worldwide perspective has also resulted in a greater desire by our students to submit to the lordship of Jesus Christ, especially with respect to His call on their lives to missions. Some of our students are headed toward missionary service. Others are not sure, but they are opening themselves to the call of God. The exciting dimension is that students are becoming more informed about and committed to the work of God throughout the world, and they are starting to see their lives in this respect.

How spiritually mature must a student be to participate in mission trips?

Sonlife Ministries has attempted to answer this question.

Their conclusions may surprise some people. Though normal developmental maturity is necessary for mission trips, depth of spiritual maturity, as demonstrated in a willingness to express one's faith in a vulnerable manner, may not be as necessary for mission trips as for personal witness among peers.

The following chart suggests levels of spiritual maturity that may be evidenced by various types of mission involvement. M1 represents the lowest level and M8 the highest level of spiritual maturity necessary for the types of service described. As in other kinds of development, people can function at all levels below their stage of development but probably will not function above that level. For example, a person at the M4 level can also participate comfortably at levels M1 through M3 but will not be willing to serve at levels M5 through M8.

Ministry as an Indication of Spiritual Maturity

M1 Cross-Cultural Group Experience in Foreign Setting
M2 Same Culture Group Experience Outside the Church
M3 Urban Group Experience (farther than 100 miles from the church)
M4 Cross-Cultural Individual Experience
M5 Urban Individual Experience (farther than 100 miles from the church)
M6 Local Individual Ministry to a Different Age Group
M7 Local Group Ministry to Peers
M8 Local Individual Ministry to Peers

SOURCE: Sonlife Ministries. M7 was added to the Sonlife chart by the editors.

The point Dann Spader's organization is attempting to make is that youth ministers who lead mission trips should not confuse participation in trips with spiritual maturity per se. Instead, such trips should lead to other activities that give evidence of greater progress in one's spiritual journey.

FOR FURTHER READING

ACMC (Advancing Churches in Missions Commitment). P.O. Box ACMC, Wheaton, IL 60189.

Anthony, Michael J., ed. 1994. *The Short-Term Missions Boom*. Grand Rapids: Baker.

Borthwick, Paul. 1988. *Youth and Missions: Expanding Your Students' Worldview*. Wheaton, Ill.: Scripture Press.

_____. *How to Plan and Develop a Youth Missionary Team*. Grace Chapel, 3 Militia Drive, Lexington, MA 02173.

_____. *The Missions Training Manual*. Grace Chapel, 3 Militia Drive, Lexington, MA 02173.

Burns, Ridge, and Noel Becchetti. 1990. *The Complete Student Missions Handbook*. Grand Rapids: Zondervan/ Youth Specialties.

Campolo, Tony. 1983. *Ideas for Social Action*. Grand Rapids: Zondervan/Youth Specialties.

Eaton, Chris, and Kim Hurst. 1991. *Vacations with a Purpose*. Colorado Springs: NavPress

Youthworker. 1989. (Fall). Missions issue. Youth Specialties, 1224 Greenfield Drive, El Cajon, CA 92021.

The Short-Term Mission Handbook. 1992. Evanston, Ill.: Berry.

Stepping Out: A Guide to Short Term Missions. 1992. Seattle: YWAM.

30

How Can Mentors Be Used in Youth Ministry?

Lavon J. Welty

As parents, we believed that we had good, open communication with our teenagers. Yet we knew they were struggling to establish their identities separate from us. We also knew they lived in a cultural context where parents are often looked on as not being "with it" or "cool."

Consequently we were always so glad that our church encouraged mentoring relationships for every youth in the church. Although the strength of the relationships differed somewhat between our teenagers and their mentors, we knew that their mentors would be there when they were needed. We give much credit and gratitude to those caring adult mentors for how our teenagers turned out. They gave time and energy to listen, to care, to love unconditionally, when our teenagers needed them.　　　　　　　　　　　　　　　　—A parent

✝ ✝ ✝

Today is Monday, and, empty coffee mug in hand, Mark sighs heavily as he turns the ignition of his car. The good news is, the car started—this has recently become a less common occurrence. The bad news is, the car started—Mark now has no excuse for going back to bed for another hour of much needed sleep. He would rather be golfing like the senior pastor who gets Mondays off. As youth pastor, Mark must wait until Thursday.

Mark stops for his usual coffee and donuts. Today he decides he will delay the inevitable list of phone calls to be returned and finish his breakfast at the donut shop. His thoughts return to last evening's youth group meeting. It did not go well.

His recollections are interrupted by the sound of a recognizable voice. An elderly member of the church, Joe Hankins, is sitting two booths over, talking to a man Mark has seen before but does not know. The voice has gotten his attention, but it is the topic that keeps it.

JOE:	Did you hear about Mel's son—who got arrested for possession of drugs last week?
JOE'S FRIEND:	Yeah. I did. Sure is too bad. Mel must really be taking it hard.
JOE:	I suppose so. But what can parents do anymore? Kids won't listen. Just do what they want and think that they'll never get caught.
JOE'S FRIEND:	When we were raising our kids, we never even heard of drugs. Never would have thought we would have them here in our town, much less in a good Christian family like Mel's. When we were growing up we did some pretty dumb things [laughs], but we never would have done anything like drugs.
JOE:	You don't think so? I wonder. If they would have been available, what would have kept us from it?
JOE'S FRIEND:	We had some morals back then. Kids today don't have morals and don't have parents who will punish them if they do wrong.

JOE: I had something else. Once my dad caught me smoking. He really tanned my hide. Made me mad! But my uncle took me out behind the barn and sat me down and talked to me. Told me about smoking and how he thought it was a filthy habit. Told me why he decided to quit. Said he wanted to quit a long time before he finally did but just couldn't because he was so hooked. He was hard on me, but deep down I appreciated it. I knew my uncle was really worried about me.

JOE'S FRIEND: Kids don't respect adults anymore. And we got to understand that today's kids don't have anybody like your uncle around. Teachers, parents, Sunday school teachers, coaches, youth pastors—you know they all care, but none of them really has time for them. Besides, most adults are such authority figures the kids don't trust them anyway.

JOE: I have to agree with you 100 percent. The adults are too busy, the kids are too busy, nobody has any real time for each other. If a kid is in trouble or even about to get into trouble, who takes the time to be with him, to listen to him, to teach him *how* to make his own decisions? Who can he turn to?

"Youth pastors . . . authority figures . . . too busy." The words hit him like a shot from a cannon. Last evening Mark had related to students in a highly authoritarian manner. In his own words, he had "lost his cool" when they became rowdy in the middle of his Bible study. In the students' own words, he "really came down on" them.

Mark is experiencing conflict about his role. He feels distressed as he considers his dilemma. *As a youth pastor, I am supposed to be there for them. But after last night I am not even sure how much I want to be with them! Nor am I sure they want to be with me. I just cannot keep up with the demands of this job. So many needs among the students—so many limitations on my part.*

Mark's thoughts race as he reflects on his students. He is painfully aware of what Mel's son, Gary, is experiencing. Gary is not the exception either. Several others in the youth group have been in trouble recently. There was Ann's pregnancy and Tom's DUI arrest. Here come the conflicting and stressful thoughts again! Mark knows how desperately each student needs a caring, listening adult who will love him and help him with his struggles. Just as the man said, "They don't have anyone."

But how much can a youth pastor realistically do? It seems to take fifty hours each week just to keep the ministry going. Mark soon realizes that much of his tension results from his anger boiling over onto the group last night. And then he recognizes that he was not so much angry at the students as he was venting frustration. He has become increasingly disturbed over his perceived inability to respond meaningfully to the needs that are so blatantly apparent in the students' lives.

What can a youth pastor do in response to needs that are bigger than he is? What can a youth pastor do to ensure that a student has someone to turn to when he is either unavailable or for some reason interpersonally disconnected from that student? Where does a youth ministry leader go for help?

THREE CONGREGATIONS: ONE BOLD CONCEPT

St. John Church is a typical church located in a large urban area in the Midwest. With 700 members, it has fifty-five young persons of high school age, about half of whom participate actively in its youth group. St. John employs a youth pastor.

St. Paul's Church is a small church located in the same city. It has 75 members and only six high school youth. Some of its members look enviously across town at St. John, wishing they too could employ a youth pastor. There just is not enough money.

Grace Church is located in the same town, with a membership of 125. Its youth sponsors want to find a way to provide more availability and depth of relationships between the adults in its congregation and the students in the youth group.

Although these three congregations face different circumstances, they all turn to one strategic solution. Each decides to incorporate mentor relationships into its ministry with youth. As they explore the possibilities, the congregations recognize that mentoring relationships can be used to address the lack of adult care, support, and guidance that so many students experience.

DEFINING MENTORING RELATIONSHIPS

Many adults can look back on their childhood and teenage years and think of an adult who became a friend, one who took special interest in them. It may have been a relative, a godparent, a teacher, or someone else who simply cared for and showed they loved them. These persons were mentors, though they would never have described themselves as such. Will today's youth be able to look back and pick out one or two adults who took interest in them like that? Will they recall adult friends outside their families who were available when they needed someone to talk to and were too embarrassed or afraid to talk with their parents?

Many will not. Too many will reflect on their teen years with disappointment and anger because of the absence of meaningful relationships with parents and other adults. Churches that provide mentor relationships as part of their youth ministry not only assist parents but also fill gaps in the adult community's relationship with its adolescents.

In the mentoring process, leaders work carefully with parents, the young person, congregational leaders, and members to identify an adult who will be a mentoring friend in a young person's life. What once happened naturally is made intentional as part of the larger youth ministry program. It can happen in small congregations as well as large.

GETTING MENTORING RELATIONSHIPS STARTED

All three congregations mentioned were deliberate in considering mentor relationships. Their first step was to send several persons to become fully versed in the philosophy and mechanics of developing mentor relationships. St. John sent its youth pastor along with the education commission chair to a youth ministry workshop. St. Paul's sent two lay persons to the same workshop, and Grace Church sent their youth sponsors. Then each congregation sent these persons to visit an out-of-state congregation that had started mentor relationships with its youth. They returned to explain the program to appropriate congregational leaders. In all three, the senior pastor was enthusiastic. At St. John, the education commission was sold on the idea and became the vehicle to gain the support of the church board and elders.

With less organizational structure at St. Paul's, the church board received the report and became the primary sponsor of the idea. The same process moved the idea along at Grace.

SELECTING A MENTORING PROGRAM COORDINATOR

Once the leaders in the three churches were supportive of initiating mentor relationships, the next step was to select the person or persons who would coordinate the program. At St. John, it seemed to fit naturally into the task of the youth pastor. While the youth pastor would continue to have direct contact with youth in other ways, this would fit well into the equipping function of the ministry. At St. Paul's, the two persons who had researched the program agreed to fill this role. The sponsors were selected at Grace.

These coordinators began their new role with ten initiatives for which they would be responsible, ten tasks that would be the foundation upon which an ongoing mentoring ministry would be built. A brief listing and description of each initiative is provided as an explanation of how you can start and sustain adult mentoring ministries for your students.

Initiative One: With congregational leaders, choose a target group for beginning mentoring relationships.

In some congregations, particularly larger ones, it may be best to begin with only the younger youth, such as those entering grades six, seven, and eight. Interested high school youth can be included, but since many are already overcommitted, they may be less open to such involvement.

Initiative Two: Draw up a list of expectations for mentors.

The essential purpose of mentor relationships is to provide caring support for youth, and any adult in the congregation is a potential mentor. The primary expectation for mentors is to meet regularly with the youth. Some congregations give the mentor-youth pairs complete freedom to choose their own activities. A minimum level of interaction for such a relationship to develop and be sustained is a once-per-month activity. The range of possibilities for doing things together is endless.

Some congregations see mentor relationships as a setting for specific educational purposes. For example, a mentor can be a special guide through catechism experiences or preparation for baptism. Some congregations have used the relationship to focus on life planning, with emphasis on planning for life after high school. A curriculum is found to help guide this focus.

Mentors will be expected to attend activities planned for the entire group of mentor-youth pairs. They will also be open to informal contacts as opportunity permits. This may be a brief conversation after worship services or a telephone call now and then. An excellent time for such contact is just before or after an activity significant to the young person, such as a music program or athletic event. As time goes on, if the relationship develops smoothly, the youth may take the initiative in seeking out the mentor for conversation after services, in phone calls, or in stopping by.

Mentor relationships are expected to last in a formal, intentional sense at least through high school. Often, meaningfully developed relationships will extend many years after graduation. Obviously there are circumstances when they will not be of that length. In our mobile society, some mentors will move away. At times a pairing may not work out as well as hoped for. Added responsibilities in church or work for the adult may necessitate dropping out. These, however, should be exceptions. The best experiences are those that last over the years. Mentors should be aware when they begin that they are making a serious commitment.

The single greatest problem in mentor relationships occurs when mentors agree to enter a relationship but fail to give time to it. Most youth, although they may not show it, are eager for such a relationship. When a mentor fails to follow through, it leaves the youth disillusioned and frustrated because promises are not kept.

Initiative Three: Meet with the parents and carefully explain the program to gain their approval and support.

It is crucial that parents are given special attention to be sure that they understand the basic approach in mentor relationships and how they are carried out. Some parents, especially where there is a high degree of family dysfunction, feel threatened when they think of their son or daughter relating to another adult. They must understand that a mentor simply stands alongside to help. Parents should be assured that they will be part of the process at every step along the way. Mentors will never take the parental role. Mentors support and encourage, listen and care. Most often when parents understand the objectives of a mentor relationship, they become its strongest supporters.

When the program is first initiated in a congregation, it is good to invite all parents to meet together. In subsequent years, as the program continues, brief telephone calls can be made to see if the parents of youth coming into the program have any questions about it.

Initiative Four: Meet with the youth in the target group to explain the program to them.

The coordinator needs to describe the mentoring program to the targeted youth. This could be done at a special meeting to which all youth in the target group are invited—with pizza, of course. Or he could take a few minutes in a group meeting or Sunday school class. Another approach is to invite all students and their parents to meet together. Although not all youth must participate in order to have a successful program, asking the young people present at this meeting whether they would *like* to have a mentor is to be discouraged. The potential for one student's negative attitude to affect others' interest levels is real. It is better to ask for this commitment in a later contact with each youth individually.

MENTORING ACTIVITIES
LAVON J. WELTY

Here are some ideas for mentor-youth activities:

☐ Attend an amusement park
☐ Go to church together sometimes
☐ Bake/cook
☐ Clean someone's house or rake his or her leaves
☐ Attend a movie together and discuss it
☐ Fix a meal for someone
☐ Go bowling
☐ Attend a concert
☐ Study the Bible together
☐ Visit a museum together
☐ Attend a major league sport event
☐ Wash cars

Adapted from Steve Ropp, *One on One: Making the Most of Your Mentoring Relationship*. Newton Kans.: Faith & Life; Scottdale, Pa.: Mennonite. Used by permission.

Initiative Five: Describe mentor relationships to the entire congregation.

Since any adult in the congregation could be asked to serve as a mentor, it is important that all members have some level of understanding of the program. One way to do this is for the coordinator to request a few minutes in a worship service to describe the program. An article in the congregational newsletter or in a special written communication to the entire congregation is also a good way to inform the body. Some church leaders not only want to describe it to the congregation but to receive formal approval in a business meeting. The idea here is that if the congregation gives its formal endorsement, they will be more supportive of the program.

Initiative Six: Arrange for the matching of each young person.

When mentor-youth relationships are first initiated, matching each youth with a mentor will likely be the most time-consuming task. The coordinator will need to do this carefully. The following steps are suggested:

1. Meet with the young person and his parents together. Review briefly the objectives of the program and check for any remaining questions. Now is the time for the young person to say whether he wants to participate or not. If there is any hesitation on the part of a parent or the youth, proceed with caution. Try to discern the cause of the hesitation and speak to it if possible.

   If the youth decides to participate, ask him or her to choose at least three adults in the congregation he or she would see as acceptable mentors. Discourage naming any relatives. Adults already paired with another youth are not eligible, since a mentor will relate only to one young person. The youth's parents may suggest possible mentors, and you as coordinator may also have some to suggest. What is important here is to be certain that the young person is comfortable with all three suggestions without necessarily any order of priority.

2. After receiving the names of three persons, it may be well to check with the pastor and other leaders to see if any view one as a better fit than the others. Approach only one adult from the list at a time, suggesting that he or she take at least one week to consider the opportunity. Encourage the person to pray about it and possibly to counsel with a trusted friend or the pastor as to whether he or she would do well to assume this responsibility.

3. When an adult agrees, you have the happy privilege to inform the youth that he or she has been paired with a mentor! When all the youth have been paired, arrange a brief commissioning service. This can be a time during a worship service when each pair is introduced, along with a special prayer of dedication and commissioning.

RELATIONSHIP-BASED
MINISTRY MODEL
DANIEL J. WEYERHAEUSER

In the last ten years of youth work, I have learned important lessons about ministry (many as a result of doing things the wrong way). Beyond the obvious daily lesson of my need to "be strong in the grace that is in Christ Jesus" (depending upon Him in prayer and reading His Word), there has been no lesson more significant than coming to see the crucial value of *relationship* as a vehicle through which to train up a teen in "the way he should go." In other words, more than the weekly program we run, there is nothing more important we can do for our students than to train adults and, through them, provide significant relationships for as many students as possible.

The principle I see operating again and again is that, as a youth worker, my ability to impact a student goes hand in hand with how deeply involved I am in that student's life. And yet even as a full-time worker, I can't have a significant relationship with more than a few guys in any given year.

As I've gone back to the Word over the years, I find this principle in operation throughout the history of God's call for His people to minister to each other. Note Paul's *heart* for his people, for example (1 Thessalonians 2:8; 3:9; Philippians 4:1; 2 Corinthians 2:4). He not only taught them as students in a class, he enjoyed and embraced them as dear brothers and sisters in a relationship.

It seems as well that this relational approach to ministry also dovetails beautifully with the transitional issues of adolescence, since teens have begun to differentiate from their parents and are *looking* for relationships outside of the home as a testing ground for their developing sense of identity. It is a unique time for the "community" to play a significant part in that young person's life. I continue to be amazed at how naturally these relationships blossom and the power they have as a tool of the Lord for shaping young hearts and minds for Him.

As a result of this lesson, we have developed a ministry model that seeks to provide these relationships for as many students as possible. In addition to our weekly meeting and Sunday school, we've recruited up to twenty adults who each meet with two students weekly for at least a year-long discipling relationship. (We would define *discipleship* as a "purposeful relationship" with an older Christian. It is not a class, study, or small group, but a significant relationship that has a purpose: life training.) These adults also form one of our church's small groups, so that I can meet with them weekly for training and encouragement. Without a doubt, the most powerful and long lasting changes we have seen happen in ministry have taken place in the context of these relationships.

How do you get adults involved? In a word, "Vision." Most adults who love the Lord are exhilarated when they realize the impact they *can* have on teens. Many are hindered by myths that keep them from ministry, like "I have to be young, athletic, and like rock music for a teen to care about what I think," or "I can't have impact unless I receive a lot of training." In truth, if an adult truly loves Jesus and is willing to love a few students and spend quantity time with them, those students' lives will never be the same. It's a model I believe any church could adopt if the key leaders

> (even if they are volunteers) have a vision for it and know how to pass that vision on to other adults. And when it comes to the teenagers' desire to be discipled, we have found that if you offer relationship, they will come.

Initiative Seven: Provide support for the mentors.

Some mentors will be highly confident in relating to their young people. Some, however, will struggle. Some may discover that they really do not know how to relate to a teenager as easily as they thought. Others may lack communication skills. Still others may wonder if they are doing what they should be doing because they receive so little response from the youth. Phone calls to mentors, group meetings to discuss their feelings and experiences, retreats for training, and special luncheons to celebrate mentors are effective means of providing encouragement. Furthermore, your support for them provides an excellent model for their roles as mentors of students.

Initiative Eight: Arrange for group meetings of all youth with their mentors.

Occasional group meetings of mentors and youth can be an important part of the program. In small congregations this can be as often as monthly, thus supplementing or even replacing some youth group meetings. In larger congregations, group meetings may be scheduled less often. These extended meetings can be primarily fun and games, with refreshments. However, they also provide an excellent opportunity to invite a special guest to talk about an issue of concern in the church or community. The input can give mentors and youth some important agendas for dialogue.

Initiative Nine: Conduct an annual evaluation of the program.

Typically the "year" in congregational life is concurrent with the school year. Toward the end of the year, evaluating the experiences of the youth-mentor pairs is an important part of the total program. Such evaluation can be as extensive as taking time to talk with each mentor and youth. Or it can be a more casual checking in with them. The purpose is to find out how things went, giving both mentors and youth opportunity to voice any concerns that they have as they look back over the year. For example, an evaluation will help to identify mentors who are frustrated because their young person will not talk—or young people frustrated because their mentors do not give them opportunity to talk!

An evaluation may identify those pairs that, sadly, are not working out for a variety of reasons. If, for example, the mentor has agreed to serve but seems not to have time for following through, some intervention can be undertaken. This may go to the extent of deciding to name a new mentor. An evaluation will also bring to light situations where a young person who was reluctant to express dissatisfaction directly to his or her mentor might actually disagree with the mentor's responses to the coordinator.

An evaluation need not only identify problems in relationships. It can also bring out the best of the experiences that have happened with youth-mentor pairs. These can in turn be the basis of reporting to the rest of the congregation in an annual report. Much of the activity between youth and mentors will have taken place behind the scenes. Congregational leaders will be interested to hear how things are going.

Initiative Ten: Develop an annual budget for the program.

There will be some costs in carrying out a mentor relationship program. Travel, mailing, and phone expenses will be incurred. Other expenses will include training events, group meetings or retreats, and curriculum materials as needed. These expenses should be part of the congregational budget as a portion of the congregational investment in youth ministry. It will be a concrete way for the congregation to show that it cares for its young people.

MENTORING:
A CALL FOR EFFORT AND EXCELLENCE

Following the above procedures for initiating a mentoring program does not guarantee success. At St. John and St. Paul's

the mentoring ministry of adults became a significant component in the lives of both congregations. At Grace Church,
however, the program hit an insurmountable roadblock. In a
meeting of all the parents (Initiative Three), several banded
together and stood solid in their opposition. These parents
could not conceive of sons or daughters relating in this way to
another adult in the congregation.

This was a group that was generally opposed to *any* new
ideas in the congregation. The "other side" knew full well
that the families in this group were not happy, healthy ones.
They knew they feared that "family secrets" would get out.
Yet, no amount of explaining could convince this negative
group that mentors would never take over a parenting role.
Sad to say, they fought any attempt to make such relationships available to any of their youth. So the leaders of Grace
Church finally gave up.

The experience of Grace Church should serve to challenge
to excellence rather than discourage to complacency. The
intergenerational bridge between youth and adults in many
congregations is fragile and needs strengthening. Mentor relationships provide a meaningful support system for youth.
Carried out carefully, they also have the potential for infusing
new life into tired, run-down congregations as the teenagers
also give life back to adults! Mentor relationships are worth
the effort—just ask the young people at St. John and St.
Paul's. Better yet, wait ten years and ask them who, other than
their parents, most influenced their lives when they were
teenagers.

(If you and your church leaders are interested in exploring
this exciting adventure, the ten initiatives are described in
much greater detail in my book, *Side by Side, Mentoring
Guide for Congregational Youth Ministry* [1989; Newton,
Kans.: Faith & Life; Scottdale, Pa.: Mennonite].)

FOR FURTHER READING

McPherson, Miles, with Wayne Rice. 1995. *One Kid at a
Time: Mentor Handbook*. Colorado Springs: Youth Specialties, David C. Cook, Church Ministries Resources.

Ropp, Steve. 1993. *One on One, Making the Most of Your Mentoring Relationship.* Newton, Kans.: Faith & Life; Scottdale, Pa.: Mennonite. An excellent resource for youth-mentor activities.

Varenhorst, Barbara B. 1988. *Training Teenagers for Peer Ministry.* Loveland, Colo.: Group. Although written as a training tool for youth-to-youth relationships, it provides excellent help for training mentors in how to relate to young people.

Welty, Lavon J. 1988. *Blueprint for Congregational Youth Ministry.* Newton, Kans.: Faith & Life; Scottdale, Pa.: Mennonite. Sets the mentoring relationship in the larger context of the congregation's ministry with youth.

_____. 1989. *Side by Side, Mentoring Guide for Congregational Youth Ministry.* Newton, Kans.: Faith & Life; Scottdale, Pa.: Mennonite. A basic guide for setting up mentor relationships in the congregation.

31

HOW CAN WE MAKE SMALL GROUPS EFFECTIVE IN YOUTH MINISTRY?

Jana L. Sundene

Karen, a high school junior and a volunteer in her church's junior high ministry, leads a weekly Bible study with three sixth-grade girls. Karen's time with these girls includes not only the scheduled one-hour Bible study but also time spent going to the girls' school sporting events, taking them Christmas shopping for their families, and occasionally hosting slumber parties. If anyone asked the three twelve-year-olds, "Who do you want to be like when you grow up?" the answer would be unanimous: *"Karen!"*

Jeremy, a high school senior, considers the highlight of his week to be his Wednesday night accountability group meeting. The group consists of Jeremy, three of his best friends, and Paul, a college student serving as a youth ministry intern at Jeremy's church. The five guys began the group to support their commitments to sexual purity in their relationships with girls. What has developed is much more, however. They have found themselves sharing and praying about every area of their lives. Jeremy's friend Walt summarized everyone's feelings last week when he said, "I don't know how I could make it without you guys."

Henry is a basketball coach at the local high school as well as being a volunteer in a parachurch ministry on campus. Eight years ago he made an arrangement with a local church to use its gym facilities as a vehicle for outreach. For the last six years, guys from the neighborhood have been invited to take part in a six-week summer basketball league. As a part of their participation, Henry requires them to commit to weekly small groups he and volunteers from the church lead. The small groups are evangelistic, exploring basic truth from the Scripture concerning the person of Jesus and the nature of salvation. As the teenagers become more interested, or in many cases come to a personal relationship with Christ, Henry makes use of church and parachurch leadership resources to take them to the next step in their spiritual journey.

Henry is particularly gratified when he observes Levon, a high school senior who came to Christ through the basketball outreach ministry three years ago. Levon now leads a small group of younger guys and next year plans to go to college to prepare for his own future as a youth minister and coach.

✝ ✝ ✝

Small groups—they seem to be everywhere, in every shape and in every form. You can find small-group Bible studies on public transportation, over computer on-line services, in middle school classrooms before and after school, in offices over lunch. They *are* everywhere (Hunt 1984, 9–10). Youth ministry is no exception. One youth pastor recently touted small group ministry as "the most essential tool for discipleship in the youth ministry today." Because of their recognized contribution to personal lives and youth group growth, small groups have become the norm rather than the exception for the practice of Christian youth ministry.

WHY SMALL GROUPS?

So what is the *big* deal about *small* groups? Furthermore, how important are they in the context of youth ministry? These questions can be answered by suggesting several unique contributions small groups can make in the lives of students.

1. *Small groups provide an opportunity for relational intimacy.* Meaningful, open, and committed relationships are increasingly rare. In a society filled with dysfunctional homes; technology that promises instant and continual psuedo-intimacy through television, movies, and computer forums; and a youth culture that is increasingly isolated from significant intergenerational relationships, many students find themselves in defective, unsatisfying relationships. These students look for love but soon despair of discovering a friend's love that will touch them at their deeper, personal levels. In a such a barren relational desert, a small group can be an oasis standing in stark contrast to the mirages that have promised but failed to deliver the relief and refreshment of interpersonal intimacy.

2. *Small groups provide a context for learning through the sharing of ideas and life experiences.* The teacher's "telling" may never produce what the student's "experiencing" accomplishes. Small groups encourage the interactive exploration of ideas and options rather than the more traditional educational approach which is built upon a teacher-to-group handing down of information. Many learn better in the environment small groups provide, but adolescents are particularly needful of those contexts because of their developmental stage in life.

3. *Small groups provide an opportunity for youth leaders to mentor students "life on life" within the context of community and the diversity of the body of Christ.* Because of the dynamics of the first two contributions above, well-developed small groups become what youth ministry veteran Kevin Cobb describes as "safe" arenas where students can share deeply. In small groups, students are engaged at their point of spiritual need and offered understanding, encouragement, challenge, and—most important to them—support. The end result is that students become increasingly aware of their need for dependence on God, interdependence on one another, and

responsibility for taking ownership of their personal spiritual growth.

When one combines the valuable contributions of small groups with an understanding of the spiritual values and expectations of Generation X and the Millennial Generation, the question is no longer *should* we be doing small groups in youth ministry but *how* can they be done most effectively?

EXPLORING THE OPTIONS

Literally dozens of methods for incorporating small groups can be identified. As a guide for exploring the plethora of options that exist, eight major kinds of small groups will be discussed. Although this is not a comprehensive list, the types are a comprehensive representation of what can be found.

Discipleship Groups

Discipleship groups are those groups that have as their focus training believers in principles of the Christian faith that will enhance growth and/or obedient practice of the disciplines of the faith. In other words, discipleship groups focus on the familiar emphases of personal Christian growth.

Some discipleship groups incorporate Bible study, prayer, and accountability. But there are also *Bible study groups* and *prayer and accountability groups,* which tend to focus more heavily on one aspect or another of the growth process. In a discipleship group a mature Christian adult or student is responsible for the group's learning experiences. The leader's role is to direct, guide, and facilitate the members' steps toward spiritual growth.

Discussion Groups

Discussion groups are generally formed to aid in the exploration of issues that affect spiritual growth. They are often used within a large ministry event to divide big groups into more appropriate settings for personally exploring a topic or idea. These groups may or may not have an assigned leader, but someone will assume responsibility for focusing and directing the conversation toward the discussion of the chosen topic.

CHOOSING A CURRICULUM
BARRY ST. CLAIR

Christian publishers churn out hundreds of new products every year, producing a sometimes dizzying array of options for small group leaders. How can we choose the best material? Here are some ideas.

PLACES TO GO

1. Go to God in prayer. He knows the type of curriculum you need.
2. Get wise counsel.
   a. After you have decided on your topic and purpose, ask your pastor, staff, and informed lay people about the best books they have seen on the topic. A glowing report from a reader is better than a glowing advertisement on the back cover.
   b. If possible, find others who have taught a similar topic and ask them for their evaluation of what they used.
   c. Call your denomination or organization's headquarters to see what material they have to offer. Their theology and approach to ministry may closely match yours.
3. Browse in your local Christian bookstore. An informed manager or worker can lead you to the appropriate section of the store and may even tell you which books or authors people rave about.
4. Do a search of *Christian Books in Print* (the bookstore should have this reference work). This guide will list all the Christian books in print by author, title, or subject. Go first to the subject listing and think of a few possible key words that may highlight your topic. You can

do the same thing for titles. If you subscribe to an on-line service, you may be able to search books through your personal computer.

QUESTIONS TO ASK

1. *What type of curriculum do I want?* Some target such small groups as Sunday schools, training classes, or vacation Bible schools. Sunday school materials have long-term goals you will want to understand. For example, some want to expose small groups to each book of the Bible over a period of years. Others deal with a biblical response to issues.

   Other small group series are broader in nature, providing studies to fit many kinds of small groups. They often consist of short paragraphs followed by questions and blanks for group members to complete. Still other books can be read alone or used with small groups. They usually have questions at the end of each chapter and/or an accompanying leader's guide.

2. *Is the content compatible with where my group is headed?* One youth worker chose discipleship material to use for a youth lock-in. Afterward she couldn't understand why her students yawned through her spiritually rich sessions. Perhaps she forgot the proverb, "Hope deferred makes the heart sick" (Proverbs 13:12). If youth come to an event with the expectation of fun and games, the Sermon on the Mount probably won't fly.

   Look at the back cover and introduction of a book to find its purpose. Does it coincide with the purpose of your group? Look at the chapter titles. Do they fit the topics you want to cover each week? Is there an appropriate number of chapters for the number of weeks your group plans to meet?

3. *Is this book compatible with my theology and approach to the Scriptures?* Certain presses cater to certain theological persuasions. If you are unfamiliar with a certain publisher, ask your pastor.

4. *Is this book helpful for small group discussions?* Do good discussion questions follow each chapter? Is there a leader's guide? Are the questions open-ended enough to provoke discussion? Are the chapters of appropriate length to be given as assignments?

5. *Is the cost prohibitive for some members of my group to purchase?* Often bookstore owners will give volume discounts.

6. *Is this book well written?* Is it organized well? Does it capture attention? Are issues clearly explained? Are points well argued?

7. *Is this resource suitable for the age group I am leading?*

Such discussion groups can be particularly effective at an outreach event. More personal contact with leaders and peers allows the spiritually sensitive youth to ask questions or react to the Christian truths that have been presented. Similarly, discussion groups are effective in meetings aimed at promoting growth in Christian students. Students find the small group context to be a place where they can meaningfully relate the content to their own world of home, school, extracurricular activities, and needs.

Additional contributions made by discussion groups include facilitating a sense of community or better communication among volunteer staff in a leaders' meeting. Small group discussions also enable students to connect interpersonally with persons they would not normally know well. Both of these latter contexts demonstrate the community-building power of dialogue as individuals share ideas and feelings with one another.

Evangelistic Outreach Groups (Apologetic)

Evangelistic outreach groups may be formed from students who have attended a parachurch ministry activity or a coffeehouse ministry where intellectually curious students are likely to gather. Other groups emerge as youth workers or teachers make their way onto the school campus and befriend students who do not know Christ. Providing a forum atmosphere, these groups set the stage for an exchange of ideas and emotions among those who are sincere seekers and those who are mature believers.

Given the thirst for relationship connections and the atmosphere of religious diversity, students, particularly late adolescents, are often eager to explore matters of spirituality in such forums. These groups are necessarily led by mature, biblically grounded Christians who are prepared to take the role of listener to students and apologists for the faith. Students will have many challenging questions. Leadership, therefore, must be comfortable with the process of sojourning with the students as they think critically about the foundational propositions of the Christian faith. The reward, of course, will be that Jesus is proclaimed in a manner that is truly relevant to seeking hearts. Joy will come as the Holy Spirit removes the "veil" and students enter into a personal relationship with the Way, the Truth, and the Life, Jesus Christ.

Short-Term Groups (Parent-Teen, Retreat, New Believer)

Groups that meet for a designated, relatively short period of time also have a significant place in youth ministry. One common example of this type of group is the small group format used in a retreat setting. Retreats are short-term, intense opportunities for students to relate to others and consider spiritual issues that impact their lives. Many decisions are made at retreats—from salvation decisions to relational reconciliation decisions to life direction decisions. Small groups are one of the ways to channel the intensity and energy that is often generated on those retreats.

Of course, there is an infinite number of ways in which students and adults are joined together for a short, previously determined time period with a clear, specific focus that shapes the direction and the experiences of the group. For example, a parent-mentor-teen small group can result in more healthy communication between adults and students (Habermas and Olshine 1995). These groups may need to be formed for a short time only, so as not to overextend the patience of either the parents or the teens!

New believer follow-up groups are often short-term commitments as well. If a rather large group of students comes to Christ at one time, they may need to be brought into small groups to introduce them to the basics of Christianity and ensure that they receive support as they begin their walk of faith. An important benefit of new believer small groups is the obvious opportunity to "graduate" into a more long-term discipleship group.

Short-term small groups can also assist youth ministry leaders in handling intense areas of ministry and growth or special student needs. For instance, a small group can be formed to assist students entering high school or about to graduate from high school. Short-term small groups can be a productive way to prepare students for a missions or service project.

As is evident from these descriptions, with a clear focus and a little creativity, short-term small groups can be used effectively to produce long-term results.

Focus Groups

The function of a focus group is to perform a particular task for the ministry. Perhaps the most common example is the youth group steering committee or planning committee. However, focus groups may also plan an upcoming event, or brainstorm for the future of the student ministry, or do some special problem solving for the ministry, but they serve as more than an idea generator or planning group.

Properly designed and managed, these groups enable adults and students to learn in the context of community what it is to serve God. They are a place to instruct and encourage students and leaders alike in the fine art of functioning as a working body of Christ. Keeping this big picture in mind is essential. Otherwise a meaningful opportunity for shaping lives is unnecessarily lost in the process of shaping programs.

Peer Counseling Groups

Peer counseling groups first became popular in the public school system, but many ministries have adopted the concept. Students are trained in basic listening skills, problem identification processes, and crisis intervention techniques. Equipped students are then mobilized to initiate groups with peers seeking a place to explore their personal issues. The process is neither as simple as it sounds nor as complex as some might imagine. Students are naturally drawn to relationships with one another, so the concept works. However—and this is critical—these groups only work well if there is adequate training, supervision, and support of the youthful counselors. Otherwise more problems than benefits can develop. Leaders seeking to put these groups into place should do their homework before offering peer counseling groups.

Special Support Groups

A special support group is not the same as a peer counseling group. A special support group should be led by a qualified adult, one with special training in the field of counseling support groups and the particular issue the given group is exploring. A professional counselor is not necessarily required, but a lay support group leader must be more than someone who "just loves students." Several community and Christian counseling/social work agencies offer training for lay adult leaders of support groups.

A special support group would be composed of adolescents in the youth ministry who are struggling with a particular issue. For example, when a ministry I was involved in presented a series of talks about various youth issues, we discovered that a number of female students were struggling with the beginnings of eating disorders. To respond to this situation, we asked a professional who was a part of our church to lead a series of small group meetings with these girls in order to prevent some potentially serious problems from developing.

Another example might be initiating a short-term grief support group if a well-known student has suddenly died. Issues such as homosexuality, abuse, eating disorders, divorce, violence, suicide, and addictions such as substance abuse and pornography are all among the topics leaders could consider dealing with through support groups and other special resources. In fact, if these concerns are to be dealt with in a significant way in the teaching ministry, leaders have the responsibility of offering support groups or additional places of referral to students who are secretly carrying the wounds of these issues.

Leadership-Building Groups

The small group context is invaluable when mobilizing and sustaining the volunteer leaders of a ministry. Leaders need opportunities to connect, to laugh, to commiserate, to encourage, to be encouraged, and to participate in problem solving with peers who share the same passions and responsibilities. A leadership small group that is participant-bonded leads to leadership development rather than mere task delegation.

Small group times for leaders may include planning retreats as well as fun socials. At other times leaders may join each other as attendees at a conference, with small group times interspersed to debrief their experiences. Or leaders may find that a "breakfast club" once a week provides sharing of selves as well as program responsibilities. Whether choosing to focus on training or spiritual nurture as the goal of this kind of group, leaders are well advised to include time for the team to simply relate to one another and experience Christian community. Learning to make a volunteer-led small group meaningful and refreshing will significantly impact a team's ability to minister effectively.

IMPLEMENTING SMALL GROUPS

The eight categories of small groups listed above are not to suggest that a ministry must have all or even most types of small groups in operation for ministry to be effective. Instead, the list is intended to suggest a number of starting points for using small groups.

Exploring the options or examining creative adaptations of the types just presented is only the first step in implementing a quality small group ministry. Three additional issues are necessary, moving from the dream to the reality: *purpose, preparation,* and *leadership.*

Purpose

Given the variety of small groups that exist, it would be tempting to choose the one type that seems most interesting or least difficult. However, implementing a small group ministry must always be preceded by the questions, Why are we forming this small group? In what way does it help us accomplish our mission? How will it enhance or overlap with the other programs that already exist? The leader of the larger ministry and the small group leaders need to know the purposes of the small groups. Other leaders also need to know how they can be supportive. The vision for the use of small groups should be articulated to all the leaders in the ministry.

Strategic planning needs to occur on the individual small group level as well. What do leaders hope to see happen in their small group after a certain period of time? If the group will exist for a semester or for an entire year, what reasonable expectations might they have for their group members? Small group leaders will be well advised to consider how the ultimate goal of the group can be broken down into manageable segments.

It is far too easy to stray from the purpose of a group if clear, assumable steps are not taken. Without smaller steps to evaluate progress, leaders may begin to prepare something new and unrelated each successive week (especially the procrastinators among us!). Moreover, change almost always occurs in small steps. Skipping randomly from topic to unrelated topic is unlikely to bring about the desired change. Leaders must be trained to develop a strategic approach to encouraging growth in members' lives. The necessity of a strategic approach points to the importance of adequately preparing small group leaders.

USING SMALL GROUPS
WITH JUNIOR HIGHERS
SAUNDRA HENSEL

I began in youth ministry by spending thirteen years working with high school students. During those thirteen years, I always pitied those who worked with junior highers—and prayed for them, that someday they might be able to do "real" youth ministry! A friend of mine, Regina, kept trying to recruit me into junior high ministry by making plans to do something with me and then surprising me by having her small group come along. I don't admit this to many people, so please don't spread it around, but on one of those occasions, I somehow ended up at a Wham concert with Regina and six eleven-year-old girls from her group. Believe me, watching eleven-year-olds scream at George Michael did not make junior high ministry appealing to me!

Several years later I was working at my church's summer camp, having taken a year off from structured ministry. During one of the junior high sessions, as I wondered again why anyone would voluntarily work with these kids, Ginny, a woman on the staff of the ministry, tried to recruit me as a leader. Again, I resisted, but she finally broke me down by placing me in a role where I would be shepherding and training the volunteers who led the small groups; I wouldn't be leading a small group myself.

Of course, what she didn't mention was how often a small group leader's car would break down the morning we had meetings or a leader would get sick or oversleep—and I would have to fill in and lead a small group. The first time it happened, I was terrified. I sat in the circle with the girls, and they were laughing and fighting and giggling and snoozing. Once more, I questioned the concept of junior high ministry.

Then I started asking the group the questions for the morning's small group time. It was the beginning of the year, so the questions focused on what they were looking forward to for the coming ministry season. "Meeting new boys . . . the band . . . playing games . . . sleepovers . . ." "Aren't any of you excited about learning more about who God is this year?" I naively asked. Blank stares were all I received until one girl finally said, "Not really." As I drove home later that day, I began to rejoice in the freedom the girls felt to be real and transparent.

Obviously, I now have a passion for junior high students that I didn't have before. What caused the change? Well, I believe Ginny knew what she was doing when she put me in a position that forced me to spend time in small groups with the students. I follow that example today as a ministry director. When I am trying to recruit a new leader, I don't start her off attending an activity. I have her sit in on a small group. It's the rare person who can spend some time with junior highers in a small group and not develop the desire to impact the students' lives in some way.

Would the realness and honesty I experienced in that first small group have taken place in the midst of games, activities, and busy programs? I don't think so. Junior highers, with their seemingly limitless energy, will play games and be active until you drop from exhaustion. They won't be the ones to initiate intimacy and depth. This is why I believe that small groups are essential for effective junior high ministry. Within a healthy small group, junior highers can grow and stretch in a safe environment. They learn interpersonal skills that are vital to their development.

Because they are still junior highers, their small groups have to be appropriate to who they are. For instance, I recently started a group for five junior high girls where we meet for an hour and a half each week to go through the book of Romans. If you know junior high girls at all, you know that one of their major needs is to talk. So the first forty-five minutes of the group we spend eating dinner and just talking about our week so far. Then we get into the Bible. Small groups are truly the most effective strategy for life-change in junior high ministry.

Preparation

If small groups are an important aspect of facilitating growth, discovery, and change among students, then it is worthwhile to spend time making sure the leaders of those groups can effectively minister within them. Leaders will need assistance in four crucial areas: *vision, skills, prayer,* and *accountability.*

Vision

Leaders must have an adequate idea of the crucial role their small group plays in the purpose and mission of the ministry of which they are a part. Small group leaders will deepen in passion for their role if they cultivate a vision for what their leadership might contribute to the growth of the students. Providing a sense of ownership will help them feel the importance of their role and encourage them through the difficult times their groups may encounter.

Skills

A part of learning to lead a small group takes place as the group leaders actually interact with the students. That is not to suggest that everything should be learned by trial and error.

A few critical skills with which they can be armed are: identifying group needs, preparing appropriate content (whether it be creating Bible studies, adapting curriculum to fit group needs, ordering the use of time, or opening and closing a discussion), discussion leading, learning styles, understanding and facilitating group dynamics, troubleshooting, and relationship building.

Prayer

Leaders need to be spiritually prepared as much as or more than they need to be skilled. It is axiomatic that spiritually prepared group leaders will be more likely to facilitate spiritual change than leaders who are skilled but not empowered by the Holy Spirit. Those who oversee and develop small group leaders should ask, "Have I prayed with them so that they know they can lead their groups in partnership with the Holy Spirit and not rely entirely on their own resources?"

Praying with small group members will remind them that God is concerned with the lives of the students they will be in contact with and that He will help them. Pointing to His promises, helping them to rely on His empowerment, looking to His leading, and resting in His partnership are meaningful by-products of time spent in prayer.

Accountability

Procrastination is a prevalent disease among highly relational youth workers! Small group leaders need someone to talk to them about how their group is developing, to meet with them to look over preparation plans for their group meetings, and to remind them of the importance of what they are doing. This can be done in a formal or an informal way, but it should be done. The potential impact of small group leaders on their students is too important to let the leaders experience the discouragement and sabotage that can occur as a result of not having anyone demonstrate consistent care for their group leading.

Leadership

Who should lead small groups? Knowing the impact these

groups have on students, high standards must be set for the leaders with respect to spiritual consistency, relational consistency, commitment, and godly character. Students will look to their group leader as a model of more mature Christian growth—leaders should be able to provide that.

It is unlikely that youth ministry leaders will find perfect small group leaders. Nobody has a flawless walk with God or a spot-free relationship to others. But do the small group leaders model consistency in dealing with those flaws in a responsible manner and with a commitment to making things right? Remember, competence can be developed through ongoing training, but consistency and commitment are qualities necessary from the beginning.

Students do not need super group leaders; they need real human beings struggling responsibly in their commitment to carry out God's call as His children on this earth. Standards must be high, but humanly realistic too.

What about student leadership? Should the more mature students be allowed to lead groups? It is difficult to answer this question without knowing what kind of group is being formed. Of the eight kinds previously listed, some are more conducive to student leadership than others. For example, students are not the appropriate facilitators of support groups, but they are the only appropriate choice for a peer counseling group. In general, there is much value in allowing mature, consistent, committed high school students to lead a group. However, those teenagers should be provided for in a way that is appropriate to their developmental stage. They are mature youth, not yet adults. They need more training and help with content; they also need much more support.

Accountability for the small group leader was suggested earlier in this chapter—double it for teenage leaders! Students in high school are still forming their identities and self-concepts as persons and as Christians, and a success or failure in this type of leadership situation may have a strong effect on that process. Furthermore, student leaders who are not getting the right kind of support and supervision can confuse or mislead their peers—and do so with the adult leader's apparent endorsement!

That means that adult leadership must be well acquainted with what the students are teaching and how they are leading. Student leaders should be related to in a manner that matches their life stage, not as "junior adult" leaders. Everybody wins—including the student small group leader—when the adult leader takes his role seriously in this discipling process.

SUMMARY

Small groups are an important resource for the ministry that hopes to relate to and reach the present generation of students. There are many ways to make use of them, as well as many kinds, many contexts, many combinations. Leaders should dream, be creative, and initiate small groups that contribute to the overall purposes of their youth ministry programs. The relationships formed and facilitated in small groups will most certainly make a significant impact.

WORKS CITED

Habermas, Ron, and David Olshine. 1995. *Tag Team Youth Ministry*. Cincinnati: Standard. A short book not specifically focused on small groups, this resource has some good ideas about creative ways to use groups with parents/adults/teens.

Hunt, Gladys. 1984. *You Can Start a Bible Study*. Wheaton, Ill.: Harold Shaw.

FOR FURTHER READING

Campus Crusade for Christ. 1995. *Leading a Small Group: The Ultimate Road Trip*. Orlando, Fl.: WSN. A Generation X–style user-friendly handbook for small group leaders. If your volunteer small group leaders are college age, they will really grab hold of the style and material presented in this manual.

Gorman, Julie. 1991. *Let's Get Together*. Wheaton, Ill.: Victor. An eight-session resource for launching a small group. Not specific to youth ministry, this book suggests helpful ideas for beginning small groups.

_____. 1993. *Community That Is Christian: A Handbook on Small Groups.* Wheaton, Ill.: Victor. A thoughtful and insightful resource considering the power and importance of the mission of small groups in Christian growth.

Griffin, Em. 1982. *Getting Together.* Downers Grove, Ill.: InterVarsity. A classic on small group dynamics. It introduces basic small group theory from a Christian perspective.

LeFever, Marlene. 1995. *Learning Styles.* Colorado Springs: David C. Cook. This book examines four learning styles that may be present in a small group and gives lots of good suggestions about how to create a small group study that will reach all four.

Long, Jimmy, et al. 1995. *Small Group Leaders Handbook: The Next Generation.* Downers Grove, Ill.: InterVarsity. This is a book on small group ministry written by a small group! Its special emphasis is on reaching the next generation of students. Although this IVP book is mainly about ministry to college students, it is helpful for senior high small groups as well.

Sturkie, Joan, and Siang-Yang Tan. 1993. *Advanced Peer Counseling in Youth Groups.* Grand Rapids: Zondervan. An outstanding resource for implementing peer counseling ministries.

Veerman, David. 1992. *Small Group Ministry with Youth.* Wheaton, Ill.: Victor. This book describes some of the hows and whys of effective small group ministries and provides profiles of successful small group models being used in various ministries around the country.

PART SEVEN

THE FUTURE IN YOUTH MINISTRY

32

✝

LOOKING AHEAD TO
THE NEXT MILLENNIUM

Richard R. Dunn
Mark H. Senter III

RICK—Reflect on what our authors have written as well as on
the *Complete Book of Youth Ministry* (the book that came
before this book). Then put that within the framework of
your book, *The Coming Revolution in Youth Ministry*. Can
you give me a snapshot of what we might be looking at in the
future of youth ministry?

MARK—No. There is no way we can paint an accurate picture
of the future. Events usually catch people by surprise. All I
can do is suggest some possibilities, and you could too.

RICK—You first. Give me one—one that particularly represents your thinking about the future of youth ministry.

MARK—OK. This is a subtle but profound shift. Youth ministry will need to think more about itself from an ecclesiologi-

cal perspective—understanding itself within the doctrine of the church. By that I mean youth ministry should not be handled as a spiritual parenthesis but as a continuity with biological and faith families.

RICK—What does a *parenthesis* look like? What does *continuity* look like?

MARK—A parenthesis is—it has a hand-off effect. Three years of middle school (then hand off), four years of high school (hand off), then four years of college. I handle them for three years, you handle them for four years, somebody else handles them for four years; then they become what Levinson might call novice adults . . .

RICK—. . . and we wait for them to get married and have children.

MARK—That's right. And then hope they return to the church. That's a hand-off effect. It's like some sort of relay race.

RICK—So who is winning?

MARK—Nobody! That's just the problem. And I don't think that's what the church is all about. Christian relationships are built on continuity, not discontinuity. What we need to start thinking about is a group of people staying together not just for four years but for an extended period of time—ten years, twenty years, or longer.

RICK—Sounds good in theory, but has it ever happened?

MARK—Young Life in Brazil found that though they started some marvelous Young Life clubs, kids did not end up in local churches.

The people who had begun their nurturing in their walk with Christ were in Young Life. To complicate matters, the staff workers could only support themselves through money sent from the United States. How were they going to solve that problem?

They decided to start *associations*. I think that's what they called them. Those associations looked like churches, acted like churches. They fellowshipped like churches; they taught like churches. There were a lot of elements that were *church*, though they didn't call themselves churches. What happened was that the Young Life leaders grew up leading clubs, then these shepherding associations came into play, and twenty-five years later people are still being nurtured by associations that are really churches. That's continuity.

RICK—Now in the United States we're different. We hand them off. Parachurch and youth groups alike say, "OK, youth group, we will disciple you into the church." It is that hand-off effect. Has it ever worked?

MARK—In my opinion, no! Young Life and Youth For Christ have struggled with this for years. And now church youth groups struggle with it as well.

We need to think strategically about the church youth group becoming a long-term church-planting strategy. In the last twenty years, it's been done four times that I know of in the Chicago area. These people have stayed together, have become bonded in a sense of mission. They in fact have built churches.

RICK—The system seems widespread when we think about immigrant churches—second generation, English-speaking youth groups who evolve into their own church because of the language barrier between the first and second generations.

MARK—So what happens there, Rick?

RICK—In those churches there are two basic models. One is the parallel model, where, for example, an Asian senior pastor will hire an associate or youth pastor who will preach and lead the "English-language-speaking congregation." They share the building but because of the language barrier have parallel services.

The other model is the branching off—where that young pastor takes that English-speaking group and begins to develop it as a new congregation. The dynamics are similar. There are difficulties, though. The difficulties do not result from continuity of relationships among peers but from discontinuity in relationships between generations. Those English-speaking individuals are cut off from the first generation.

MARK—If that happens, it is faulty ecclesiology. You've got to have intergenerational church.

RICK—So you're suggesting that there should be a continuity among the peer group and also continuity among the church as a whole, among the generations.

MARK—I would hope we would find a continuity between the mother church and the daughter church, where there is sharing of board members, finances, and other resources.

RICK—Another difficulty I see is that students go away during college. If we adopt this model, we will have to deal with the fact that much of what we have been doing in youth ministry has been to simply get them through the high school years. If we are to provide continuity, we'll have to begin preparing them for the university and young adulthood. How do we think about that?

MARK—There are two sides to the issue, Rick. About 65 percent of people in the United States go to college. That leaves about one-third of the population who will not. So by definition, there are a lot of people who will remain here locally. Now, generally, youth groups have not geared themselves to this group of people. Some will say you can't build a church around the non–college-bound kids because they're not leaders. I have a problem with that kind of reasoning.

On the other side, continuity with the person who goes away becomes an extremely attractive feature, since youth groups will now have to begin thinking of the people who've gone as still being part of them. There will be a greater responsibility for the youth pastor and the volunteers to maintain continuity with those people once they've left—phone calls, E-mail, letters, personal visits . . .

RICK—I see. They've not handed them off—they're still a part of us.

MARK—That's right. At the same time I think there will be greater incentive for those young people to come home because they're part of something that's building.

RICK—Many of our students—whether they go to a secular or Christian college—don't get involved meaningfully in local churches during their college experience. I would think they would welcome the opportunity to stay attached to people who loved them through high school.

But let me pull us in a different direction . . .

MARK—OK.

RICK—It seems to me that if we accept the descriptions of young people today, we have a postmodern, post-Christian, post-absolute generation that has been dubbed Generation X. Soon we will begin dealing with the Millennial Generation. I think we're looking at some cultural discontinuity between the previous generation and this one. This generation doesn't appear to embrace, accept, and engage traditional values in the same way the previous generation has. Nor in many cases do they have the same values.

MARK—How is this generation different from its predecessors?

RICK—One of my students recently said, "Since we're postmodern, don't we have to approach the Scriptures as postmodern people before we can accept them as rational and linear?" You can see that type of thinking.

MARK—Are you afraid young people are becoming irrational in how they make decisions?

RICK—I would describe them as a-rational and experiential. I wouldn't say irrational, because you can be experiential and dealing with life as it comes to you—by relationship, by experience, by motive in responses—so that images, stories, real-life experiences become the medium by which content is assimilated. They're very capable of rational thought, and they're very perceptive. If you hang around the coffee houses, you're going to hear some insightful observations.

MARK—Where do you see them as vulnerable, then?

RICK—Probably in the way that this generation thinks about morality and values, and the difficulty they have in holding to a worldview that includes absolute truth and absolute moral standards. Many students are struggling to make sense out of their worldview in light of the plurality of religions, moral options, and choices—the entire way in which they encounter those things.

MARK—Let me add three more factors in their decision-making process. One is community—now you alluded to community . . .

RICK—I didn't use the word, but that's it.

MARK—The fact is that most of the Generation X and the Millennial Generation are saying, "I hear what you say. I understand the logic of what you say. But show me it lived out in the lives of a group of people that are different from the people I know. Otherwise, it's just words." And so a living, vibrant community of faith is extraordinarily important in the mix of things.
    A second factor is the visual, artistic element.

RICK—Imagery?

MARK—Imagery. I think visual impressions—not just verbal images, but physical images in art and in media—express concepts that they probably would not respond to in a linear fashion. These images have the ring of truth when viewed on the screen or in picture form.

The third thing I would mention is crisis. The growth point for people may be the point of crisis—tragedy, broken dreams, problems. A few years ago I did some interviews with youth specialists in Atlanta, and what we concluded was that most of them found their spiritual life changed because of hard times.

RICK—The youth workers themselves?

MARK—The youth workers themselves. I've explored that concept for years since that time. I find that spiritual life more frequently comes alive in response to hard times than out of a linear process. Yet the linear process is the groundwork for responding.

RICK—You introduced another concept—our theological understanding of spiritual maturity in youth ministry. This means that to have good grounding in the Word of God there must be an entry point. What I would suggest as our entry point is their questions about life experiences. Our job must be to help them make sense of their experiences in light of who God says He is and what He has to say about stuff in Scripture and how He reveals Himself.

MARK—OK. Give me a snapshot on that one.

RICK—What I don't mean to suggest is simply to address topics—how to live life better, how to have more friends, how to have a better dating relationship, how to succeed in your work . . .

MARK—Don't forget sex and satanism. That will bring them in.

RICK—There are distinct ways in which kids think about their world and make decisions. They make sense out of who they are in relationship to other people. There are ways to bring out the purpose of life, to come alongside those issues and bring what God has revealed to bear on those very meaty issues.

Here's maybe the best example I could give. Let's say we are talking about sexuality. We do a three-week series so that they know the basic facts, know the principles, and then are asked to apply them. It might be a whole lot better to spend a longer time on that—make it a three-month series and take apart love and look at love in the culture. Look at love from the perspective of past generations. Give them a sense of how to think about all that and interact with it and find that the Bible really does have meaning for their lives—and not just one verse here or one verse there. What I'm trying to say, Mark, is, we need not only to educate them in the Bible but to train them to think Christianly, theologically, about life. Because they're going to need that. It runs counter to the world they live in.

MARK—Point well made. But let's get a little more concrete about what youth ministry needs to look like in response to this generation. We've been talking primarily about similar kids—kids in the church and those who are similar to the kids in the church. But there are a lot of kids who don't have contact with the church right now. And furthermore, the high school is much more fragmented than it was when we created the current models of youth ministry. How are we going to reach individual subpopulations of the high school or junior high?

RICK—Let me give you an example—a snapshot—in our area. There are some graduates from the college and some current students who developed a vision for a coffee house for alternative kids. These would be kids who are not in the mainstream—kids who are not going to show up at the youth groups. One student got the idea of making it "totally nonthreatening and safe." "We'll come alongside," he said, "and spend time with kids and use casual conversations to introduce the gospel and invite them to a Bible study outside of that. The coffee house will remain in place just for the exchange of ideas." That's the sort of thing these kids were into. They liked to drink coffee and exchange ideas.

So the Christians developed this ministry. And this set of kids who were alternative kids by their attitude started coming and would stand out in the cold in the Chicago winter waiting for somebody to come out so they could go in. They wanted to be a part of what was going on.

Then after a football game, some of the players and cheerleaders decided to try out the coffee house. That almost ruined it because the alternative kids didn't want them. The reason the jocks came was because a dance got canceled. So the kinds of kids who would go to a school dance didn't have anywhere to go, and they decided to come to the coffee house. It really, really irritated the alternative kids, who were trying to get away from the school-spirit types. And it created a great dilemma. I think that speaks to the fragmentation you're talking about.

MARK—So our high school society is built on an antagonism between groups that we've got to deal with. Now a Christian perspective brings them together ultimately but not initially.

RICK—Not initially. And not when we're talking about outreach. This happens further down the road when kids have matured and grown.

MARK—Let me give you a series of snapshots. The junior high kid who's really into alternative music—has no interest in the church, has no contact with the church. How are we going to reach him?

RICK—Junior high kid, alternative music, no interest in the church. Probably not through a lock-in.

MARK—I tend to agree with that.

RICK—Probably not through summer groups. Probably not through the standard ways. Somebody's going to have to build a relationship with that kid. Somebody's going to have to listen to and learn a little bit about alternative music. Or get to know a little about it.

I once went to a youth group to speak for a weekend, and the youth pastor told me how his youth group had changed and the membership had changed dramatically since the last guy. Well, come to find out, the last guy had been an athlete. *This* guy was a musician. The last youth group consisted of jocks. *This* youth group—everybody was in the band.

MARK—Yep.

RICK—So if that's true, we're going to have to find leaders who can build relationships with that kid and with his friends and be there. We have to be willing, I believe, to think of youth *ministry* as separate from youth *group*.

MARK—The next snapshot. The computer nerd. In every high school there's a group of people who are computer geeks. Their social skills may not be great, but they are quite good at what they do and are very happy to talk about it. And it drives a lot of their life. How are you going to reach those people?

RICK—Well, there's a selfish reason for reaching that kid, because someday he may invite you to his weekend mountain retreat or maybe give you a job.

MARK—The Bill Gates mentality, huh?

RICK—That's right. My thought is this. You can use the same relational principle. Computers are a wonderful source of media and a wonderful source of performing certain tasks related to organization and administration—to creating, whether it be fliers, multimedia for an event, or whatever. Ask the kid to come along and contribute his expertise to your learning. Or work with you on how to develop something that could fold into the group—not in a way that's using the kid in any way, but that says, "I really want to learn from you." And, "Can you teach me some of this?" And, "What things could you do?" Because if we put ourselves into the position of being a learner of his computer skills, he may put himself in the position of being a learner of life skills.

MARK—Let's take the reverse view. If we're looking at snapshots a few years hence, what are the things you *fear* may show up in those snapshots?

RICK—I'm awfully fearful of professionalization.

MARK—What do you mean by professionalization?

RICK—In our attempt to become more sophisticated, to think more accurately, to try new things, to be innovative and all that—we become so enamored with youth ministry that we forget about youth.

MARK—OK. The difference I hear is success orientation versus a ministry orientation.

RICK—Yes, that, and even just—sometimes I feel people are in love with the idea of youth ministry more than they love kids.
    Another concern I have is that in our desire to come alongside these students in their life experiences, we might not be aware of how much our culture is shaping us. Even we in the Christian mainstream tend to be shaped by the values of our culture, and we may actually redefine the gospel in terms comfortable to us sociologically and culturally rather than letting the gospel address and critique *it*. So there's a sense in which we need to be priests to our kids and priests in our churches. We also need to be prophets. And I think it's a lot more popular to be a priest now than it is to be a prophet.

MARK—One of my own tragic snapshot fears is that the evangelical kids will be mirror images of society at large, and there will be no way to distinguish them because you will find just as many pregnant girls and just as many promiscuous boys, just as many people who are playing with drugs and hurting other people. There will be no ethical difference. There will be just as many Christian kids who take advantage of the referee in a basketball game as would be the case among kids on the street.

RICK—Let me give one more snapshot. Youth workers are some of the busiest people I know—including me. It's scary to think that we might be so busy creating change—trying to usher in revolution—that we miss what God is wanting to do and to speak to our hearts. And we're not spending time in prayer, seeking after Him and hearing the heart of God so that we are caught by His Spirit rather than being caught up in the movement. At some point we're going to have to seek the face of God, and we're going to have to listen and catch His agenda for what He wants to do.

What about for you?

MARK—One of the snapshots I fear would be that everybody in the picture is well-to-do. The only people who can afford the kind of youth ministry that has been emerging is people who are well-heeled financially. The camps are getting more expensive. The trips are getting more expensive. The social activities are more expensive. The Bible study materials are more expensive . . .

RICK—Yes.

MARK—The cost of hiring quality youth pastors is becoming more expensive. And Christian concerts are getting more expensive.

RICK—And those are professionalization issues, in a sense.

MARK—Yes. So that's one of the things that I fear. And I don't have an alternative for it.

Another fear I have is that there's an absence of passion. That we're doing things not for Spirit-driven reasons but for reasons that are more related to self-esteem and maybe a reflection of the culture at large.

RICK—I guess another snapshot of fear in relation to youth ministry is that youth workers would all be very young and very inexperienced. I think it takes a few years to come to the point of discovering what leadership is. I've often said that in my first few years in youth ministry I tried to do everything. My next few years I was struggling with feeling bad because I couldn't do everything. I think I'm just starting to mature to the point where I'm starting to be happy that somebody else can do most of it.

MARK—And then when you get to my stage, you're looking back, and you're saying, "I hope I *did* something."

RICK—On the positive side, I'm pleased with the courage among youth workers to be realistic and honest. I think that's why I like what Mark DeVries suggests in his discussion of family-based youth ministry. He has the courage to say, "You know what? This doesn't work. I mean it looks good, but we're gonna sacrifice the goose that laid the golden egg if we don't do something different."

MARK—Another good snapshot is youth ministry in living color. By that I mean people and systems of youth ministry being *generated* by people of color rather than their adapting models and styles of youth ministry created in the Anglo culture.

RICK—You spoke of that in *The Coming Revolution in Youth Ministry.*

MARK—I believe it is even closer today. Churches in the Pacific Rim, Latin America, and sub-Saharan Africa are already sending out missionaries; and it won't be long before some youth worker types will have the audacity to come into the Anglo world—and when they do, something new and exciting will begin to happen.

RICK—How about another snapshot?

MARK—Older people reentering youth ministry! There are a lot of people who did youth ministry at some point in life and may have left it because they couldn't afford to raise their family on the salary they were able to gain. But they still have a love for young people. They still have those skills and abilities to communicate with kids. And they are secure enough financially that they don't have to spend as much time working, and they've got some discretionary time on their hands. So they begin to look at some of the young people and hang out with them. They can't beat kids in basketball anymore. They can't go one-on-one with them. But they still know how to connect with them in some sort of way.

RICK—Reminds me of a man I met at a retreat. He's a retiree. And he decided that he wanted to be a grandfather at the local high school. So he just became a part of it—became a part of the sports teams—you know, taking up tickets. Started eating in the cafeteria. Volunteered for anything he could do. Little short guy, bald head. I mean, you'd never catch him on the cover of any *Youthworker* magazine. But kids call him when they need help. "My mom's kicked me out of the house, and I have nowhere to go." He and his wife go down and pick up the kid and bring him home. This is the way he lives in retirement.

He wrote me recently. He went to a home basketball game with his wife. Some kids stopped him at the door just to talk. It was kind of like they were delaying him. He couldn't figure out what was going on. Until he walked into the gym. They had the entire place decorated. They had a table set up, and they brought him over before the game started and honored him and his wife—a standing ovation from high school students. And if you looked at that man, not many people would say, "Now that's the guy I'd want to be doing youth ministry."

MARK—Yeah.

RICK—But kids see it differently. Wayne Rice once said that junior high kids will gravitate toward the oldest person who will love and accept them.

MARK—Let me give you a snapshot that comes out of some of my conversations with people in England. They have what they call secular youth ministers. These happen to be Christian people who are employed by social welfare agencies. School counselors, that sort of thing. I think this is a type of youth ministry we may want to consider. And public school teaching. All college students who are taking education classes should begin to think in terms of mission as well as pedagogy.

RICK—I had a number of students at the college where I was teaching who did that very thing. Education kids would come into my office and say, "I want to learn youth ministry 'cause I want to make an impact on my school by teaching."

MARK—How about law enforcement? There are some people, by God's grace, who really need to be in the law enforcement business to bring salt and light to it. And some of those people should be fabulous youth workers if they don't get hardened in the whole process.

RICK—There are other kinds of people in secular youth ministry. I think of those who employ young people and could have a tremendous shaping influence on them. Franchise operators for some of the fast-food chains survive on employing young people. They could use their job of teaching them how to make money in order to gain entry into their world and somewhere along the line talk about Jesus Christ.

MARK—Obviously people who are associated with sports. And people who are associated with record stores, where a lot of young people hang out because they like to do the music stuff.

RICK—As we conclude this book, we must recognize there's a distinct possibility that it could be a part of the problem rather than a part of the solution in youth ministry as we go into the twenty-first century.

MARK—Only time will tell. How can we avoid being part of the problem?

RICK—I hope by initiating people into thinking about youth ministry from a proactive mind-set—seeing themselves as people who can create and who can think and who can move in ways that you and I could never dream of. The best ideas in youth ministry have yet to come. They're still out there ready to emerge. And probably, Mark, they are not going to come from you and me.

MARK—I agree with you.

RICK—We are really, really needing God's instruction, God's discipline, God's wisdom—and if this book or any other book takes the form of *the* encyclopedia or *the* how-to book, we're in a lot of trouble. If it takes the form of stimulating ideas, of giving people a sense of some principles that are both biblical and effective, of being able to identify those themes that are central and essential—and then people take off in new directions—the book and our ministry will be significant. Hopefully you and I can give encouragement and give a sense of our past and teach from our mistakes, but it's going to fall to the readers to make youth ministry what it can be in the twenty-first century.

MARK—I do see our role as being cheerleaders. I want to be able to step back and be a cheerleader for people who spin off. I have an old framework. I try to be a reader of current trends, but I still bring with me something that was formulated in the fifties and the sixties. And I need to liberate other people to go for the brass ring. I would like to become a mentor to the activists.

RICK—And my experience comes out of the seventies and eighties. Whoever is making ministry happen right now will be shaped by the paradigm shifts of the nineties and the first decade of the twenty-first century. I think that's what it means to hand off leadership. But I want to hand it off in such a way that we're still carrying some of the load and are still involved. We don't know what's going to emerge on the other side. And it would be easier if we did. But if we did, we would just start working to make that happen and not enjoy some of the things God's going to do along the way.

It is possible, however, that someone may read this book fifteen years from now and say, "Well, those two guys—I mean, they weren't even close. Those snapshot things were good ideas and stuff, but you remember what happened in 2001, or remember when God brought that revival and, you know, kind of wiped everything out." And you know what? That would be all right with me.

MARK—That would be all right with me, too.

Index of Subjects

NOTE: *Figures are indicated by boldface type*

Index of Persons

Moody Press, a ministry of Moody Bible Institute,
is designed for education, evangelization, and edification.
If we may assist you in knowing more about Christ
and the Christian life, please write us without obligation:
Moody Press, c/o MLM, Chicago, Illinois 60610.